The Wines of Spain

The Wines of Spain

by Julian Jeffs

MITCHELL BEAZLEY

The Wines of Spain
by Julian Jeffs

First published in Great Britain in 2006
by Mitchell Beazley, an imprint of
Octopus Publishing Group Limited,
2–4 Heron Quays, London E14 4JP.

Cartography: Encompass Graphics Ltd

The author and publishers will be grateful for any information that will assist them in keeping future editions up-to-date. Although all reasonable care has been taken in the preparation of this book, neither the publishers nor the author can accept any liability for any consequences arising from the use thereof, or the information contained therein.

ISBN 13: 978 1 84533 100 9

ISBN 10: 1 84533 100 1

A CIP catalogue record for this book is available from the British Library.

Set in Berkeley Book and Trade Gothic

Printed and bound in England by Mackays, Chatham

Contents

Acknowledgments

So many Spanish wine-growers have helped with information and hospitality that if I attempted to list them there inevitably would be unfortunate omissions, so I have taken the easy way and named none. My wife Deborah came with me on innumerable visits to Spain, did a good deal of the driving, and helped in all sorts of ways. The Spanish Commercial Office in London has given every possible sort of help, especially in digging out information from Spanish sources and in providing me with its invaluable Education Notes. Many members of the wine trade also have helped, and I should specially mention John Hawes of the specialist importers Laymont & Shaw, and Nicholas Burridge of Burridges of Arlington Street. Harold Heckle was with me on one trip and has given lots of help. I am profoundly grateful for the pioneering work of Jeremy Watson, who wrote the first edition of the *Education Notes* and whose great book, *The New and Classical Wines of Spain,* has been a most useful guide. It is hardly possible to thank John Radford enough. He succeeded Jeremy Watson in preparing the *Education Notes,* and his pioneering and exemplary researches have been a guide and inspiration to all who have written about Spanish wines, not least myself. He arranged a memorable tasting of 600 wines that he allowed me to attend, and his book, *The New Spain*, now in its second edition, has helped me no end. I also have been given very valuable guidance by the Guía Peñin and by La Guía of TodoVino. I have accessed all the websites of the listed bodegas. I am grateful to Professor Jocelyn Hillgarth for supplying fascinating literary and historical references. Many others have helped with information and advice, and I am grateful to them all. Mistakes are mine alone.

Introduction

Writing a book that attempts to cover all Spanish wines has been a fascinating experience and an exhausting one. The area is vast and, of course, there have been problems. It has been difficult to know whether to use Spanish names or English ones where these are available: Navarra or Navarre, Mallorca or Majorca, Cataluña or Catalonia? Not without hesitation I have decided to use the Spanish names throughout. In many books the Spanish word for pink wine, *rosado*, is translated as rosé, but I can see no reason to substitute a French word for a Spanish one, though Spaniards often do. There have been problems, too, with genders, particularly with the names of vines, which can often be either masculine or feminine, depending on where you are and whom you are talking to. I have generally used the masculine form, but it should be remembered that growers may use either.

For each district I have given the basic information at the beginning of a chapter: geography; climate; soils; grapes; planting; vineyard area; authorized yield; wines; production; and vintages; with occasional omissions where the information is not available. In a country where the wine scene is changing so rapidly, though, figures are often revised and can never be completely up to date. The Spanish authorities classify vintages as regular (1), average (2), good (3), very good (4), or excellent (5). The first used to be called poor, but optimism prevails. If occasionally the authorities err on the side of benevolence, the assessments are generally fair and the best going. Vintage assessments, though, can often be misleading, as those who buy claret, for instance, know only too well. There are always a few disappointing wines even in a very fine vintage, and it is great fun to find good ones (and there usually are some) in vintages that have generally failed. This certainly applies to districts such as Rioja, where the large area and irregular terrain provide many microclimates. However, Spanish sunshine means that there are far fewer failures than in more northerly countries.

I have not attempted to explain abbreviations, Spanish words, or wine-making terms in the text (apart from where necessary in the first chapter), but I have attempted to put them all into the Glossary. Spain grows a great many grape varieties, some of which are unique to specific areas, but most are grown in several. Often, to complicate matters further, they have different names in each, sometimes more than one in a single area. I have set out the grape varieties, all the names for them that I can trace, and the areas in which they are grown (either officially or unofficially) in the last chapter.

SPANISH NAMES

Readers may be perplexed by the formation of Spanish names. The Spaniard uses the surnames of both parents, putting the father's first. The two names may or may not be joined by "y" (or in Catalan "e"), meaning "and". Thus if Sr Fernández married Srita Gómez and they had a son whom they christened Pedro, his full name would be Pedro Fernández (y) Gómez. In normal speech and informal writing, the second name is generally omitted unless it is necessary for clear identification. To complicate matters, some Spanish names are double-barrelled.

A Spanish lady retains her maiden name after marriage but adds her husband's surname. Thus if Ana López married Sr Castillo, she would become Ana López de Castillo, and would be referred to as Castillo's señora. If her husband were to die, she would describe herself as his widow, *viuda*.

To the British the system sounds rather complicated, but it is much more logical than ours.

SPANISH ADDRESSES

In the past, visitors to Spain have been surprised to find a remote house or even a church displaying a plaque with "27" or some such number. As these were manifestly meaningless they have been dropped and many buildings, especially large ones, are simply s/n, *sin numero* (no number). A useful way of locating buildings has been adopted relying on the kilometre posts that are along all Spanish main roads. Thus Carretera "Ollauri – Nájera km 2" means the bodega is by the 2 kilometre post of the road between Ollauri and Nájera. Post codes (zip codes) are all in numerals.

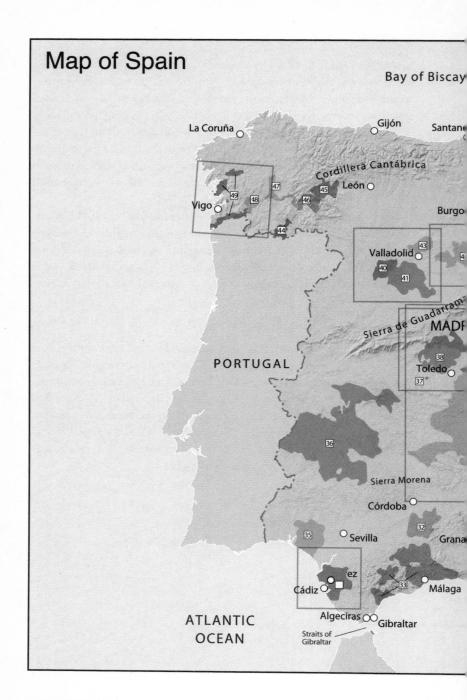

Map of Spain

Bay of Biscay

La Coruña

Gijón

Santan

Cordillera Cantábrica

León

Burgo

Vigo

47

49

48

45

46

44

Valladolid

43

4

40

41

Sierra de Guadarram

MADR

38

Toledo

37

PORTUGAL

36

Sierra Morena

Córdoba

32

35

Sevilla

Grana

ez

33

Cádiz

Málaga

ATLANTIC
OCEAN

Algeciras

Gibraltar

Straits of
Gibraltar

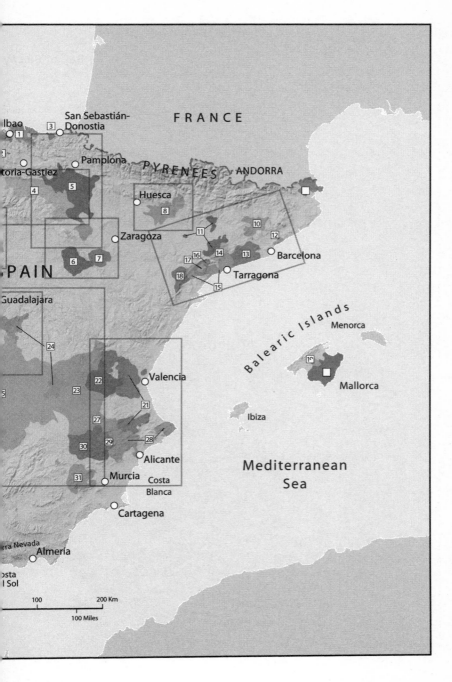

1

The Spanish wine scene

It has been positively exciting to taste Spanish wines over the past forty years. They have been transformed at a rate that has been accelerating all the time, and fine new wines are still emerging. This achievement should be set in its context. The Civil War had left the country ruined. It was followed by World War II, with nearly all export markets cut off. In those days, most wines were made in conditions that now look primitive, with the must being fermented in huge earthenware (or later concrete) *tinajas* that made bodegas look like stage-sets for *Ali Baba and the Forty Thieves*, though good wines were made that way and some still are.

In 1960, the only Spanish wine well known internationally and acknowledged to be world-class was sherry. Vega Sicilia was legendary but very expensive and very hard to find, like the burgundies of Romanée-Conti. Within Spain the great table wines were from Rioja, but in the UK they appeared only in their humblest form at the lowest end of the market, mislabelled as Spanish Chablis and Spanish Burgundy. And most of the wines so labelled did not come from Rioja at all, but were simply table wines of doubtful origin. There also was Spanish Sauternes, which was very sweet and rather nasty. Within Spain you could buy fine Riojas, and if you could not afford them you bought a Valdepeñas. There were some other good wines but, for the most part, these could be bought only locally. And there were some good sparkling wines, now called cava but in those days mislabelled Champaña.

How things have changed! Riojas were the first fine wines to break into the UK market. In the 1960s, if you went to the right wine merchant, you also could find an occasional Valdepeñas or even an Alella, but not much else. The best wines were expected to come from France or Germany. Most of those to get excited about today simply did not exist or were made only in very small quantities for local sale, just finding their way on to the wine lists of the best restaurants in Madrid and Barcelona.

A number of things led to the revolution – for revolution it was. Perhaps the most important was Spain's increasing prosperity, which brought an important national market for fine wines and people with money for investment to make them. Another was an increasingly international outlook, so that oenologists got their training in such places as Bordeaux and Davis, California. Their values became absolute rather than local and insular. And at the same time they could be provided with the modern tools of their trade, notably cool fermentation in hygienic stainless-steel tanks. Delicate wines of great finesse could be made in hot places – previously the fermentations had been tumultuous and uncontrolled, so that many elements of flavour and aroma were driven off and lost forever.

Another very important development was a new willingness to experiment with vine varieties and to match them with the soils and microclimates. The acknowledged pioneer was Miguel Torres, who virtually created Penedès as a fine wine area. He brought in foreign vines such as Cabernet Sauvignon, Pinot Noir, and Gewürztraminer and found out where to grow them. The use of international varieties led to controversy, and the debate still goes on hotly. Some were originally Spanish and never ceased being grown there: Garnacha, for instance, called Grenache in France, and Cariñena, which the French call Carignan. Spain has other grapes of its own which are among the best in the world: Tempranillo, for instance, is at last becoming international.

Some Spanish varieties practically disappeared, and while a number of these will not be missed there could well be others that could contribute something special. Some enlightened growers, like Miguel Torres, are cultivating them and trying them out. But the real argument is whether Spain should concentrate on producing wines from native varieties, wines that are uniquely Spanish, or from international varieties that produce yet another Cabernet Sauvignon or Chardonnay. The danger lies in saying "yet another". The style of wine that a vine produces depends on four things: the clone; the soil; the microclimate; and the way the wine is made. And quite apart from that, vines are remarkably adaptable plants that develop characteristics of their own, depending on where they are grown. No vine demonstrates this more than Tempranillo. So just as Garnacha has produced great wines in Châteauneuf-du-Pape, Cabernet Sauvignon has produced great wines in, for instance, Penedès and Navarra. And an admixture of Cabernet Sauvignon can add backbone and finesse to a Tempranillo in Spain just as it can to a Syrah (Shiraz) in Australia. Great wines can never be lookalikes; their greatness lies in their individuality. They usually come after years of devotion and experimentation. In being too nationalistic, or too international, one can cut off one's nose to spite one's face and prevent the emergence of something special. Spanish wine-growers have generally avoided the pitfalls and have produced some very fine wines, adopting the approach best suited to where they are. Growers in areas untrammelled by tradition – Penedès, Somontano, or Navarra, for instance – had most freedom in making good use of international varieties, though they have not neglected the native ones. But this in itself brings difficulties as the name of the district no longer implies a particular style of wine.

New prosperity has brought a mushrooming of boutique bodegas, ones that the French sometimes refer to as *garagistes*. They are now found in all the main districts and make some of the very finest wines. At the same time many of the big names have chosen to diversify and buy or plant vineyards in new places, taking their experience with them and creating excellent wines, often in places with potential they recognized but which were not known as fine wine regions.

In surface area, Spain is the second-biggest country in western Europe, ranking after France; and in terms of vineyard area it is the biggest, but in production only fourth. There are several reasons for this. Spain is very sparsely populated so the pressure to produce large yields did not exist. After Switzerland it has the highest average altitude in Europe and is very rocky and infertile, so that in many places only vines and olive trees will grow. In most vineyards there is a shortage of water, especially in the summer, but irrigation is fortunately now allowed in very dry areas, and also to save the lives of very young vines, or more generally in years of serious drought. Moreover many vines are over forty years old, which greatly reduces yield. And in the DO districts it is generally reduced deliberately in the interests of quality, though in some this could go further. Garnacha vines, for instance, tend to produce very dim wines if the yield is high, but can produce great ones in the right place if it is kept very low.

Whatever the vine, quality is protected in the *Denominacion de Origens* (DOs) by decrees of *rendimiento*. If grapes are pressed to yield the last drop of juice, the resulting must is of very poor quality; hence each district sets a limit to the amount that can be abstracted. This is between sixty-five and seventy per cent, and should perhaps be enforced more rigorously. Nowadays grapes are tested when growers deliver them to a bodega. A mechanical arm is lowered into the middle of a truckload and a sample taken that is analyzed immediately by an electronic device to measure sugar and acidity, which have to be in balance if the grower is to get the highest price.

Another feature is the remarkably wide variety of the vines grown. This comes from Spain's sheer size, stretching from the Atlantic to the Mediterranean and from the Pyrenees to Tarifa, not to mention the islands. It also is very mountainous, with several massive ranges, and ascends from the coast to the high central Meseta. The north Atlantic coast is cool and damp. The Mediterranean coast is agreeably warm, though it can be very hot in summer as you get further south. The mountains behind are much cooler, especially at night. And the whole of the central Meseta is horribly cold in winter and very hot indeed in summer. There are as many soils as there are microclimates and an enormous choice of vines. It has everything, and in terms of wine, it produces practically everything.

While the quality of the best wines is above reproach and the value offered by the wines in general is remarkable, there are still some problems to be addressed. Spanish wines have the unfortunate reputation of being over-oaked – Spaniards certainly love the taste of oak, but in an international context it is less appreciated. Happily this has been recognized and fewer wines can be criticized in this way. Another problem is over-extraction. The colour and many of the elements of flavour in red wines come from their skins. An analogy can be made with the use of tea bags. Left in the pot for too short a time the tea is weak and watery, left too long it becomes a sergeant-major's brew. So it is with grape skins. If the extraction is too long the wine is dark and dense. Such wines are often impressive when young, and tend to win competitions, but do not age well and do not complement food. This also has been recognized, but to some extent still persists.

AGEING

The way wines are aged has a profound effect on them. The traditional way in Spain was to use large oak casks and the wine sometimes spent years in them. Some casks were infected and imparted taints; some made the wines taste very woody; some had been in use so long that they had become practically impermeable to air and the wine might just as well have been in tanks. Happily this is now in the past. The ways in which wines mature became the subject of intense study, and experiments are still going on in all the major bodegas.

There are two ways wines age. The first is by oxidation, when the wine is in cask and oxygen permeates through the wood and between the staves. The second is by reduction, when the wine is in bottles or airtight tanks. Ageing in oak is quicker and also extremely complex. The wine takes in tannins, vanillin, and other flavouring elements from the wood. Just how quickly it is oxidized and what these elements are depend on the wood used, how big the casks are, and how they are made. The larger the cask, the smaller the area of contact between the oak and a given volume of wine. Some winemakers use American oak, some French, and some a combination of the two. In the past Slovenian oak was favoured and is now coming in again, with Russian and other eastern Mediterranean oaks. There also is some Spanish oak, but this is in such short supply as to be insignificant.

American oak, *Quercus alba*, has been the most popular for years. It imparts more of an oaky flavour than does French oak, particularly vanillin. Those who favour it say it is best suited to the native wines. Others use it for an initial part of the ageing and then go over to French, or use French for ageing a part of their wines and blend them together. In American cooperage the staves are sawn, while in Europe they are split into shape (if European oak is sawn the staves tend to leak), and this also makes a difference. Among the many experiments going on are those to make casks from American oak but by European methods. And some winemakers aim at getting the best of both worlds by using American casks with French ends or vice versa.

There are two principal kinds of French oak: Limousin and Allier. Sometimes one finds Nevers or Tronçais referred to, but these, like Allier, come from the centre of France and are virtually indistinguishable. French oak is of a different kind from American, or rather of two different kinds, *Quercus sessilifora* and *Quercus robur*, but in practice no distinction is drawn between them. French oak, of whatever kind, is less aggressive, which may or may not be a good thing: it depends on the wine and what you are looking for.

Other factors influence the effect of casks, regardless of the oak of which they are made. The first is the way the wood is seasoned. This can be hastened artificially or left to time and nature. The latter is considered best and, to make sure, some bodegas buy in wood and season it themselves before having it coopered. The second is the degree of "toast". In making a cask the staves are bent by placing a partly assembled cask over a fire, which burns in the middle; water is then thrown on, making it possible to bend the staves into shape. The fire chars the wood to give casks of high, medium, or low toast. The higher the toast, the less the penetration of the wine, which therefore tastes less woody and tannic, but the char also imports flavours of its own.

Then there is the question of size. In the past the practice was to use enormous casks that provided a low surface-to-volume ratio. Nowadays DO regulations stipulate that casks have to be less than 600 or even 330 litres (in the past it was 1,000) although, following French practice, most bodegas now use *barricas* of 225 litres. Finally (at any rate for the purposes of this brief description), there is the age of the cask. New casks impart the most flavour. Indeed, if the wine is very delicate (for instance in a light vintage), it may be unwise to use new casks at all. But generally the tannins and vanilla overtones that they bring are desirable and are used, at least in part, for maturing new wines, while some are actually fermented in new casks. After four or five years, though, the flavouring matters have been absorbed and what is left is simply slow oxidation. Casks can be revived to some extent if they are taken apart and shaved, but this is not often done. Older casks are desirable for some wines and particularly for the later stages of maturation. Too long in a new cask can be altogether too much of a good thing and is a mistake that the new wave of winemakers is learning to avoid, after some unfortunate experiences.

CLASSIFICATION BY AGE

Wines are classified according to the amount of ageing they are given:

Noble – wines with a year in oak of not more than 600-litre capacity or bottle.

Añejo – "mature"; wines must have two years in cask or bottle.

Viejo – "old"; wines must be three years old and show oxidative ageing.

Joven – also called *vino del año*, *sin crianza*, or (rarely but officially) *con simple garantía de origen*, but the authorities are encouraging the term *joven*. They are made for drinking immediately and have either spent no time in cask or less time than that needed to qualify them as *crianzas*.

Semi-crianza or roble – not an official term but one increasingly found on labels for wine that has been given some oak ageing, usually about six months, but not enough to be classified as a *crianza*.

Crianza – usually translated as "breeding", but in this context a better translation might be "bringing up" or "education". Reds must be aged for at least two full years after the vintage, of which a period, usually at least six months but sometimes a year, as in Rioja and Navarra, must be in oak casks of not more than 330 litres. Whites and *rosados* must spend at least a year in the bodega with at least six months in oak.

Reserva – reds must have at least three years' ageing, of which at least one must be in oak. Whites and *rosados* must be aged for at least two years, of which at least six months must be in oak.

Gran reserva – these are allowed to be made only in good vintages. Reds must be aged for at least five years, of which at least eighteen months (it used to be two years) must be in oak. Whites and *rosados* are rare and must be aged for at least four years, of which at least six months must be in oak.

The above ageing periods must all be in the bodega; time spent at a merchant's does not count, though of course it can make a profound difference to the maturity of the wine. Time spent in tanks does not count either; when not in cask it must all be in bottle. These periods are subject to local variations, but normal ageing rules are assumed in the chapters below unless otherwise stated.

GEOGRAPHICAL ORIGIN

Nothing is more important than the geographical origin. Official delimitation has long been established in Spain – for instance the *consejo regulador* for sherry was established in 1933 – and is continuing apace. New areas are being defined continually. The authority responsible is INDO – Instituto Nacional de Demoninaciones de Origin – whose responsibilities are not confined to wine. As Spain is part of the EU, it conforms to European rules, but precise geographical limitations are left to the member nations. In the EU regulations there are only two categories: "table wines" and "quality wines". The latter are classified as "quality wines produced in specific regions" (QWPSR) or, in Spanish, *vinos de calidad producedos en regiones determinadas* (VCPRD). Each country is left to formulate its own laws within the rules. In Spain, there are four categories: *vino de mesa* (VdM), *vino de la tierra* (VdlT or VT), *vino de calidad con indicación geográphica* (VCIG), *denominación de origen* (DO), and *denominación de origen calificada* (DOC, DOCa, or in Catalan DOQ).

Vino de mesa simply means "table wine". These are grown in unclassified vineyards or are blended from two or more different regions, which automatically become table wines under EU law and which may not carry a vintage date nor a geographical identification. There used to be two other categories: *vino comarcal* (VC or CV), which meant a "local wine", and *vino de mesa de* [followed by the province or region] (VdM de…), but these have been abolished and fall within the VdlT.

All but two of the Spanish quality wines have the status of *denominación de origen* (DO). Each is carefully mapped out, though it is not always easy to get a copy of the map, sometimes owing to disputes around the edges. And each is governed by its own *consejo regulador*, which is government-controlled but run locally by a board that includes representatives of winegrowers and bodegas. Each has its own strict set of rules that are summarised in the chapters that follow. The two exceptions are Rioja and Priorato, which have been promoted to *denominación de origen calificada* (DOC, DOCa, or in Catalan DOQ), the former in 1991, the latter in 2002. This is a new category created in 1988 to correspond to the Italian DOCG. If that category does not mean much in Italy, at present it seems to mean even less in Spain. It is based on quality, reputation, and the cost of the grapes. No one could deny that Rioja and Priorato qualify on all counts, and further regulations are under discussion that may give real meaning to a DOCa, but at the moment it means no more than a DO. There have been various suggestions – such as a further classification of areas within the DOCa, like in Bordeaux or Burgundy – but so far these have come to nothing. And one can only wonder, if these are special cases, why not Jerez, Ribera del Duero, Rias Bajas and… But where is one to draw the line? That is the trouble and perhaps things are best left as they are.

A new development, dating from 2003, is the creation of *pago* wines, which are single vineyard wines – all the grapes must be grown in that vineyard. It was thought up by the regional government of Castilla-La Mancha, but is now general and is granted only to estates of outstanding reputation. If within a DO or DOCa, this can be added. Two estates, Dominio de Valpusa and Finca Eléz, have been granted DOs of their own. Several estates are aspiring to similar status.

There is one odd anomaly in the DO rules: cava. This covers Spain's finest sparkling wines, which are made by the same method as Champagne (though the French will not let them say so) and the denomination was originally concerned only with the details of this method. Now it does have geographical limitations, but the principal thrust is still concerned with method rather than with geography, and the vineyard area is not put on the label.

2

CATALUÑA

Cataluña (Catalonia in English and Catalunya in Catalan), is the north-east part of Spain, and stretches about 240 miles down the Mediterranean coast. Although it was one of the first of Spain's Roman possessions – forming part of Hispania Tarraconensis – there is strong evidence that wine was made there long before the Romans arrived. The region's own language Catalan – part old French and part Castilian – is easier to read than to understand when spoken. Although actively suppressed during the Franco years, Catalan has returned with a vengeance and is now the language of choice for those who speak it (though they all speak Castilian too). Vines are grown right up to the French border, in the DO Ampurdan-Costa Brava – as well as along the Costa Brava, where the once remote and beautiful coastline has not yet been destroyed by tourism and development. Travelling south, the next DO area is Alella, hidden amongst the northern suburbs of Barcelona.

Cataluña's capital Barcelona is a wonderful city, and the second most important in Spain – though the Catalans would certainly put it first. There are many excellent restaurants where the local wines can be enjoyed to the full. Anyone exploring the vineyards should pause here for as long as possible.

As a vineyard, Cataluña has re-created itself, beginning in the 1950s, accelerating in the 1960s, and continuing to this day. The process is reflected in the histories of the bodegas that follow. Cavas were the main-stay of the trade, after they were invented at the end of the nineteenth century, while the table wines used to be poor, dominated as they were by

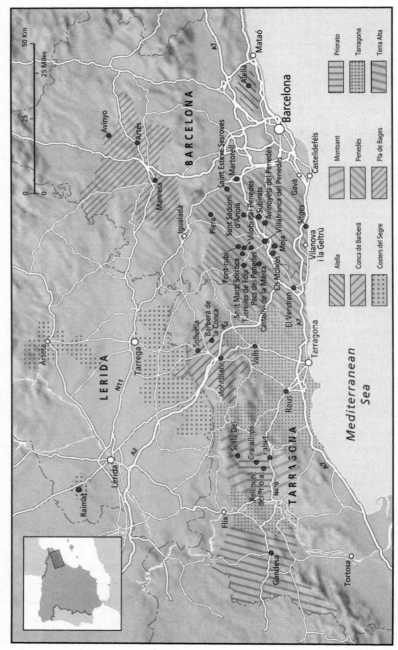

i Cataluña

oxidised *rancios* and nondescript *rosados*. Made by small growers, these can still be found. The major DO, Penedès, lies to the south-west of Barcelona; in addition to table wines, it's home to some of Spain's best cavas and brandies. Behind it to the west lies the DO Conca de Barbera and beyond that, the DO Costers del Segre.

Travelling further down the coast one comes to the DO Tarragona. , Like Barcelona, the city of Tarragona is well worth visiting. The DO Montsant is an enclave within Tarragona and Priorato, in turn, is surrounded by Montsant. One of the most beautiful of all wine-growing districts, Priorato produces some of the finest wines in the world. They are also, alas, among the most expensive. Farther inland, and to the south-west of Tarragona, there is the DO Terra Alta.

All of these are Catalan, though, a line firmly taken by the proud Catalans. Some thought the individual DOs a pedantic nuisance and cheerfully brought grapes from are to another, to the annoyance of the authorities. The solution introduced – in 1999 (but not immediately implemented) – was to create a catch-all DO, simply After some initial resistance, the new DO came about: it seems a good idea, affording DO status to wines that for one reason or another are part of the smaller DOs. There is an obvious parallel with Bordeaux, where wines lying outside specifically denominated areas fall within the general appellation.

Cataluña provides a wonderful range of wines of practically every conceivable kind, several often appearing within a single DO. The Catalans are individualists and although there are some very great names, no one predominates. There can be a huge estate, and next to it a whole lot of small growers, just as there can be a great winery and, just down the road, a boutique one producing wine on the smallest possible scale. It is a fascinating place to visit.

PENEDÈS

Geography

Although the nearest great city is Barcelona, the capital of the wine-growing area is Villafranca del Penedès, inland to the north-northwest of the coastal town of Sitges. The three vineyard areas are: Baja- (Baix-) Penedès (Low Penedès); Medio- (or Mitja-) Penedès (Middle Penedès, and Penedès Superior (or Alt-Penedès) (High Penedès). The first is low-lying, from sea level to 250 metres (820 feet), the second is on rolling hills from 250–500 metres (820–1,640 feet) above sea level, and the third runs into the foothills of the mountains behind the coast and extends to 800 metres (2,625 feet).

Climate

The hottest area is Baja-Penedès, though the heat is moderated by proximity to the Mediterranean. Temperatures vary between 2.6°C (36.7°F) and 27.8°C (82°F) with a mean of 14.4°C (58°F). Rainfall is 500–600 millimetres (19.6–23.6 inches), with 2,548 hours of sunshine. The other areas are cooler, with the Medio-Penedès at 12°C (53.6°F). Being further from the sea, they are more continental, with higher peaks and lower troughs of temperature; but as they are hilly there are many significant microclimates.

Soils

All three areas have deep soil that drains well, with about twenty per cent calcium carbonate, as limestone in the lowerground and chalk in the higher. The lower vineyards tend to be sandy while the higher ones have more clay.

Grapes

There are 121 identified varieties. Most are not even of academic interest, but some may well be revived.

Red varieties: Tempranillo (here called Ull de Llebre); Garnacha Tinta (Lladoner or Aragonés); Monastrell (Alcayata); Cariñena (Mazuelo); Merlot; Cabernet Sauvignon; Pinot Noir; Syrah; and Samsó.

White varieties: Parellada; Xarel.lo (Pansá Blanca); Macabeo (Viura); Chardonnay; Riesling; Gewurztraminer; Chenin Blanc; Moscatel de Alejandría; Subirat-Parent (Malvasía Riojana).

Experiments continue and other varieties can be found.

Planting

Old vineyards were densely planted with up to 7,000 vines per hectare. New thinking reduced that figure to less than half, but the experimental work of Miguel Torres has shown that best quality is achieved with 4,500–5,000, and this density is generally adopted in new vineyard – though experiments continue. Traditionally, the vines were grown *en vaso,* but newer vineyards, particularly those growing foreign varieties, use wires or trellises and are pruned cordon, Guyot, or Royat.

Vineyard area

28,000 hectares.

Authorized yield

55hl/ha for red and *rosado* wines, 65hl/ha for white wines.

Wines

All colours are grown: red; *rosado*; and white, including some sweet whites; a little of the old-style *rancio;* and some sparkling wines classified as *espumoso* (not the same as cavas, though most of the best cavas are grown in Penedès). The usual regulations for ageing apply: *vino joven* (*vi novell*) is young wine for immediate drinking; *vino de crianza* requires two years' ageing, with at least six months in oak. Red *reservas* age for three years, with at least one in oak. White and *rosado reservas* age for two years with six months in oak, and *gran reservas,* at least two years in oak and three in bottle.

Production

1,709,000 hectolitres (1989).

Vintages

The official ratings are:

	whites	reds		whites	reds
1980	3	3	1992	3	3
1981	3	3	1993	4	4
1982	4	3	1994	3	4
1983	4	4	1995	3	4
1984	3	4	1996	4	4
1985	4	5	1997	3	4
1986	2	2	1998	4	5
1987	3	3	1999	4	4
1988	4	4	2000	4	4
1989	3	4	2001	4	4
1990	4	4	2002	3	3
1991	3	3	2003	4	4

Penedès lies on the coast, from about thirty kilometres (18.5 miles) south of Barcelona, extending for forty-five kilometres (28 miles) to a point about sixteen kilometres (10 miles) east of Tarragona. Sitges is about halfway, stretching inland for some thirty-five kilometres (21.5 miles). All distances are approximate, as wine districts are not neatly rectangular. Shape and position are shown on the map.

One of the greatest European cities, Barcelona is much frequented by tourists. Sitges is still a delightful little place despite much modern development; it was a favourite resort of twentieth-century English writer GK Chesterton, to whom a monument has been erected. Well worth a visit, it has some delightful museums, one of which contains a couple of El Grecos. The wine capital is Villafranca del Penedès. At first sight it seems rather nondescript, but its centre has the remains of an old town with a maze of narrow streets and some fine houses. There is also an excellent wine museum which is not devoted entirely to wine, and includes a fine display of plates and tiles, a fourteenth-century primitive, and some good modern paintings. Wine lovers will be most interested in the Roman-era amphorae used for transporting and exporting wine, proof of the area's historical importance as a wine-growing district.

Like so many parts of Spain, Penedès has always been a wine region: recent excavations suggest viticulture dates to pre-Phoenician days. A beautiful piece of countryside with old farms, pine woods, olive groves, cypress and nut trees, and of course vines, it has a most agreeable climate. The mountains of Montserrat shelter Penedès from the cold northern winds. It's no surprise that it was favoured by rich Romans who had villas here; the many remains of amphorae indicate that wine was exported as well as drunk locally. The sweet *rancio* wines that are still made in small quantities are said to date from that era. After the Romans left, wine-making vanished into obscurity for centuries. What wine was made was drunk locally and not much more is known. As late as the eighteenth century there were virtually no roads linking inland areas with the coast, hence no carts, so everything was carried by pack animals. Any wine made inland for sale was usually distilled. In the seventeenth century, wine began to appear in export statistics. It went to most parts of Europe, but the main market was Latin America. These wines came from Baja-Penedès and were generally fortified for export – even the strongest of them. The most famous was the Moscatel from Sitges.

In the nineteenth century, bulk wines were exported to France following the devastation wrought by phylloxera there, but most came from Catalan areas other than Penedès. Phylloxera arrived in 1887, reaching its peak of destruction in 1890. Its inexorable progress continued until 1910, by which time it had spread everywhere, destroying many vineyards. Many were then replanted with hybrid vines that gave atrocious wines. From the 1870s to the 1960s, the history of wine-making is largely that of cava, which is covered in a separate chapter.

No nationally or internationally recognized table wines were grown until the Torres family began a revolution that was to give the region a completely new dimension. Trained in France, Miguel Torres's outlook was international, and he judged wines by absolute standards. He planted the classic varieties from France and Germany as well as the best of the Spanish ones. Before growing anything he meticulously investigated the soil and the microclimate to see that each variety was grown where it would perform best. Not least, he brought back with him the latest and best wine-making techniques. In the nineteenth century, wines generally had been fermented in underground pits where the temperatures could rise alarmingly and all the aromas could be lost. Others were soon to climb on his bandwagon. The variety and quality of the wines available were totally transformed, and Penedès is now a leading area for table wines judged by world standards.

The importance of imported varieties must not, however, be exaggerated. They still form only a small, though crucial, part of the total. Most vineyards are planted with the traditional varieties originally grown to make cavas. But the new varieties have had a profound effect on the development of the Spanish wine trade and have spread to many other areas.

Like so many of the places in Spain where fine wine is made, Penedès is beautiful. Baja-Penedès is the least attractive. It lies on the coastal plain and, like nearly the whole of the Spanish Mediterranean coastline, it has been developed - built over with modern high-rises. Most of the vineyards have disappeared beneath the concrete, but there are still some left. A good way to see where they begin is take the train from Barcelona to Villafranca del Penedès as it is much easier to see them from the train than from the road.

Medio-Penedès lies in a great broad valley behind a range of hills. To describe it as a valley is rather misleading, though, for it is an area of small hills, streams, and gorges. In such a place there are inevitably many microclimates, and some are much better for vine-growing than others. There is mixed farming and many other crops, notably delightful orchards of nut trees with their beautiful blossom in spring. Penedès Superior lies in the foothills of the mountains, though most of the vineyards are on relatively flat pieces of land, and there is the same variety of microclimates.

Baja-Penedès is the hottest of the three areas, despite the moderating influence of the sea, and also the wettest. Storms are few, and all in all it is an easy climate to grow vines in. Historically it was an area of Malvasía and Moscatel vines, and its most famous wine was the Moscatel of Sitges; but sweet fortified wines have fallen out of favour and these vines are not grown much today. Recently many vineyards have been replanted with red wine grapes, usually Garnacha, Cariñena, Monastrell, and Tempranillo.

Medio-Penedès is in the hills 250–500 metres (820–1,640 feet) above sea level, so that the moderating influence of the sea is less apparent, making it warm in summer and cooler in winter – quite a lot cooler, with snow from time to time. It is the best area for most vine varieties, and all the red and white wine grapes are grown. There are vineyards of Chardonnay and Chenin Blanc, but imported white varieties on the whole tend to do better higher up.

Penedès Superior, at 500–800 metres (1,640–2,625 feet), is colder in winter and snow is commonplace, but it can be hot in summer and there is plenty of sunshine to ripen the grapes. Current climatic statistics are not available, and in the mountains they are likely to be unreliable anyhow. It is where the imported white wine varieties come into their own. Of the native varieties, the most important here is Parellada. It is too cool for Cabernet Sauvignon. At the height of summer, when the temperature on the coast is 30°C (86°F) by day and only falls to 25°C (77°F) by night, in Penedès Superior it may rise to 40°C (104°F) by day and fall to 15°C (59°F) by night. In Penedès, though, more than in most areas, the emphasis should be on the wide varieties of microclimates, allowing growers to plant any grape variety in the right place in any of the districts – and they do.

Statistics for the number of vines planted in Penedès are meaningless, as figures vary annually. Malvasía, for example, is declining, while Cabernet Sauvignon (along with most of the other imported varieties) is rapidly increasing. It is worth noting that the principal product is not table wine but cava, and that grapes are also grown for another important product: brandy. While the big cava producers and some larger wine-makers (notably Torres) have huge vineyards, the average holding is small at 2.5 hectares, with growers selling to the long-established and important houses and cooperatives.

If a hundred years ago Penedès produced bulk wines that were very southern in style – flabby, short on acid, and lacking in aroma owing to the hot fermentation that had driven off all the volatile elements – the position today is the very opposite. The revolution is complete. Old-style wines such as Moscatel de Sitges (which is good when you can find it) are still produced in small quantities, as are some *rancios,* which have their aficionados, but temperature-controlled vinification is now the order of the day and highly trained oenologists create table wines to the best international standards. Full use is made of the native grapes, but supplementing them with the imported varieties has created a whole new range of wines and has added new dimensions to the old ones. The whites were first to be recognized internationally, as one might expect from an area well versed in making good base wines for cavas. These are now among Spain's best, but so are the *rosados* and the reds. The *rosados* are often vinified from Garnacha, but there are also excellent ones from the imported varieties, notably Merlot. The reds fully realize the potential of the native varieties, but these are often enhanced by blending with the imported ones, which can add backbone and complexity – Tempranillo, for instance, blends very well with Cabernet Sauvignon. And many growers produce excellent reds made from the imported varieties alone, notably Cabernet Sauvignon and Merlot, or combinations of the two. Since the 1970s, Penedès has been a most exciting region and many of the wines of all descriptions produced today are world class.

Some leading bodegas

ALBET I NOYA

Can Vendrell de la Codina, 08739 Sant Pau D'Ordal, Barcelona.
Tel: +34 938 99 48 12; Fax: +34 938 99 49 30;
Email: albetinoya@albetinoya.com; Website: www.albetinoya.com
This story began in 1903 when the Albet family moved in to replant the vineyard after phylloxera. They are still here, now in their fourth generation, having bought the business in 1986. The forty-six hectare vineyard is cultivated organically, and other grapes are bought in from local growers taught to use the same methods. Can Vendrell de la Codina is 300 metres (984 feet) above sea level on the western slopes of the Ordal mountain range. White varieties planted include the usual local ones together with Chardonnay, Viognier, and Sauvignon Blanc. Black varieties include Cabernet Sauvignon and Tempranillo, but also Syrah, Petite Sirah, Caladoc (a cross between Merlot and Garnacha), and Arinanoya (a cross between Merlot and Petit Verdot). Apart from these, Albet i Noya is experimenting with seven grape varieties that flourished before phylloxera but have now almost disappeared. It makes a rather bewildering number of wines including varietals from Xarel.lo, Chardonnay, Tempranillo, Cabernet Sauvignon, Merlot, and Syrah. The labels are Can Vendrell, Lignum, Noya, and for its top range, Col.lecció, made only in good years. The excellent

Reserva Marti is made from sixty per cent Tempranillo, thirty per cent Cabernet Sauvignon, and ten per cent Syrah. These are certainly among the best in the district and the leading wines deserve bottle age.

ALEMANI I CORRIO

Melió 78, Villafranca del Penedès, Barcelona. Tel/Fax: +34 938 17 25 87; Email: sotlefriec@totpenes.com

Established in 1999 with a modest eight-hectare vineyard, this boutique bodega has developed a formidable reputation for the quality of its wines.

BACH

Carretera Martorell – Capellades km 20.5, 08635 Sant Esteve de Sesrovires, Barcelona. Tel: +34 937 71 40 52; Fax: +34 937 71 31 77; Email: codinfo@codorniu.es; Website: www.grupocodorniu.com

The Bach family fortune came from selling cotton to the French army in World War I. The profits were ploughed into building a great mansion in the middle of a 350-hectare estate. In 1975, it was bought by the great cava maker Codorníu and, like all the properties of that illustrious concern, it is immaculately kept up. It has eighty hectares of vineyard in Penedès Superior at the foot of Montserrat, and other grapes are bought in. The wines are good, and there is an enormous range of them. The whites include Extrísimo, made in 2003 from eighty per cent Xarel.lo and twenty per cent Macabeo with twelve months in American oak, and the notably good Extrísimo Seco made in 2004 from seventy per cent Xarel.lo and fifteen per cent each of Macabeo and Chardonnay with no wood ageing. The *rosado* in 2004 was made from fifty-four per cent Tempranillo, forty-one per cent Cabernet Sauvignon, and five per cent Garnacha. The red *reserva* 1994 had forty-five per cent Cabernet Sauvignon, twenty-five per cent Tempranillo, seventeen per cent Cariñena, and thirteen per cent Merlot. Its reds include good varietals: Cabernet Sauvignon, Tempranillo, and a particularly good Merlot. *See also* Cataluña.

RENÉ BARBIER

Partida Torre del Gall s/n, 08739 Sant Cugat de Sesgarrigues. Tel: +34 938 91 70 90; Fax: +34 938 91 70 99; Email: renebarbier@renebarbier.es; Website: www.renebarbier.es

This large bodega was founded in 1880 by a Frenchman, Léon Barbier, from a wine-growing family at Avignon, but is now owned by the great cava house Freixenet. It has vineyard holdings of 250 hectares, which include thirty hectares of Cabernet Sauvignon. Good wines are made in a great many styles.

Varietal whites include Chardonnay and Xarel.lo, and there is a red Cabernet Sauvignon. One of its best known wines is the good white Kriliner, made in 2002 from forty per cent Xarel.lo, thirty per cent Macabeo, and thirty per cent Parellada. The red *crianza* 2001 was made from seventy per cent Tempranillo, twenty per cent Cabernet Sauvignon, and ten per cent Merlot. The *reservas* usually have eighty-five per cent Tempranillo and fifteen per cent Cabernet Sauvignon. There is no connection (other than through membership of the founding family) with the Priorato bodega of René Barbier Fill.

CAN FEIXES-HUGUET

Finca Can Feixes, 08785 Cabrera d'Anoia, Barcelona. Tel: +34 937 71 82 27; Fax: +34 937 71 80 31; Email: canfeixes@canfeixes.com; Website: www.canfeixes.com

This great domaine at Cabrera D'Anoia, whose history dates to the fourteenth century, has been making wine since 1690 - though its present owners do not claim to trace their history further back than 1768. It has eighty hectares of vines in the hills, up to 400 metres (1,312 feet) above sea level, where there is a considerable difference between day and night temperatures. They sell some of the grapes but use most to make very good wines. The Blanc Selecció 2003 was made from forty per cent Parellada, thirty-five per cent Macabeo, twenty per cent Chardonnay, and five per cent Pinot Noir, fermented in stainless steel and given no oak. The varietal Chardonnay 2001, however, was given nine months in French oak. The red Reserva Especial 1999 was made from sixty-five per cent Cabernet Sauvignon and thirty-five per cent Merlot. The Negre Selecció 2002 was made from forty per cent each of Merlot and Cabernet Sauvignon with the rest Tempranillo and spent a year in oak, ninety per cent French. The top red wines are excellent and have very good ageing potential.

CAN RAFOLS DELS CAUS

Can Ràfols del Caus s/n, 09739 Avinyonet del Penedès (Barcelona). Tel: +34 938 97 00 13; Fax: +34 938 97 03 70; Email: canrafols@seker.es

Founded in 1980 in an old *masía* (farm or country house), this estate has a substantial vineyard of fifty-eight hectares and makes some of the best wines in the DO. Most are sold as Petit Caus and Gran Caus. Imported grape varieties predominate and for the reds these are combined in the Bordeaux manner; for instance Gran Caus 1988 was made from forty-one per cent Cabernet Sauvignon, thirty-four per cent Merlot, and twenty-five per cent Cabernet Franc, while Gran Caus Crianza 1989 was made from fifty-three per cent Cabernet Franc, thirty-two per cent Cabernet Sauvignon, and fifteen per cent Merlot. Caus Lubis is a varietal Merlot. Its varietal whites include Vinya La Calma from Chenin Blanc, an excellent expression of that grape, and not least Vinya El Rocalís, from the rare Incroccio Manzoni vine, a Pinot Blanc x Riesling cross from Italy: unusual and very good.

CASTELL DE VILARNAU
Ctra D'Espiells km 1.4, "Finca Can Petit", 08770 Sant Sadurní D'Anoia, Barcelona. Tel: +34 938 91 23 61; Fax: +34 938 91 29 13; Email: castelldevilarnau@castelldevilarnau.es; Website: www.gonzalezbyass.es

Founded by the great sherry house Gonzalez Byass in 1982 to make cava, this bodega now markets a range of excellent table wines that are sold under the name Les Planes. The Chardonnay is a varietal that is twenty-five per cent barrel-fermented, which gives just the right touch of oak. The *rosado* 2005 was made with fifteen per cent Syrah, as was the Cabernet Sauvignon 2003 – the Syrah adding a dimension. These wines are excellent value.

CAVAS GRAMONA
Industria 26, 08770 Sant Sadurni D'Anoia, Barcelona. Tel: +34 938 91 01 13; Fax: +34 931 18 32 84; Website: www.gramona.com

This family-owned bodega, now in its fourth generation, was founded in 1881 and has 29 hectares of vineyard. Principally known for its cavas, it also makes a wide range of very good table wines, often from unusual varieties, as well as marc. The whites include Gessamí from seventy per cent Muscat and thirty per cent Sauvignon Blanc, and varietals from Chardonnay, Riesling, Gewürztraminer, and Sauvignon Blanc. The *rosados* have forty per cent Syrah and thirty per cent each of Pinot Noir and Merlot. The very good red Merlot & Co 2001 was made from seventy per cent Merlot and thirty per cent Syrah.

CAVAS HILL
Bonavista 2, 08734 Moja, Barcelona. Tel: +34 938 90 05 88; Fax: +34 938 17 02 46; Email: cavashill@cavashill.com; Website: www.cavashill.com

The original Joseph Hill came from England to settle in Cataluña in 1660, but the present bodega was founded in 1887. It has 50 hectares of vineyards at an altitude of 200 metres (656 feet), and makes a notable range of good value table wines. The white wines include blanc de blancs made from fifty per cent Xarel.lo and varietals from Chardonnay and Sauvignon Blanc. The Masía Hill *rosado* is from sixty per cent Tempranillo and forty per cent Garnacha. The reds include Gran Reserva with sixty per cent Cabernet Sauvignon, thirty per cent Tempranillo, and ten per cent Syrah. Gran Civet is made from fifty per cent Tempranillo, thirty-five per cent Cabernet Sauvignon, and fifteen per cent Merlot. Its best known red is the massive but quaffable Gran Toc, made from sixty per cent Tempranillo, twenty-five per cent Cabernet Sauvignon, and fifteen per cent Merlot. Slightly sparkling wines (*vinos de aguja*) are sold under the name Timon.

JEAN LEON

Pago Jean León, 08775 Torrelavit, Barcelona. Tel: +34 938 99 55 12; Fax: +34 938 99 55 17; Email: jeanleon@jeanleon.com; Website: www.jeanleon.com

This bodega, along with Torres, led the way with imported vines. Jean León (his original name was Ceferino Carrión) was born in Santander and became a successful restaurateur, owning La Scala Restaurant in Beverley Hills. He wanted his own wines to serve in his restaurant – wines that would please his American clientele – and thought of growing vines in France, but fortunately took advice from the great Professor Amerine of the wine school at Davis, California. In 1963 he found the right place at Torrelavit, and bought it. French vines were (and are) all the rage in America, and he set out to get the best. His Chardonnay came from Corton, his Cabernet Sauvignon from Château Lafite, and his Cabernet Franc from Château La Lagune. His first vintage was in 1969. The wines were spectacularly successful and became legendary. There are now 61 hectares of vineyard growing Cabernet Sauvignon, Cabernet Franc, Merlot and Chardonnay in five separate *pagos* that are identified on the labels. The bodega is moving toward organic viticulture. In 1995 the enterprise was bought by Miguel Torres, (*see* below), who was a great friend. If some of the followers of Jean León had doubts, these were groundless: the wines are better than ever. It is one of the few places growing really good Chardonnay. Tarrasola is a very successful blend of eighty-five per cent Chardonnay and fifteen per cent Garnacha Blanca with three months in oak. Its greatest wines are the reds. These include varietal Merlots and Cabernet Sauvignons. The superb Gran Reserva 1996 Cabernet Sauvignon, which included fifteen per cent Cabernet Franc, had two years in French oak and three in bottle before release, and carries a striking label by the artist Josep Guinovart. Cabernet Franc has not been used in later vintages of the Gran Reserva. These wines are produced only in the best vintages. The same grape mix went into the 1999 Reserva. The top wine is Zemis, the 2000 *crianza* being a blend of sixty per cent Cabernet Sauvignon, thirty per cent Merlot, and ten per cent Cabernet Franc; the composition is likely to vary from year to year. For its Terrasola range *see* Cataluña.

ANTONIO MASCARO

Casal 9, 08720 Villafranca del Penedès, Barcelona. Tel: +34 938 90 16 28;
Fax: +34 938 90 13 58; Email: mascaro@mascaro.es

This admirable bodega was founded in 1945 by Narciso Mascaró Marsé as a distillery and is now owned by his son Antonio Mascaró Carbonell, who is ably assisted by the third generation, his daughter Montserrat. It is still perhaps principally known as a distillery and its pot-still brandies are among Spain's best. It then branched out into making good cavas. The family owns two estates with some sixty hectares of vineyards. But Don Antonio is an enthusiastic wine man, with a great love of Bordeaux. When others set the example of growing Bordeaux varieties he decided to grow his own. He planted Cabernet Sauvignon in the thirty-five-hectare vineyard at his Mas Miquel estate in 1980, and the first wine was released in 1991. There is a varietal Cabernet Sauvignon from the El Castell vineyard, but the top of the range is a *gran reserva* Anima, ninety per cent Cabernet Sauvignon and ten per cent Merlot, made only in the best years and aged for three years in Tronçais casks, initially in new ones but racked into old wood. It improves with further time in bottle and is best drunk at ten to twenty-five years. Its red wines are its best.

PARES BALTA

Masía Can Baltà, 08796 Pacs del Penedès, Barcelona.
Tel: +34 938 90 13 99; Fax: +34 938 90 11 43;
Email: paresbalta@paresbalta.com; Website: www.paresbalta.com

The family has owned this property since 1790, but founded the bodega in 1934. It has an extraordinarily large vineyard holding of 637 hectares in five different places, four ranging from 180–205 metres (591–673 feet), but the biggest of 500 hectares at between 680–750 metres (2,231–2,460 feet). They are fertilized by grazing sheep. All of the wines are good and the best are very good indeed. Mas Pons is a varietal Chardonnay, but perhaps the most interesting white is the slightly sweet Honey Moon, made from late harvested Parellada. The *rosado*, Ros de Pacs, is made form Cabernet Sauvignon and Merlot. Mas Petit is the best varietal Cabernet Sauvignon, aged in Allier oak. Mas Elena is a Bordeaux blend of Cabernet Sauvignon, Merlot, and Cabernet Franc. But in the best years there are also special releases. Mas de Carol is a Chardonnay grown at 680 metres (2,231 feet). Mas Irene is made from Merlot and Cabernet Franc. Absis 2000 *reserva* is made from Tempranillo, Merlot, Cabernet Sauvignon, and Shiraz. Wines from this house are worth seeking out.

JOAN RAVENTOS ROSELL

Heretat Vall-Ventós s/n, Carretera Sant Sadurní d'Anoia – Mesquería km 6.5, 08783 Masquefa, Barcelona. Tel: +34 937 72 52 51; Fax: +34 937 72 71 91; Email: correu@raventosrosell.com; Website: www.raventosrosell.com

Founded by a member of the Raventós family in 1895, this bodega has 100 hectares of vineyard growing Parellada, Macabeo, Xarel.lo, Chardonnay, Sauvignon Blanc, Chenin, Cabernet Sauvignon, Merlot, and Pinot Noir. It goes in very much for varietals. In whites there are Chenin, Chardonnay, and Sauvignon Blanc; in *rosados* a Merlot and a Pinot Noir vinified as a blanc de noirs (with minimal skin contact); in reds Tempranillo, Merlot, and Cabernet Sauvignon. The Chardonnays are well balanced and not over-oaked. The Cabernet Sauvignons and Merlots are well structured and deserve bottle age. There are also blends. In whites, the Blanc Primer has Chardonnay and Chenin, while the Rosat Primer has Pinot Noir and Merlot. The best red of all is the Reserva, which in 2000 had fifty per cent Cabernet Sauvignon, thirty per cent Merlot, and twenty per cent Syrah with twelve months in American and French oak.

JOSEP MARÍA RAVENTÓS I BLANC

Plaça de Roure, 08770 Sant Sadurní D'Anoia, Barcelona. Tel: +34 938 18 32 62; Fax: +34 938 91 25 00; Email: raventos@raventos.com; Website: www.raventos.com

This bodega was founded by a rebellious member of the Raventós family (that owns Codorníu) who went off to do his own thing on land owned by his family since 1497. It is now run by his son. He followed the family tradition in putting up some striking and beautiful buildings, in 1986, and in making good cavas. There are eighty-eight hectares of vineyard. The white wines include a varietal Chardonnay and El Preludi, made from the same mix as the Cava Gran Reserva: fifty per cent Xarel.lo, thirty-five per cent Macabeo, and fifteen per cent Chardonnay. Premium Vi Blanc is made from sixty per cent Macabeo and forty per cent Muscat. The *rosado*, La Rosa, is a Merlot. The reds include Isabel Negra with equal parts of Merlot and Cabernet, given fifteen months in French and American oak, and L'Hereu from sixty per cent Tempranillo, thirty per cent Merlot, and ten per cent Cabernet Sauvignon.

MIGUEL TORRES

M Torres 6, 08720 Villafranca del Penedès, Barcelona. Tel: +34 938 17 74 00; Fax: +34 938 17 74 44; Email: webmaster@torres.es; Website: www.torres.es

Old-established companies seldom lead revolutions – but this one did, thanks to the inspiration and energy of the fifth generation of the family,

Miguel Torres Jr, who had a fine foundation to build on. Today Torres is the most famous table-wine bodega in Spain, its wine exported to eighty-five countries and found on the lists of two-thirds of the Michelin two-star restaurants in France. (No one can be more insular than the French, but even they have been convinced). The fame is bolstered by high-class, family-run wineries in California and Chile, so the operation is truly international.

Old documents suggest that the family has been growing wine in Penedès since 1628, but no such date is claimed for the company. Jaime Torres emigrated to Cuba in 1855. After a distinctly shaky start he made good in the newly burgeoning petroleum industry and in shipping. In 1870, he came home a rich man and joined his brother Miguel, a viticulturist, in founding the company. He had big ideas and he realized one of them when he commissioned the largest wine vat in the world: 600,000 litres, a good deal bigger than the famous Heidelberg tun. In 1904, King Alfonso of Spain visited the bodega and put this monstrous vessel to a bizarre use by having lunch inside it. Jaime Torres died in the same year, unmarried, and left his share to his brother, who himself died two years later. It has been handed on from father to son ever since. Miguel, the fourth generation, took over in 1932 at the age of twenty-three, following the early death of his father. Four years later the Spanish Civil War broke out and the bodega was taken over by the Republican Workers' Committee. In January 1939 it was accidentally bombed, the bomb having been intended for the railway station next door. All was ruin. Everything, including the great vat, was destroyed. Miguel Torres, however, was undaunted. In 1940, with the war ended, he set about rebuilding the bodega and re-establishing the business. He also made one very important decision: to cease from selling wine in bulk and to sell it only in bottles. A new opportunity then arose. In 1941 Hitler invaded France and French wines were no longer available in the United States. Miguel and his wife crossed the Atlantic (a highly dangerous undertaking at the time) and set about selling their wines. They did no advertising but hawked the bottles around restaurants, insisting that the restaurateurs should try them. Stories are told of having three dinners in an evening and of Sra Torres always carrying a bottle in her handbag. A trade was established and has never been lost. Miguel lived until 1991.

Miguel Torres of the fifth generation was born in 1941. After reading chemistry at Barcelona University he went to the University of Dijon to study viticulture and oenology. Meanwhile, in 1956, his father had introduced the brands Sangre de Toro, Viña Sol, and Coronas. Miguel Jr came into the company in 1962, full of ideas and well equipped to carry them out. Fortunately, he was allowed to do so. In 1966 he started to plant imported vines, at first Chardonnay and Cabernet Sauvignon, to be followed by Merlot, Pinot Noir, Gewürztraminer, and Riesling. Since 1975, the bodega has been practising ecological viticulture, and instead of using insecticides it has attacked pests by introducing their natural predators. It also started to use stainless steel for fermentation. All sorts of combinations of grapes were used experimentally, and it is rather confusing to try and look back. But the great breakthrough came in 1979 when Torres Black Label 1970 (later called Gran Coronas Mas La Plana and then simply Mas La Plana), won the Cabernet section of a blind tasting, in the French Gault Millau Wine Olympics, beating Château Latour 1970 into second place and leaving other illustrious names well behind. Torres wines had to be taken very seriously and Penedès, as a wine-growing area, was firmly put on the map. This wine is made only in good years; there was no 1986 nor 1992, for example.

Miguel Torres took a new look at everything, and not least at the relationship between the vine and the site, matching one to the other after studying the soil and microclimate. He also studied planting density and training the vines. Torres now has thirteen vineyards in the various Catalan DOs making a total of 930 hectares. Of these some 500 hectares are trained on wires and are suitable for mechanical harvesting. The debate between those who favour hand picking and those who prefer machinery is a hot one that shows no sign of abating. In climates like that of Penedès, where the weather can be very hot at the time of the vintage, machinery has the real advantage that it can be used at night, when the grapes are relatively cool, so avoiding premature fermentation. The company's own vineyards provide half its requirements. The other half (entirely native varieties) is bought in. Each variety is vinified separately. Apart from the commercial vineyards, Miguel Torres is keen to examine and, if they prove good enough, to grow local varieties that are almost extinct. He is cultivating about a hundred.

In oenology, he made two particularly important changes: the use of controlled temperature fermentation and maturing the wine in small oak casks for a carefully limited period, as has long been the practice in Bordeaux, but was unknown in Cataluña. Cultivated yeasts are used and the company grow some of its own.

In 1967, Miguel Torres married an accomplished German artist, Waltraud Maczassek. She helps with the sale of Torres wines in Germany and the Riesling is named in her honour.

The range of Torres wines is so extensive as to be rather bewildering, made all the more so by the fact that both names and grape mixes have changed from time to time over the years. Until recently it thought the Torres name was enough and did not bother with the DOs. Now these are being used, so many of the wines fall within Conca de Barbará and the new DO Cataluña.

Torres now claims to be the biggest wine exporter in Spain. All its wines are good and fully deserve their high reputation. Indeed, most are very good. The Mas La Plana vineyard was planted with Cabernet Sauvignon in 1966 and the first harvest taken in 1970. The Gran Coronas Mas La Plana of that year, which beat Château Latour in the tasting mentioned above, had ten per cent Monastrell and twenty per cent Ull de Llebre, and was aged for twelve months in American oak. By 1975, the Cabernet Sauvignon was showing its real quality and the wine of that year, which only had ten per cent Cabernet Franc in the blend, was aged for eighteen months in American oak. In 1981, the style was changed, with reduced yields, made as a varietal Cabernet Sauvignon, and given twenty-one months' ageing in fifty-fifty American and French oak. Although highly successful in the export markets, it was very intense and a bit too much so for the local taste, so from then onwards the style was gradually softened. In 1991, it was matured in 100 per cent new French oak, as it has been even since, with the name changed to Mas La Plana. It is very fine indeed, with great ageing potential. Gran Coronas is a fine blended red made from eighty-five per cent Cabernet Sauvignon and fifteen per cent Tempranillo. Gran Viña Sol is a white with eighty-five per cent Chardonnay and fifteen per cent Parellada, one third barrel-fermented in French oak.

MASÍA VALLFORMOSA

Apartado de Correos No 327, 08720 Villafranca del Penedès, Barcelona.
Tel: +34 938 97 82 86; Fax: +34 938 97 83 55;
Email: vallformosa@vallformosa.es; Website: www.vallformosa.es

This is a family-owned bodega in Vilobí del Penedès, established in 1865, whose nine vineyards make an impressive total of 307 hectares. It is well known for its cavas but also makes some good table wines. The varietal Chardonnay, made without malolactic fermentation, is fresh and good. Viña Blanca is made from the traditional cava grapes, Macabeo, Xarel.lo, and Parellada. Its *rosado*, Viña Rosada, is made from Garnacha and Cariñena. Its varietal reds include Tempranillo, Syrah, Cabernet Sauvignon, and Merlot. Its best Cabernet Sauvignon is Clos Maset Selección Especial. The good Vall Reserva red has 85 per cent Tempranillo and 15 per cent Cabernet Sauvignon. Its semi-sparkling wines are sold under the name Marina.

JANÉ VENTURA

Carretera de Calafell 2, 43700 El Vendrell, Tarragona. Tel: +34 977 660 118;
Fax: +34 977 661 239; Email: janeventura@janeventura.com;
Website: www.janeventura.com

A family-owned bodega with a history of evolution. The present proprietor's great-grandfather began making wine for local sale in 1914, then the bodega was formed in 1930, and eventually, in 1985, the wine began to be bottled. It has gone from strength to strength ever since. It has twelve hectares of vineyards in two plots, one at 250 metres (820 feet) and the other at 450 metres (1,476 feet). Other grapes are bought in. There is a young white made from ninety per cent Xarel.lo, eight per cent Parellada, and two per cent Subirat-Parent, and a barrel-fermented Macabeo, Finca El Camps, with five to ten per cent Xarel.lo. A *rosado* is made from ninety per cent Tempranillo and ten per cent Cabernet Sauvignon. There are several reds. Vinya Palfuriana is made from equal parts of Tempranillo and Merlot, while Margalló has fifty per cent Tempranillo and twenty-five per cent each of Merlot and Cabernet Sauvignon. The top reds are Finca El Camps and, best of all, Mas Vilella, both varietal Cabernet Sauvignons. These are all good wines and well worth looking for.

ALELLA

Geography

The vineyards are only about fifteen kilometres (under 10 miles) north from the centre of Barcelona, which is one of the most densely populated cities in Europe and expanding rapidly. The result is that many of the traditional vineyards have been built over, mostly with the agreeable houses of rich Barcelona businessmen. Surprisingly for such a small DO, there are really three districts: the coastal area up to 90 metres (295 feet); the traditional area from 90–150 metres (295–492 feet); and now new sites have been opened up higher in the foothills of the Cordillera Catalana, though they go up to only 260 metres (853 feet). The vineyards are generally planted on slopes facing the sea. The style of the wine so far, despite the building and planting of new vineyards, does not seem to have altered.

Climate

The traditional slopes, going up to ninety metres (295 feet), are typically Mediterranean: mild winters and hot summers. The average temperature is 15.8°C (60.4°F), the rainfall 500–600 millimetres (19.7–23.6 inches), and the sunshine 2,500 hours. The new and higher vineyards are generally rather cooler but, especially when sheltered from the sea breezes, rather more continental. This area is protected from cold winds by the Sierra de Parpers. There is, however, a serious frost risk, especially in the new, higher vineyards.

Soils

Light and sandy topsoil. The old vineyards are on sauló, a porous sandy soil over granite, and the new ones over limestone that is very suitable for wine-growing.

Grapes

White varieties: Pansá Blanca (meaning white grape, a clone of Xarel.lo); Garnacha Blanca; Chardonnay; Pansá Rosada; Picapoll; Parellada; Chardonnay; Sauvignon Blanc; Chenin; Malvasía; and Macabeo. Of these, the first two are the most widely planted.

Red varieties: Tempranillo (Ull de Llebre); Garnacha Tinta; Garnacha Peluda; Merlot; Pinot Noir; Syrah, and Cabernet Sauvignon. Again, the first two are the most widely planted.

Planting

The lower vineyards are planted mostly with Garnacha Blanca; the intermediate heights, from 90–160 metres (295–525 feet) are planted with Pansá Blanca, together with the red varieties; and the new, higher vineyards are planted with Pansá Blanca. Old vineyards grow bush vines trained *en vaso*, but newer ones are double cordon (particularly Chardonnay) on wires.

Vineyard area

In 1956 there were 1,500 hectares, but owing to the spread of the city this was reduced to 560 hectares by 1990, even including the new areas. It fell even further, to 380 hectares, though it has now risen to about 500 hectares, making it one of the smallest DOs.

Authorized yield

45.5hl/ha.

Wines

Red, *rosado,* and white (11.5–13.5% ABV), but most of the production is white. The traditional Alella was a white vinified from 100 per cent Pansá.

Production

4,720 hectolitres. (1990).

Vintages

1990 (4); 1991 (5); 1992 (4); 1993 (5); 1994 (4); 1995 (4); 1996 (3) (but some good Chardonnay); 1997 (5); 1998 (5); 1999 (4); 2000 (5); 2001 (5); 2002 (4); 2003 (4).

Although wine-growing in this beautiful, hilly countryside goes back for many centuries, traditionally making sweet white wines, the vineyards were wiped out by phylloxera at the end of the nineteenth century. They continued as smallholdings, but they were not re-created commercially until after the end of the Spanish Civil War, so as vineyards go they are comparatively modern. They got off to a good start. In the days when most Spanish white wines were heavy, flabby, and oxidized, these (together with some in the northwest) were the conspicuous exceptions: light, fresh, delicious, and usually with just a touch of sweetness. They are still undoubtedly among Spain's best and need a year in bottle before they show to full advantage. Some have a trace of carbon dioxide, but no more than a spritz. The *rosados* and reds are good without being exciting. Unfortunately, many of the vineyards were, and are, small – just a couple of hectares or so, cultivated as a hobby by people who work in Barcelona. This, coupled with the great demand for building land from the 1960s onward, has led to the vineyards' tragic reduction and to their movement to higher ground. As would be expected of an area so close to Barcelona, where much of the modern bodega equipment is made, vinification is completely up to date.

Some leading bodegas

ALELLA VINÍCOLA CAN JONC

Angel Guimerà 62, 08328 Alella, Barcelona. Tel: +34 935 40 38 42; Fax: +34 935 40 16 48; Email: commercial@alellavinicola.com; Website: www.alellavinicola.com

This estate began as a cooperative in 1906, and unlike most was housed in a very beautiful building. It is now a company with 100 shareholders and 150 hectares of vines: much what it was before, but reconstructed. Recently it has been facing competition from private bodegas, nevertheless it continues to make good wines and to sell them under the trademark Marfil.

ALTA ALELLA

Cau D'En Genis, 08391 Tiana, Barcelona. Tel: +34 934 64 49 49;
Fax: +34 934 64 24 0; Email: carmenet@carmenet.es

A small bodega and a newcomer, founded in 2000 with a modest ecological vineyard holding of eight hectares. It has made great strides and its wines are very highly regarded, particularly its red Orbus, a varietal Syrah.

PARXET

Mas Parxet s/n, 08391 Tiana, Barcelona. Tel: +34 933 95 08 11;
Fax: +34 933 95 55 00; Website: www.parxet.com

This privately owned bodega is housed in a beautiful 16th-century farmhouse, and beneath it lies a maze of fascinating tunnels, many of which are used to mature its excellent cavas. Next door is a modern vinification plant. It first bottled its wines in 1920 and created its leading brand, Marqués de Alella, in 1981. It owns 40 hectares of vineyards, planted mostly with Pansá but also with some Chardonnay and a little Chenin. It also buys from some 80 growers, whose average holdings are less that two hectares – and this puts it in control of about half the DO's wine. Most of its table wine is white, with a little *rosado*. The wines include Classico, made from Pansá Blanca, an unoaked Chardonnay, and Chardonnays matured in Allier oak. These are very good wines.

ROURA

Vall de Rials s/n, 08328 Alella, Barcelona. Tel: +34 933 52 74 56;
Fax: +34 933 52 43 39; Email: roura@roura.es; Website: www.roura.es

Founded as recently as 1987, this bodega has already made a name for itself by planting its 45 hectares with Sauvignon Blanc, Chardonnay, Cabernet Sauvignon, Merlot, and Tempranillo, and it also buys from twenty small growers. It matures its Chardonnays and reds in American and Allier oak. In whites there are varietals from Xarel.lo, Sauvignon Blanc, and Chardonnay, the latter given six months in Nevers oak. Its *rosado* is a varietal Merlot. Its reds, which are perhaps the best made in the DO, include a *sin crianza* (another term for *joven*) and a *crianza*, both from equal parts of Tempranillo and Cabernet Sauvignon, the former given American oak and the latter part American and part French. It also makes varietal Merlots. The Merlot Reserva 1996 was given 12 months in the vat and 18 in Allier oak, while the Merlot Especial 1996 was given eighteen months in vat and twenty-four in Allier oak. The Merlots are especially good; despite the maturation given before release they deserve several more years in bottle and need decanting, as they are apt to throw heavy deposits.

AMPURDAN-COSTA BRAVA

Empordà-Costa Brava is its Catalan name and the locals would call it nothing else.

Geography

This is where the Pyrenees meet the Mediterranean, and the vineyards stretch inland practically from the coast to an altitude of about 200 metres (656 feet). They adjoin the French wine areas of Banyuls and Côtes du Roussillon, which Catalans protest are parts of their country. Some vineyards, with a fine disregard for politics, straddle the border.

Climate

Mediterranean, ranging from 1.5°C (34.7°F) in winter to 29°C (84.2°F) in summer, but the average is 16°C (60.8°F) and slightly less in the higher vineyards. The rainfall is 600–700 millimetres (23.6–27.5 inches) and there are 2,400 hours of sunshine, but it is windy and the cold northern Tramontana can reach gale force twelve.

Soil

Light brown with some limestone, especially in the foothills of the Pyrenees.

Grapes

Red varieties: Cariñena; Garnacha; Tempranillo (Ull de Llebre); Cabernet Sauvignon; and Merlot. Cariñena is by far the widest planted.
White varieties: Garnacha Blanca; Macabeo; Moscatel; Xarel.lo; and Chardonnay. The first two are the most widely planted.
Other vines are being tried experimentally: Syrah and Cabernet Sauvignon for reds, Chenin, Riesling, Gewürztraminer, and Parellada for whites.

Planting

Most of the vines are grown traditionally as bushes, but absolutely everything is being tried in the experimental vineyards. Whichever way they are grown, though, they need strong support against the gales.

Vineyard area

2,033 hectares.
Authorized yield

49 hl/ha.

Wines

Reds and *rosados* reach 11.5–13.5% ABV and whites 11–13% ABV. There is also an unusual, traditional wine – the orange-red, sweet, long-lived Garnatxa d'Empordà, made by drying Garnacha grapes in the sun before pressing to give a strength of 15% ABV with a sugar content of five Baumé. These may be compared with those grown across the border in France. Most of the table wines, especially the *rosados*, of which there are many, are made to be drunk young, but increasingly there are *crianzas* and above as the area is going in for fine wines. There have also been experiments with Vino Novel del Ampurdán (in Catalonian Vi Novell del'Empordà), made in the style of Beaujolais Nouveau, but these have been received with modified rapture.

Production

65,000 hectolitres (1994).

Vintages

1994 (3); 1995 (4); 1996 (4); 1997 (2); 1998 (5); 1999 (4); 2000 (4); 2002 (3); 2004 (4).

The Pyrenees, snow-capped through all the cooler months, make a wonderful backcloth to the agreeable, rather flat countryside that lies behind the populous beaches. It is here that the best vines grow, with the greatest concentration in the north and stretching into the valleys of the foothills. Most of the vineyards are small, some of them beautifully tended, but others are dire. With so many small growers, it is not surprising that most of the winemaking is in the hands of cooperatives. Although these are showing signs of entering the modern world, lethargy prevails; the mediocre local *rosados*, made from the Cariñena grape, can be sold so easily to the holidaymakers. Things are rapidly looking up, though, with vineyards being replanted and serious experiments with new varieties taking place.

Some leading bodegas

CASTILLO PERELADA VINOS Y CAVAS

Plaça Carme 1, 17491 Perelada, Gerona. Tel: +34 932 23 30 22; Fax: +34 932 23 13 70; Email: perelada@castilloperelada.com; Website: www.castilloperalada.com

A family-owned company now in its third generation and housed in a striking castle, Castillo Perelada has long been a leader in producing quality wines. In white wines, its blanc de blancs has Macabeo, Xarel.lo, and

Chardonnay, but it also makes varietals from Chardonnay and Sauvignon Blanc. Its standard *rosado* is from Garnacha, Cariñena, and Tempranillo, but again there is a varietal, from Cabernet Sauvignon. In reds, the *crianzas* are made from Garnacha, Cariñena, and a little Tempranillo with twelve months in seventy per cent American and thirty per cent French oak. The *reservas* are made from Cabernet Sauvignon, Garnacha, Merlot, and Cariñena with equal quantities of the two oaks. The red Gran Claustro is made from Cabernet Sauvignon and Merlot with small amounts of Cariñena and Garnacha. Its best wines, though, are the single-vineyard wines and those with the label Ex Ex. The former include Finca Malaveïna from Merlot, Cabernet Sauvignon, Garnacha, Cabernet Franc, and Syrah. The Ex Ex wines began as experiments but the best of them were bottled in limited editions, with the abbreviation now standing for exceptional experience, and they are. The Ex Ex 2 1988 was a varietal Cabernet Sauvignon. Since 1987 there has been an international music festival in the castle, with a special festival wine each year.

PERE GUARDIOLA

Carretera GI-602 km 2.9, 17750 Capmany, Gerona. Tel: +34 972 54 90 96; Fax: +34 972 54 90 97; Email: vins@pereguardiola.com; Website: www.pereguardiola.com

Founded in 1989 with 38 hectares of vineyards, this bodega makes reliable white, *rosado,* and red wines under the label Floresta. The reds are particularly good. The *crianza* 1999 was made from fifty per cent Tempranillo, thirty-five per cent Cabernet Sauvignon, and fifteen per cent Cariñena, matured in eighty per cent French and twenty per cent American oak.

CELLERS SANTA MARÍA

Plaza Mayor 6, 17750 Capmany, Gerona. Tel: +34 972 54 90 33; Fax: +34 972 54 90 22; Email: ridi@ctv.es

Although the family set up this company in 1955, it has a history stretching much further back and they are proud of a medal won in 1877. The present proprietor's grandfather discovered phylloxera locally and wrote a paper about it in 1889. The family tree goes back to 1767. The bodega has twelve hectares of vines, including Garnacha, Cariñena, Macabeo, and Cabernet Sauvignon. It operates on a small scale and everything is done by hand. The little cellar is said to be at least 370 years old and is one of the most beautiful it is possible to imagine, with Gothic and Romanesque vaults – the latter probably being a good deal older. It makes *rosados,* but its reds are *crianzas* and *reservas* made from Cariñena, Garnacha, Tempranillo, Cabernet Sauvignon, and Macabeo. They are sold under the mark Gran Recosind.

CONCA DE BARBERA

Geography

The vineyards are planted in an undulating valley some 200–500 metres (656–1,640 feet) above sea level, making it about equal to the Middle Penedès. Most of them are planted around the town of Montblanc in the valleys of the rivers Francolí and Auguera, which provide excellent drainage, and are sheltered by the mountain ranges of Tallat to the north, Prades to the east, and Montsant to the south. They are also planted in *concas* – basin-shaped valleys that provide shelter and, at the same time, exposure to the sun.

Climate

Mediterranean, but away from the moderating influence of the sea, so summer temperatures go up to 35°C (95°F) and in winter there are frosts. The average is 14°C (57.2°F), with 2,500 hours of sunshine and 450–550 millimetres (17.7–21.6 inches) of rainfall. The humidity tends to be relatively high. At night it is cooled by winds from the sea.

Soil

Light with some chalk over limestone.

Grapes

Red varieties: Trepat (Garnacha-Trepat); Tempranillo (Ull de Llebre); Garnacha; Cabernet Sauvignon; Merlot; Pinot Noir; Syrah; Cariñena; and Monastrell.
White varieties: Macabeo; Parellada; Chardonnay; and Sauvignon Blanc.

Planting

Old vineyards (the vast majority) are planted in a rectangular pattern with 1.2 metres (four feet) between vines and 3.4 metres (eleven feet) between rows, trained *en vaso*, but new ones are on wires with a possibility of mechanical harvesting in the future. There are 2,000–4,500 vines per hectare.

Vineyard area

5,871 hectares.

Authorized yield

49 hl/ha.

Wines

Red (10.5–13% ABV), *rosado* (10–12% ABV), white (10–12% ABV), and white Parellada (10–11% ABV) are entitled to the DO. The whites and *rosados* are made as *jóvenes,* and a malolactic fermentation is avoided so as to preserve their fresh acidity. The *rosados* were traditionally made from the local Trepat grape. Some of the reds are also made as *joven*, but others are fermented in oak to provide *crianzas* and above. Many of the grapes are grown for cavas.

Production

250,000 hectolitres.

Vintages

1992 (3); 1993 (3); 1994 (3); 1995 (4); 1996 (3); 1997 (4); 1998 (5); 1999 (4); 2000 (4); 2001 (4); 2002 (3); 2003 (3); 2004 (4).

Barberá de la Conca, after which the district is named, is a very odd and rather undistinguished little hill town with many narrow alleyways, its different levels linked by flights of stone steps; it has a rather sinister atmosphere and is full of cats and dogs. On the other hand Montblanc, the capital, is a really delightful little place, full of things worth seeing, and any visitor to the area simply must take some time off to see the Monasterio de Santa María de Poblet.

Conca means a basin, and this is the impression one gets in the vineyards, surrounded as they are by distant mountains. They are very well tended. One of them, Castillo de Riudabella, is exceptionally beautiful and has a castle in the middle, which is a family house with holiday accommodation. The surrounding vineyards are run by Codorníu, of Penedès, which grows some of its best Chardonnay there. Torres also grows some of its best Chardonnay here in the vineyard of Milmanda.

The region has developed a cunning technique for dealing with its Chardonnay: "double vintaging". The grapes are grown on sites where they ripen early and are picked with plenty of acidity to give fresh, young wines. After the bodega plant has been used to make these, it is used again for the main harvest, with obvious economic advantages.

Some leading bodegas

BODEGAS CONCAVINS

Carretera Montblanc-Barberà s/n, 43422 Barberà de la Conca, Tarragona.
Tel: +34 977 88 70 30; Fax: +34 977 88 70 32;
Email: info@bodegasconcavins.com; Website: www.concavins.com

A large, well-equipped bodega that was originally a cooperative but is now privately owned. It has forty hectares of vineyard and buys in from its former members. It sells most of its wines under the trademarks Clos Montblanc and Castillo de Montblanc. They are well made and reliable. Varietal whites include Chardonnay and Sauvignon Blanc. Varietal reds include Cabernet Sauvignon, Tempranillo, Pinot Noir, and Syrah. There are also blends including Cabernet/ Merlot, generally seventy per cent and thirty per cent.

CAVAS SANSTRAVÉ

C/de la Conca 10, 43412 Solivella, Tarragona. Tel: +34 977 89 21 65; Fax: +34 977 89 20 73; Email: bodega@sanstrave.com; Website: www.sanstrave.com

A family bodega founded in 1985. It has twenty hectares of vineyard growing Chardonnay, Tempranillo, Merlot, and Cabernet Sauvignon, and its wines reflect these mainly French varieties. They are sold under the names Sanstrave and Gasset and include a varietal Syrah. Gasset Negre Sansatravé red *reserva* is made from sixty per cent Cabernet Sauvignon, thirty per cent Tempranillo, and ten per cent Merlot.

CELLER MAS FORASTER

Camino Ermita de Sant Josep s/n, 43400 Montblanc, Tarragona.
Tel: +34 977 86 02 29; Fax: +34 977 87 50 37; Email: foraster@teleline.es

Founded in 1988 with twenty-two hectares of vineyard, this bodega is developing a good reputation with its red wines. The *joven* 2003 had eighty-five per cent Tempranillo and fifteen per cent Cabernet Sauvingon, but the more usual mix is eighty to ninety per cent Tempranillo and the rest Cabernet Sauvignon.

MIGUEL TORRES

See Penedès, p.22.

Miguel Torres has long been growing some of his finest wines in this DO, but until recently eschewed selling under DO labels and just used his own name, so the wines were often thought of as Penedès, home to his headquarters. He has two vineyards here, Milmanda of fifteen hectares and Gran Murales of thirty-two, which produce eponymous wines. The former is his leading Chardonnay, the latter a fascinating blend of native varieties, including two that are now very rare and that he has been bringing back: Garró and Samsó, as well as Cariñena, Monastrell, and Garnacha, which are aged in French oak. The result is a big wine with a unique, slightly smokey flavour that needs ten years to show its best and will go on developing longer. These are undoubtedly two of the very best Catalan wines.

COSTERS DEL SEGRE

Geography

The meaning of this name is "the banks of the Segre", a river that rises in the Pyrenees and flows through Lérida (Lleida in Catalan). There may be some poetry to the name, but there is little reality in it as the vineyards are separated into six parts. The smallest, Raïmat, is the most important historically and in the quality of its wines. It lies to the northwest of Lérida, near the border of the province of Huesca, and is separated from the others. Pillars Jussà (which embrases the former VdlT area of Conca de Tremp) is to the north of Lérida. Segrià lies to the northeast, as does Artesa de Segre, actually by the river. Valls de Riucorb and Las Garrigas are to the southeast, next to each other and within the Province of Tarragona. The altitude above sea level is 200–350 metres (656–1,148 feet).

Climate

Continental, rising to 35°C (95°F) in summer and falling to zero (32°F) or below in winter, with an average of 14–15°C (57–59°F). There is a big drop at night: at Raïmat in summer it falls from 32–35°C (90–95°F) to 17–18°C (62–64.5°F). The climate is harshest in Artesa, which has a long, cold winter. Rainfall is 300–440 millimetres (11.8–17.3 inches), but is unusually unpredictable – in 1995 the total at Raïmat was only 160 millimetres (6.3 inches), but in January 1996, 180 millimetres (7 inches) fell in one month. There are 2,800 hours of sunshine.

Soil

Very alkaline. Sandy topsoil over limestone.

Grapes

Red varieties: Garnacha; Tempranillo (Ull de Llebre or Gotim Bru); Cabernet Sauvignon; Merlot; Monastrell; Trepat; Mazuelo; Cariñena; Syrah;

and Pinot Noir.

White varieties: Macabeo; Parellada, Xarel.lo; Chardonnay; Garnacha Blanca; Riesling; Sauvignon Blanc; and Albariño.

Planting

There are still old vineyards planted *en vaso*, but modern ones are planted on wires for mechanical harvesting, the height of the trellises varying with the vine variety. The average density is 2,000 per hectare. At Raïmat the Chardonnay is on trellises 1.1 metres (3.6 feet) high, with 3.2 metres (10.5 feet) between rows and 1.7 metres (5.6 feet) between vines, whereas the Cabernet Sauvignon is on trellises 90 centimetres (2.9 feet) high with 2.1 metres (6.9 feet) between rows.

Vineyard area

4,144 hectares.

Authorized yield

70 hl/ha for vines planted *en vaso* and 120 hl/ha for vines grown on wires.

Wines

Reds 11–14.5% ABV, *rosados* and whites 9–13.5% ABV. Most whites and *rosados* are sold as *jóvenes,* but reds can go as high as *gran reserva*. Many of the wines are sold as varietals. There are also sparkling wines from 10.8–12.8% ABV, *vino de aguja* from 9–12% ABV, and natural sweet wines from 9–13.5% ABV.

Production

87,919 hectolitres (2002).

Vintages

1988 (5); 1989 (4); 1990 (5); 1991 (4); 1992 (3); 1993 (5); 1994 (5); 1995 (5); 1996 (4); 1997 (4); 1998 (4); 1999 (4); 2000 (4); 2001 (4); 2002 (4–5); 2003 (4); 2004 (5).

This DO cannot be summed up in a few words; it is too complex. Yet a great deal of it can be summed up in one word: Raïmat. Traditionally it was an area of small growers. And like other districts it usually made rather rustic wines, often vinified by cooperatives, from Spanish grape varieties. But the rise of Raimat, making world-class wines and exporting a substantial part of them, changed the whole picture. Now, at one end of the scale there are still the cooperatives, at the other end Raïmat, and in between a whole gamut of privately owned wineries, ranging from the boutique to the substantial, and most of them anxious to emulate Raimat's success. An interesting area to watch, the wines are usually worth looking at.

The story of the creation of Raïmat is an extraordinary one: it is the story of a far-sighted entrepreneur and wine-lover. Manuel Raventós Doménech was a member of the family that owns the great cava house of Codorníu at Sant Sadurní de Noya in Penedès. He knew the area that is now Raimat, which in those days was just a desert – though wine had been grown there many years before. But he learned that an irrigation canal had been cut through it in 1910, bringing water from the Pyrenees. He thought that with·irrigation the ground would blossom – and how right he was. But it was not so simple as that. In 1914, he bought an estate of 3,200 hectares with a castle and one tree standing next to it. The rest of the land was bare and 300–350 metres (984–1,148 feet) above sea level. The castle has foundations dating back to the Moors, but was substantially rebuilt in the seventeenth century – a beautiful place. (As a sideline of history, Franco took the castle over and stayed in it during the crucial battle of the Ebro). On the castle was a coat of arms with a bunch of grapes (*raïm* in Catalan) and a hand (*mat*), pointing to its ancient connection with wine-growing, hence the name he gave to his new property. And he created not just an estate, but a whole village complete with houses for his workers, a school, and even a railway station. The irrigation was put in hand, but the ground was no good for vines as it was infertile and salt-laden, so his first crop was mainly lucerne, followed by pine trees. These put things right and in due time were grubbed up. Then the vines followed.

Raïmat is by far and away the largest and most important bodega; without it there would be no DO. Others are following and are beginning to compete, but most of the wines produced by the small growers still go into cava.

Some leading bodegas
CELLER DE CANTONELLA
Avenida de les Garrigues 26, 25471 La Pobla de Cérvoles, Lérida.
Tel: +34 973 58 02 00; Fax: +34 973 71 83 12;
Email: info@castelldelremei.com; Website: www.cervoles.com
This is an offshoot of the Cusiné family that made its fortune in agricultural machinery and owns Castell del Remei (*see* below). It is kept as a separate enterprise that grows the family's most prestigious wines. They are very

good indeed, sold under the name Cérvoles. It has thirty-two hectares of vineyard in the area of Les Garrigues. Eighty per cent of the casks are Allier. The Cérvoles Blanc, fermented in new Allier, is a fifty-fifty mixture of Chardonnay and Macabeo. Reds typically are made from forty per cent Tempranillo, thirty-one per cent Cabernet Sauvignon, eighteen per cent Garnacha, and eleven per cent Merlot. The Selecció en Vinya has fifty-nine per cent Cabernet Sauvignon, twenty-one per cent Tempranillo, and twenty per cent Garnacha, and spends twenty-two months in new Allier oak.

RAÏMAT

Afueras s/n, 25111 Raïmat, Lérida. Tel: +34 973 72 40 00;
Fax: +34 973 72 40 61; Email: info@raimat.com; Website: www.raimat.com

Much has been written above because the story of the DO is so closely bound up with Raïmat. In 1918, when his land had been prepared but before there was a single grape, Manuel Raventós optimistically built the winery, and he did it magnificently. The family has always had a feeling for architecture, and the buildings at Codorníu itself are described in the cava chapter. At Raïmat he commissioned Rubió Bellver, one of the great Gaudí pupils and followers, to design a huge avant-garde building in reinforced concrete, the first in this material to be built in Spain. It has worn very well indeed. The fine wines that were to fill it took some time to come though. At first the traditional Penedès varieties were planted: Macabeo, Parellada, and Monastrell, for cava. But the family had noticed what was going on in the rest of the world and took advice from the universities of Davis and Fresno, in California, which suggested they should experiment with Cabernet Sauvignon and Chardonnay. They did, but these were not successful until, with continuing advice from California, they found the right rootstocks and methods of planting. Cabernet Sauvignon and Chardonnay were being grown successfully by 1975, Merlot and Tempranillo by 1980. The area has expanded to 2,245 hectares and experiments continue with other varieties, including Albariño, Garnacha, Cariñena, Sauvignon Blanc, Syrah, Malbec, Petit Verdot, Verdejo, Godello, and several others including some Italians. The rest of the land is planted with fruit trees and cereal crops.

Driving from Lérida you know at once by the vast and perfectly tended vineyards when you have reached the edge of the Raïmat estate. Suddenly there is a large vineyard that looks totally chaotic and you assume it belongs to someone else. But no! It is an experiment with minimal pruning, which is being tried in Jerez, too. Experiments are continuous on this estate.

Most of the vineyards are designed for mechanical harvesting, which can be done at night – a good thing here in view of the heat during the day at vintage time – and it takes an average of only eighteen minutes to get the grapes to the press. Cultivation is almost entirely organic. There is a certain amount of irrigation in hot weather however, from eighteen reservoirs. Vintaging usually starts in mid-August, beginning with Chardonnay picked at eight degrees of alcohol for sparkling wine followed by Chardonnay picked at thirteen degrees of alcohol for "table wine".

As the vineyards expanded, the original winery, large though it is, proved inadequate and a new one was added. Architecturally this fully maintained the aesthetic traditions of the Raventós family. Designed by Domingo Triay and built in 1988, it is as ultra-modern as the old winery was in 1918 and will wear as well. To build it, a hill was excavated to ninety metres (295 feet) and much is below ground. What one sees is a glass structure in the shape of a pyramid with the top cut off, or a Mexican pyramid; and on the flat top there is a vineyard of Cabernet Sauvignon. It is original to the point of eccentricity, but none the worse for that; and it is extremely efficient.

Of the whites, only the Chardonnays see oak, but the reds are generally oak aged. The casks are 300 litres rather than the usual 225, so as to limit the oakiness imparted. Regardless of where the oak comes from, they are all coopered in Spain and are kept for a maximum of six years. American oak is used for Cabernet Sauvignon and Tempranillo, French for Pinot Noir, and both French and American for Chardonnay, while Merlot starts in American and finishes in French.

There is an exceptional range of high quality "table wines". The whites include a straight Chardonnay without oak and an oak-fermented Chardonnay Selección Especial, and both are exceptionally good. The most widely distributed of the reds is Abadia, which used to be a blend of sixty-five per cent Cabernet Sauvignon, twenty-five per cent Tempranillo, and ten per cent Merlot. But this has evolved and the 1998 was sixty-five per cent Cabernet Sauvignon, fifteen per cent Merlot, ten per cent Tempranillo, and five per cent Pinot Noir, while the 2000 was made from just Cabernet Sauvignon and Tempranillo. These are fermented separately, producing a fine, well-balanced wine with some complexity and good length that ages well and is sold at a very competitive price. The top range includes excellent varietals of Merlot, Pinot Noir, Tempranillo, and (exceptionally good) Cabernet Sauvignon, which has ten to fifteen per cent Merlot blended in. The top red is 4 Varietales, a *gran reserva* which in 1994 was made from fifty-one per cent Cabernet Sauvignon, twenty-six per cent Merlot, fifteen per cent Tempranillo, and eight per cent Pinot Noir. There is also an excellent sparkling wine from Chardonnay with thirty per cent Pinot Noir. It used to be sold as a cava but is now sold under the DO as Raïmat *gran brut*.

CASTELL DEL REMEI

Castell del Remei, 25333 La Fuliola, Lérida. Tel: +34 973 58 02 00; Fax: +34 973 71 83 12; Email: info@castelldelremei.com; Website: www.castelldelremei.com

The bodega, southwest of the town of La Fuliola, was founded in 1780, or perhaps 1871, but it has only really taken off since it was bought by the Cusiné family in 1982. Although they have another mark, Cérvoles, for some of their most prestigious wines (see above) this should not denigrate their Castell del Remei wines, which are excellent and sometimes better. The bodega has a forty-hectare vineyard and is a beautiful place with a castle, a chapel, and a restaurant. Its wines include Blanc Planell made from fifty per cent each of Chardonnay and Sauvignon, and Oda Blanc, a barrel-fermented blend of Chardonnay and Macabeo. Its red wines are particularly good. Gotim Bru used to be the top wine, from Tempranillo, Cabernet, and Merlot, with ten months in American oak barrels in their third and fourth years: a big, complex wine that is a delight to drink. Taking a step up, the very good Oda *crianza* is made from Merlot, Cabernet Sauvignon, and Tempranillo, matured for twelve months in new American oak and unfiltered. The top wine is 1780, from Cabernet Sauvignon, Tempranillo, and Garnacha vines over forty years old and matured in new American oak for twelve months. These are worth seeking out and deserve further ageing.

PLA DE BAGES

Geography

Before this DO came into being in 1995 the wines were sold under local names, notably Artés. The principal town is Manresa, toward the south of the DO in its narrowest part. It lies to the northwest of Barcelona, in fairly mountainous country, isolated from the other Catalan DO areas. The vineyards are planted at altitudes of 200–600 metres (656–1,968 feet), averaging 400 (1,312 feet).

Climate

Mediterranean, with limited rainfall. But owing to the mountainous terrain there are wide variations and significant microclimates. It is driest in the northeast and wettest in the southeast. The average temperature is 13°C (55.4°F) and rainfall 500–600 millimetres (19.7–23.6 inches).

Soils

These again vary significantly from place to place, but are generally loam with clay or sand and some chalk.

Grapes

Red varieties: Garnacha; Tempranillo (Ull de Llebre); Merlot; and Cabernet Sauvignon. Pinot Noir and Cabernet Franc are also grown.
White varieties: Macabeo; Parellada; Picapoll; and Chardonnay. Sauvignon Blanc is also grown.
Sumoll is also grown locally, but this is not suitable for quality wines and is used for non-DO reds.

Planting

2,000–4,500 per hectare on a pattern of 1.4 metres x 2.8 metres·(4.6 feet x 9.2 feet) with cordon pruning.

Vineyard area

550 hectares.

Authorized yield

Of grapes, 5,000 kg/ha for reds and 7,500 kg/ha for whites.

Wines

Reds of 12.5% ABV, rosados of 12% ABV, and whites of 11.5–12% ABV, with a small production of sparkling wines.

Production

16,000 hectolitres (2002).

Vintages

1996 (4); 1997 (4); 1998 (5); 1999 (4); 2000 (5); 2001 (4); 2002 (4); 2003 (4); 2004 (4).

Wine-growing throughout Cataluña has an ancient history, and no doubt this area has one like the rest, but little seems to be known about it. The name Bages is derived from the ancient Roman city of Bacassis, which in turn was said to have been named after Bacchus, the Roman god of wine; but it would be unwise to build any theories on this. What is more certain is that in the recent past many of the wines were destined for cavas. More recently still the growers have decided to develop a market for table wines, and there is no doubt that the potential is there, notably for reds. Recent plantings have largely been of French varieties. How this new DO will develop remains to be seen. The wines have certainly not yet reached the top flight, but it is certainly worth watching.

Some leading bodegas

CELLERS COOPERATIVA D'ARTÉS
Carretera Rocafort 44, 08271 Artés, Barcelona.
Tel: +34 938 30 53 25; Fax: +34 938 30 62 89
Founded in 1908, this is the biggest as well as the oldest established bodega, a cooperative with 250 members having 3,000 hectares of vines between them – six times the area of the DO. Most of its wines are no more than table wines, but the DO wines are sold under the name Artium. They include a varietal white Picapoll, a varietal Cabernet Sauvignon *crianza,* and a red *crianza,* Artium Rocas-Albas, made from seventy per cent Tempranillo, twenty per cent Merlot, and ten per cent Sumoll.

ABADAL MASIES D'AVINYÓ
08279 Santa María D'Horta D'Avinyó, Barcelona. Tel: +34 938 75 75 25;
Fax: +34 938 74 83 26; Email: info@abadal.net; Website: www.abadal.net
A small, modern bodega founded in 1983, with 70 hectares of vineyard, making the best wines in the DO. It is part of the Roqueta group. Its whites include a fresh varietal Picapoll and a varietal Chardonnay. Reds include Cabernet Sauvignon and Merlot varietals. The very good Selecció 2001 was made from forty per cent Cabernet Sauvignon, forty per cent Cabernet Franc, and twenty per cent Syrah. The best *reservas* are sold as Abadal 3.9. The fragrant and well-balanced 1999 had eighty-five per cent Cabernet Sauvignon with a year in seventy per cent French and thirty per cent American oak.

PRIORATO
Geography
The vineyards are in the mountains, ranging from 100–700 metres (328–2,297 feet) above sea level with an average altitude of 450 metres (1,476 feet). Although there is a little flat land in the valley of the river Siurana, most of the vineyards are on terraces carved out of fifteen per cent or even thirty per cent slopes and are terribly hard to work.

Climate
The climate is unique and helps to distinguish this DO from all the others in Cataluña. It is sufficiently inland to be continental, but high in the mountains so that it can freeze in winter to about 6°C below zero (21°F). The summer maximum is 35°C (95°F), but it sometimes rises to no more than 26°C (78.8°F). The mean annual temperature is 15°C (59°F), and the mean summer temperature is 24–26°C (75–78.8°F). It is affected by cold north winds and warm, moist winds from the Mediterranean. The rainfall averages 600 millimetres (23.6 inches), but the rain falls only in limited periods: October–November and March–April. There are 2,600 hours of sunshine.

Soil
The area is of volcanic origin and the topsoil, of quartzite and slate, looks grey, sometimes almost black. Bits of quartzite sparkle in the sun. Underneath there is a base of "llicorella", a reddish slate with particles of quartzite (mica), through which the roots of the vines penetrate deeply. In the higher vineyards there is a subsoil of schist, which passes in a stratum beneath central Spain to re-emerge in the port vineyards of the Douro.

Grapes
Red varieties: Garnacha Tinta (the most favoured); Garnacha Peluda; Cariñena; Cabernet Sauvignon; Merlot; and Syrah.
White varieties: Garnacha Blanca; Macabeo; Pedro Ximénez; and Chenin Blanc.

Planting
En vaso, with some on espalier double cordon Royat.

Vineyard Area
1,820 hectares.

Authorized yield

42hl/ha, but in practice this is never even approached in the most serious vine-yards where the vines are often very old and the yield is minuscule: 5-6hl/ha.

Wines

Practically the whole of the production is red, which ranges from *joven* to *gran reserva*, and the regulations are rather different from the normal ones. *Crianzas* must have a minimum of twelve months in oak and twelve months in bottle, *reservas* twelve and twenty-four, *gran reservas* twenty-four and forty-eight. All are unusually strong (13.75–18% ABV). American and French oak are used. The whites and *rosados*, which are no more than ten per cent of the total, are all *jóvenes*. But in addition to these there are also two kinds of traditional wines: *generosos*, mostly from Pedro Ximénez (14–18% ABV) and *rancios*, which must be aged for at least four years (14–20% ABV).

Production

10,546 hectolitres (1993), but 66,000 hectolitres may in future be expected in a good year.

Vintages

1980 (3); 1981 (4); 1982 (4); 1983 (3); 1984 (3); 1985 (4); 1986 (3); 1987 (3); 1988 (3); 1989 (3); 1990 (3); 1991 (3) (quantity reduced by hail); 1992 (4); 1993 (5); 1994 (4); 1995 (5); 1996 (5); 1997 (3); 1998 (5); 1999 (4); 2000 (5); 2001 (5); 2002 (3); 2003 (4) 2004 (4)

Priorato (in Catalan Priorat) is a very special place. Up in the mountains, the scenery is indescribably beautiful, and the wines are some of the finest grown anywhere in the world. It is an exciting place to be, too. The wine-makers are enthusiasts, aiming for the heights and scaling them. Their efforts have been well recognized, and in one respect this is unfortunate, for their wines are not only among the best anywhere, they are also among the most expensive.

There is a long tradition of wine-growing stretching back, as it so often does, to a monastery. There is a story that a shepherd tending his flocks in the valley of the river Siurana had a vision of angels rising as if up a staircase to the heavens. He told a travelling order of Carthusian monks, who established a monastery on the spot in 1162, and of course made wine. Another version ascribes the vision to a monk. In the landscape and atmosphere of Priorato, one can believe it. The monastery was called Priorat de Scala Dei –

the Priory of the Staircase of God – from where Priorato takes its name. Today it is a beautiful ruin, but the old monastic cellars are still in use.

It is here that Garnacha shows what it can do if the yield is kept low enough and the wine well made. Far from oxidizing easily and having a short life, the best Priorato wines need to be kept until they are eight to fifteen years old before they show their best and will clearly last much longer. However, they can be drunk with pleasure when they are five or six years old, especially if they are given time to breathe. They are best decanted. In the past they had the reputation of being practically black, enormously strong, heady, and unsubtle. They were used for blending, and in Bordeaux made a cheaper substitute for Hermitage. Nevertheless there were some good examples, which were sought out by people who knew about them. Some are still being made in the old-fashioned way, mostly by the cooperative, which was formed by amalgamating several small ones, and is well equipped, producing over half of the wine.

The revolution came with an influx of young winemakers that began in the 1970s in the high country at Gratallops. They appreciated the area's enormous potential at a time when it looked as if it would be abandoned. Vines were dying and not being replaced, while the countryside was becoming depopulated. They had their first success with the creation of the DO in 1975. Then they set about making fine wine. Above all they worked for very low yields from very old vines pruned short. And they were at pains to keep the yield down rather than to increase it. Tasting the wine from seventy-year-old Garnacha vines, one can see at once how much better and more concentrated it is than wines made by the same winemaker from fifteen-year-old vines. Most of the growers do not irrigate at all, despite the climate; the exception is Mas Martinet, which uses a sophisticated and unusual system producing a fine spray on the surface. The vines reach for water by growing roots down twelve or even twenty metres (39.3–65.6 feet) – but some of them die. The newcomers have harvested the grapes earlier, while they still have enough acidity to secure a good balance. They see, too, that the addition of small proportions of foreign varieties add new dimensions of complexity. The Syrah, for instance, is hard to grow here, where it is planted towards the top of the slopes, but is well worthwhile. A small proportion of Cabernet Sauvignon also helps, and is grown on the cooler sites, sometimes on north-facing slopes. But the major grape is still Garnacha. Cariñena gives a higher yield and good colour, but less intensity and is not greatly favoured by the new winemakers. Picking the grapes at perfect maturity sometimes involves as many as twelve passes through the vineyard.

The whites and *rosados* are mostly cold fermented in stainless-steel tanks, though some are fermented in Limousin casks; they do not have a malolactic fermentation. Some of the reds are also made in stainless-steel, with others, in epoxy-lined cement tanks; and they are all put through a malolactic fermentation before cask ageing. In the boutique wineries of Gratallops, where the exquisite new-style wines are made, everything is of the latest, though some growers have fibreglass as well as stainless steel. The old-fashioned wines are then matured in American oak, but for the new ones there is also French oak. René Barbier, for instance, uses only French oak. The strength of the new wines is generally kept down to a modest 13.75% ABV, but does sometimes go up to 16% ABV.

In 2003, it joined Rioja in becoming a DOCa – or in Catalan a DOV. Watch this space, as they say. New growers have arrived and others are on their way – notably Torres.

Some leading bodegas

BUIL & GINÉ

Ctra Gratallops – Vilella Baixa km 11.5, 43717 Gratallops, Priorato.
Tel: +34 977 83 98 10; Fax: +34 977 83 98 11;
Email: info@builgine.com; Website: www.builgine.com

In 1996 the Buil i Giné family, who had been engaged in groceries but whose ancestors had been wine-growers, decided to return to their roots and set up in Priorato with thirty-two hectares of vineyard. Their white Blanc Giné is good: big but very fresh. There are three red wines. Giné Giné is from Garnacha and Cariñena, half from young and half from old vines. Joan Giné Giné is from Garnacha, Cariñena, and Cabernet Sauvignon, the first two from vines over twenty-five years old and the last from five to eighteen years old, matured for twelve months in French and American oak. The top wine, Pleret, is from Garnacha, Cariñena, Cabernet Sauvignon, Syrah, and Merlot. The first two come from vines over forty years old, the last three, which are in minor proportions, from vines ten to twenty years old. It has two to fourteen months in new French oak.

CELLER DE L'ENCASTELL

Carrer de Castell 13, 43739 Porrera, Tarragona. Tel/Fax: +34 977 82 81 46;
Email: roquers@roquers.com; Website: www.roquers.com

An enthusiastic boutique bodega, founded in 1999, with 7.5 hectares of vineyard very high up. Its Roquers de Porrera 2001 was made from sixty per cent

Garnacha, twenty-five per cent Cariñena, with Cabernet Sauvignon and Merlot, matured in French oak. Its second wine, cheaper but still very good, is Marge, which in the same year had fifty per cent Garnacha, twenty per cent Cabernet Sauvignon, fifteen per cent Merlot, and fifteen per cent Syrah.

CELLER DEL PONT

Del Rue 1 Baixos, La Vilella Baixa, Tarragona. Tel/Fax: +34 977 82 82 31; Email: cellerdelpont@mixmail.com

A boutique bodega, in fact more of a *garagiste*, on the ground floor of an old village house. It was founded by seven enthusiastic local partners who had five hectares of vineyard – half of the vines being over fifty years old – growing Garnacha, Cariñena, Cabernet, and Syrah. The excellent wine Lo Givot, is matured in ninety per cent French and ten per cent American oak, and is sixty-five per cent Garnacha and Cariñena in equal parts, twenty-five per cent Cabernet Sauvignon, and ten per cent Syrah.

CELLERS DE SCALA DEI

Rambla de la Cartoixa s/n, 43379 Scala Dei, Tarragona. Tel: +34 977 82 70 27; Fax: +34 977 82 80 6; Email: codinfo@codorniu.es; Website: www.grupocodorniu.com

This is one of the largest and oldest established bodegas, founded in 1973 in the delightful village of Scala Dei, and housed in old monastery buildings. The date 1692 appears above the cellar door. In 2000, the cava house Codorníu bought a twenty-five per cent share and took over the winemaking. The monks used to control the fermentation temperature by circulating water round the fermentation tanks in the cellar. It took centuries to reinvent that process, but now everything is up-to-date and thermostatically controlled. It has ninety hectares of vineyards, which are unusual in including Chenin, and even more unusual here in being trained on wires. The Cartoixa *crianza* 2000 was made from forty-eight per cent Cabernet Sauvignon, forty-seven per cent Garnacha, and five per cent Syrah, with a year in French oak, while the Negre 2003 was a varietal Garnacha *joven*. Though this bodega helped to lead the way for the region, it got left behind when new, young winemakers stole the glamour, and their tiny-production wines took the edge. Perhaps the new management will bring it to the fore again.

CLOS FIGUERAS

Carrer La Font 38, 43737 Gratallops, Priorato. Tel: +34 977 83 17 12; Fax: +34 977 83 17 97; Email: europvin@infonegocio.com

Established in 1996, this boutique bodega, owned by Bordeaux-based broker Christopher Cannan, already has a high reputation. The red Font de la Figueras is based on Garnacha (forty to fifty per cent) with Cariñena (thirty to forty per cent), Syrah (ten to fifteen per cent), and a minor contribution from other varieties. The top Clos Figueras is made in very small quantities from a similar grape mix.

CLOS MOGADOR

Carní Manyetes s/n, 43737 Gratallops, Tarragona. Tel: +34 977 83 91 71; Fax: +34 977 83 94 26; Email: closmogador@terra.es

Run by René Barbier with his wife and son in an old grange, this is a real family concern: a perfect example of a small, dedicated winery. Barbier is Spanish but of French descent and is a member of the family that owned the eponymous bodega in Penedès, which is now part of the Freixenet group, but there is no connection. This is a beautiful little bodega surrounded by twenty-five hectares of vineyards on a superb mountain site: a little bit of paradise, but very hard work. It is practically a one-wine bodega, producing a superb red wine, Clos Mogador, from Garnacha, Cabernet Sauvignon, Syrah, and Cariñena, matured in French oak. It has no fining or filtration, but precipitates naturally when the door is opened in winter to let the cool air in. It also makes 200 cases of wine a year from a friend's vineyard, Clos Erasmus, which is based on Cariñena.

COSTERS DEL SIURANA

Camí Manyanetes s/n, 43737 Gratalops, Tarragona.
Tel: +34 977 83 92 76; Fax: +34 977 83 93 71;
Email: info@costersdelsiurana.com; Website: www.costersdelsiurana.com

Privately owned by Carles Pastrana and Mariona Jarque, who bought the property in 1984-5 and got going in 1987, this bodega produces superb wines from four vineyards, amounting to 100.5 hectares, which supply all its needs. An enormous amount of trouble is taken in planting, fitting each variety into the most appropriate aspect and microclimate. The couple introduced Cabernet Sauvignon, Merlot, and Syrah, while retaining the indigenous varieties and restoring a vineyard of fifty-year-old Cariñena to health. The flagship wine is Clos de L'Obac, first made in 1989 from thirty-five per cent each of Garnacha and Cabernet Sauvignon, and ten per cent each of Syrah, Merlot, and Cariñena matured in 100 per cent new French oak. These five varieties are still used. Miserere, first created in 1990, comes not far behind it, from one of the old vineyards of the priory, Mas d'en Bruno, made from Tempranillo, Garnacha, Cabernet Sauvignon, Merlot, and sometimes Cariñena. It is matured in fifty per cent new oak, the remainder being of the second year. There is also a white wine that is made in very small quantities for friends and restaurants and which came about rather by chance, simply because the grapes – Garnacha Blanca, Macabeo, Moscatel de Alejandría, and Parellada – happened to be there. Fermented in Limousin oak, it is dry and very good, but very oaky, at any rate when young. Finally there is a very small production of a delicious sweet red wine – Dolç de L'Obac – first made in 1991 with very ripe grapes from the Clos de L'Obac vineyard: eighty per cent Garnacha; ten per cent Syrah; and ten per cent Cabernet Sauvignon. It is really what the Germans would describe as a *beerenauslese*. It is fermented in new French oak and the skins are taken out through a large hole in the top after the fermentation and maceration: a unique method. The fermentation is blocked with one per cent alcohol and cooling. It is strong stuff at 16% ABV.

MAS MARTINET VITICULTORS

Ctra Falset-Gratallops km 6, 43730 Falset, Tarragona. Tel: +34 629 23 82 3; Fax: +34 639 12 12 4; Email: masmartinet@masmartinet.com; Website: www.masmartinet.com

The Pérez i Ovejero family has a wine-growing tradition and founded this bodega in 1982, with fifteen hectares of terraced vineyard. Unlike most of the younger generation of growers, this bodega does not avoid irrigation, and is in fact proud of its own system, which produces a very fine spray and does not appear to dilute the wines – the wines taste anything but diluted. Only reds are produced. The best grapes – about forty per cent – are used for Clos Martinet; the second wine is Martinet Bru. Both are matured in Allier oak, the latter in three-year-old casks. While the Martinet Bru is a good wine, the Clos Martinet is very good indeed, and as the vineyard is still young, one can only suppose that it will get better and better. The grape mix has changed some-what over the years, but for Clos Martinet in 2001 it was forty per cent Garnacha, twenty-five per cent Syrah, twenty per cent Cabernet Sauvignon, and fifteen per cent Garnacha, while for Martinet Bru it was forty per cent Garnacha with thirty per cent each of Cabernet Sauvignon and Merlot.

ALVARO PALACIOS

Afores s/n, 43737 Gratallops, Tarragona. Tel: +34 977 83 91 95; Fax: +34 977 83 91 9; Email: alvaropalacios@ctv.es

Alvaro Palacios, a scion of the famous Rioja family, is one of the best and most dynamic of the new wave of young winemakers. His unusually wide knowl-edge and experience includes a stint in the Napa Valley and another at Château

Pétrus, so his sights are aimed high. Instead of taking the easy course and going into the family bodegas, he wanted to do his own thing, and looked for a vineyard outside of Rioja where he could grow world-class wine. He found it in Priorato. For his bodega he acquired a little, old, disused theatre where the proscenium arch rises mysteriously behind the fermentation tanks. Arriving in 1989, he in fact found and bought two vineyards: L'Ermita and Finca Dofí. L'Ermita, 550 metres (1,804 feet) above sea level, was planted with very old Garnacha vines. It slopes northeast, so it does not get a very great exposure to the sun, and this results in unusually fragrant wines. He is now establishing new vineyards on terraces prepared with an enormous amount of work. Most of the oak used is French but there is a small proportion of American, which adds an element of creaminess. The various vine varieties are fermented separately. L'Ermita is generally eighty per cent Garnacha and twenty per cent Cabernet Sauvignon. The Finca Dolfi 2002 was made from fifty-five per cent Garnacha, the rest from Cabernet Sauvignon, Syrah, and Merlot. Les Terasses is more competitively priced and very good value. It has fifty to sixty per cent Cariñena, thirty to forty per cent Garnacha, and ten per cent Cabernet Sauvignon, sometimes with a little Syrah. L'Ermita is one of the most expensive wines in the world, and it is not overpriced. Production is very small.

CELLER VALL LLACH

C Pont 9, 43739 Porrera, Tarragona. Tel: +34 977 82 82 44; Fax: +34 977 82 83 25; Email: celler@vallllach.com; Website: www.vallllach.com

This boutique bodega was founded by a lawyer and a singer in 1997 and has thirty-eight hectares of vineyard, mostly very old vines but with some new plantations of Merlot, Cabernet Sauvignon, and Syrah. It makes three wines. Vall Lach is from the oldest vines and has sixty-five per cent Cariñena, twenty-five per cent Merlot, and ten per cent Cabernet Sauvignon. It is expensive. Idus de Vall Lach is forty per cent Cariñena, twenty per cent Merlot, twenty-five per cent Cabernet Sauvignon, ten per cent Garnacha, and five per cent Syrah. Embruix de Vall Lach is from the young plantations and has thirty per cent each of Cariñena, Garnacha, and Cabernet Sauvignon, with ten per cent Syrah. The Vall Llach is initially rather oaky and tannic, needing bottle age – as they all do – but should grow into something very good.

TARRAGONA

Geography

The DO stretches inland east and west of the ancient city of Tarragona. New regulations approved in 2001 intend to do away with the old subdivisions, but as these still exist geographically and have distinct characteristics, they will be described. Tarragona Campo (in Catalan, El Camp) surrounds the ancient city in an arc of approximately thirty kilometres (18.5 miles) and in altitude ranges from sea level (though the lowest vineyards are at about forty metres, or 131 feet) to about 200 metres (656 feet) where the mountains begin and the vineyards end. Ribera de Ebro (in Catalan, Ribera d'Ebre) was originally considered a subdivision of the larger area of Falset but most of this has been hived off into the new DO Montsant, (see below). In the river valley the vineyards are at an altitude of 100 metres (328 feet) though they go up to 450 metres (1,476 feet).

Climate

Tarragona has a most agreeable climate: the average temperature is 16°C (60.8°F), falling to 3°C (37.4°F) in winter and rising to 35°C (95°F) in summer. Rain falls mainly in September and October and averages 465 millimetres (18.3 inches) in El Campo, and 305 millimetres (12 inches) in Ribera de Ebro, though in some districts it goes up to 650 millimetres (25.6 inches). There are 2,600 hours of sunshine.

Soils

In El Campo these are generally dark brown with some limestone and, in the highest ones, granite. In Ribera de Ebro they are more fertile and alluvial along the river.

Grapes

Red varieties: Garnacha (Garnatxa); Cariñena; Tempranillo (Ull de Llebre); Cabernet Sauvignon; Merlot; and Syrah.
White varieties: Macabeo; Xarel.lo; Parellada; Garnacha Blanca; Chardonnay; and Moscatel.
Additional varieties, however, are certainly grown and the new regulations envisage growing the red Sumoll.

Planting

The grapes are grown *en vaso* in the older vineyards and on wires in the newer ones, but there is a unique, local rectangular pattern: fourteen vines by seven, with 1.4 metres (4.6 feet) between the vines and 2.8 metres (9.1 feet) between the rows.

Vineyard area

7,400 hectares (1994).

Authorized yield

El Campo: white 70hl/ha, red 59.5hl/ha. Elsewhere: 52hl/ha.

Wines

There is a bewildering variety. All table wines are from 11–13% ABV. Tarragona Clásico Licoroso has a minimum of 13.5% ABV (it can go up to 23%) and must be aged in oak vats of less that 2,000 litres for a minimum of twelve years. Rancio wines must have a minimum of 14% ABV with an age of not less than four years divided between wood and bottle. But there are many versions of each category. All the white and *rosado* wines are sold as *jóvenes*. Some of the red wines and *vinos de licor* are aged according to a unique local system. Traditional *rancios* are still made in demi-johns and are fully oxidized.

Production

450,000 hectolitres (2003).

Vintages

Some are said to be better than others, but there is really little variation owing to the equable climate. All the vintages from 1999 to 2003 were classified as "4" with the exception of 2002 (a very wet year) which was "3".

Tarragona is one of the biggest and the least distinguished Catalan DOs. A journey through it shows that most of the land does not look promising for growing fine wines. Yet until the rise of Penedès and cava in the 1960s it was the only Catalan wine that drinkers in the UK had ever heard of. And it had a terrible reputation. In the nineteenth century it was sold as "Tarragona port" and was known as "poor man's port" or, more commonly, "red biddy". These were the red *vinos de licor*, imported to be sold very cheaply. A few are still made, and the best have a certain quality about them with some matured on the *solera* system. The area also has a remarkable and very long tradition of making wines for the church, which lays down a very strict specification, though some of this activity has now passed to Montsant. Some wines are sold in bulk to France to form the base wines for proprietary apéritifs and for strengthening weak wines: a very ancient trade. It is an area that can, and does, grow practically everything, but is not generally associated with quality wines. Though this is changing, especially as wines that were once taken to other areas for blending are now being sold under the DO, and some will doubtless be sold under the new DO Cataluña, though there is still a big trade in wine for cavas. Tarragona *clásico* is generally 100 per cent Garnacha, which can ripen so as to achieve seventeen degrees of alcohol unaided and still leave sugar in the wine, which is certainly remarkable. The table wines range from the fairly light to the massive. I have yet to find an amateur of Tarragona wines, yet the potential is there. It would have needed a very far-sighted person visiting the Penedès in the 1950s to predict where they are today.

Leading bodega

DE MULLER

Camí Pedra Estela 34, 43205 Reus, Tarragon. Tel: +34 977 75 74 73; Fax: +34 977 77 11 29; Email: export@demuller.es

Established in 1851, this family-owned bodega is the most important in the DO, with its business founded on wines for the church. It is noted for its *vinos de licor*, but it makes a complete range of very good-value table wines. It has 132 hectares of vineyards and a new, modern winery at Reus. It is also active in Priorato and Terra Alta. Its varietals include Chardonnay and Muscats in whites, a *rosado* from Pinot Noir, and reds from Pinot Noir, Cabernet Sauvignon, and Merlot. Its *licorosos* include Solera 1851 and Solera 1926, made from the two colours of Garnacha, surprisingly light and totally delicious.

TERRA ALTA

Geography

Remote in the mountains in the southernmost part of the province of Tarragona, Terra Alta borders with Zaragoza and Teruel, its vineyards on rolling hills from 300–500 metres (984–1,640 feet).

Climate

Continental, with very hot summers and very cold winters, moderated only slightly by the influence of the Mediterranean. Temperatures range from -5 –35°C (23–95°F), the average being 16.4°C (61.5°F), with rainfall of 400–600 millimetres (15.7–23.6 inches) and 2,700 hours of sunshine. A key influence is the dry *cierzo* wind from the Ebro Valley that keeps the vines healthy.

Soils

Deep and well drained with some limestone and variable amounts of clay.

Grapes

Red varieties: Garnacha; Cariñena; Garnacha Peluda; Syrah; Cabernet Sauvignon; Merlot; and Tempranillo, of which the first two cover three quarters of the vineyard. There are small plantations of other varieties including Pinot Noir and Pinot Meunier.

White varieties: Macabeo; Garnacha Blanca; Parellada; and Moscatel; with very small quantities of Chardonnay; Viognier; and Colombard. The first accounts for sixty-nine per cent.

Planting

Generally *en vaso,* but with trellises taking over. 2,800–3,000 per hectare.

Vineyard area

8,200 hectares.

Authorized yield

56hl/ha, but in practice a good deal less.

Wines

Table wines are 12–15% ABV, *rancios* and *mistelas* 15–20% ABV.

Production

202,670 hectolitres (2003).

Vintages

1988 (5); 1989 (3); 1990 (4); 1991 (4); 1992 (4); 1993 (4); 1994 (3); 1995 (4); 1996 (4); 1997 (4); 1998 (5); 1999 (4); 2000 (5); 2001 (5); 2002 (3); 2003 (4); 2004 (4).

This area is almost as beautiful as Priorato, and before the roads came it must have been just as remote. It is high in the mountains, and on the horizon there are misty mountain ranges, with more mountain ranges rising behind them. Some of the vineyards, as in Priorato, are on terraces fashioned by massive work, while others, more manageable, occupy plateaux. This used to be, and to some extent still is, a backwoods area with very old, low-yielding vineyards producing fortified *rancios* and clumsy table wines of staggering strength. These have clearly had their day. The *consejo regulador* saw that the future lay in making lighter wines and encouraged the replanting of vineyards to increase the yield, which had fallen to eleven hectolitres per hectare, and the trial of new varieties. Many of the wines are made by cooperatives, and it is worth making the journey just to see the wonderful Art Nouveau buildings of those in El Pinell de Brai and Gandesa, designed by Cèsar Martinell, a follower of Gaudí. Many of their wines are sold in bulk to the cava houses. This is clearly an area with real potential, as yet unfulfilled, though some agreeable, modern, light wines are already being made and boutique wineries are moving in. A place to watch, it will be interesting to see how many of the wines grown here finish up with the new DO of Cataluña.

Some leading bodegas

CELLER XAVIER CLUA
Vall de Sant Isidre 41, 43782 Vilalba dels Arcs, Tarragon. Tel/Fax: +34 977 43 90 03; Email: info@cellerclua.com; Website: www.cellerclua.com
The Clúa family has twenty-six hectares of vineyard, which include Garnachas of both colours from thirty to seventy years old and all the other usual varieties plus Sauvignon Blanc, and they are experimenting with Pinot Noir. They sell *jóvenes* under the mark, Mas d'en Pol, but it is their *crianzas* that are best. The white is Vendemia and is made from Garnacha with ten per cent Chardonnay. The red Mil.lenium is made from sixty-five per cent Garnacha, twenty per cent Cabernet Sauvignon, fifteen per cent Tempranillo, and a trace of Pinot Noir. The sweet red Mil.lenium Dolç is made from late-gathered Garnacha.

CELLER BARBARA FORES
Santa Anna 28, 43780 Gandesa, Tarragona. Tel: +34 977 42 01 60; Fax: +34 977 42 13 99; Email: info@cellerbarbarafores.com
An old firm that was reconstituted and modernized by the Ferrer family in 1994. It has twenty-four hectares of vineyard, some of the vines forty years old. The whites include El Quinta, a barrel-fermented varietal Garnacha Blanca, and a white made from eighty-five per cent Garnacha Blanca, with fifteen per cent Viognier. The *rosado* is made from equal parts of Garnacha Tinta and Syrah. Bárbara Forés Crianza 2001 was made from sixty per cent Garnacha, twenty-five per cent Syrah, and fifteen per cent Cariñena. The top wine is Coma d'En. The 2001 was made from thirty per cent Garnacha, thirty per cent Cabernet Sauvignon, twenty-seven per cent Syrah, and thirteen per cent Merlot.

CELLER COOPERATIU GANDESA

Avenida Cataluña 28, 43780 Gandesa, Tarragona. Tel: +34 977 42 62 34;
Fax: +34 977 42 04 03; Email: gandesa@ccae.es

The fine building that houses this cooperative has already been mentioned. Its members have 850 hectares, and it has moved forward to make a range of good-value wines that include Cariñena and Cabernet Sauvignon varietals.

CELLER VINOS PINOL

Avenida de Aragón 9, 43786 Batea, Tarragona. Tel: +34 977 43 05 05; Fax: +34 977 43 04 98; Email: info@vinospinol.com; Website: www.casapinol.com

Founded in 1945, this bodega has forty-two hectares of vineyard relatively high up at 400–500 metres (1,312–1,640 feet), and makes some of the best wines in the DO. Among the reds the leader is L'Avi Arrufi, an oak aged red, the 2002 made from thirty per cent Cabernet Sauvignon, twenty per cent Merlot, twenty per cent Garnacha, and fifteen per cent each of Syrah and Tempranillo. Its sweet wines are good, too, named Mistela Josefina Piñol – the white a varietal Garnacha Blanca and the red Garnacha with ten per cent Syrah.

MONTSANT

Geography

Montsant is in the shape of a horseshoe practically surrounding Priorato, with a gap in the east. It was taken from vineyards formerly in the DO of Tarragona, particularly the sub-region of Falset. It is a notably beautiful place. The average altitude of the vineyards is 360 metres (1,181 feet) but some go up to 700 metres (2,297 feet).

Climate

Although inland, it is sheltered and not extreme. The temperature ranges between 1°C (33.8°F) in winter and 31°C (87.8°F) in summer, with 2,600 hours of sunshine and rainfall of 400–600 millimetres (15.7–23.6 inches).

Soils

Mostly lime clay but sandy with some granite and slate.

Grapes

Red varieties: Cabernet Sauvignon; Mazuelo; Garnacha; Garnacha Peluda;

Merlot; Monastrell; Picapoll; Syrah; Tempranillo; and Trobat.
White varieties: Chardonnay; Garnacha Blanca; Macabeo; Moscatel; Pansal (Xarel.lo); and Parellada.

Planting
Vines are grown *en vaso* in older vineyards and on wires in newer ones.

Vineyard area
2,091 hectares.

Authorized yield
57hl/ha, but usually much less.

Wines
Minimum strengths: white 11.5% ABV; *rosado* 12% ABV; and red 12.5% ABV.

Production
67,807 hectolitres (2003).

Vintages
As for Tarragona.

This new (as of 2001) DO was carved out of Tarragona and surrounds Priorato, taking in some of the best vineyards in the sub-region of Falset – so it got off to a flying start. Although it does not pretend to reach the heights of its neighbour Priorato, it is undoubtedly a very serious wine-growing area with wines sometimes approaching the quality of Priorato, but not yet the price. So there is good value to be had, though prices are rising.

Some leading bodegas
AGRICOLA A FALSET-MARÇA
Miquel Barceló 31, 43730 Falset, Tarragona. Tel: +34 977 83 01 05; Fax: +34 977 83 03 63; Email: afalma@falsetmarca.com; Website: www.falsetmarca.com
A cooperative dating from 1913 and formed by the amalgamation of the two cooperatives Falset and Marça. Its members have over 200 hectares of vineyard growing Garnacha, Cariñena, Syrah, Cabernet Sauvignon, Tempranillo, and Merlot, among them some very old vines. It makes everything from the traditional *licorosos* and *rancios* to a vermouth, but is strong in table wines sold

mostly under the Etim brand. The Negre red is from Garnacha, Cariñena, Syrah, and Tempranillo. The *rosado*, Rosat, is two-thirds Garnacha and one-third Syrah. The white is from Garnacha Blanca, ten per cent of which is barrel-fermented in French oak. Top of the range is Castell de Falset from Garnacha, Tempranillo, old vine Cariñena, Cabernet Sauvignon, and Syrah. Its sweet wines include Etim Verema Sobremadura from vines over 70 years old – late-harvested, 60 per cent Garnacha and 40 per cent Cariñena – and a white from Garnacha Blanca.

CELLER DE CAPCANES

Llebaria 4, 43776 Capçanes, Tarragona. Tel/Fax: +34 977 17 83 19;
Email: cellercapcanes@cellercapcanes.com

This began as a cooperative in 1933, but recently became a company with its 142 members as shareholders. Between them they have 270 hectares of well-established vineyard. It was they who pressed for a new DO for their wines which they rightly thought a cut above Tarragona. There are some excellent reds including Cabrida, an oak-aged varietal Garnacha; Flor de Primavera, made from forty per cent Cabernet Sauvignon, forty per cent Garnacha, fifteen per cent Tempranillo, and five per cent Cariñena; and Mas Tortó, from seventy per cent Garnacha, and ten per cent each of Cabernet Sauvignon, Merlot, and Syrah. But all their reds are worth trying. They even make a red kosher wine.

CELLER LAURONA (PREVIOUSLY EUROPVIN FALSET)

Carretera de Bellmunt-Sort dels Capellans Pol 21, 43730 Falset, Tarragona.
Tel/Fax: +34 977 83 17 12; Email: europvin@infonegocio.com

This really is a boutique bodega, founded in 1999 with only five hectares of vineyard farmed on organic principles; but its wines, made by René Barbier (*see* Priorato) are already famous. Laurona is made from thirty per cent Garnacha, thirty per cent Cariñena, fifteen per cent each of Merlot and Syrah, from vineyards planted fifteen to forty years ago, and ten per cent Cabernet Sauvignon. The top 6 Vinyes de Laurona is from eighty per cent Garnacha and twenty per cent Cariñena, from (as its name suggests) six vineyards with vines from fifty to eighty years old. Both are matured in French oak.

JOAN D'ANGUERA

Mayor s/n, 43746 Darmós, Tarragona. Tel: +34 977 41 80 06; Fax: +34 977 41 83 02; Email: anguerabeyme@teleline.es; Website: www.cellerjoandanguera.com

A family business established in 1820 and now in its sixth generation. It has thirty-two hectares of vineyard, including the first Syrah to be planted here, which is now mature. Its wines include El Bugader, from seventy per cent Syrah and fifteen per cent each of Garnacha and Cabernet Sauvignon, and

Finca L'Argata, from forty per cent Syrah, thirty-five per cent Cabernet Sauvignon, fifteen per cent Garnacha, and ten per cent Cariñena. The former is matured in French oak, the latter in American and French.

VENUS LA UNIVERSAL
Carretera Porrera, 43730 Falset, Tarragona. Tel/Fax: +34 977 83 05 45.
A boutique bodega established in 1999 with 4 hectares of vineyard. Its wines include Dido, from 40 per cent Merlot and 30 per cent each of Cabernet Sauvignon and Garnacha, and Venus, from equal parts of Syrah and Cariñena, matured in new French oak.

CATALUÑA
Geography
The area is vast, taking in all the parts of Cataluña where wines can be made and incorporating all the existing DOs described above.

Grapes
Red varieties: Cabernet Franc; Cabernet Sauvignon; Garnacha; Lladoner; Garnacha Peluda; Garnacha Tintorera; Merlot; Monastrell; Pinot Noir; Samsó; Crusilló; Mazuelo; Trepat; Tempranillo; and Syrah.
White varieties: Chardonnay; Garnacha Blanca; Macabeo; Moscatel de Alejandría; Moscatel de Málaga; Riesling; Sauvignon Blanc Xarel.lo; Pansá Blanca; Gewurztraminer; Malvasía; Pedro Ximénez; and Picapoll.

Vineyard area
3,872 hectares, excluding all the DO vineyards described above.

Authorized yield
51hl/ha.

Wines
Whites from 10–13% ABV, *rosados* from 10.5–13.5% ABV, and reds from 11.5–14.5% ABV. This very useful "catch all" DO, created in 1999, includes all the DOs described above and almost 4,000 hectares of land outside them. Its name in Catalan is Catalunya, in English, Catalonia. (This book uses the Castillian, Cataluña). It is vast, stretching throughout the whole of this part of northeast Spain. Growers within a specific DO can still use it, and generally do, but it regulates a long-standing practice of the Catalans to move grapes from one district to another, taking the robust line that they are all Catalan, and

blending them to suit their tastes and markets. Now they can use this DO and operate within the law. Wines that have long been associated with DOs to which they were not entitled have now come out into the open. It is a very useful DO with which cava makers can sell their still wines.

Some leading bodegas

BOHIGAS
Finca Can Macià, 08711 Odena, Barcelona. Tel: +34 938 04 81 00; Fax: +34 938 03 23 66; Email: export@bohigas.es; Website: www.bohigas.es
In the family for 400 years, the estate has been making wine for sale only since the Spanish Civil War - still old by most standards. Cava is the main product of its sixty hectares, though there are some good still wines. These include a varietal barrel-fermented Chardonnay, a varietal Cabernet Sauvignon, and good reds up to a *reserva* made of Bordeaux grape varieties.

JEAN LEON *See* Penedès.
Apart from the Penedès wines already described, this excellent bodega produces wines in this DO with the name Terrasola. These include a Sauvignon Blanc, which is blended with 25 per cent Garnacha Blanca, and a blend of 83 per cent Syrah and 17 per cent Cariñena.

MAS GIL
Afueros de Calonge – Apartado 117, 17251 Calonge, Girona. Tel: +34 972 66 14 86; Fax: +34 972 66 14 62; Email: oguevara@closdagon.com
This 12-hectare bodega was bought by Englishman Reggie Williams and his wine-maker wife Phoebe. By 1968 her whites were fetching twice the price of her neighbours. Now under local ownership, it produces excellent reds called Clos d'Agon. The 2001 was 60 per cent Cabernet Sauvignon and twenty per cent each Merlot and Syrah. There is also a young white from 46 per cent Viognier, 36 per cent Roussanne, and eighteen per cent Marsanne.

MIGUEL TORRES *See* Penedès.
Miguel Torres was one of the earliest advocates for creating this DO. To use it he has created a new range of wines, Nerola. The white is half Xarel.lo and Garnacha Blanca, the red from 80 per cent Syrah and 20 per cent Monastrell. He also uses it for his De Casta *rosado*, from Garnacha and Mazuelo, and for his famous red wines – Coronas, from Tempranillo and Cabernet Sauvignon, and Sangre de Toro and Gran Sangre de Toro, both from Garnacha and Cariñena. All Torres' wines are worth seeking out.

3

Aragón

The Romans liked Aragón so much that when the legions left Spain many of the citizens remained here. One can see why. It is a beautiful place, dominated in the north by the Pyrenees, and well watered. As you go south, though, the landscape changes and becomes practically a desert. The scenery is extremely varied, and so, of course, are the wines. The area is steeped in history. Indeed the history of modern Spain really began here in 1469 when Ferdinand married Isabella, Queen of Castile. In 1479 he succeeded to the throne of Aragón, and the two kingdoms were united under the Catholic Kings. The Moors were expelled and America was discovered. Their daughter, Caterina, known to history as Catherine of Aragon, married Prince Arthur, heir to the English throne; and when he died she married his brother King Henry VIII. So a good deal of English as well as Spanish history had its roots here.

Its political importance gave Aragón a ready market for its wines, and they were counted among the best in Spain right into the nineteenth century. The leading vineyard then was Cariñena, and its best vines spread over the border into France, where they became known as Carignan and are still widely grown. If one looked at Aragón in the 1980s, one felt it had somehow got left behind and had failed to share in the prosperity of the rest of Spain. It has now caught up. Somontano led the way and is a success story; its wines rose from being practically nothing to become world class. But the other regions are exciting, too. The town of Calatayud has had a remarkable renovation, and its vineyards are producing good, well-balanced wines. In Campo de Borja the wines are bigger-bodied and perhaps inclined to be rather more rustic; and Cariñena is gradually regaining its old reputation.

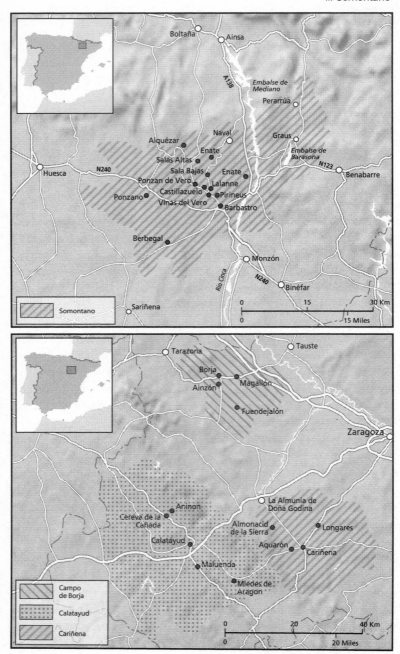

iv Calatayud, Campo de Borja & Cariñena

CALATAYUD

Geography

Calatayud is in the province of Zaragoza, south of Navarra and Campo de Borja and west of Cariñena, which it joins. It is a hilly area with several small rivers, and the motorway from Barcelona to Madrid passes through the middle. The vineyards are high, officially at 550–880 metres (1,804–2,887 feet) above sea level, though some growers claim to have vineyards at 1,000 metres (3,280 feet). There are high winds, and corresponding wind breaks.

Climate

Although this is continental, with cold winters and a high frost risk, the summer heat is kept down by winds to an average of 22–24°C (71.5–75°F). It can go as high as 40°C (104°F) in summer, but the average in winter is 2–6°C (35.5–43°F). It has many microclimates and the rainfall varies from 300–550 millimetres (11.8–19.7 inches), depending on where you are; the average is 336 millimetres (13.2 inches). There are 1,800 hours of sunshine.

Soils

Brown, loose, and stony limestone and loam over gypsum, with marl in the north and slate in the south.

Grapes

Red varieties: Garnacha (the local clone is known as Garnacha Tinta del Monte); Tempranillo; Mazuelo; Merlot; Cabernet Sauvignon; Syrah; and Monastrell.
White varieties: Viura (Macabeo); Malvasía; Chardonnay; Garnacha Blanca; and Moscatel.
There are also old vineyards of Cariñena, Juan Ibáñez (also called Miguel de Arco), and Robal.

Planting

Traditionally in *marco real* with 2.2 metre spacing (7.2 feet), but some of the more recent vineyards are *en espaldera* with a 3 x 1.5 metre (10 x 5 feet) spacing. The *espaldera* method has been a great success, producing very healthy grapes, and irrigation is installed in forty per cent of these vineyards. The vine density is 1,500–2,400 per hectare.

Vineyard area

5,940 hectares.

Authorized yield

Whites 56hl/ha, reds 49hl/ha, but in practice usually very much less.

Wines

Minimum strengths: white 10.5% ABV; *rosado* 11.5% ABV; red 12.5% ABV; and Calatayud Superior red 12.5% ABV. Most are sold as *jóvenes,* but whites are authorized up to *reserva* and reds up to *gran reserva.* Calatayud Superior is a new category made from Garnacha vines over thirty years old.

Production

59,947 hectolitres (2003).

Vintages

1999 (3); 2000 (4); 2001 (4); 2002 (3); 2003 (4); 2004 (4).

The name Calatayud is a corruption of *Qualat Ayub* – the castle of Ayub, or Job, a Moorish governor. The countryside is planted with fruit trees and is particularly famous for its peaches. The poet Martial, whose vinous epigrams are often quoted, was born and died nearby, but spent most of his life in Rome. Most of the winemaking is done by the cooperatives, which have brought themselves up to date with stainless-steel and are making very much better wines. These used to be hefty and short-lived, sold in bulk and exported to France or drunk in bars. But since the establishment of the DO in 1990, things have changed, and the best whites and *reserva* reds show there is real potential here. In particular, blending in Cabernet Sauvignon or Syrah gives the reds the backbone they need, and in some more modern wines Cabernet Sauvignon predominates. This is a place to look for value.

Some leading bodegas

BODEGA NINO JESUS

Las Tablas s/n, 50313 Ariñon, Zaragoza.

Tel: +34 976 89 91 50; Fax: +34 976 89 61 60.

Officially this is SAT 2563 Niño Jesús, founded in 1978 with 150 members who between the have 330 hectares of vines, most thirty to forty years old at 650–880 metres (2,132–2,887 feet) above sea level and very low yielding. It also deals in cherries, almonds, and olive oil. It began selling wine under the mark Estecillo in 2000. Owing to trademark difficulties, the mark Tinto Figaro is used in the USA. The white is a varietal Macabeo and the *rosado* a varietal Garnacha. The red 2003 (a year of high alcohol) is from seventy-five per cent Garnacha with twenty-five per cent Tempranillo, but the very promising Legado Viñas Viejas of the same year was a varietal Garnacha and was given three months in American oak. The 2000 *crianza* was eighty-five per cent Garnacha and fifteen per cent Tempranillo with two years in oak, forty per cent third use French and the rest American: a big, generous wine.

BODEGAS SAN ALEJANDRO

Carretera Calatayud–Cariñena km 16, 50330 Miedes de Aragón, Zaragoza.
Tel: +34 976 89 22 05; Fax: +34 976 89 05 40;
Email: bodegas@san-alejandro.com; Website: www.san-alejandro.com

Otherwise known as Cooperativa San Alejandro, founded in 1962, this is a cooperative with 600 members. Collectively they have 1,400 hectares, from 650–800 metres (2,132–2,625 feet) above sea level, and one is said to be at almost 1,000 metres (3,281 feet) – the highest in the DO. It grows mostly Garnacha, but has some Cabernet Sauvignon, Merlot, and Syrah. It has taken huge strides in the past few years and its wines have been trans-formed, turning it from a good average cooperative into a high flyer. A few years ago it reduced its range of labels from five to two. The good commer-cial wines are Viñas de Miedes, a white varietal cold-fermented Macabeo, a varietal Garnacha *rosado*, and two Garnacha varietal reds – the basic red and the Viñas Viejas, made from vines over forty years old. Its top wines have taken the name of a seventeenth-century local poet, Baltasar Gracián. The *crianza* is made from seventy per cent Garnacha, twenty per cent Tempranillo, and ten per cent Syrah with a year in fifty-fifty French and American oak. Baltasar Gracián Garnacha Viñas Viejas is a very fine wine indeed. The Varietales is made from fifty per cent Syrah, thirty-three per cent Tempranillo, thirteen per cent Merlot, and four per cent Cabernet Sauvignon, given six months in new French oak. The vines it is made from are still relatively young, but it is a good wine and will get better still as it ages. The excellent Expresión is fifty-three per cent high-altitude Garnacha of 75-80 years, nineteen per cent Tempranillo of 15-20 years, and twenty-eight per cent young Syrah, given six months in French oak.

CASTILLO DE MALUENDA

Cortés de Aragón 4, 50300 Calatayud, Zaragoza.

Tel: +34 976 88 92 51; Fax: +34 976 88 92 52.

Email: informacion@castillodemaluenda.com; Website: www.castillodemaluenda.com

Founded in 1999, this used to be the Cooperativa del Campo San Isidro, and conducts some of its activities as Bodegas y Viñedos de Jalón. It is in the village of Maluenda, just south of Calatayud. It sells its wine under the marks Castillo de Maluenda and, in the USA, Viña Alarba. It is the largest producer in the DO with 500 members and 1,645 hectares of vineyard.

COOPERATIVA SAN GREGORIO

Carretera Villalengua s/n, 50312 Cervera de la Cañada, Zaragoza. Tel: +34 976 89 92 06; Fax: +34 976 89 62 40; Email: montearmantes@bodegasangregorio.com; Website: www.bodegasangregorio.com

Another big cooperative, established in 1965 with 500 members and 950 hectares of vineyard. Its wines, sold under the mark Monte Armentes, include varietals from Garnacha and Tempranillo. Its top red wine, Carmesí, is from equal parts of Tempranillo and Garnacha.

VIRGEN DE LA SIERRA

Avenida de la Cooperativa 21, 50310 Villaroya de la Sierra, Zaragoza.

Tel: +34 976 89 90 15; Fax: +34 976 89 91 32.

This highly successful bodega, founded in 1954, produces extremely good-value varietals of Macabeo and Garnacha sold under the mark Cruz de Piedra.

CAMPO DE BORJA

Geography

Campo de Borja is contiguous with Navarra to the northwest, but is separated historically, being in the province of Zaragoza, and climatically. The beautiful Sierra de Moncayo lies to the west, and the vineyards reach into the foothills of the Cordillera Ibérica at altitudes of 300–750 metres (984–2,460 feet). To the east there are rolling hills. The twelfth-century Monasterio de Verula lies at the edge of the region. No longer a monastery, but used for promotional purposes and concerts, it includes a wine museum and is well worth a visit; it is a beautiful building with a memorable tomb.

Climate

This is continental with extremes of temperature. In 1990, for example, the highest temperature was 40°C (104°F) and the lowest -7°C (19.4°F). In winter there is a dry north wind called the *cierzo,* and frequent severe frosts extend into the spring. The average temperature, however, is 14.3°C (57.7°F) and there is plenty of sunshine: some 2,800 hours. But the nights, even in summer, are cool, which makes all the difference. The average rainfall is 434 millimetres (17 inches), but there is little rain for much of the year.

Soils

Mostly sandy over limestone; stony and well-drained.

Grapes

Red varieties: Garnacha; Tempranillo; Mazuelo; Cabernet Sauvignon; Merlot; and Syrah.
White varieties: Macabeo; Moscatel; and Chardonnay.
The traditional variety for the area is Garnacha and this still fills seventy-five per cent of the vineyard, but Tempranillo is encouraged and is being more widely planted. Macabeo comes second.

Planting

Traditionally *en vaso*, *marco real* with 2.2 metre (7.2 feet) spacing, and growing the vines low in this way is essential on the windier sites; but some new vineyards are being planted in *en espalderas*, spaced 3 x 1.5 metres (10 x 5 feet). The density of planting is 1,600–2,500 vines per hectare.

Vineyard Area

7,940 hectares.

Authorized Yield

49hl/ha for reds and 56hl/ha for whites.

Wines

Whites and *rosados*, minimum strength 11% ABV, reds 12% ABV or 12.5% ABV for *crianzas* and above. In a DO red, at least fifty per cent must be Garnacha. In addition to these DO wines, some sweet *mistelas* with a strength of 17.5% ABV are made from Moscatel.

Production

184,100 hectolitres (2003).

Vintages

2000 (5); 2001 (4); 2002 (3); 2003 (3); 2004 (4).

Campo de Borja means the field, or territory, of Borja, named after the noble family that owned it. One member, Alfonso de Borja, became pope as Calixtus III and, moving to Rome with his notorious family, Italianized his name to Borgia. His nephew, Rodrigo de Borja, became Pope Alexander VI in 1492, and apportioned the New World between Spain and Portugal. He also was the father of Cesare and Lucrezia. Happily their exploits are irrelevant to this book. Their great castle can still be seen in ruins above the town.

Although wine has been grown here from time immemorial, it was heady plonk from the traditional Garnacha. Easily rising to 14% ABV, thanks to the hot summers, it was sold in bulk for drinking in bars and for blending and bottling elsewhere. Vineyards are small (there are more than 2,500 growers), and nearly all the wine is produced by six cooperatives; but the leaders have recently taken a leap forward, experimenting and setting out to make quality wines. They have succeeded. The DO was established in 1980 and since then progress has been rapid. The best wines today are good and, not surprisingly, resemble those from neighbouring Navarra. They are gradually establishing a reputation and are very good value.

Generally speaking, the lower vineyards are planted with Garnacha and those on the higher slopes with Tempranillo and the foreign varieties. There is no irrigation, nor is there ever likely to be, owing to shortage of water. Some old wooden and epoxy vats remain, but these are steadily being replaced with stainless steel, in which all the best wines are made. Some of the red *jóvenes* are made by carbonic maceration.

Some leading bodegas

BODEGAS ARAGONESAS

Carretera Magallón s/n, 50529 Fuendejalón, Zaragoza. Tel: +34 976 86 21 53; Fax: +34 976 86 23 63; Email: bodegasaragon@bodegasaragonesas.com; Website: www.bodegasaragonesas.com

The company was founded in 1984 to sell the wines of the Cooperativa San

Juan Bautista, founded in 1955 at Fuendejalón. It was joined in 1984 by the Cooperativa Santo Cristo at Magallon. In 1994 the Aragón government became a shareholder and a new bodega was built in 1995, which has since been expanded. The members have some 3,500 hectares of vineyard, most of which is Garnacha but there is twelve per cent Tempranillo and experimental plantings of the other varieties including twenty-five hectares of Cabernet Sauvignon plus Merlot, Mazuelo, and Syrah. It is now the largest producer in the DO, accounting for about sixty-five per cent of the total and makes very good wines. Since 1995 all have been fermented in stainless steel. Red wines account for eighty per cent, *rosados* for fifteen, and whites for five per cent. The brands are: Crucillón; Viña Tito; Don Ramón; Mosén Cleto; Coto de Hayas; Duque de Sevilla; and Fagus. Viña Tito is used for the basic *jóvenes*, Don Ramón and Coto de Hayas for the next step up. The Coto de Hayas white *joven* is from fifty per cent Chardonnay, forty-five per cent Macabeo, and five per cent Moscatel; the *rosado* from ninety-five per cent Garnacha, with five per cent Tempranillo; and the red from fifty per cent Garnacha, twenty per cent each Tempranillo and Syrah, and ten per cent Cabernet Sauvignon. The Duque de Sevilla *reserva* is from eighty per cent forty-year-old Garnacha and twenty per cent twenty-year-old Tempranillo, with twelve months in American oak. The best of all is Fagus, a varietal Garnacha from vines forty to fifty years old, matured in French oak, and is one of the finest expressions of that grape found anywhere.

BODEGAS BORSAO

Ctra Nacional 122 km 63, 50540 Borja, Zaragoza. Tel: +34 976 86 71 16; Fax: +34 976 86 77 52; Email: info@bodegasborsao.com; Website: www.bodegasborsao.com

This is the trading name of the Sociedad Cooperativa Ltda Agrícola de Borja, dating from 1954, though the bodega itself was founded in 1958. Another of the big players, it combines three cooperatives and is a general cooperative for local farmers, with extensive interests in olive oil, almonds, tomatoes, asparagus, and other crops. Its wines are very good. The members have 1,200 hectares of Garnacha, 100 hectares of Tempranillo, twenty-five hectares of Cabernet Sauvignon, ten hectares of Mazuelo, and twenty-five hectares of Macabeo. It makes reds, some *rosado,* and a very little white. The *jóvenes* come from the lower vineyards, the *crianzas* and *reservas* from the higher ones. Its bestseller is Tres Picos, a varietal Garnacha *joven*, as is Primitzia. The Borsao *joven* 2003 was from seventy per cent Garnacha, twenty per cent Cabernet Sauvignon, and ten per cent Tempranillo. The *crianzas* are sixty to sixty-five per cent Garnacha, twenty per cent Cabernet Sauvignon, and fifteen to twenty per cent Tempranillo, matured in American oak. The very good *reserva* 2000 was from fifty per cent Garnacha, the rest equal proportions of Tempranillo and Cabernet Sauvignon, matured in seventy per cent French oak.

CRIANZAS Y VINEDOS SANTO CRISTO
Carretera de Tabuenca s/n, 20570 Ainzón, Zaragoza.
Tel: +34 976 86 96 96; Fax: +34 976 86 80 97;
Email: info@bodegas-santo-cristo.com; Website: www.bodegas-santo-cristo.com
A cooperative founded in 1955 with 1,185 hectares of vineyard. Its cheaper range is sold as Viña Collado. Its better wines are sold as Viña Ainzón: the *crianzas* from Garnacha, Tempranillo, and Cabernet Sauvignon, with ten months in American oak; the *reservas* from eighty per cent Tempranillo and twenty per cent Garnacha with fourteen to twenty-eight months, and are well worth seeking out. The 1998, with twenty-eight months, was very good indeed. Peñazuela is modern, high expression, varietal Garnacha with four months in American oak. There is also a Viña Ainzón varietal Garnacha with eighteen months in American oak. A highly regarded sweet wine, Moscatel Ainzón, is from Moscatel de Grano Menudo.

CARIÑENA

Geography

To the southwest of Zaragoza and to the east of the ajoining DO of Calatayud, Cariñena is an attractive region of high plains and small hills. In the foothills of the Sierra de Algairén, which form part of the Cordillera Ibérica, the vineyards rise from 400–800 metres (1,312–2,625 feet).

Climate

Continental hot summers, up to 38°C (100°F), but it cools down at night. In cold winters it goes down to -8°C (17.5°F), but the yearly average is 15°C (59°F). It is relatively dry, with a rainfall of 300–350 millimetres (11.8–13.7 inches) and averages 2,800 hours of sunshine. Drought and hail are hazards, as is the cold, northerly *cierzo* wind.

Soils

Ochre-coloured limestone with slate in places and some alluvial soil.

Grapes

Red varieties: Garnacha; Tempranillo; Cariñena; Juan Ibáñez; Monastrell; Cabernet Sauvignon; Merlot; and Syrah.

White varieties: Viura (Macabeo); Garnacha Blanca; Parellada; Moscatel Romano; and Chardonnay.

Garnacha occupies fifty-five per cent of the vineyard, followed by Viura with twenty per cent, and Tempranillo with fifteen per cent. It is ironic that the local Cariñena grape, which is widely grown in France under the name Carignan, and is known elsewhere in Spain as the Mazuelo, is now down to six per cent.

Planting

Marco real with 2.2 metres (7.2 feet) spacing and *espaldera* with 3 x 1.5 m spacing (10 x 5 feet). The latter is being encouraged in new or replanted vineyards, as those on the high plains are very suitable for mechanical harvesting. The density is 1,500–3,000 vines per hectare.

Vineyard area

16,676 hectares.

Authorized yield

Whites 52hl/ha, reds 45.5hl/ha, but usually rather less.

Wines

Minimum strengths: whites and *rosados* 11% ABV, reds 12% ABV, *rancios* 15% ABV (and with three years in oak), and *vinos de licor* 17.5% ABV. The last two are made only in very small quantities. Most of the wines are *jóvenes*, with reds predominating, but about thirty per cent are made as *crianzas*, *reservas*, and *gran reservas*, the last only being produced in the best years.

Production

320,000 hectolitres (2003).

Vintages

1999 (3); 2000 (4); 2001 (5); 2002 (4); 2003 (4); 2004 (4).

This has never been regarded as a fine wine district, but always as a reliable one; though in 1824 Al Henderson wrote of Spanish wines in general: "That which is obtained from the species called Garnache… is in highest repute; and the growth of Cariñena are preferred to all others." Traditionally it made sweet wines of enormous alcoholic strength and colour by picking the grapes very late. Happily, the bodegas have been brought up to date with stainless steel and the wines are now very well made, so that the lusty and unsubtle styles of the past have disappeared and new, lighter ones have taken their place. The reds are the best and are very good value at all levels. The *consejo regulador* has an admirable little museum that is well worth a visit. Among other things it shows the work of Jules Lichenstein, who had a bodega here (as did several French wine merchants at the end of the nineteenth century) and who described the life-cycle of phylloxera before his death in 1886, so that when it arrived in 1901 everyone knew what to do.

Some leading bodegas

BODEGAS ANADAS

Carretera Aguarón km 47, 50400 Cariñena, Zaragoza. Tel: +34 976 79 30 16; Fax: +34 976 62 04 48; Email: bodega@carewines.com

This small bodega, established as recently as 2000, has already gained a formidable reputation for the quality of its wines, sold under the name Care. It has 100 hectares of vineyard growing Merlot, Cabernet Sauvignon, Syrah, Garnacha, Tempranillo, and Chardonnay – but no Cariñena. Its *rosado* and red *jóvenes* are made from equal parts of Tempranillo and Syrah, but the *crianzas* have sixty to sixty-five per cent Garnacha from eighty-year-old vines, with thirty-five to forty per cent Cabernet Sauvignon from twenty-five-year-old vines, and spend fourteen months in French and American oak.

BODEGAS GRAN DUCAY

Ctra Zaragoza–Valencia km 46.2, 50400 Cariñena, Zaragoza. Tel: +34 976 62 04 00; Fax: +34 976 62 03 98; Email: bsv@sanvalero.com; Website: www.bodegasanvalero.com

Formerly called San Valero, this is a large cooperative with 700 members having 4,000 hectares of vineyard, founded in 1945. In 1983 Bodegas Gran Ducay was founded, originally for making cava, and both are now combined in the Grupo BSU. It makes two complete ranges under the brands Don Mendo and Monte Ducay, going up to *gran reservas*, with Villalta for young wines and Marqués de Tosos for some of its best. The Monte Ducay wines are the best known on the export markets and offer very good value. The reds are made from combinations of Tempranillo, Garnacha, and Cariñena, but the Monte Ducay *gran reserva* is from Tempranillo, Cabernet Sauvignon, and Garnacha. The top wine is Imperial Carinus from Merlot, Syrah, and Cabernet Sauvignon given fourteen months in fifty-fifty French and American oak.

BODEGA IGNACIO MARÍN

San Valero 1, 50400 Cariñena, Zaragoza. Tel: +34 976 62 11 29; Fax: +34 976 62 10 31; Email: comercial@ignaciomarin.com; Website: www.ignaciomarin.com
One of the few substantial private bodegas, this family concern was founded in 1903 and has 117 hectares of vineyard. Its air-conditioned bodega is as modern as can be and its wines are very highly regarded. They are sold under the marks Barón de Lajoyosa, Castillo de Viñaral, and Duque de Medina. The *crianzas* are from sixty per cent Garnacha and twenty per cent each of Cariñena and Tempranillo, sometimes with a little Cabernet Sauvignon. The Baron de Lajoyosa *gran reserva* is fifty per cent Garnacha, thirty per cent Tempranillo, and twenty per cent Cabernet Sauvignon, while the Duque de Medina *gran reserva* has fifty per cent Tempranillo, thirty per cent Garnacha, and twenty per cent Cariñena. There is also a varietal Moscatel.

COVINCA SOCIEDAD COOPERATIVA

Carretera Valencia s/n, 50460 Longares, Zaragoza.
Tel: +34 976 14 26 53; Fax: +34 976 14 24 02; Email: covinca@rsc.es
This young cooperative, founded in 1988 by the amalgamation of two older ones, whose members have 3,000 hectares of vineyard, is one of the best known, making very sound wines under the brands Marqués de Ballestar, Torrelongares, and Viña Oria.

GRANDES VINOS Y VINEDOS

Ctra Valencia km 45.7, 50400 Cariñena, Zaragoza. Tel: +34 976 62 12 61; Fax: +34 976 62 12 53; Email: info@grandesvinos.com; Website: www.grandesvinos.com
Formed in 1997 by the amalgamation of six cooperatives - the best known of which was Cooperativa San José, it has 1,000 members and some outside shareholders including the government of Aragón. With 5,800 hectares, it is the biggest bodega in Aragón. The wines are made at the individual cooperatives under the supervision of oenologists from headquarters. Not surprisingly, it has a bewildering number of wines and marks. The most widely distributed are Monasterio de la Viñas and Valdemadera. Corona de Aragón is sold only to restaurants. Viña Rotura is based on Garnacha and San Valero is made from the oldest vines. The Monasterio de las Viñas range includes varietals from

Tempranillo, Cabernet Sauvignon, and Garnacha. Its reds are from Garnacha, Tempranillo, Cariñena, and, in *crianzas* and above, Cabernet Sauvignon. The 2000 *crianza* was from forty-five per cent Garnacha, thirty-five per cent Tempranillo, ten per cent Cariñena, and ten per cent Cabernet Sauvignon. The top wine is Anayón from the oldest vines of Cabernet Sauvignon, Tempranillo, and Merlot. The wines are very well made and completely reliable. The top wines are excellent.

SOLAR DE URBEZO

San Valero 14, 50400 Cariñena, Zaragoza. Tel: +34 976 62 19 68; Fax: +34 976 62 05 49; Email: info@solardeurbezo.es; Website: www.solardeurbezo.es

This modern, family-owned bodega founded in 1995 has already earned a great reputation. It has 100 hectares of vineyard growing Cabernet Sauvignon, Syrah, Tempranillo, Garnacha, Cariñena, and Chardonnay. The wines are matured in American, French, and Russian oak. Its varietal Chardonnay is very cold fermented at 8–10°C (46.4–50°F) and has twenty days in new French oak. The red *joven* is made by a form of carbonic maceration from forty per cent Garnacha, thirty per cent Tempranillo, and thirty per cent Syrah. There is a Cariñena/Syrah blend. The 2000 *reserva* was from Cabernet Sauvignon, Cariñena, and Merlot.

SOMONTANO

Geography

Somontano means "under the mountains", referring to the Pyrenees. The main town is Barbastro, 80 kilometres (50 miles) south of the French border. The vineyards surround it, but lie mainly to the west and north, in the Pyrenean foothills, between 350–650 metres (1,148–2,133 feet). Unlike most Spanish vineyards, these are in a lusciously green, hilly area within Huesca, in the old kingdom of Aragón. The *consejo regulador* has a wine museum.

Climate

Far from the moderating influence of the sea, it is continental, with temperatures up to 40°C (104°F) in the summer and falling to -10°C (14°F) in the winter. Nevertheless it is more moderate than most, sheltered from the cold north winds by the Pyrenees, with a modest yearly average of 11°C (51.8°F),

500 millimetres (20 inches) of rainfall, and 2,700 hours of sunshine. The summers are dry and arid. Hail can be a big problem.

Soils

Thanks to a high proportion of sandstone and clay, these are red-brown to the eye, but contain a good deal of calcium.

Grapes

Although a long-established wine region, it has relied historically on the local red Moristel and white Alcañón grapes. It is experiencing a renaissance and, unfettered by tradition, all sorts of varieties are being tried, most of them successfully. Others will undoubtedly be tried in the future and it may well be many years before a set pattern emerges.

Red varieties: Moristel; Garnacha; Tempranillo; Parraleta; Cabernet Sauvignon; Pinot Noir; Merlot; and Syrah.

White varieties: Macabeo; Alcañón; Garnacha Blanca; Chardonnay; and Gewurztraminer.

Planting

Various patterns are used depending on the highly irregular sites and the grape variety, but typically they are planted in a rectangular pattern and trained *en vaso* or single or double *cordon*. Many vineyards have water spraying equipment to counter the risks of frost in March and April. The density is 1,500–3,000 per hectare.

Vineyard Area

4,055 hectares.

Authorized yield

Reds 59hl/ha, whites 67hl/ha, but in practice less.

Wines

Whites from 10–13.5% ABV with, exceptionally, late-gathered Macabeo varietals up to 16% ABV. Light reds and *rosados* from 11–13.5% ABV and reds from 11.5–14% ABV. Sparkling wines 10–13.5% ABV.

Production

135,307 hectolitres (2003).

Vintages

1985 (5); 1986 (3); 1987 (4); 1988 (5); 1989 (4); 1990 (3); 1991 (4); 1992 (4); 1993 (5); 1994 (5); 1995 (5); 1996 (4); 1997 (3); 1998 (5); 1999 (4); 2000 (3); 2001 (5); 2002 (4); 2003 (4); 2004 (4).

Somontano is a most beautiful place, with the peaks of the Pyrenees, snow-capped for much of the year, making the perfect backdrop to the vineyards. The ancient city of Barbastro, unlike most Spanish towns, has agreeably resisted development and has a good, small sixteenth century cathedral. Alquézar, a most attractive hilltop village in the north of the DO area, is well worth a visit. It is one of the most exciting wine-making regions in Spain. A few years ago no one had ever heard of it. It made light, rustic wines that travelled into and over the Pyrenees. Then, in 1984, it achieved DO status. It took off and has been expanding rapidly ever since. For all practical purposes, in wine terms, it was virgin territory. Young winemakers with ample capital and all the latest equipment poured in, transforming old cooperatives and creating superb modern bodegas. They brought with them foreign vines. The French vines assumed a different personality in their new environment; Spanish varieties that had been little grown, such as Tempranillo, flourished; and new blends were created, some of them using the old native varieties. The wines spoke for themselves: well balanced and delicious, some of the best in Spain. The bodegas are full of energy and enthusiasm, and as they are untrammelled by the traditions of an established market, they can experiment as they like, which they have done to very good effect.

Some leading bodegas

BLECUA

Ctra Barbastro–Naval km 3.7, 22300 Barbastro, Huesca. Tel: +34 974 30 22 16; Email: marketing@vinasdelvero.es; Website: www.bodegablecua.com

A boutique offshoot of the excellent Viñas del Vero (*see* below), it was set up in 2000 to make just one red wine of the highest possible quality, and that is what it does. It has its own bodega and a fourteen-hectare vineyard, though it is not limited to this and can use special selections from the best seven of the Viñas del Vero holdings. New French Allier oak is used for the fermentation and maturation, the wines being bottled without stabilization or filtration. The first vintage, 1997, was made from equal parts of Merlot,

Cabernet Sauvignon, Garnacha, and Tempranillo. The 1998 was principally Cabernet Sauvignon and Garnacha. No wine at all was sold of the 1999 vintage. The 2000 was thirty per cent each of Cabernet Sauvignon, Merlot, and Tempranillo, with ten per cent Garnacha. The exact proportions vary each year, but the results are marvellous, up-front wines of a slightly New World style that need cellaring for ten years to show their true quality.

BODEGAS BORRUEL SAT – OSCA

La Iglesia 1, 22124 Ponzano, Huesca. Tel: +34 974 31 90 17; Fax: +34 974 31 91 75; Email: bodega@bodegasosca.com; Website: www.bodegasosca.com

Bodegas Borruel has roots that stretch back to a family firm founded in 1903, but now has a new image. Osca, its most-noted brand, is now part of the bodega name. It operates modestly with twenty-five hectares and makes some good and interesting wines. Its white varietals include a barrel-fermented Chardonnay, a Macabeo, and an Alcañón; its reds a Moristel, a Merlot, and a Cabernet Sauvignon. The first is given eight months - and the others, fifteen - in American and French oak. Mascún is a mark used for varietals of Garnacha and Merlot. The *rosado* is made from Tempranillo and Moristel. The *crianzas* are from Tempranillo and Cabernet Sauvignon, with twelve months in American and French oak. Its top wines are a very good *crianza* from the same varieties, sold as Castillo de L'Ainsa, and a *reserva*, Gran Eroles, from the same varieties, given twenty-four months in oak. There is a second range sold under the L'Ainsa brand.

BODEGAS PIRINEOS

Ctra Barbastro–Naval km 3.5, 22300 Barbastro, Huesca.
Tel: +34 974 31 12 89; Fax: +34 974 30 66 88;
Email: info@bodegapirineos.com; Website: www.bodegapirineos.com

Starting life in the 1960s as the Bodega Cooperativa de Somontano, in 1993 it was totally transformed. It became a company and invested an enormous amount in latest technology. The change was visionary. It pioneered the development of Somontano as a fine wine area by selling bottled wines. With 130 hectares of vineyard and another 400 owned by its shareholders, it makes a number of varietals. In whites there are Chardonnay, Gewürztraminer, and Macabeo (including a barrel-fermented late-harvest wine); in reds Garnacha and, most unusually, the two local varieties Moristel and Parraleta. Its blended wines include Merlot/Cabernet Sauvignon, in equal measure. The bodega name is used for most of the wines, but its old brand name, Montesierra, is used for some. The *crianzas* are fifty per cent Tempranillo, twenty-five per cent

Moristel, and twenty-five per cent Cabernet Sauvignon. Its *reserva* Señorio de Lazan is fifty per cent Tempranillo, forty-five per cent Cabernet Sauvignon, and five per cent Moristel. Its excellent top wine is Marboré, a blend of Tempranillo, Merlot, Cabernet Sauvignon, Parraleta, and Moristel. Local varieties are put to good use here, and contribute their own elements to the complexity.

BODEGAS SIERRA DE GUARA

Ctra Abiego km 0.2, 22124 Lascellas, Huesca. Tel/Fax: +34 974 31 93 63; Email: info@bodegassierradeguara.com; Website: www.bodegassierradeguara.es

A newcomer established in 1997, it has eighty-five hectares of vineyard in a fine location at an altitude of 600 metres (1,968 feet), not all of which is at present planted. There are twenty-eight hectares of Tempranillo, twenty of Merlot, and twelve of Cabernet Sauvignon. There are only three wines: a Chardonnay, a Merlot *rosado,* and a *roble* red from fifty per cent Tempranillo, twenty-five per cent Cabernet Sauvignon, and twenty-five per cent Merlot. All have won high praise. French oak is used for ageing. This is one to watch.

ENATE – GRANDES VINOS DE ESPANA

Ctra de Barbastro a Naval km 9, 22314 Salas Bajas, Huesca. Tel: +34 974 30 25 80; Fax: +34 974 30 00 46; Email: bodega@enate.es; Website: www.enate.es

No bodega could be more up to date than this: Enate is firmly in the twenty-first century. Everything is spacious, clean, and computer controlled. From the very start the aim was to produce top-quality wines, and it has done just that. It is a family-owned company founded in 1991, but the bodega building was not started until 1992 and was opened in 1993. It acquired forty hectares of vineyard and now has 400 on chalky-clay soil with large stones, in the hills, 500 metres (1,640 feet) up. One is used for experimental varieties. A large reservoir provides irrigation, the water pumped up by solar power. Neither herbicides nor insecticides are used and the grapes are hand harvested. While it produces mostly reds, the *rosado* and whites are notable. All are sold under the brand name Enate, and the bottles have striking modern labels. The whites include a Chardonnay, fermented in new French oak – the casks later used for maturing red wines – left on the lees, which are stirred every two weeks, and undergo malolactic fermentation. The alcohol content is a lusty 13.5% ABV, but thanks to its big flavour it is in perfect balance, does not taste over-oaked, and benefits from three to four years' bottle age. Chardonnay 234 is made from grapes grown in the 234 hectare vineyard. The varietal Gewürztraminer is impressive, having none of the potential blowzy trait of this grape's wines. The superior *rosado* is a varietal Cabernet Sauvignon. Enate Tinot is a blend of equal parts Cabernet Sauvignon and Merlot, while the *crianza* is seventy per cent Tempranillo, with thirty per cent Cabernet Sauvignon and is worth keeping for a year or two to give extra bottle age. The Varietales are mainly Merlot, Tempranillo, and Cabernet Sauvignon. A varietal Cabernet Sauvignon Reserva with twelve months in French oak has plenty of tannin and is worth laying down for several years. There is also a varietal Merlot called Merlot-Merlot. The excellent Reserva Especial wines have fifty to sixty per cent Cabernet Sauvignon (depending on the vintage) and the rest Merlot. It is a superb range of wines, and most of the vineyards are still relatively young. It can only get better.

VIÑAS DEL VERO

Finca de San Marcos, Varretera Barbastro–Naval, km 3.7, 22300 Barbastro, Huesca.
Tel: +34 974 30 22 16; Fax: +34 974 30 20 98;
Email: info@vinasdelvero.es; Website: www.vinasdelvero.es

This is also a producer of top-quality wines, founded in 1986 as Compañia Vitivinicola Aragonesa (COVISA) by the local Aragón development agency, and owned by the savings banks, the government of Aragón, and a private company. Its first wines were sold in 1990. A building, which has been admirably restored and extended, was bought from the old-established company of Lalanne, and large vineyards were acquired, together with planting rights. It is now the biggest vineyard owner in Somontano, with 750 hectares. These are semi-organic, and disease is generally avoided, but the bodega will spray if it has to. Some grapes are machine-picked. The yield is deliberately kept down to thirty-six hectolitres per hectare. One vineyard surrounds the bodega, while another is in a beautiful position on top of a hill. There are all the traditional local varieties and a number of experimental ones. Again it is worth noting that most of the vineyards are still relatively young: their full quality is developing.

Everything in the bodega is state of the art and computer controlled. Its height allows wine to be moved by gravity. American oak is used for maturing Tempranillo and Moristel, but French Allier is used for Merlot, Cabernet Sauvignon, Pinot Noir, and Chardonnay. A complete range of top-quality wines is produced. The white varietals are a very good and agreeably restrained Gewürztraminer, and two Chardonnays, one including a small part that is barrel-fermented, while the other spends six months in new Allier oak. There is also a basic white from Macabeo and Chardonnay. The *rosado* is Tempranillo, Moristel, and Cabernet Sauvignon. The red is Merlot, Cabernet

Sauvignon, and Moristel, with four months in French and American oak; the *crianza* is Tempranillo and Cabernet Sauvignon matured in American oak. The reds varietals are Tempranillo, Pinot Noir, Merlot, and Cabernet Sauvignon. The Tempranillo is made by carbonic maceration, but all the others, along with the Gewürztraminer and the oak-aged Chardonnay, form the superior range Los Vinos de Colección. The Chardonnays are among Spain's best. But perhaps the most interesting is the Pinot Noir. This difficult variety is given eighteen months in French oak and is excellent, tasting rather like a spicy Burgundy. The Merlot is also very good. At the top of the range is Vinos de Autor. The particularly good Gran Vos Reserva is made from equal quantities Cabernet Sauvignon and Merlot, and five per cent "others" (mostly Pinot Noir), given eighteen months in Allier oak, eighty per cent of which is new. The white Clarión, from selected but unspecified grapes, is not barrel aged. The superb Secastilla is from very old Garnacha vines grown at a height of 700 metres (2,296 feet). *See* also Blecua, above.

OTHER WINES

The ancient kingdom of Aragón extended further than the present *autonomia*, which includes the provinces of Huesca, Teruel, and Zaragoza. The DO wines of Calatayud, Campo de Borja, Cariñena, and Somontano have been described, but wine is made all over the place. Travelling around, one can find agreeable local wines that are mostly strong, lusty, and rustic, but good vineyard soil can be found and it's a lot cheaper than in the DOs. Serious local wine-makers may emerge before long. Seven areas enjoy VdlT status: Bajo Aragón; Campo de Belchite; Muniesa; Ribera del Gállego-Cinco Villas; Tierra Baja de Aragón; Valdejalón; Valle de Jiloca; and (not yet a VdlT) Valle del Cinca, but no wines from these areas have yet established a national – let alone international – market. The last appears the most promising.

Codorníu, the great cava house, has invested in a new property called Nuviana in Belver de Cinca, 11 kilometres (6.8 miles) from San Miguel. It has built a magnificent, modern bodega with a modest 3.4 hectare vineyard, but is fed with grapes from six estates and 435.5 hecatres growing Cabernet Sauvignon, Tempranillo, Merlot, Syrah, and Chardonnay. It launched its first wine in 2002 and currently makes three: a varietal Chardonnay; a blend of fifty-five per cent Tempranillo and forty-five per cent Cabernet; and a blend of sixty per cent Cabernet Sauvignon and forty per cent Merlot. The two reds get five months in American oak. This is certainly one to watch and could turn into another Raïmat.

4

Rioja

Sheltered by the Pyrenees and far enough north that the sun is not too hot, this part of Spain is very well placed for growing top-quality table wines. Of the two great areas - Rioja and Navarra - the former was the first off the mark with world-class wines and is not resting on its laurels – its great bodegas look to the future.

Geography

The Rioja wine district is in the centre-north of Spain and should not be confused with the *autonomia* La Rioja, the capital of which is Logroño. The total area is 61,993 hectares, stretching 120 kilometres (74.5 miles) along the Ebro Valley, never more than 50 kilometres wide (31 miles), sheltered in the north by the Sierra de Cantabria and in the south by the Sierra de la Demanda. The greater part of the vineyards are within La Rioja, but 7,000 hectares lie within the province of Alava and 4,000 hectares within the province of Navarra. It is divided into three parts: Rioja Alta; Rioja Alavesa (the part that lies within Alava, on the edge of the Basque country); and Rioja Baja.

Climate

Alta and Alavesa are in the highlands, 400-500 metres (1,312–1,640 feet) above sea level, where the altitude and a certain Atlantic influence gives an average temperature of 12.8°C (55°F) and an average rainfall of 450 millimetres (17.7 inches). Hot spells in summer do not usually last long. The Baja subdistrict is lower, at about 300 metres (984 feet), and has a more Mediterranean climate with an average temperature of 13.9°C (57°F) and 370 millimetres

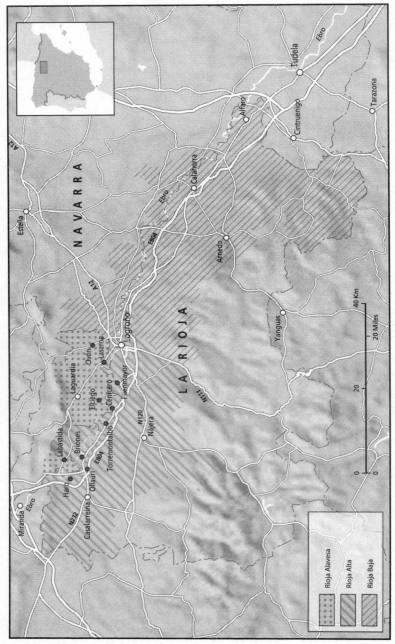

v Rioja

(14.5 inches) of rainfall, though at its southern extremity it reaches into the foothills of the mountains and there are some vineyards with a more continental climate. All three have some vineyards that are higher than the average, and these are increasingly favoured. Sheltered from north winds by the mountains, all three regions have hot summers, long and mild autumns, but cold winters with a considerable frost risk in the Alta and Alavesa that extends into the flowering and can seriously reduce yield. Snow is apt to fall there between the middle of January and the second half of February, and there can be unpleasant freezing fogs. There is little frost and snow, however, in the more Mediterranean climate of the Baja. In the summer the wine districts look arid, and crossing the mountains to the north reveals a greener, cooler world that is quite different and generally unsuitable for wine-growing. The average hours of sunshine are 2,750, though higher figures of over 3,000 are sometimes given, as are lower ones, down to 2,000. It undoubtedly varies considerably from place to place. About forty-three per cent of the vineyards are in the Rioja Alta, twenty per cent in the Alavesa, and thirty-seven per cent in the geographically much larger Baja.

Soils

In both Alta and Alavesa they are calcareous clay, though there are some ferruginous and alluvial soils in the former. In Alavesa in particular there is a problem with rocks, which have to be removed laboriously if a new vineyard is to be planted. In Rioja Baja, on the other hand, the land is generally flat, with mainly ferruginous clay and alluvial soils. The light-coloured calcareous clay, which may contain as much as forty-five per cent calcium carbonate, is the best, certainly for red wines. A map showing exactly where each kind of soil is to be found is so complicated that it looks like a jigsaw puzzle.

Grapes

The forty or so varieties that were grown in the eighteenth century have been reduced to seven.

Red varieties: Tempranillo (sixty per cent of the vineyard); Garnacha (nineteen per cent); Mazuelo; and Graciano. Cabernet Sauvignon is grown too and led the drive for quality in the nineteenth century, but now forms only one per cent of the vineyard and cannot be mentioned on back labels, being classed as "*emperimental*", which is rather absurd. There have been moves to add it to the official varieties and to introduce Merlot, Syrah, and Pinot Noir, but although the door has been left open, this has not happened yet, and there is a strong lobby to develop the local varieties. The French vines are listed disparagingly as "other varieties". There is a research product to revive old, semi-extinct local varieties, the most notable so far being the red Maturana; there is also a white Maturana, which is now being grown commercially by Bodegas Viña Ijalba. Some wine-makers, however, continue to favour Cabernet Sauvignon to give added structure to their wines. Traditionalists say Graciano can do this just as well, but not much is grown. **White varieties:** Viura (fifteen per cent); Malvasía Riojana; and Garnacha Blanca. A number of other white varieties are being grown experimentally and probably illegally. These include Roussanne; Marsanne; Sauvignon Blanc; Viognier; and Chardonnay. The authorities are not currently giving permission to plant new white wine vineyards, so the old ones may fetch up being more valuable than the reds.

Planting

En vaso, with 2,850–4,000 vines per hectare. Some recent vineyards are, however, being trained on wires and pruned by the Guyot method. There is no mechanical harvesting.

Vineyard area

24,457 hectares in Rioja Alta, 12,050 hectares in Rioja Alavesa, and 20,907 hectares in Rioja Baja. Although some major shippers have large vineyard holdings, the average size is still only 4.4 hectares.

Authorized yield

Red 45.5hl/ha, white 63 hl/ha, but usually less.

Wines

Red, *rosado*, and white. Rioja *joven* (formerly known as *sin crianza*, a term still often used) has seen at most three or four months of oak and may not have seen any at all; it is released in its first or second year. Rioja *de crianza* can be released in its third year (which is not necessarily three full years after the vintage) and must have spent at least six months in 225-litre oak *barricas* if white, and twelve months if red. These wines, particularly in Spain, used to be labelled simply "third year", but nowadays are sold with their vintage and have to be labelled with it if they are for export. At least eighty-five per cent of the wine must come from the vintage specified; this has been so since 1981. Rioja *de reserva* must have the same minimum oak ageing, but cannot be released until its fourth year. The highest category is Rioja *de gran reserva*, made only in exceptional years. Recently some winemakers have been producing *corta crian-zas,* or *semi crianzas,* with about six months in oak, so that they are fresh but have oak overtones; this description is not allowed on labels. White and *rosado reservas* must spend at least six months in oak, but wines of these colours are very rarely made as *gran reservas.* Red *gran reservas* must spend at least twenty-four months in oak and thirty-six in bottle. They can be released after five years. Many bodegas, especially the old-established ones, mature the wines in wood for much longer than the minimum period. Some of the modern bodegas, although producing *crianza* and *reserva* wines, refuse to label them as such because they think it sounds old-fashioned.

The minimum strength allowed depends on where the wine is grown. For white wines it is 11% ABV in Alta and Alavesa, 11.5% ABV in Baja. *Rosados* can be 0.5% ABV less, but reds must be 0.5% ABV more. A Garnacha grown in Baja can attain an awesome 16% ABV, but most wines are shipped at about 13% ABV.

Production

Average 2,600,000 hectolitres.

Vintages

The following are the official classifications:

1970 (4); 1971 (1); 1972 (1); 1973 (3); 1974 (3); 1975 (4); 1976 (3); 1977 (2); 1978 (4); 1979 (2); 1980 (3); 1981 (4); 1982 (5); 1983 (4); 1984 (2); 1985 (3); 1986 (3); 1987 (4); 1988 (3); 1989 (3); 1990 (3); 1991 (4); 1992 (4); 1993 (4); 1994 (5); 1995 (5); 1996 (4); 1997 (3); 1998 (4); 1999 (3); 2000 (3); 2001 (5); 2002 (3); 2003 (3); 2004 (5).

With such a large area and several varieties of vine, there are always excep-tions to the rule and the above classifications can only be taken as indicative.

La Rioja is a very beautiful place, but it does not reveal itself immediately. The town of Haro at first seems nondescript, but the oldest part, in the cen-tre, has some fine stone houses bearing proud escutcheons, though most are tumbledown and there are far fewer than there were thirty or forty years ago. Logroño is bigger and, like so many other Spanish towns, is rapidly becom-ing a concrete jungle; but it has some good things such as the eighteenth century church of Santa María de la Redonda. Many of the small towns and villages, though, remain unspoiled. Laguardia, in Rioja Alta, succeeds in keeping cars out and is exquisitely preserved, with a wonderful view to the mountains. It is worth going to Rioja just to look at the hilltop villages such as Briones. The countryside in Alta and Alavesa is beautiful, too, packed with vineyards and revealing unexpected vistas as you drive through the hills. The mountains are all around, still snow-capped at the beginning of May. In the autumn, after the vintage, the leaves on the Tempranillo, Graciano, and Mazuelo turn into wonderful colours of red and brown. Rioja Baja, however, is not beautiful, nor is it so densely planted with vines. On leaving a vineyard you often have to travel quite a way to find the next.

Like most of the major Spanish vineyards, Rioja has a long and complex history, but the early years are rather obscure and the wines we know today only really go back to the beginning of the nineteenth century. The first known written use of the word Rioja was in 1092, and it is said to be derived from the Rio Oja (*oja* means leaf), a very small tributary of the Ebro; probably it originally referred only to a limited area, but it came to cover the whole. There are records of wine being exported in the sixteenth century. At that time, the wines grown were almost entirely white and these were the most expensive; the reds were the cheapest and in between were some *vinos claretes*. Wine-growing increased considerably during the seventeenth century, but there was little hope of building up a significant export market as the roads were terrible and the area isolated. Two of the best vines currently used for making red wine – Tempranillo and Mazuelo – became prominent in the eighteenth century, and with them the *claretes*; but the Spanish economy was in a dreadful state, and at the end of the century so much bad wine was being produced there was a problem selling it.

In the old days the small growers used to make their wines in the way practised all over the north of Spain, in *lagos*. Spanish/English dictionaries translate *lago* as lake, which indeed is right: that is the usual meaning. On a visit to Spain I was once surprised when an English-speaking wine-grower told me that in the past every house had its own lake. But in the context of wine the meaning is different. A *lago* is a tank, usually underneath the house, made of stone or plastered brick. Everything was tipped in: grapes, stalks, and all. Then they were lightly pressed by foot and a violent fermentation – known as the tumultuous fermentation – soon started. There was no way of controlling the temperature, which could rise to heights that today would be regarded as alarming. After a week, the first wine – *vino de lágrima* – was run off into a smaller tank. Most of the grapes were still intact, though, and these were turned over. Then there was another fermentation, producing *vino de corazón* (the heart wine), which was considered the best. Then the contents of the *lago* were pressed and the wine of the first, light pressing was added to the heart wine. The must was run into large oak casks where it completed its fermentation over a period of months. This method of winemaking is still used by a few small growers who supply wines to the local bars and is really a primitive form of carbonic maceration (*maceración carbónica* or, in France, where it is widely used, *maceration carbonique*). In a more advanced form the grapes are destalked first.

Changes came in the nineteenth century and were brought about by a number of factors, some of them far-sighted improvements and others fortuitous. The first of the pioneers was a local priest, Manuel Quintano y Quintano, who was born in Labastida, where he was to become the incumbent and a canon of Burgos cathedral. At the end of the eighteenth century he visited Bordeaux and saw how wine was made in the leading châteaux. He and his brother began to experiment with the French method and made some of the best wines so far seen. In 1795 he successfully sent his new wine to Cuba, but the local growers would have none of it and did their best to obstruct him. Then came the problems of the Napoleonic Wars. Quintano gave up and went back to his cathedral.

The far-reaching change that led to international success was finally brought about by the two great *marquéses*: Murrieta and Riscal, whose wines have made them immortal. Luciano de Murrieta y García Lemoine was born in Peru in 1822. Of small stature but great spirit, he was a henchman of General Baldomero Espartero, who was ennobled as the Duque de Vitoria for his services in the Carlist War and later became Regent of Spain, but was deposed by a coup and driven into exile in London, where he lived from 1843–48, taking Murrieta with him. While there Murrieta took a liking to French wine and went to study it in Bordeaux, arriving in Logroño by 1850, where he produced his first wine in a bodega owned by the duke.

The Marqués de Riscal de Alegre, Camilo Hurtado de Amézaga, had also been in exile after being on the wrong side in the Carlist War and learned his trade in Bordeaux. When he returned to Spain he brought Cabernet Sauvignon vines with him and made his first vintage in 1860.

The authorities evidently approved of the new wines, for in 1862 the provincial government employed a Bordelais wine-grower, Jean Cadiche Pineau, from Château Lanessan, to teach the new methods of winemaking; but the peasants again would have none of it – indeed some of them still make their wine today as they made it then. Although he made some excellent wines, various things militated against him: his methods called for ageing wines in casks. Likewise he added Cabernet Sauvignon to the Spanish varieties, adding an element of individuality and complexity.

French winemaking methods were a great advance, but it was events in France itself that completely changed the history. In 1852 the fungus Oidium (now called powdery mildew or *Uncinula necator*), originating in the USA, struck French vineyards. French wine merchants sought new supplies in Spain and naturally tried the north first. Rioja had obvious potential and it was not far over the Pyrenees. Oidium was not long confined to France, though. It arrived in Rioja via Portugal and wrought havoc between 1855–62, sometimes reducing the yields almost to zero, before it was eventually conquered by the use of sulphur on the vines. France had worse to come. Phylloxera, also originating in the United States, struck the vineyards in 1867, and although it reached Portugal only a year later, at least some of the French growers held the extraordinary belief that it would be unable to cross the Pyrenees. They, together with négociants, came in droves, establishing vineyards and bodegas in which they actually matured the wine before shipping it. This in itself was a revolutionary change, as the peasant growers had been wont to throw away any wine left from the previous vintage when a new one came along. They did not have the capital to invest in casks for maturation even if they were aware of the technique. Phylloxera did eventually reach Rioja in 1899, but in the meantime the French led the way to establish a new world-class vineyard.

The decade 1870–80 was dynamic. Rioja took off. One of the old problems that has already been mentioned was inaccessibility. In 1790 there had been a movement to build a new road to the coast, but nothing came of it, thanks to the Napoleonic invasion, the Carlist wars, and the devastation brought by a visitation of cholera. The nineteenth century, however, was predominantly the era of railways. They spread throughout the world, revolutionizing life and industry. In Rioja the Madrid–Irun railway, constructed in 1862, passed through Miranda de Ebro, but 1880 brought the vital link from Haro to Bilbao. Many of the grand new bodegas were built near the railway station, where they can still be found. And the trade with France was reinforced in 1882, when a Franco–Spanish treaty reduced duties on wine imported from Spain into France. Another old problem was that the wine was not well made, was too weak, and would not travel. Valuable improvements in the making and ageing of wine followed from the advice of the Estacion de Enologia, established by royal decree in 1888. It is still there. The trade fluctuated, peaking at more than nine million litres in 1891 but down to two million in 1894. Many of the great bodegas that still flourish today date from this time.

Trade was good in Spain, too. Rioja was the wine to serve on special occasions. But in Spain's Belle Epoque the fashion was for things French, and Rioja came to be labelled Cepa Chablis (for dry white wines), Cepa Sauternes (for sweet ones), Cepa Borgoña (for the fleshier reds), and Cepa Burdeos (for the lighter reds). The word "*cepa*" was itself misleading, though, for it means "vine", and others used the more descriptive "*tipo*", or "style". Another name used for this new style of wine was Médoc Alavés. Not surprisingly this unfortunate usage was carried forward into the export markets, and until Spain's entry into the EU it was only too common to find wines labelled Rioja Chablis, Rioja Burgundy, and so on. The growers also had to face fraud, as it was only too easy for a restaurateur to refill a Rioja bottle with cheaper wine from elsewhere. To counter this, they started to put wire cages, or *alambiaclos*, round the bottles so that drinkers could see if they had been tampered with. However, it is said that some of the growers themselves were not above fraud, watering the wine and bringing the strength back up with industrial alcohol imported from Germany. From the beginning the embryo *consejo regulador* addressed its mind to this.

Then everything went wrong. By 1890 many of the French vineyards had been reconstructed and this major export market was lost, a position exacerbated when in 1892 France doubled the duties on imported wines in retaliation for Spain's protectionist policy initiated by Canovas. Other valuable export markets went when Spain lost Cuba and the Philippines in 1898. Between 1901–05 phylloxera spread and ravaged the vineyards. Of the 50,000 hectares, 36,000 had been destroyed by 1909 and much of the land was returned to cereals. In that year the vineyards began to be reconstructed, with advice from an agronomist, Francisco Pascual de Quinto, appointed by the provincial government; but the lowest trough of production was not reached until 1912, just as the reconstructed vineyards were beginning to yield fruit. The growers then got a chance to rebuild their fortunes two years later when the outbreak of the World War I cut off supplies of wine from France to the USA and opened new markets. By 1935 there were 35,000 hectares of vineyard, but the following year the Spanish Civil War started and as soon as that was over World War II came. The only substantial exports were to neutral Switzerland.

Every wine-growing district in Europe has found the need for some degree of official regulation, and this applied to Rioja as much as to the others. A *consejo regulador* was set up in 1926, the first in Spain, and at about this time cooperatives were established, which have played a very important part in the trade ever since. But the *consejo regulador* was not a success and a second was set up in 1945, which did not work either. Then a third was established in 1953 and given teeth: effective legal sanctions to enforce its regulations. It needed them, for in the good years of 1964, 1968, and 1970, more young wines were sold than were grown. This is unlikely to ever happen again, for in 1976 everything was tightened up and further reorganized in 1981. It is now sufficiently funded and there is a close control over every aspect of wine-growing and making.

By the 1970s trade was flourishing, helped by a surge in French wine prices, which caused drinkers to expand their horizons, and this brought a second spate of new bodegas of every possible size, from the huge to the boutique, and the number is continuing to grow. In 1982, 148 bodegas were licensed to age wine, and this figure rose to 286 in 2003. And there was money enough for them to be supplied with all the latest equipment their oenologists needed.

In 1991, Rioja became the first DOCa (*denominación de origin calificada*) and as such subject to very tight control throughout the winemaking and ageing process. The promotion could have prompted a radical revision of the rules, and several suggestions have been made, for instance the creation of smaller geographical areas, the exclusion of *jóvenes* from the DOCa, and the demotion of wines from DOCa to DO that do not pass a specially stringent tasting test. But these options were eliminated on the grounds of practicality and the politics of the wine trade. It is doubtful if they would have added much anyhow. In reality, little has changed and one relies on the reputations of the individual bodegas.

Rioja is now exported all over the world. The largest export market is the UK, which in 2004 imported 22,899,954 litres at an average price per litre of €4.29, followed by Germany with 11,826,738 litres at an average price of €2.82, and Switzerland with 6,210,043 litres at an average price of €4.66. Sales to the UK are rising, while those to Germany, previously the principal importer, are going down and are directed mostly to the cheapest end of the market.

So far as the major shippers are concerned the Bordeaux production-method took over in the nineteenth century and has remained in use ever since. There have been developments, though. Until the 1960s the wines were matured in old oak casks, many of them very big, where they remained for a long time. In those days *reservas* had to have at least six years maturation and *gran reservas* at least eight. They tasted strongly of vanilla and were oxidized. It is not surprising that they had their detractors. The red wines stood up to this surprisingly well, but the whites came as a shock to those used to the light wines of the north. They were deeply coloured, did not have much fragrance (and that was largely oak), and lacked acidity. A revolution began in the 1970s.

Nowadays nearly all the bodegas are completely up-to-date, with stainless-steel tanks where the fermentations are carried out under controlled temperatures – though it is interesting to note that some are going back to concrete vats, which they say can now be temperature controlled better than stainless steel, and to modern versions of the old vertical presses.

Maturation is in 225-litre casks of American, French, or (recently) Baltic oak, some of them combining two kinds, for instance with American bodies and French ends, many of them new. However the lighter white wines and some of the red *jóvenes* do not see oak at all. Here, as in most of the Spanish fine wine districts, there is argument as to which kind of oak to use, but Spanish oak is generally not favoured, and the use of oak chips is strictly forbidden. Cool fermentation, long maceration, concentrating on Tempranillo vines, and the judicious use of oak produce the new generation wines.

Their makers refer to *alta expresión* (high expression), displaying the qualities of grape and place – the description was concocted by a journalist and is now falling out of favour. But if they think the wines made by the older houses lacked either, they must be crazy. Those of the old school decry them as, for instance, over-extracted or lacking the personality of old-style Riojas. They sell well, though, and have attracted very discriminating drinkers who avoided Rioja in the past. It would be wrong to think that there are two distinct styles, though. The boundary between them is very blurred, and some of the old shippers who were strong in their criticism seem to approach the new style with their top-flight wines. And some of the new shippers, looking rather embarrassed, say that they find large barrels or even cement tanks best for fermentation, provided you control the temperature, which can be done easily now. Also, basket presses, that look remarkably like the old ones, are sometimes seen to be replacing the pneumatic stainless steel ones, and even the most modern bodegas make a point that some of their wines are barrel-fermented.

As in Bordeaux, the complexity of the wines reflects the combination of a number of different grape varieties, but it also reflects the blending of wines from different vineyards and areas. The old practice used to be to plant all the varieties that the grower needed for his wines in his vineyard. These were usually picked and vinified together. Nowadays each variety is kept separate, picked at the right time, and vinified separately. Each has its own characteristics of flavour. For the red wines, the leading vine is the Tempranillo, a native that is undoubtedly one of the greatest in the world, and forms the basis of the finest Riojas. It gives powerful yet well balanced, subtle, fruity wines of great fragrance and ageing potential. The amount planted is going up, mostly at the expense of the Garnacha.

The Garnacha, though, is a very fine vine, as the French have discovered. Too often trained to produce excessive yields, it tends to be underrated; but trained to produce a moderate yield it gives strong, full-bodied, fruity wines of great charm. It is particularly good for making *rosados*.

The Mazuelo gives rather tannic, though not very alcoholic, wines that keep their colour well and can be important in a blend intended for long ageing. The Graciano (which is the same as the Monastrell of Cataluña) gives wines that are rather weak in alcohol, but high in tannin, colour (though the colour tends to turn brown rather quickly), and acid, with floral overtones, ageing very well and particularly useful for including in *gran reservas*. There is a government subsidy for planting Mazuelo and Graciano.

Cabernet Sauvignon forms only one per cent of the whole, but is important in some vineyards and is notable for its characteristic aroma and backbone; it has long formed part of the tradition of Marqués de Riscal, though that bodega is now relying largely on Tempranillo.

Of the white grapes, the leader is undoubtedly the Viura (the same as the Macabeo), which is productive yet of good quality, giving white wines that do not oxidize easily and hence are ideal for cask ageing. Although it ripens rather late, it can become overripe and the wines are then dull; but picked at the right time they are fresh and fruity. It is sometimes blended into red wines to give lightness and freshness. The Malvasía Riojana (which is the same as the Subirat-Parent of Penedès) is not very widely grown, but has a fragrance all of its own, though the wines tend not to age very well. The Garnacha Blanca gives strong wines, not very high in acidity, which used to be regarded as rather dull, but it has been transformed by modern, low-temperature fermentation and now produces fresher and more aromatic wines.

A typical combination for red wines in Rioja Alta is traditionally sixty per cent Tempranillo, twenty-five per cent Garnacha, and fifteen per cent Graciano and Mazuelo. In Rioja Alavesa it is ninety per cent Tempranillo and may include a little Viura. In Rioja Baja the Garnacha predominates and may be 100 per cent. But in practice a wide variety of combinations is used, as set out in the descriptions of the individual bodegas that follow; and, increasingly, varietal wines are being made.

The fact that there are three distinct sub-districts and eight different vine varieties gives some idea of the large choice of wines. As in all major wine-growing areas throughout the world, much depends on the precise site in which the grapes are grown. Each sub-district, however, has its own general style. Rioja Alta produces wines of good acidity that require ageing. Rioja Alavesa provides softer wines that mature more quickly and sometimes have a slightly earthy taste. Rioja Baja, where the Garnacha predominates, gives big fruity wines that do not need much age and some of which are sold straight off for early consumption in the bars. But there are many exceptions. For instance Rioja Alavesa has some firm wines that age very well, and the best vineyards in Rioja Baja produce wines of considerable character and quality. And one must remember that what matters is where the vines are gown, not where the bodega is.

The types of wines made are listed at the beginning of this chapter, and specific wines are described below under the names of individual shippers, but there are some generalisations that should be mentioned first. Although some are grown in specific estates, the majority of wines are blended from various vineyards and districts to give the house styles of the individual shippers. There are two basic styles of red: *clarete*, generally lighter in style and bottled in Bordeaux bottles; and *tinto*, bigger bodied and softer, bottled in Burgundy bottles. But there is no rigid distinction between them. It all depends on the practice of the individual shipper and the shape of the bottle is not a sure guide.

In the 1980s, in the new wave of prosperity, it must be admitted that some bodegas lost their way, even one or two of the great names, and at the bottom end things were made worse by price cutting. Up till then the wines had certainly tended to be very woody, and one of the early Masters of Wine told me fifty years ago, "I don't like Rioja. I like wine, not wood." He could not make that generalization today, but it was justified at the time. At the bottom end the wines were cheap and cheerful, at the top they were often superb, but in the middle there were some disasters: sweet with overripe grapes, flabby with lack of acid, dumb from hot fermentations and too long in large casks, and sometimes frankly unclean. At the same time the bodegas were faced with the competition of burgeoning quality vineyards from all over Spain and, not least, from the New World. The wines made in Rioja were different, of course, but people were worried. New prosperity enabled both old and new generations of winemakers to change all that, and they succeeded abundantly. One solution was to produce young, *joven*, wines, without ageing, sometimes made by carbonic maceration, and lacking any vanilla oakiness. This was certainly good for cash flow, but time has shown that greater ageing is generally more popular, and the majority of the red wines are still *crianzas*, with smaller quantities of the older *reservas* and *gran reservas*.

There is a heated debate going on between the traditionalists and those that think of themselves as international. The traditionalists want Rioja to taste like Rioja and not to produce yet another Cabernet Sauvignon or Chardonnay. One does see the point. But the younger generation of winemakers says that the combination of grapes is not writ in stone. In Bordeaux, for instance, it has changed notably over the years. And in Rioja a little Cabernet Sauvignon adds backbone and structure to a red wine, while Chardonnay can add grace to a white wine and make it more acceptable in world markets. The traditionalists say that the same or better results can be achieved my making wiser use of local grapes, for instance by using more Graciano rather than Cabernet Sauvignon. There is strength in both points of view.

Of the whites, the older, traditional style still has a large connoisseur following. Exemplified by such wines as the excellent whites of Marqués de Murrieta and López Heredia, they are dry but very full bodied, deep with vanilla overtones; almost unique in the world of white wines. The only others that can be compared with them are the white Rhônes from Châteauneuf-du-Pape and Hermitage, which compliment highly flavoured foods. The new style whites, pioneered by Cune, Faustino Martinez, and Marqués de Cáceres, are now made almost everywhere and are totally different: fresh, fruity, light, and crisp. The Cáceres wines now include an oak-fermented white, though. The *rosados* too, should be looked at. In the past they were not worth taking seriously, but are now very well made and often delicious.

Red Riojas are among the longest lived of wines and most are drunk before they reach their peak, which is apt to happen ten, twenty, or even thirty years after the vintage. In the past, vintage years were not taken very seriously, and one of my Spanish friends joked many years ago that a shipper had registered "Vintage 1929" as a trade mark; but this is certainly no longer so, nor was it ever so with the leading shippers, and they can be relied on. The oldest red that I have tasted so far was Marqués de Murrieta 1925. Drunk in England in 1982, it was still full of fruit and had a magnificent, lingering flavour, with no signs of decay. The same shipper's 1931, bottled in 1934 and drunk in Spain in 1996, was still wonderfully young, packed with fruit, and marvellously complex: one of the finest wines I have ever tasted. I have no doubt that the best of the wines being made today will last every bit as well.

It is now almost impossible to buy a bad Rioja. Though to mention every good shipper would be impossible; the number is vast and it is increasing, especially following the repeal in 1989 of the law that prevented a bodega from being a *Bodega de Crianza* unless it had at least 500 casks and produced 2,250 hectolitres of wine. Now small producers can provide *crianzas, reservas,* and *gran reservas.* This opened the way for those bodegas that the Americans describe as boutique and the French, more disparagingly, as *garagiste.* Those listed below have been chosen because of their historical or commercial importance, or for the sheer quality of their wines, or often for a combination of all these things. Some that deserve a mention have undoubtedly been left out.

A recent development is a superb new wine museum just outside the delightful little town of Briones, created by the Vivanco family. It is full of good and original things, both technical and artistic, and enormously worth a visit, though it is often necessary to book in advance. It is not confined to Rioja, but covers all wines and has a vineyard with 300 varieties from all over the world, and an excellent library. It also has a very good restaurant and a hotel is being planned.

Some leading bodegas

BODEGAS AGE
Barrio de la Estación s/n, 26360 Fuenmayor, La Rioja. Tel: +34 941 29 35 00; Fax: +34 941 29 35 01; Email: bodegasage@byb.es; Website: bodegasage.com
A large bodega dating from 1881, when Félix Azpilicueta y Martínez founded a company that in 1967 merged with two others: Cruz García and Entrena. Its name is taken from the initials of the three companies. It uses a number of trademarks including Azpilicueta for its best *gran reserva* and Marqués de Romeral for its second best; but its most popular wines are sold under the name Siglo and include Siglo Saco, which is sold in a burgundy-shaped bottle covered with sacking. The wines tend to be thoroughly sound and reliable rather than exciting. It has been a member of the big Bodegas y Bebidas group since 1995, part of a subsidiary called Iverus, which also includes Bodegas Juan Alcorta and Bodegas Ysios in Rioja, and has bodegas in Ribera del Duero, Rueda, Rías Bajas, Castilla, Navarra and Chile, now part of the Allied Domecq group. Its great old bodegas in Fuenmayor have been knocked down and its wines are made in the Juan Alcorta bodegas in a beautiful position on the edge of Logroño, 100 metres (328 feet) above the Ebro Valley. *See* also Campo Viejo and Ysios.

BODEGAS ALEJOS
Poligono "El Sequero" Parcela 27, 26509 Agoncillo, La Rioja.
Tel: +34 941 43 70 51; Fax: +34 941 43 70 77;
Email: b.a.alabanza@teleline.es; Website: www.bodegasalejos.com

One of the new wave of bodegas, founded in 1988 with twenty-five hectares of vineyard, to make modern wines of high quality. The Selección wines are the best of all with three per cent Graciano.

FINCA ALLENDE

Plaza Ibarra 1, 26330 Briones, La Rioja. Tel: +34 941 32 23 01; Fax: +34 941 32 23 02; Email: allende@finca-allende.com; Website: www.finca-allende.com

This bodega was founded in 1995 by a family of established wine-growers with forty-two hectares of vines, mostly Tempranillo, but some Graciano and small amounts of Garnacha, Viura, and Malvasía. Its wines are exceptionally good. Those sold as Allende are varietal Tempranillos. The top range, sold as Aurus, with fifteen per cent Graciano, and the Calvario *crianzas*, with eight per cent Garnacha and two per cent Graciano, are particularly good, among the very best Riojas. Both ranges are matured in French oak, the former for two years and the latter for fourteen months. The Aurus, in particular, rewards keeping. The barrel-fermented white is unusual in having forty per cent old vine Malvasía.

BODEGAS ALTANZA

Ctra N232 km 419.5, 26360 Fuenmayor, La Rioja.
Tel: +34 941 45 08 60; Fax: +34 941 45 08 04;
Email: altanza@bodegasaltanza.com; Website: www.bodegasaltanza.com

A fine new bodega established in 1998 to make varietal Tempranillo wines, *reserva* and above, but in 2000 it also made a *crianza*. The wines are sold under the brands Altanza and Lealtanza, the Club Lealtanza being made from the oldest vines.

ARTADI – COSECHEROS ALAVESES

Carretera de Logroño s/n, 01300 Laguardia, Alava. Tel: +34 945 60 01 19;
Fax: +34 945 60 08 5; Email: info@artadi.com; Website: www.artadi.com

Founded as a growers' cooperative at Laguardia in 1985, with the appropriate name of Cosecheros Alavesas, its grapes came from nine growers with seventy hectares. In 1992 it turned itself into a company and then tacked on the name of its most famous wine, Artadi. It began modestly, just intending to market young wines, but these turned out to be very good, and the rest followed. It is modern, well-equipped, and is producing wines of very good quality and value under the marks Artadi and Artadi Viñas de Gain. The Artadi Pagos Viejos Reserva is particularly good, made from old vines and generally a varietal Tempranillo, though in some years minor proportions of

Mazuelo and Graciano have been added. The very top wine is Viña el Pisón. These are powerful, concentrated, intensely flavoured wines that will age magnificently for many years.

BARON DE LEY

Ctra Mendavia–Lodosa km 5.5, 31587 Mendavia, Navarra. Tel: +34 948 69 43 03; Fax: +34 948 69 43 04; Email: info@barondeley.com; Website: www.barondeley.com

A very up-to-date bodega, founded in 1985 at Mendavia, in the province of Navarra, in an old monastery that has been meticulously restored. In 1997 it became a public company and is in the same group as El Coto de Rioja (*see* below). It is a single estate with 160 hectares of vineyard including some Cabernet Sauvignon, which are matured in new or nearly new oak, eighty per cent American and twenty per cent French. It also makes whites. Its red wines are the ones to try, with backbone and ageing potential provided by the Cabernet Sauvignon. Its top wine is Finca Monasterio, with a good contribution from Cabernet Sauvignon. Not least, it offers remarkably good value.

BERBERANA/ARCO BODEGAS UNIDAS

Ctra de Vitoria km 182–3, 26360 Cenicero, La Rioja. Tel: +34 941 45 31 00; Fax: +34 941 45 31 14; Email: info@berberana.com; Website: www.berberana.com

The Berberana bodega was founded in 1877 at Ollauri by the Martínez Berberana family. The beautiful old building there remains, housing some of the finest wines, but the main bodega has been at Cenicero since 1975. After various vicissitudes of ownership, including a period in the Rumasa group, it has now become a quoted public company, with five cooperatives having minority shareholdings, and is associated with some other famous names: Marqués de Griñón, Bodegas Lagunilla, Dominio de Súsar (all of which have separate entries in this section, the last as Marqués de la Concordia), Viñedos y Bodegas de Malpica (Castilla y León), and Marqués de Monistrol (Penedès). In 2004 it formally changed its name to Lagunilla (*see* below), but the Berberana name is used for its separate range of wines. It also is part of the Haciendas de España enterprise that is establishing hotels and bodegas all along the Duero Valley. The fifty hectares of vineyard that it owns is enough only for a small part of its needs, so it also buys in grapes and has first call on its shareholder cooperatives, who are free to sell off anything it does not want.

The beautiful old cellars were carved out of the living rock by Galician and Portuguese stonemasons in the seventeenth century, and they are perfect for maturing wine, with a temperature of between 12–14°C (53.6–57.2°F) throughout the year and a humidity of ninety per cent, giving a slow evolution. The company owns Lagunilla, which it brought from IDV in 1994, and the joint venture with Carlos Falcó, Marqués de Griñón, also dates from that year. All the wines are now made and bottled in Cenicero, with the old Lagunilla bodegas being used for table wines which, by law, are not allowed to enter Rioja bodegas. Everything is as clean and as up to date as it is possible to be, with temperature-controlled fermentation, though, as the fermentation bodega faces north, cooling is not often necessary. *Remontaje* is computer controlled with interior levers moving the caps. The casks are nearly all American oak, though some French is used, principally for Marqués de Griñón wines. Some reds are varietal Tempranillo, but the *reservas* and *gran reservas* (including the Viña Alarde and Carta de Oro) are blended with twenty per cent Garnacha. The wines from this bodega are consistently good in taste and value. Its associated company Berberana Vinícola in Fuenmayor produces good non-DO wines, including a white from the unusual Pardina grape variety, which is not authorized for Rioja.

BODEGAS BERCEO

Cuevas s/n, 26200 Haro, La Rioja. Tel/Fax: +34 941 31 07 44;
Email: bodegas@gurpegui.es; Website: www.gurpegui.es
This is one of the oldest bodegas in every sense, founded by the French in 1872 and named after Gonzalo de Berceo, a monk who was the first person known to have written Spanish. It was bought in 1980 by the Gurpegui family, who have substantial wine interests in Navarra (*see* Chapter Five) and Chile. Situated in the old part of Haro, where the ground rises to the castle, it has two secret passages, one to the castle and the other to the main square. Because it is against a hillside, the old stone buildings are constructed in five levels with the top and bottom levels in different roads; it is quite a long journey to go from one to the other outside the building. It has the advantage, though, that everything can be done by gravity: grapes in at the top and bottles out at the bottom. There is also the enchanting eccentricity that it has an experimental vineyard on top in its roof garden. Apart from this the family owns 300 hectares of vineyard with part in each of the three sub-divisions of the Rioja; and it has recently added some at Baños de Ebro that were planted in 1870 on sandy soil that phylloxera could not penetrate, so are ungrafted. There is now an additional and very modern bodega at San Adrián. There are two versions of the white Viña Berceo, one completely modern, fresh, and ultra-cooled, the other cask fermented and given five months in oak; it is not ultra-cooled and is wonderfully complex. The *joven* and *rosado* are sold under the mark Viñadrián and

have some Garnacha. The Viña Berceo mark is used for the *crianzas* and *reservas,* but the *gran reservas*, made only in the best years, are sold as Gonzalo de Berceo and have some Mazuelo and Graciano. They can be as much as twenty years old when they are put on the market. The ungrafted vines are used to make a varietal Tempranillo called Los Dominios de Berceo Prephylloxérico. They make very good wines, especially the *reservas* and *gran reservas*.

BODEGAS BERONIA

Carretera Ollauri–Nájera, km 1.8, 26220 Ollauri, La Rioja. Tel: +34 941 33 80 00; Fax: +34 941 33 82 66; Email: beronia@beronia.es; Website: www.beronia.es

With this bodega one gets straight back into the twentieth century. Founded in Ollauri in 1970, it first operated on a very small scale, expanded in 1974, and in 1982 became associated with Gonzalez Byass, of Jerez, who invested heavily and built a new, up-to-date bodega complex outside the town on the road to Nájera. It has ten hectares of vineyard next to the bodega, at an altitude of 540 metres (1,772 feet); other fruit is bought from growers within ten kilometres, as it likes the soil and microclimate and can supervise the growing carefully. The white wines are made almost entirely from Viura, while Tempranillo predominates for the reds, but there are very small experimental plantings of Cabernet Sauvignon, Merlot, and Chardonnay. It ferments in an unusual way: it puts some wine of a previous year into the tanks so that they start a liquid of about four degrees of alcohol; a very slow fermentation, lasting about 120 days, is then induced with cultured yeasts.

The reds are made principally from Tempranillo and some Mazuelo, with a little Garnacha in the *crianzas* and Graciano in the *reservas*. The 2000 *reserva* was made with six per cent Mazuelo and five per cent Graciano. The *gran reserva* had two per cent more Mazuelo. Two innovations are a varietal Tempranillo fermented in 225-litre American oak casks, and Rioja's only varietal Mazuelo Reserva; the 1991, aged for two and a half years in American oak, was powerful, rather astringent and very long, while the 1999 was a very worthy successor, well balanced and well worth laying down. The Reserva de la Familia is particularly good. The top wine is rather curiously named "III aC" and the 2001 was made with seven per cent Graciano and five per cent Mazuelo. It comes in very modernistic packaging and is excellent. The whites include new style wines and some that are barrel-fermented and then left on the lees to give complexity of flavour. It makes good wines that age well.

BODEGAS BILBAINAS

Estacion 3, 26200 Haro, La Rioja. Tel: +34 941 31 01 47;

Fax: +34 941 31 07 06; Website: www.grupocodorniu.com

This is one of the largest bodegas in Haro, high on the hill behind the railway station, with a beautiful garden. It was founded in 1901 by a Bilbao wine merchant, Santiago Ugarte, who took over some of the assets of a French company, Sauvignon Frères, which had been founded in 1850, but went out of business in the changes that took place at the beginning of the twentieth century. Some of its oak vats are still in use. More versatile than the other Rioja houses, it also makes notable cava and brandy. The phylloxera that was rampant at the time did not prevent Sr. Ugarte from investing heavily in vineyards, and it now owns no fewer than 278 hectares, mostly on the slopes immediately behind the bodega buildings. These are not enough to supply all its needs, and thirty per cent of the grapes are bought in, but all the *reservas* and *gran reservas* come from its own vineyards. Some years ago this well-established house appeared to be in a decline, but a controlling interest was acquired by the major cava house Codorníu, in 1997, which has invested a very large sum of money in equipment and vineyards, bringing it back to the forefront. Its plantings include some Cabernet Sauvignon. The vineyard names have now become as famous as the names of wines produced from them: Viña Pomal, Viña Zaco, and Viña Paceta. Viña Pomal is produced as a *crianza,* a *reserva* and, in the best years, as a *gran reserva*. It has recently gone over toward the new style, and the 2000 *crianza* is a varietal Tempranillo. La Vicalanda is a seven and a half hectare plot within Viña Pomal, which gives its name to a *reserva* made exclusively from Tempranillo grapes grown there and introduced for the first time as a *reserva* of the 1981 vintage. The *reserva* has one year, and the *gran reserva* two, in new French oak. These wines are exceptionally good. Viña Zaco is a rather softer style with fifteen per cent Garnacha and twelve and a half per cent each of Graciano and Mazuelo. The latest addition is Vicuana from an eleven-hectare vineyard by the river Ebro. The first vintage, with twenty-five per cent Graciano, had fifteen months *crianza* in Allier oak, and was bottled *en rama* (without stabilization or filtration), so is intended to throw a deposit.

BODEGAS RAMON BILBAO

Avda S Domingo 34, 26200 Haro, La Rioja. Tel: +34 941 31 02 95; Fax: +34 941 31 08 32; Email: info@bodegasramonbilbao.es; Website: www.bodegasramonbilbao.es

The bodega was established in 1924, but it became a public company in

1972 and in 1999 was taken over by the Groupo Zamora, which also has interests in Rias Bajas, and which injected large sums of money, totally transforming this estate. It owns fifty hectares of vineyards with a further 500 under contract. The wines come, rather confusingly, in both the traditional and modern styles. The *crianzas*, which are varietal Tempranillos, and the *reservas*, which have five per cent Graciano and five per cent Garnacha, are traditional, but the Viña Turzaballa and the Mirto de Ramón *crianza* are in the modern style. The Edicion Limitada is made from old vine Tempranillo; it is made only in good years and comes in numbered bottles. These fine reds are well worth laying down. There is also a barrel-fermented Viura.

BODEGAS BRETON CRIADORES

Ctra de Fuenmayor km 1.5, 26370 Navarrete, La Rioja.

Tel: +34 941 44 08 40; Fax: +34 941 44 08 12;

Email: info@bodegasbreton.com; Website: www.bodegasbreton.com

This bodega was founded in 1983 at Logroño by an old wine-growing family and some friends. They engaged the services of a first class manager, Miguel Angel de Gregorio, who is also the technical director and was able to design the bodega from scratch to meet his very exacting requirements. This has now been supplemented by an additional bodega, opened in 2004 and dedicated to ageing Alba de Bretón. His first wine was made in 1985 and sold in 1988. He left in 1995 to found Allende (*see* above). The bodega is in the very top flight, producing superb wines headed by Alba de Bretón and the single-vineyard Dominio de Conte, which are made only in the best years (there was none in 1992 or 1993) and are closely followed by the complete Loriñón range. It owns 106 hectares of vineyard and began planting in 1985, but these supply only seventy per cent of its needs, the rest being brought in, including grapes from eighty-year-old vines. Aiming only at the top end of the market, the wines are made with enormous enthusiasm and meticulous care. This is illustrated by the way in which the bodega gets its casks. Initial experiments were with French oak and with American oak from Missouri, Ohio, Lousiana, and Virginia. The last was eventually chosen as giving the best results, but instead of buying the casks, it buys wood that is kept for three years before it is made up by a local cooper, who also supplies Alejandro Fernández of Ribera del Duero fame. It is careful not to overdo the oak, though, aiming at fruit and fragrance. It is one of the few bodegas producing a barrel-fermented Viura, which is given about one day's skin contact (the amount depending on the year) and is fermented with selected yeasts, but there is no *bâtonnage* as the lees from Viura are described as "very hard in the mouth". An unusual feature is that the casks of white wine are left out in the winter. It also produces stainless-steel-fermented whites. *Crianzas* are given 14–18 months in cask, *reservas* 24–30, and *gran reservas* forty. The authorized grape varieties are used.

Alba de Bretón is a varietal Tempranillo, but the Dominio de Conte 2001 was made with ten per cent Graciano, while the Loriñon *gran reservas* are made with five per cent Garnacha, five per cent Mazuelo, and five per cent Graciano. Pagos de Camino is an excellent varietal Garnacha from vines planted in 1930. Wines from this bodega age noticeably well and repay laying down.

BODEGAS CAMPILLO

Ctra de Logroño s/n, 01300 Laguardia, Alava. Tel: +34 945 60 08 26; Fax: +34 945 60 08 37; Email: info@bodegascampillo.es; Website: www.bodegascampillo.es

Part of the Faustino Martinez group, this bodega at Laguardia was started from scratch in 1987 and officially inaugurated in 1990 in a vast new building happily constructed in the traditional style. Its grapes come from fifty hectares of Tempranillo vines owned by Faustino Martinez, but it leads a totally separate life. Its white is fermented in French oak and has some Malvasía. The *rosado* is a varietal Tempranillo, as is the *crianza*, which is matured in American oak. The *reservas* have ten per cent Graciano and fifteen per cent "experimental varieties", for which read Cabernet Sauvignon, matured in French oak, as is the *gran reserva*, which is a varietal Tempranillo. The Reserva Especial has no less than forty per cent "other varieties", but these include some Graciano. These are fine, serious wines, the best given backbone by the disputed Cabernet Sauvignon, and it is most encouraging to find a grower uninhibited in the use of this variety. It is also experimenting with a single-vineyard Tempranillo Peludo for a wine called Reserva Pago Cuesto Claro Raro, which will undoubtedly need long bottle ageing.

CAMPO VIEJO

See Bodegas Juan Alcorta.

BODEGAS LUIS CANAS

Ctra Samaniego 10, 01307 Villanueva, Alava. Tel: +34 945 62 33 73; Fax: +34 945 60 92 89; Email: bodegas@luiscanas.com; Website: www.luiscanas.com

The Cañas family had been growing grapes for a couple of centuries, then started making wine, and eventually in 1970 started to bottle it. They own ninety hectares of vineyard. The bodega makes a complete range of wines, all of which are good and the top ones very good indeed. It uses seventy per cent French and thirty per cent American oak. The good barrel-fermented white has ten per cent Malvasía, the red *crianza* five per cent Garnacha, the *reserva* and *gran reserva* five per cent Graciano. The 1999 Reserva Seleccion de la Familia was made from ninety-five per cent Tempranillo, three per cent Graciano, and two per cent Garnacha. The show wine is Hiro Tres Racimas made from old vine Tempranillo and matured in French oak. Amaren is a varietal Tempranillo *reserva* also matured in French oak. The most interesting of all is a varietal Graciano *crianza*.

VINEDOS DEL CONTINO

Finca San Rafael s/n, 01321 Laserna, Alava. Tel: +34 945 60 02 01; Fax: +34 945 62 11 14; Email: laserna@contino-sa.com; Website: www.cvne.com

Hidden away beyond the village of Laserna in Rioja Alavesa, Contino must be one of the most difficult bodegas to find, but its wines are among those most worth finding. Vines have been grown on the site since medieval times, which is not surprising as it has a perfect microclimate, the vineyards sloping down to a curve in the river Ebro. The bodega itself is housed in a fine old stone building. It is among the most beautiful estates in Rioja. Contino was founded in 1974 and the great house of Cune has a half-share, but it is allowed to go its own way and makes its wines exclusively from its own sixty-two-hectare vineyards: seventy-six per cent Tempranillo, nineteen per cent Graciano, three per cent Mazuelo, and two per cent Garnacha, so it makes only reds, and it makes them only in the good years; in 1993, for instance, it sold its grapes. No grapes or wine is bought in, and sometimes there is a surplus, sold to Cune. The vineyards slope at about seven degrees, so they are well drained and catch the sun. Those at the bottom are full of big stones and are very suitable for Graciano, of which it is planting more. For maturing it used to have equal numbers of French and American oak casks, but they are now about seventy per cent French, twenty per cent American, and ten per cent Hungarian, which have proved very successful. A typical grape mix is eighty-five per cent Tempranillo, ten per cent Graciano, and five per cent Mazuelo, but it was also the first bodega to produce a varietal Graciano: an excellent wine. Viñedo de Olivo is a very fine wine made from a special plot round an old olive tree, ninety per cent Tempranillo and ten per cent Graciano, but the proportion of the latter will be increased. These wines are unusual in the Alavesa in that they mature only very slowly – and very well. In the best years they certainly repay keeping until they are twenty years old and benefit from breathing for a while before being drunk. They are definitely in the top flight.

EL COTO DE RIOJA

Camino Viejo de Oyón, 01320 Oyón. Tel: +34 945 62 22 16;

Fax: +34 945 62 23 15; Email: cotorioja@elcoto.com; Website: www.elcoto.com

Founded in 1970, after various changes of ownership this vast bodega is now part of the Barón de Ley group (*see* above). It has over 300 hectares of vineyards and makes good wines under the brands El Coto, Coto Real, and Coto de Imaz. The *rosado* is half Tempranillo and half Garnacha. Most of the reds are varietal Tempranillos, but Coto Real 2000 Reserva had twenty per cent Garnacha and ten per cent Graciano. Its *reservas* and *gran reservas* are especially good.

COMPANIA VINICOLA DEL NORTE DE ESPANA/CUNE

Barrio de la Estación s/n, 26200 Haro, La Rioja. Tel: +34 941 30 48 00;

Fax: +34 941 30 48 15; Email: marketing@cvne.com; Website: www.cvne.com

Known generally by its initials CVNE, or more usually still by its corruption into Cune, which it uses as one of its principal brand names, this is one of the biggest and most traditional of Rioja establishments, strategically sited in the cluster of bodegas above the railway station at Haro. It was founded in 1879 by two brothers, Eusebio and Raimundo Real de Asúa; it is still run by Eusebio's descendants, now in the fifth generation. It has expanded into a group that includes Viña Real and Contino (*see* separate entries). Cune wines have long been among the most popular in Spain and in many export markets; but they can be sold for a higher price in Spain than, for example, in England, so it is not surprising that it concentrates on the Spanish market. Its vineyard holdings are among the largest: five vineyards with a total area, including some under contract, of 600 hectares, planted with the authorized varieties together with minute experimental plots of one hectare Chardonnay and 0.1 hectare Cabernet Sauvignon. It would have more Chardonnay if it could, but if this is allowed it lies in the future. Nevertheless these large holdings are only enough for sixty per cent of its needs, and the rest are bought in. Although among the oldest established, it is not merely up to date, but is in the forefront of technology. Everything is done by gravity, while the internal logistics look like something out of science fiction. The results are admirable. One of its great pioneering efforts was the dry, white Monopole, the first of the new generation of light, modern wines. If this no longer occupies the pre-eminent position it once did, it is not because it has gone off, but because a brilliant idea has caught on. It has now been joined by a barrel-fermented version. The standard version, which is given a year in oak, has the grape mix of seventy per cent Viura, fifteen per cent Malvasía, ten per cent Garnacha Blanca, and a rather mysterious five per cent "other varieties". For the barrel-fermented version the first-picked grapes are used, mostly Viura and Malvasía, with new American oak. There is also a good semi-sweet white, Corona, and an excellent *rosado* made from Garnacha. Reds are the most important wines, though, accounting for eighty per cent of the production. All are given wood ageing, using eighty-five per cent American oak, which is preferred, and fifteen per cent French, varying in age from new to twenty-five years. The very popular basic red Cune has a grape mix of seventy per cent Tempranillo, twenty per cent Garnacha, and the rest made up from Mazuelo, Graciano, Viura, and Garnacha Blanca. At the top of the range there are fine reds. The benchmark wine is Imperial (named after the imperial pint in which wine exports from Bilbao to England used to be measured), which comes only as a *reserva* and as a *gran reserva*. It is one of the best and most highly respected of all red Riojas, made typically with ten per cent Graciano, and five per cent each of Mazuelo and Garnacha, grown entirely in Rioja Alta and mostly from the Villalba vineyard, which is protected by the mountains and has a special microclimate. It has recently been joined by Real de Asúa Reserva, vinified separately in its own little bodega. The 1995, with five per cent Graciano, ten per cent Mazuelo and Garnacha, was memorably excellent. The 2000 has the simpler mix of ninety-five per cent Tempranillo and five per cent Graciano. These wines mature well in bottle and are worth laying down.

BODEGAS DARIEN

Avenida Mendavia 29, 26006 Logroño, La Rioja. Tel: +34 941 25 81 30; Fax: +34 941 27 03 52; Email: info@darien.es; Website: www.darien.es

Founded in 1999 as a rich man's hobby, this has become a bodega of fine wines, housed in a striking, perhaps even startling, modern building. Originally called Viñedos y Bodegas XXI it changed its name in 2004 to Darien, its brand name, in honour of the somewhat obscure French author Georges Darien. It has sixty-six hectares of vineyard, including one at Pradolagar at a height of 380 metres (1,247 feet) overlooking the Ebro, and another at 550–600 metres (1,804–1,968 feet) on the slopes of Mount Yerga. Its best wines are those from *crianza* upward. The *crianza* 2001 had seventeen per cent each Garnacha and Mazuelo and six per cent Graciano, while the Darien Selection 2001 had ten per cent Graciano, eight per cent Mazuelo, and seven per cent Garnacha. The top wine is Delius, named after the English composer, which is made only in good years and typically has twenty-five per cent Garnacha, aged for two years in mostly French oak. It is certainly an *alta expresión* wine and is intended for ageing.

BODEGAS DOMECQ
Carretera de Villabuena s/n, 01340 Elciego, Alava. Tel: +34 945 60 60 01; Fax: +34 945 60 62 35; Website: www.domecqbodegas.com

In 1970 the great sherry and brandy house Pedro Domecq decided to branch out into "table wine" and, as would be expected, went about it in a very scientific way. After a brief partnership with the international House of Seagram in Bodegas Palacio, it set about exploring various possibilities. The choice fell on Rioja Alavesa where, in 1973, it bought a large tract of land and built a magnificent new bodega in Elciego. In 1984 Domecq was taken over by Allied Lyons to become Allied Domecq, with worldwide ramifications. In July 2005 it was bought by Pernod Ricard and its position remains unclear. Nothing was wanting in either expertise or in capital, and the results are impressive. The vineyards had to be cleared of rock, much of it beneath the surface, and planted – mostly with Tempranillo, but with some Graciano, Mazuelo, and Viura. The 300 hectares or so are all on the best chalky soil, but this holding, the largest in Rioja Alavesa, provides only half the grapes required. American oak is used. The cheaper wines are sold under the mark Viña Eguia and are excellent value, but at present are sold only in Spain. The top end of the range is sold internationally under the brand Marqués de Arienzo (the marquis is a real person) and the wines are very good indeed, particularly the *reservas* and *gran reservas*. The usual grape mix for the reds has 2.5 per cent each of Mazuelo and Graciano. The Marqués de Arienzo Reserva Especial is made only in the best years, and in 1998 had twenty-five per cent Graciano. There is also a modern style white made as a varietal Viura.

LA ENCINA BODEGAS Y VINEDOS
Ctra Nacional Logroño–Vitoria 124 km 45, 26290 Briñas, La Rioja.
Tel: +34 941 30 56 30; Fax: +34 941 31 30 28;
Email: info@laencinabodegas.com; Website: www.laencinabodegas.com

When you enter La Rioja from the northwest this is the first thing you see: a very modern, minimalist building of striking architecture on top of a hill. When you get there the views over the Conchas de Haro and on to the mountains are stunning. It is a small but forward-looking bodega founded in 1999 and had its first vintage in 2002. Its has five hectares of vineyard just by the bodega with a further fifteen owned by a partner, the rest coming from two growers. It uses equal quantities of French and American oak, and has the idea of marketing two-bottle packs of wine matured in the one and the other, which should be very interesting. The Tobelos range includes a varietal Garnacha, from an old mountain vineyard one kilometre away (two-thirds of a mile). Tobelos generally has five per cent Garnacha. The Tahon de Tobelos *reservas* and *gran reservas* are varietal Tempranillos. They aim to fall between the styles of the old and the modern Riojas, which is a very sensible approach, and these are very promising wines.

BODEGAS FAUSTINO

Ctra Logroño s/n, 01320 Oyón, Alava. Tel: +34 945 62 25 00; Fax: +34 945 62 21 06; Email: info@bodegasfaustino.es; Website: www.bodegasfaustino.es

Founded in 1861 at Oyón in Rioja Alavesa by Eleuterio Martínez Arzoc, who already owned vineyards, it is still run by the family, now in the fourth generation. It started to bottle wine in 1930. It specializes in *reservas* and *gran reservas,* which it exports all over the world. It has 500 hectares of vineyard in some of the best soils of the district, which makes it self-sufficient for *reserva* and *gran reserva* wines; it is also the largest family-owned estate in the region, but can still supply only forty per cent of its total needs. It has experimented with various kinds of oak and has found that wine in American oak oxidizes more slowly than in French, which gives more chocolate and caramel flavours, and wines in French oak oxidize faster in Limousin than in Allier, which gives finer tannins. As a result mostly American oak is used, with 20–25 per cent medium-toast French for the *gran reservas*. New casks are bought each year, but are never used for the *reservas* or *gran reservas* until they are two years old. They are kept for a maximum of fourteen years and have an average of seven. The *gran reservas* are given 30–36 months in cask and a minimum of four years in bottle before sale.

Faustino I is the brand used for *gran reservas*. The grape mix varies from year to year; for example in 1987 there was twelve per cent Graciano and three per cent Mazuelo, while in 1995 there was ten per cent Graciano and five per cent Mazuelo. These excellent wines age particularly well. Faustino V is used for *reservas* and again the grape mix varies from year to year but is essentially Tempranillo with 3–10 per cent Mazuelo and 0–12 per cent Graciano. The same brand is also used for reds, *rosados,* and whites, some of which are *crianzas* and are barrel fermented, made from 100 per cent Viura. The emphasis is on Tempranillo in the *rosados*. Faustino VII is used for reds and whites of second-tier quality, mostly intended for the home market, and for *rosados* made from Garnacha. At the other end of the scale is the top wine of all and the only one not to have a number: Faustino de Autor Reserva Especial. The 1998 was made with twelve per cent Graciano and three per cent Cabernet Sauvignon. Beyond doubt it is one of Rioja's very best.

It also makes cavas. One of the best producers, its wines are consistently good. Apart from Campillo (*see* above), the group also includes Marqués de Vitoria (*see* below) and a non-DO bodega producing the very successful range of Don Darius wines.

BODEGAS FERNÁNDEZ DE PIEROLA

Ctra Logroño s/n Finca el Somo, 01322 Moreda, Alava. Tel: +34 945 62 24 80; Fax: +34 945 62 24 89; Email: bodegas@pierola.com; Website: www.pierola.com

One of the new wave of bodegas, founded in 1996 with its first commercial vintage in 2000, it has a fascinating modern building, which looks rather like an enormous ship's bridge, on a hill with superb views. All its grapes come from over eighty hectares of old vines surrounding the bodega at an altitude of 350 metres (1,148 feet). Its wines are modern, too, and very well made with excellent balance. The *crianzas* mature for six months in new French oak and twelve in three- to four-year-old American. The *reservas* are divided equally between French and American. An unusual feature is using wild ferments, even for the whites, which many winemakers avoid. The whites have an unusual degree of finesse, though the oak is very evident. These and most of the reds are sold under the bodega name. The reds are varietal Tempranillo and need some bottle age, so the 2001 *crianza* was not put on the market until 2005. The top of the range is Vitium and is excellent. The 1998 Reserva Especial spent eight months in new French oak and eight in new American. It will age very well.

FINCA VALPIEDRA

El Montecillo s/n, 26360 Fuenmayor, La Rioja. Tel: +34 941 45 08 76; Fax: +34 941 45 08 75; Email: info@fincavalpiedra.com; Website: www.martinezbujanda.com

In 1973 the Martínez Bujanda family bought this vineyard from Bodegas Montecillo when the rest of the enterprise was bought by Osborne, of sherry and brandy fame. At first they used the vines for their own range of wines, but the intention was always to make a single-vineyard wine from this unique eighty-hectare plot in Rioja Alta on the banks of the Ebro. This was realized with the 1994 vintage, and the aim has always been to let the vineyard express itself in its highest form: a single *reserva* wine from a single vineyard, though in poorer years it may be a *crianza*, and in the best a *gran reserva*. The results have been extremely impressive. The grapes used are ninety per cent Tempranillo, five per cent Cabernet Sauvignon, three per cent Graciano, and two per cent Mazuelo; the oak is ninety per cent French and ten per cent American.

BODEGAS FRANCO-ESPANOLAS

Cabo Noval 2, 26006 Logroño, La Rioja. Tel: +34 941 25 13 00;
Fax: +34 941 26 29 48; Email: francoespanolas@francoespanolas.com;
Website: www.francoespanolas.com

Now part of the Paternina group, Bodegas Franco-Españolas, in Logroño, traces its history back to the French connection in the nineteenth century. In 1890 Frédéric Anglade, a Bordeaux wine merchant, started growing wine in Rioja and formed a company with French and Spanish capital and with directors of both nationalities. Despite phylloxera, the company flourished, but the French interest waned; more Spanish capital was subscribed and by 1922 it was Spanish owned. In 1973 it was bought by Rumasa. This group was dispossessed by the state, which ran it for a while before selling it on to Marcos Eguizábal Ramirez. It has fifty hectares of vineyard. It is kept separate from Paternina and has its own complete range of well known, sound, commercial wines, sold mostly under the brands Bordón and Royal Bordón for the reds and Viña Soledad, Diamante, and Rinsol for the whites. Its best whites have proportions of Malvasía and Garnacha Blanca. Diamante is an agreeable semi-sweet white. Its Rosado de Lujo, made from seventy per cent Garnacha and thirty per cent Viura, is well worth seeking out. The *gran reserva* Excelso used to be its top wine, but in 2003 it went one better and introduced Baron d'Anglade, an excellent *reserva* from selected grapes and aged in Allier oak.

BODEGAS VINA IJALBA

Ctra Pamplona km 1, 26006 Logroño, La Rioja. Tel/Fax: +34 941 26 11 00;
Email: vinaijalba@ijalba.com; Website: www.ijalba.com

The story starts in 1975, when Dionisio Ruiz Ijalba planted his first vineyard near Logroño. He was a local businessman involved in gravel extraction, and the vineyard was planted on extracted land that was a near-desert, and unsuitable for any other crop. Further vineyards were subsequently planted and there are now eighty hectares of them, all cultivated ecologically and low yielding. They include one of the largest plantations of Graciano in Rioja: eighteen hectares. The very modernistic bodega was built in 1991. It produces a complete range of wines under a number of names. Genoli is an oak-free Viura white, Ijalba Blanco a white from the very rare Maturana Blanca grape with some cask ageing in French oak, Aloque a *rosado* made from equal parts of Tempranillo and Garnacha, Livor a red *joven* made from Tempranillo, Solferino also a red *joven* but made by carbonic maceration, Múrice a red *crianza* with ten per cent Graciano, Ijalba Reserva with ten to twenty per cent Graciano, and Ijalba Reserva Especial from equal quantities of Tempranillo and Graciano, with two years in new French oak. Its most exciting wines of all are its varietals: Graciano (in 1995 it made the first in Rioja) and a *joven* from the very rare Maturana Tinta marketed as Dionisio Ruiz Ijalba.

VIÑA IZADI/VIÑA VILLABUENA

Herrería Travesia 2, 01307 Villabuena, Alava. Tel: +34 945 60 90 86; Fax: +34 945 60 92 61; Email: izadi@izadi.com; Website: www.izadi.com

In 1987 this bodega was founded by a restaurateur who wanted to make quality wines, and who has succeeded abundantly. They are certainly in the top flight. He owns sixty-six hectares of vines and buys more in. There is a good barrel-fermented white, using half French and half American oak and made from eighty per cent Viura and twenty per cent Malvasía. The red *crianza* is matured in American oak and has five per cent each of Graciano and Mazuelo. The *reserva* has the same grape mix but in mostly French oak. The Selección has twenty per cent Graciano, and the top wine, Expresion, is matured in new French oak and has ten per cent of "other varieties"; but as with all growers, the proportions vary from year to year.

BODEGAS JUAN ALCORTA

Camino de la Puebla 50, 26006 Logroño, La Rioja. Tel: +34 941 27 99 00; Fax: +34 941 27 99 01; Email: info@adwes.es; Website: domecqbodegas.com

Descended from Campo Viejo, which was founded at Logroño in 1963, this is part of the big Bodegas y Bebidas group that has expanded to be one of the largest in Rioja (*see* Age, above). In 2002 it moved into a magnificent new bodega just outside Logroño, 100 metres (328 feet) above the Ebro Valley. Its old premises in Logroño have been destroyed. Its new installation is all underground with trees planted on top, so it is as cool as it is spacious; and as it is on several levels, the wine can be moved by gravity. Its 502 hectares of vineyards (fifty hectares of which surround the bodega) can supply only twenty-five per cent of its needs. It makes only *crianzas, reservas,* and *gran reservas* using a positively bewildering number of names: Azpilicueta (an Age mark, *see* above), Campo Viejo, Viña Alcorta (aimed at the on-trade), Marqués de Villamagna, Almenar, Albor, Tres Ducados, Marqués de Mudela,

Foncalada, Montés de Ciria, Selección José Bezares, and Castillo de San Ascensio. It produces a complete range of wines: new style and barrel-fermented whites, *rosados*, and every category of red. All are good, commercial wines. The barrel-fermented white is excellent, but three of its brands, Viña Alcorta, Marqués de Villamagna, and Dominio de Montalvó, are reserved for the best, which are very good. The first contains a proportion of Cabernet Sauvignon. Albor is made by a method that bears some resemblance to carbonic maceration. There is also a range of varietal wines.

LAGUNILLA

Ctra de Elciego s/n, 26350 Cenicero, La Rioja. Tel: +34 941 45 31 00; Fax: +34 941 45 31 14; Email: infointernational@lagunilla.com; Website: www.lagunilla.com

Founded in 1885 by Felipe Lagunilla San Martín. After various changes of ownership over a hundred years it became part of the Arco Bodegas Unidas group. Its reliable wines are widely distributed; the best of them, La Case de Comendador, is made from eighty per cent Tempranillo and twenty per cent Garnacha and is matured in American oak. (*See* Arco Bodegas Unidas, above).

BODEGAS LAN

Paraje Buicio s/n, 26360 Fuenmayor, La Rioja. Tel: +34 941 45 09 50; Fax: +34 941 45 05 67; Email: info@bodegaslan.com; Website: www.bodegaslan.com

Founded in 1972 in Fuenmayor, this is one of the new generation of large, very up-to-date, commercial enterprises. For a time it formed part of the Rumasa empire, but is now privately owned again and is part of the Santiago Ruiz group from Rias Bajas. It has seventy-two hectares of vineyards, notable for their large pebbles, like a miniature Châteauneuf-du-Pape, on the top of a cliff over the river. These are used for the top-of-the-range Viña Lanciano, supplemented with grapes from other growers for the rest of the wines. It produces a complete range of good wines under the names Lan and Viña Lanciano in a new, vast, and immaculate bodega. The Viña Lanciano *reservas* are particularly good. There are no white wines. From the 1994 vintage onward it has taken a firm step toward the "new style", with long maceration to give deep colour, limiting the barrel ageing to avoid oakiness, and using new barrels. It is among the bodegas using composite barrels: American bodies and French ends. The *jóvenes* and *crianzas* are made with ten per cent Garnacha and five per cent Mazuelo, while the *reservas* have ten per cent Garnacha and ten per cent Mazuelo. The Viña Lanciano wines are made with 15–20 per cent Mazuelo, but only in good years. The 1998 was matured for a year in American and six months in Allier oak. The top Culmen de Lan is produced only in the very best years, so far 1994, 1995, and 2001, from a special part of the Pago El Rincón vineyard, has its malolactic fermentation in French oak, and is matured in new French and American oak. The 1995 had twenty per cent Mazuelo and five per cent Graciano; it is likely to improve for twenty years. Contrariwise the Lan Limited Edition 2001 had ten per cent Mazuelo and five per cent Graciano from old vines and was aged in French and Russian oak, then bottled without filtration and sold after four to five months: a wine for early drinking. This bodega makes excellent wines.

BODEGAS R LOPEZ DE HEREDIA-VINA TONDONIA
Avenida Vizcaya 3, 26200 Haro, La Rioja.
Tel: +34 941 31 02 44; Fax: +34 941 31 07 88

Founded in 1877, this is one of the grand old bodegas down by the station in Haro. One cannot miss it, with its large nineteenth century buildings and enchanting tower, all in a Swiss style. Unlike most of its rivals, it has resolutely refused to move with the times, but it seems none the worse for it, as its wines are unquestionably in the first flight of traditional Riojas. It is still family owned, run by descendants of the founder, Rafael López de Heredia, who at first had a French partner. It is a law unto itself, but is willing to innovate, and to celebrate its 125th anniversary it produced a varietal Mazuelo.

To cross the threshold is to walk into the past. While the new-generation wine-makers worship cleanliness and have bodegas that are much cleaner than the average hospital, here they could not care less. There are cobwebs all over the place, which are encouraged; spiders do not get into the wine and they eat insects, including the flies that produce cork weevils, so they have their own odd cleansing function.

Viña Tondonia is the best vineyard: over 100 hectares on the right bank of the river Ebro. There are three others – Viña Cubillo, Viña Bosconia, and Viña Zaconia – a total of 170 hectares, providing all the grapes for its top wines, and very little is bought in. In the early days some French grapes such as Cabernet Sauvignon and Merlot were tried, but were rejected; and the vineyards are now planted entirely with the authorized Spanish varieties, some of the vines being seventy years old.

There is no stainless steel here, only oak. It buys American oak from the Appalachians, Ohio, and Michigan, seasons it, and makes all the barrels in its own cooperage. The emphasis is on ageing in the deep cellars, and mercifully the accountants have not got at them, so stocks are enormous. All the wines are made to last forever, and they do so wonderfully well with sufficient acidity to balance their oakiness, which gives a slightly musty aroma, much enjoyed by lovers of old-fashioned Rioja. The lightest of all the wines is the white Viña Gravonia, which is not a single-vineyard wine, but derives its name from the old "Rioja Graves"; made from the Viura grape, even this is oak aged and sold at four years old. A white wine that is really in the old tradition is Viña Tondonia Blanco, which has at least four years in cask. The *rosado*, too, is given cask ageing. The youngest red wine, Viña Cubillo, a *crianza* with twenty-five per cent Garnacha and five per cent each of Graciano and Mazuelo, is given three years' ageing with at least two in oak. Viña Tondonia Tinto is given four years in oak and is made with fifteen per cent Garnacha, five per cent Mazuelo, and five per cent Graciano; but the Garnacha comes entirely from Rioja Alta, which gives wines from this vine good ageing capabilities. The red *reservas* and *gran reservas*, which are the pride of the bodega, are sold in two styles. Viña Bosconia is the fuller in flavour and sold in Burgundy-shaped bottles; it is given at least three years in cask and is made with fifteen per cent Garnacha, and five per cent Mazuelo and Graciano combined. Viña Tondonia spends at least four years in oak and is made with fifteen per cent Garnacha and five per cent each of Mazuelo and Graciano. *Gran reservas* are not usually sold until they are at least twenty-eight years old. This is the home of really old, traditional Rioja.

UNION VITIVINICOLA, MARQUÉS DE CÁCERES

Carretera Logroño s/n, 26350 Cenicero, La Rioja. Tel: +34 941 45 40 00; Fax: +34 941 45 44 00; Email: dc.marquesdecaceres@fer.es

This bodega was founded in 1970 by Enrique Forner, whose training was in Bordeaux, where he owns Château Camensac and runs Château Larose-Trintaudon, which he formerly owned. He was advised by the great Bordeaux oenologist Professor Peynaud. The *marqués* does exist (indeed he is a grandee of Spain), but his part in the bodega is that of a benevolent bystander, taking some modest royalties that he gives to charity. The wines, though, do not attempt to imitate Bordeaux and have gained an international reputation as among the best in Rioja. They are impressively consistent. It has practically no vineyards of its own (just over two hectares), but is able to buy from excellent nearby vineyards including those that have very old vines; 170 of the growers are minority shareholders.

There are four whites: a young one in the modern style and an oak-aged *crianza* in the traditional style, both from 100 per cent Viura; Antea, mostly from Viura, but with ten per cent Malvasía, which is a *crianza* barrel fermented in Allier oak; and Satinela, a delicious sweet wine with an aroma of apricots, which is made from very ripe grapes, eighty-five per cent Viura and fifteen per cent Malvasía. There is a very fresh *rosado* with twenty per cent Garnacha, and a complete range of reds made with fifteen per cent Graciano and Garnacha; it includes all levels up to *gran reserva*. In 1994 it introduced a very special top wine from very old vines, Gaudium (Latin for joy), a traditional red Rioja of the finest quality. Its latest addition, in 2002, was MC, a varietal Tempranillo in the new style and a marvellous example. These leading wines are made only in the best years. American, French, and even a little Spanish oak is used, but *reservas* and above are matured only in French.

MARQUÉS DE GRIÑON
Carretera El Ciego s/n, 26350 Cenicero, La Rioja.
Tel: +34 941 45 31 00; Fax: 941 45 31 14
Carlos Falcó y Fernández de Códova, Marqués de Griñón, is one of the best wine-growers in Spain, who also has interests in Argentina. Apart from actually making wine, also markets wine made and matured under his supervision by others. This is how, at the moment, he produces his good Riojas; they are actually made by Bodegas Berberana at Dominio de Súsar (*see* above), but the situation is developing and foreshadows a more hands-on approach. There are only reds: a basic wine, which is always good value, a *crianza*, the Reserva Especial, and the Reserva Colección Personal, all nearly one hundred per cent Tempranillo.

BODEGAS MARQUÉS DE LA CONCORDIA
Hacienda de Súsar, Avenida del Ebro s/n, 26540 Alfaro, La Rioja.
Tel: +34 941 45 31 00; Fax: 941 45 31 14; Email: adelgado@haciendas-espana.com; Website: www.haciendas-espana.com
Now part of a loosely knit combination of interests that include ARCO, Bodegas Unidos, and the Marqués de Griñon (*see* above), together with Hacienda la Concordia, high up in the Rioja Alta and due to be opened in 2006, this bodega was founded in 1995, and made its first wine in 1999. It has been famous for growing experimental vines including Merlot and Syrah; it has found that Syrah performs brilliantly. But are these wines Rioja? And does it matter? On a more down-to-earth level it produces very good Tempranillo varietal *crianzas* and *reservas* from its fifteen-hectare vineyard made in the new style, with the emphasis on fruit rather than oak. The most interesting, indeed fascinating, wine is sold under the estate name of

Hacienda de Súsar, made from fifty per cent Tempranillo and the rest equal parts of Cabernet Sauvignon, Merlot, and Syrah, with eighteen months in French oak. It is classified as "experimental" by the *consejo* and the 2001 was memorably good, but would repay ten years' bottle age.

BODEGAS MARQUÉS DE MURRIETA

Carretera Logroño-Zaragoza km 5, 26006 Logroño, La Rioja.
Tel: +34 941 27 13 70; Fax: +34 941 25 16 06;
Email: bodegas@marquesdemurrieta.com; Website: www.marquesdemurrieta.com

The origins and early history of this great bodega have already been given, for it is tied intimately with the origins of the Rioja that we know today. It was founded in 1872 by Luciano de Murrieta y García-Lemoine, who was born in 1822 to a father who had emigrated to Peru and a Creole mother whose father owned a silver mine. His upbringing, however, was influenced by his uncle Cristóbal Pascual de Murrieta who, among other interests, was a banker in London, where he learned about good wine. After some military adventures, Luciano bought his fine estate at Ygay in 1872, just outside Logroño on the road to Zaragoza, near the border of the Rioja Alta and the Rioja Baja. By this time he knew all that was then known about winemaking. He died in Logroño a bachelor aged 89. The estate remained in the family until it was bought in 1983 by Vicente Cabrián, Conde de Creixel, who chose to live there. At that time the estate and bodega were notably old-fashioned and distinctly run down. He already owned a beautiful estate at Pontevedra, the Pazo de Barrantes, making fine Rias Bajas wines. Two more different kinds of wine are hard to imagine. Following his tragically early death, it is now owned by his son Vicente, who has continued to pour money in and to complete the modernization and extension. The estate includes 300 hectares of vineyards surrounding the bodega and notable for their enormous number of big, reddish stones. It is planted with the red varieties Tempranillo (seventy-five per cent), Mazuelo (twelve per cent), Garnacha (ten per cent), and Graciano (three per cent), and the white varieties Viura, Malvasía, and (a rare choice) Garnacha Blanca. There are many different plots and these are being evaluated with some remarkable results, such as the white Capallenía and the red Dalmau *reservas*, described below. No doubt there will be others to come.

The modern bodega equipment includes fermentation tanks equipped with French *pigeage* machines (most unusual in Rioja), which work like stirring a vast stewpot very slowly. The pressing – in large, old cage presses – is very gentle, and twenty per cent of the press wine is used in the blend. The wines, both red and white, are aged in 13,200 casks, all of which are American with the exception of 700 French; 500 are replaced every year.

This is the place for oak-aged whites, and no one produces anything remotely like them save for López de Heredia. Only a couple of decades ago Spanish white wines in general, and those from the Rioja in particular, tended to be demonstrably over-oaked, flabby, and oxidized. This was never so with those from Marqués de Murrieta, and the present range of full-bodied whites balances their oakiness with ample acidity, remarkable complexity of flavour, and great length. They are also unusual among whites in that not only do they last well, but they actually repay laying down, particularly the top wines. Even the youngest is a *reserva*, usually made from eighty-seven per cent Viura, three per cent Malvasía, and ten per cent Garnacha Blanca, with two years in oak, though the 2000 was a varietal Viura. Misela, made from seventy-nine per cent Viura, six per cent Malvasía, and fifteen per cent Garnacha Blanca, is at least three years old when sold and should be kept for another three. Top of the range is Castillo Ygay *gran* Reserva Especial, made only in the best years from ninety-five per cent Viura and five per cent Malvasía, and sold at ten years old. These have recently been joined by Capellanía, a single-vineyard wine from eighty-five per cent forty-year-old Viura, ten per cent Garnacha Blanca, and five per cent Malvasía. The unusual inclusion in most of these wines is the Garnacha Blanca, which is used in France to make the best white wines of Châteauneuf-du-Pape, and one can see the resemblance.

The red wines are equally remarkable. The first thing one notices is their intense colour. The second, with experience, is their remarkable longevity; they seem to go on for ever and actually to improve into extreme old age. The 1931, which has already been mentioned, was made with 17 per cent Garnacha, 17 per cent Mazuelo, and ten per cent Graciano; it spent five months in tanks and then twenty-nine in fairly new oak before bottling. Drunk in 1996, it was a superb old wine. But it was by no means the oldest in the cellar, which has every vintage back to 1877. These are recorked as necessary, the 1931, for example, in 1957, and 1987. Even the bottom of the range is a *reserva*. These are made with 3–10 per cent Garnacha, 4–12 per cent Mazuelo, and 2–8 per cent Graciano. Top of the range, Castillo Ygay Gran Reserva Especial, is made only in the best years with 6–14 per cent Garnacha, 7–15 per cent Mazuelo, and 1–3 per cent Graciano. Labelled "early release", some are put on the market a good deal earlier than they used to be. These have now been supplemented by the Dalmau Reserva range, made with ten per cent Cabernet Sauvignon and five per cent Graciano from vines over thirty years old. The first was the 1994, matured in American oak and bottled in 1998. The 1996 was matured half and half in new American and French oak, the 1997 entirely in French. The Cabernet Sauvignon gives these a very good structure. Beautifully balanced, they too need keeping several years to reach their peak. In 1997 came a new venture: two *jóvenes*, a white and a red, sold as Colección 2100. The white is ninety per cent Viura, five per cent Malvasía, and five per cent Garnacha Blanca, the red is seventy-five per cent Tempranillo, twelve per cent Mazuelo, ten per cent Garnacha, and three per cent Graciano. Compared with the traditional wines of this bodega they come as a shock, but they are undoubtedly among the best of their kind. To celebrate the 150th anniversary there was an Especial Anniverario Mazuelo, a single-vineyard wine of 2001 bottled in 2003.

HEREDEROS DEL MARQUÉS DE RISCAL

Torrea 1, 01340 Elciego, Alava. Tel: +34 945 60 60 00;
Fax: +34 945 60 60 23; Email: marquesderiscal@marquesderiscal.com;
Website: www.marquesderiscal.com

The importance of this bodega in the early history of Rioja has already been related. In 1860, having personally decided to engage the services of Jean Pineau, Camilo Hurtado de Amézaga, Marqués de Riscal, set about establishing a model bodega on French lines at Elciego in the Rioja Alavesa. He engaged an architect, Ricardo Bellsolá, and sent him to study *chais* in Bordeaux. When he came back he built the fine stone bodega that we see today, though it has since been extended. The most modern winemaking equipment was installed with barriques for maturing the wine, the first to be used on a commercial scale in Rioja or indeed in Spain. Within five years, medals were being won at exhibitions all over the world. Ever since then the red Riscal wines have provided a standard by which others are judged. But it must be admitted that there was a hitch. From the mid-1970s to the early 1980s the wines failed to live up to their high reputation. This was due mainly to trouble with casks; they were old and some had become tainted. There was also perhaps an element of resting on laurels. In 1985 came a big shake-up, and eighty per cent of the barrels were scrapped. Now the bodega is back on form.

In the earliest days the emphasis was on Cabernet Sauvignon, producing wines sold as "Médoc Alavesa", but for many years now the emphasis has been on Tempranillo. In the 202 hectares of vineyard there are twenty-five hectares of Cabernet Sauvignon (some of which date back to 1898), twenty-eight hectares of Graciano (perhaps the largest holding of this variety), ten hectares of Mazuelo, and the rest is Tempranillo. The bodega would like to experiment with Merlot and Syrah – and why not? – but at present the authorities will not let it. In addition, grapes are bought from 250 hectares of vineyards owned by local growers, who are meticulously supervised and who are paid more for grapes from old vines. Some Viura is used for the *rosado,* but any white wine left over is sold to other bodegas. There is no white Riscal Rioja. There are indeed white Riscals of excellent quality, but these are all grown in Rueda, and that is another story. The red grapes are divided by age of vines: under fifteen years, used principally for *rosado,* fifteen to thirty years, and over thirty years old, which are used for making wines at the top of the range. The bunches of grapes are examined by hand to eliminate any below standard. Various kinds of oak have been tried for maturation including American, Canadian, French Nevers, and Bosnian, but American has been found to be the best; it is bought as wood, seasoned, and made up into casks by the bodega's own coopers. There are no *jóvenes* with the exception of the *rosado,* made from ninety per cent Tempranillo and ten per cent Viura, and one of the best in Rioja. Nor are there any *crianzas,* only *reservas, gran reservas,* and the superb Baron de Chirel. *Gran reservas* are made every year, but only after a careful selection of grapes and wine. Baron de Chirel is made only when everything is exactly right. The Reserva 2000 was made with ten per cent Graciano and Mazuelo combined, aged in oak for twenty-five months. The *gran reserva* 1996 was made with ten per cent Graciano, five per cent Mazuelo, and twenty per cent "other varieties" (which means Cabernet Sauvignon), and aged in oak for thirty-six months; while the *gran reserva* 1987 was made with twenty per cent Graciano and thirty-five per cent "other varieties", aged in oak for thirty-two months. The 1999 Baron de Chirel Reserva was made with forty-six per cent "other varieties". The reds have excellent ageing potential, especially the Baron de Chirel, which can age for decades. Indeed the 1871 was still excellent in 1997. At the time of writing, an enormous new complex is being built, designed by Frank Gehry. It will include a restaurant, hotel, and museum. The construction makes extensive use of metal, and from afar it looks like a magnified scrap heap; but when it is finished it will it will no doubt be as impressive as another Gehry building, the Guggenheim in Barcelona.

BODEGAS Y VINEDOS DEL MARQUES DE VARGAS

Hacienda de Pradologar, Ctra Zaragoza km 6, 26006 Logroño, La Rioja.
Tel: +34 941 26 14 01; Fax: +34 941 23 86 96; Email: bvargas@jet.es

The bodega and vineyards are in an area known as "The Three Marquéses": Murrieta, Romeral, and Vargas. The marqués' family has grown grapes on this site since 1845, but used to sell them to shippers until he decided to establish his own very modern bodega in 1991 on the edge of an immaculate sixty-five-hectare estate with calcareous clay soils, poor in nutrients. It provides all the grapes used: Tempranillo, Mazuelo, Graciano, Garnacha, and Cabernet Sauvignon, which are grown without irrigation, pesticides, or herbicides, and divided into sixteen plots, each picked and vinified separately. It produces only red wines, *reservas* and *gran reservas*, without filtration or clarification (so they throw a deposit when mature and need decanting), matured in American, French, and Russian oak, the last proving very successful. The *reserva* 2000 had ten per cent Mazuelo, five per cent Garnacha, and ten per cent "others", and was matured in thirty per cent new American oak, twenty per cent new French oak, ten per cent new Russian oak, and the rest in one-year-old casks from the three places. The Reserva Privada had ten per cent Mazuelo, ten per cent Garnacha, and twenty per cent "others", from old vines in two plots and was matured in new Russian oak. The Hacienda Pradolagar, first made in that year, had ten per cent Mazuelo, ten per cent Garnacha, and forty per cent "others" from old vines in one plot and was matured in new French and Russian oak. The Hacienda Pradolagar and the Reserva Privada are made only in very good years. All are superb wines that benefit from considerable ageing, especially the top ones.

BODEGAS MARQUÉS DE VITORIA

Camino de Santa Lucía s/n, 01320 Oyón, Alava.

Tel: +34 945 62 21 34; Fax: +34 945 60 14 96;

Email: info@bodegasdevitoria.es; Website: www.marquesdevitoria.es

Beginning life as a cooperative in 1988, this has since been acquired by Faustino Martínez (*see* above). It is independent, though, with Faustino making its admirable traditional wines and Vitoria making equally admirable wines in the new style. It owns ninety hectares of Tempranillo and four hectares of Viura at 400–600 metres (1,312–1,968 feet) above sea level, plus six hectares of Tempranillo in the Rioja Alavesa cultivated organically and used to make an organic *crianza*. All its wines, apart from the white, are varietal Tempranillos. The *crianza* is matured in American oak, the *reserva* and *gran reserva* in French, while the top wine, Original, is from old vines with short maturation in both French and American oak.

BODEGAS MARTINEZ BUJANDA

See Valdemar.

BODEGAS MIGUEL MERINO

Ctra de Logroño 16, 26330 Briones, La Rioja. Tel: +34 941 32 22 63; Fax: +34 941 32 22 94; Email: info@miguelmerino.com; Website: www.miguelmerino.com

Miguel Merino founded his enchanting bodega in the historic town of Briones in 1993 and runs it in a very hands-on way. The secret of making good wines, he says, is to have old vines and new casks. He has a modest two hectares of established vineyard, but buys from four trusty friends with fourteen hectares in the village, the youngest planted in 1973. He has also planted a small experimental vineyard of 298 vines in front of the old farmhouse that is a perfect example of a boutique bodega. The grapes are not gathered when it is hot; but when they get to the bodega they are picked over by hand and generally over nine per cent are rejected. In 1999, when it rained, this figure rose to twenty per cent. He makes only *reservas* and *gran reservas*. The beautifully balanced, relatively light *Reserva* 1996 was made mostly from Tempranillo, a little Mazuelo, and a very small amount of Graciano. The Reserva 1998, with three per cent Graciano, is bigger and more muscular – an excellent wine to drink at ten years. The excellent *Gran Reserva* 1995 had three per cent Graciano and one per cent Mazuelo and was aged in fifteen Allier and four American casks. So far he has made only red wines, but in 2004 made three barrels of white from Viura. He has high expectations of the 2004 vintage.

BODEGAS MONTECILLO

Ctra Navarrete km 3, 26360 Fuenmayor, La Rioja. Tel: +34 941 44 01 25; Fax: +34 941 44 06 63; Email: comunicacion@osborne.es; Website: www.osborne.es

With a history going back to 1874, this was originally called Hijos de Celestino Navajas and was one of the bodegas established in the first boom, by two brothers, one of whom had studied in Bordeaux. It changed its name and was bought in 1973 by the great sherry and brandy house Osborne, of El Puerto de Santa María. It sold off the estate, which became Finca Valpiedra, and buys in all its grapes from local growers. The resulting influx of capital and knowledge enabled it to move into the big league. Located at Fuenmayor, it has a complete range of reliable wines, offering good value. They are varietal – Viura or Tempranillo as the case may be – and use is made of French oak, with the barrels made in its own cooperage. The Selección Especial *gran reservas* are excellent.

DAVID MORENO

Carretera de Villar de Torres s/n, 26310 Badarán, La Rioja.

Tel: +34 941 36 73 38; Fax: +34 941 41 86 85;

Email: davidmoreno@davidmoreno.es; Website: www.davidmoreno.com

David Moreno Peña, originally an automobile engineer with Seat, came back home to the Rioja and founded his boutique bodega at Badarán in 1981. He sold his first wine in 1989, mostly from his own one-hectare vineyard and from grapes bought from members of his family, who are long-established growers. He uses both French and American oak, and some of his reds are made by carbonic maceration. He produces a complete range of attractive and attractively priced wines in the modern style under his own name and under the brand Monasterio de Yuso.

BODEGAS MUGA

Barrio de la Estación s/n, 26200 Haro, La Rioja.

Tel: +34 941 31 18 25; Fax: +34 941 31 28 67;

Email: info@bodegasmuga.com; Website: www.bodegasmuga.com

It is impossible not to be enthusiastic about Muga wines. The bodega was founded by Isaac Muga Martínez in 1932, right between the two boom periods, at a time of consolidation rather than enterprise. Originally it was in the middle of Haro, but Sr Muga was planning a move to premises near the station when he died in 1969. It was inherited by his three children, who made the move in 1971, subsequently digging cellars and most recently building a tower. They began with thirty-five hectares of vineyards, but have increased this to 170 and are still expanding in this area; they aim eventually to become self-sufficient. The bodega prides itself in being "artisanal", or in other words completely traditional. Here there is no stainless steel, but plenty of oak. White wines are barrel fermented but all the reds are fermented in the old way, using 18,000-litre oak *tinos*. This does not mean that the bodega is unwilling to experiment, though. For maturation it has tried oak from Kentucky, Ohio, Rouvre, Limousin, Allier, and Spain, maturing the same wine in different barrels, side by side. It buys the wood and makes all the barrels in its own cooperage. The result so far is that there is slightly more French oak than American. New barrels are used for fermenting white wine and are then used for maturing red, until they are 8-10 years old. Any wine that does not come up to standard is immediately sold on. Muga Blanco is made from ninety per cent Viura and ten per cent Malvasía; it is barrel fermented in French oak, is bone dry and beautifully balanced, avoiding being over-oaked. The *rosado* is very pale in colour, made from sixty per cent Garnacha, thirty per cent Viura, and ten per cent Tempranillo. The emphasis, though, is on red wines, which account for ninety per cent of the production. The classic *crianzas* and *reservas* are made from twenty per cent Garnacha, and ten per cent Mazuelo and Graciano combined. The excellent Prado Enea 1995 *gran reserva* was made with twenty per cent in all of Garnacha, Mazuelo, and Graciano, spent twelve months in wooden vats, thirty-six months in oak barrels, and a minimum of thirty-six months in bottle before being released. Torre Muga, introduced in 1991 and matured in new French oak, used to be the top wine, the 2000 having fifteen per cent Mazuelo and ten per cent Graciano. Now the bodega has gone one step further with Aro, made with grapes from low-yielding old vineyards, thirty per cent Graciano, and also matured in new French oak. These top wines are made only in good years. It also makes a cava, Conde de Haro. The red wines need some age to give of their best, and their best is very good indeed.

BODEGAS MURÚA

Ctra Laguardia s/n, 01340 Elciego, Alava. Tel: +34 945 60 62 60; Fax: +34 945 60 63 26; Email: info@bodegasmurua.com; Website: www.bodegasmurua.com

Established in 1974 by Masaveu, an old-established group with widespread industrial interests that also owns Fillaboa in Rias Bajas, this bodega is self-sufficient in grapes with 110 hectares of vineyard at an altitude of 450 metres (1,476 feet): seventy-five per cent Tempranillo and fifteen per cent Graciano, the rest being mostly Mazuelo. It makes an unusually good barrel-fermented white with some Garnacha Blanca and Malvasía, but concentrates on very good reds of *reserva* level and above. It uses eighty per cent American and twenty per cent European oak, including some from the East. The usual grape mix includes fifteen per cent Graciano and ten per cent Mazuelo. Its top wines, made only in the best years, are Veguin de Murúa *reserva* made from vines over sixty years old and, since 1991, Murúa M with ten per cent Graciano. It is unusual in having a fine wine library.

BODEGAS OLARRA

Poligono de Cantabria s/n, 26006 Logroño, La Rioja.
Tel: +34 941 23 52 99; Fax: +34 941 25 37 03;
Email: bodegasolarra@bodegasolarra.es; Website: www.bodegasolarra.es

Housed in a large, elegant building on the edge of Logroño, this bodega was founded in 1972 by Luis Olarra, a steel magnate from Bilbao, and some of his friends; but in 1984 he sold his interest to another Bilbao steel family, Guibert-Ucin. It is part of a group that includes Bodegas Ondarre and

Antina Vins in Penedès. Owning no vineyards of its own, it buys from all three regions and produces a complete range of wines sold under the marks Otoñal, Añares, and Cerro Añon. Summa Añares is made with twenty-five per cent Mazuelo and fifteen per cent Graciano and is very good.

BODEGAS ONTAÑÓN

Avenida de Aragón 3, 26006 Logroño, La Rioja. Tel/Fax: +34 941 23 42 00; Email: ontanon@ontanon.es; Website: www.ontanon.es

A family-owned bodega established in 1984, it is almost as full of modern art as it is of wine. Backed by a large holding of 150 hectares of vineyard, it makes good wines, especially the *reservas*. *Crianzas* have ten per cent Garnacha, while the *reservas* and *gran reservas* have five per cent Graciano.

BODEGAS PALACIO

San Lárazo 1, 01300 Laguardia, Alava. Tel: +34 945 60 01 51; Fax: +34 945 60 02 97; Email: cosme@bodegaspalacio.com; Website: www.habarcelo.es

Founded in 1894 by Cosme Palacio, this bodega at Laguardia has had a very confused recent history. In 1972 the Palacio family sold it, and for a while it had a complicated time as a subsidiary of multinationals. In 1987, it was bought out by the management, headed by M Jean Gervais, a Frenchman who had been manager of Barton & Guestier in Bordeaux and a vice-president of Seagram Europe. He was advised by consultant Michel Rolland. In 1998 it was bought by the Spanish group Hijos de Antonio Barceló, but the management was left in place. If there is a French background, the intention is to produce the best style of Rioja using only Tempranillo and Viura, not a Spanish version of French wine. It does use French oak, though, for most of its casks. The Barceló group has poured in money, making everything modern and turning the old bodega into a luxury hotel. It offers a complete range. There are whites Cosme Palacio y Hermanos Blanco, and Regio, a white *reserva*. Glorioso is its most famous brand, the reds matured in French oak, the *crianza* for fourteen months and the *reserva* for twenty-two. The El Portico, *crianza,* and *reserva* are the only wines aged in new American oak. The Cosme Palacio y Hermanos wines are aged partly in new French oak. Castillo is one of the new *corta crianzas*, having six months in oak, which is not enough for it to be a *crianza*, and leaves it delightfully fresh. The Reserva Especial is made only in very good years from the oldest vines and matured in French oak. It is very good indeed.

BODEGAS PALACIOS REMONDO

Avenida Zaragoza 8, 26540 Alfaro, La Rioja. Tel: +34 941 18 02 07;

Fax: +34 941 18 16 28; Email: hremondo@vinosherenciaremondo.com;

Website: www.vinosherenciaremondo.com

The Palacios family has a long history in the Rioja, but this bodega was not founded until 1945. Since 2000 the wines have been made by that charismatic member of the family, Alvaro. (For his other activities, *see* the chapters on Priorato and Bierzo.) Here he has 100 hectares of vineyards in that extraordinary place in the Rioja Baja, Alfaro, where they are 550 metres (1,804 feet) high but, being in the Baja, Tempranillo loses its usual preponderance. When he took over, yields went down and quality dramatically up. Plácet is white, a varietal Viura with part cask fermentation, and it is one of the best. La Vendímia is a varietal Tempranillo *joven*. La Montesa comes as a *crianza* and as a *reserva*, both made with thirty-five per cent Garnacha and fifteen per cent Mazuelo. Propriedad is forty per cent Garnacha, thirty-five per cent Tempranillo, fifteen per cent Mazuelo, and ten per cent Graciano, from low yielding vines grown in the best part of the estate. In their very different ways, these are splendid wines bearing the mark of their maker.

BODEGAS FEDERICO PATERNINA

Avda Santo Domingo 11, 26200 Haro, La Rioja. Tel: +34 941 31 05 50; Fax: +34 941 31 27 78; Email: marketing@paternina.com; Website: www.paternina.com

Paternina is perhaps the most famous bodega in the Rioja, but has a complicated history. It was founded in 1896 by Federico de Paternina y Josué, the fifth son of an aristocratic winemaker, Eduardo de Paternina, Marqués de Terán. He decided to go it alone and established his bodega at Ollauri, with wonderful cellars dating from the late sixteenth century, carved out of the rock, where the *reservas* and *gran reservas* are still matured. In 1919, however, something went wrong, and the bodega was bought by Joaquín Herrero de la Riva, a banker from Logroño, with the backing of four Spanish families. Three years later a French winemaker was brought in, Etienne Labatut, who drove the bodega to new heights. At the same time, the premises of the Cooperativa de Sindicatos Católicos in Haro were acquired, where the headquarters are still located.

In 1972 it was bought by Rumasa, and after Rumasa's dispossession it was run by the state for a short time before being sold to a rich businessman, Marcos Eguizábal Ramíriz, who also bought Bodegas Franco-Españolas in Rioja and some of the Rumasa interests in Jerez, but most of these have been sold on. At the time of the Rumasa takeover, Paternina had acquired a special position as the supplier of the most popular Rioja in Spain: the red Banda Azul. When a Spanish family wanted a treat, that is what they bought. Then a catastrophe happened: 1972 was one of the worst vintages on record, and orders were given that the young wine from this vintage, which had not yet finished its malolactic fermentation, was to be blended in with the wine being bottled for sale. It duly completed its malolactic fermentation – but in bottle. There was a current joke that people who ordered Banda Azul were asked whether they wanted it *con* or *sin* gas, like mineral water. Unfortunately to many unsophisticated drinkers, Banda Azul was Rioja, and the whole district went under a cloud. Of course all of this is now ancient history. Rioja has recovered its image and Banda Azul has long since recovered its quality and its place as a very good buy. But it was a bad time.

Things are very different today. The bodega is thoroughly up to date and fascinating in its automation. Nearly all the wood is American. The range of wines is comprehensive. The basic white is Banda Dorada, a varietal Viura. There is a *crianza* white called Graciela with ten per cent Malvasía. A *reserva* white is made in good years from Viura, sometimes with a little Malvasía and Garnacha Blanca: a good example of a traditional white Rioja. The ubiquitous and very agreeable red *crianza* Banda Azul has thirty per cent Garnacha. One step up is the *crianza* Banda Oro, with fifteen per cent Garnacha and five per cent Mazuelo. The popular *gran reserva* Conde de los Andes has a grape mix that varies from year to year, the 1991 having ten per cent Mazuelo. The top red is the recently introduced Clos Paternina, with some Cabernet Sauvignon, made only in good years and in very small quantities, and matured in new French oak casks.

PEDRO BENITO URBINA

Campillo 33–5, Cuzcurrita de Rio Tirón, La Rioja. Tel/Fax: +34 941 22 42 72; Email: urbina@fer.es; Website: www.urbinavinos.com

A family-owned bodega of modest size at the northwestern edge of Rioja, it is now in its fourth generation and has seventy-five hectares of vineyards cultivated "traditionally" – which means not quite organically, but using the minimum of chemical intervention. No grapes are bought in. It began bottling the estate's wines in 1975. The reds are made with 5-10 per cent of Graciano and Mazuelo. It uses twenty per cent Allier oak. These are always sound wines, especially at the top of the range.

BODEGAS PRIMICIA

Ctra de Elvillar s/n, 01300 Laguardia, Alava. Tel: +34 945 60 02 96; Fax: +34 945 62 12 52; Email: albertoherrero@bodegasprimicia.com; Website: www.araex.com

This estate was founded in 1985 by the two sons of the late Julián Madrid, who had always wanted to make wines from his own forty-four-hectare vineyard, so his sons named their best wine after him. The brands are Primicia, meaning "first fruits", and Diezmo, meaning "tithes" paid by local people to the town and the church. Indeed the old building that houses the bodega was the collection point for tithes. The most unusual wine is a varietal Diezmo Mazuelo, but most, apart from a barrel-fermented Viura called Flor de Primicia, are Tempranillo-based, and are apt to contain proportions of "other varieties": the Julián Madrid 1999 has twenty per cent. The old-vine Curium is particularly good. These are good, reliable wines and not over-oaked.

BODEGAS PUELLES

Camino los Molinos s/n, 26339 Abalos, La Rioja.

Tel: +34 941 33 44 15; Fax: +34 941 33 41 32;

Email: informacion@bodegaspuelles.com; Website: www.bodegaspuelles.com

The Puelles family claims to have been growing wine from time immemorial. In 1844 it bought a seventeenth-century watermill, the Finca de Molino, where it grows nineteen hectares of Tempranillo ecologically, with additional grapes bought in. When in 1989 the regulations were relaxed to permit the establishment of boutique bodegas, two brothers of the family formed one, initially establishing a Club del Molino, to raise capital by selling whole casks of wine *en primeur*. The Reserva 1996 was excellent. The top wine is Puelles Zenus.

BODEGAS FERNANDO RAMÍREZ DE GANUZA

La Constitución 1, 01307 Samaniego, Alava.

Tel: +34 945 60 90 22; Fax: +34 945 62 33 35;

Email: fernando@ramirezdeganuza.com; Website: www.remirezdeganuza.com

A bodega of modest size but enormous reputation, founded in 1988 by its eponymous proprietor, who has fifty-four hectares of sixty-year-old vines (ninety per cent Tempranillo and ten per cent Graciano) that supply all his needs. He is an inventive man who has devised his own unique bodega apparatus and is immaculate in his methods. For instance, he noticed that the narrow ends of bunches of grapes ripen less well than the tops, so these are all cut off and used to make a wine by carbonic maceration. He uses seventy per cent American oak, the rest being from France and Eastern Europe, but does not go in for excessive oaking. His most modest wine (though it is not at all modest by most people's standards) is Fincas de Ganuza, with seventeen per cent Graciano. "R." (Erre Punto) is a *joven* made by carbonic maceration, with five per cent Graciano and five per cent "others". Then comes Trasnocho, with ten per cent Graciano, and finally his top *Reserva* with seventeen per cent Graciano. These are fine wines by any standards.

GRANJA NUESTRA SENORA DE REMELLURI

Carretera Rivas s/n, 01330 Labastida, Alava. Tel: +34 945 33 18 01; Fax: +34 945 33 18 02; Email: info@remelluri.com; Website: www.remelluri.com

It is impossible to imagine a more beautiful estate than this one, and the wines it grows are just as beautiful. It is up in the hills above Labastida, on the edge of the Sierra Toloño, 600–800 metres (1,968–2,625 feet) high, cool and with notable Atlantic influence, in the Rioja Alavesa but on the edge of the Rioja Alta. Originally belonging to the Monastery of Toloño, by the fourteenth century it was independent and growing wine. At the end of the eighteenth century some of the vineyards were in the hands of Manuel Quintino, whose part in the history of the Rioja has already been described. In the 1960s it was bought by Jaime and Amaya Rodríguiz Salis; he is Spanish and she is French. They planted vines but the grapes were initially sold to local winemakers. The first vintage was in 1971. The whole estate is 152 hectares, with 100 hectares of vineyards, planted on chalky-clay soils. The only bought-in grapes are from a one-hectare vineyard owned by the cook.

The red grapes are eighty per cent Tempranillo, with some Garnacha and Graciano, which grows very well here. Some white grapes are also grown – Garnacha Blanca, Moscatel del Pais, and Malvasía, with the "foreign" varieties Roussanne, Marsanne, Viognier, Sauvignon, and Chardonnay, but very little Viura. It does not wish to jump on the bandwagon of organic viticulture, but use no herbicides, systemic products, or chemical fertilisers, just organic compost and manure applied once in four years. Owing to its altitude, it is very cold at night here and can catch the frost; in the spring of 1997 half the crop was destroyed. For the same reason the vintage is unusually late, generally at the end of October. The yield is about half the average for Rioja, which itself is low by world standards. And it faces another rather unusual hazard: wild boar. To keep them from eating the grapes, radios are played in the vineyards and the boar think that people are about.

After the malolactic fermentation, the wine is aged for two years in oak, but any that does not reach their standards is sold off: about a quarter. Of the 4,500 *barricas*, ninety per cent are French oak and the rest American. One-year-old casks are bought from Château Latour. The wines are neither filtered nor fined. In a good vintage they are second to none and age well. Of recent vintages, the 1992 was frankly disappointing; the 1994 and 1995 were excellent and set the pattern for what followed. It used to make only red wines: *reservas* and, in the best years, *gran reservas*. The Reserva 1999 was made with five per cent Graciano and five per cent Garnacha, plus Mazuelo. But now there is a red *crianza* and a white *crianza*, made from Garnacha Blanca, Roussanne, Moscatel, Sauvignon and Viognier, as well as Petit Corbu. It is one of the best and most interesting Rioja whites, with some of the traditional oakiness but remarkable fragrance.

LA RIOJA ALTA

Avenida de Vizcaya s/n, 26200 Haro, La Rioja. Tel: +34 941 31 03 46; Fax: +34 941 31 28 54; Email: riojalta@riojalta.com; Website: www.riojalta.com

If any one bodega were to be singled out as the exemplar of the classic style of Rioja, this would have to be it, year after year producing wines of only the highest quality. The company was founded in 1890, when Daniel-Alfredo Ardanza y Sanchez got together with some friends: Doña Saturnina Garcia Cid y Gárete, Don Dionisio del Prado y Lablanca, Don Felipe Puig de la Bellacasa y Herrán, and Don Mariano Lacorte Tapia. The trademark, the Rio Oja flowing by four oak trees, was registered in 1902. After more than a hundred years the company now has many shareholders, but it remains essentially a family concern managed by the fifth-generation descendants of the founders and has now expanded to form a group that includes Torre de Oña, in Rioja, Lagar de Fornelos in Rías Bajas, and Aster in Ribera del Duero. It is one of the great bodegas by the railway station in Haro. Over the years it has accumulated 425 hectares of vineyards, which provide half its needs. It has kept up with the times and is immaculate, with temperature-controlled fermentations in stainless steel. All the wood is American with casks made in its own cooperage.

It concentrates on red wines from *crianza* upward, though it ages its *crianzas* so long that they could officially be offered as *reservas*. It has stopped making white wine since establishing its Rias Bajas vineyard. Of the red wines, the *crianza* is sold as Viña Alberdi; the 1992 had five per cent each of Mazuelo, Graciano, and Viura, with two years in barrels, but the 2000 omitted the Graciano and Viura. There is a trend here to reduce Garnacha and increase Graciano. There are two *reservas*. Viña Arana is the lighter style and in 1988 had five per cent each of Mazuelo and Graciano; after six to eight months in large oak vats it had three years in barrels. The red Viña Ardanza is a big, robust, and beautifully smooth wine, slightly more alcoholic (13% ABV as compared to 12.5%) but complex with perfect balance and great length. In 1998 the *reserva* was made with twenty per cent Garnacha. There are two extremely fine *gran reservas*. Gran Reserva 904 in the past was called Gran Reserva 1904, not to indicate a vintage, but the year when the bodega merged with one owned by one of its directors. However the possibility of confusion was obvious and the name was changed. It is a big wine and one of the best of the *gran reservas*. The 1994 had ten per cent Graciano, and was aged for four months in large oak vats and then for five years in barrels, giving an elegant wine of perfect structure and exquisite complexity. Top of the range is Gran Reserva 890. Again its name originally was 1890, the year of the bodega's foundation, but it was changed for the same reason. If the 904 is a big wine, the 890 is bigger still, with a magnificence that does not hide its subtlety. The 1989 had ten per cent Graciano and Mazuelo, and was aged for six months in wooden vats and then for no less than seven years in oak barrels.

BODEGAS RIOJANAS

Estacion 1–21, 26350 Cenicero, La Rioja. Tel: +34 941 45 40 50; Fax: +34 941 45 45 29; Email: bodegas@bodegasriojanas.com; Website: www.bodegasriojanas.com

This notable bodega, which has a charming little fantasy castle, was founded in Cenicero at the height of the French influence in 1890. Being built on a hillside enables it to move its wines by gravity. It produces a remarkably wide range of wines that tend to be rather big and old fashioned, rise from good to excellent quality, and are generally very good value. Although a quoted company, it is still run by members of the founding family. It has 200 hectares of local vineyards that supply sixty per cent of its needs. All the oak used is American. Its two best known trademarks are Monte Real and Viña Albina, the former used for the more commercial wines and the latter, the name of the wife of one of the founders, for the more expensive ones. A third, Puerta Vieja, is aimed at the restaurant and supermarket trade. About eighty-five per cent of its wines are reds, and of these, forty-five per cent are *reservas* and *gran reservas*. The Monte Real 2003 and the Viña Albina Barrica 2003 whites were both 100 per cent Viura. The grape mix for the reds generally includes fifteen per cent Mazuelo and five per cent Graciano, though the *Gran* Albina 2001 was unique in being made from equal parts of Tempranillo, Graciano, and Mazuelo. The Viña Albana *gran reservas* are very good. The *Gran* Albina 1998, with twenty per cent Graciano and ten per cent Mazuelo, is exceptionally good and has considerable ageing potential. Monte Real wines are found all over Spain and can be relied on.

BODEGAS RODA

Avda de Vizcaya, 5 Barrio de la Estación, 26200 Haro, La Rioja. Tel: +34 941 30 30 01; Fax: +34 941 31 27 03; Email: rodarioja@roda.es; Website: www.roda.es

This boutique bodega, on the hill above the station at Haro, is fantastic. It was set up in 1986 by the Rotllant-Daurella family, who are wine merchants in Barcelona, where the commercial headquarters is located. It has sixty hectares vineyards of its own, densely planted to give a small yield and organically cultivated; but these grapes are not used, nor will they be until the vines are at least fifteen years old. At the moment grapes are bought from a number of growers and have to be from vines that are at least thirty years old. When the bunches are delivered they are individually selected by hand. The site on the hill is a remarkable one, with deep maturation cellars carved out of the rock; at the end one emerges on to a balcony, hidden away on the hillside, with a glorious view over the river Ebro. Vinification is in large vats of French oak equipped with temperature control, and after the malolactic fermentation the wine is matured in French oak barrels, one third of which are renewed each year. Owing to the peculiarity of the site, everything can be done by gravity. The grapes are introduced through a door high up in the bodega wall and it all follows from there. They make only three red wines. Roda I and Roda II are the first and second quality, but the top wine is Cirsion. Anything that is not good enough for the second is sold on. Cirsion and Roda I are varietal Tempranillos: the first superb and the second excellent, and both will benefit from long ageing. Roda II is now generally made with five per cent Garnacha and three per cent Graciano, though the 1998 had twenty-seven per cent Garnacha. It is not intended for long ageing, but by any normal standards is very good indeed. When a vintage does not produce wine up to standard, none is sold: 1997 for instance. Conversely, in a very fine year there may be no Roda II: 1994 for instance.

VINOS DE BENJAMÍN ROMEO

Amorebieta 6 Baja, 26338 San Vicenete de la Sonsierra, La Rioja.
Tel: +34 941 33 42 28; Fax: +34 955 60 16 7.

This is not just a boutique bodega, but what the French would call a *garagiste*. Indeed the wines are actually made in a garage beneath a block of flats, though grander premises are being planned and there is an ageing store in the cool cellars of the church. Benjamin Romeo, who was winemaker at Artadi for eighteen years, is a one-man band, doing everything himself save for some help from his father in the vineyards. His eight hectares are divided into twenty-two parcels including one in a loop of the river; all are at high altitude. They are immaculately tended with such details as leaving wild herbs to grow, which he says influence the grapes, and buying his sheep manure two years in advance, to be used once in every three years. Everything is done according to the phases of the moon. He picks individual bunches and destems those for his best wine by hand. All his wines are matured in new French oak. The wines are bottled unfiltered and he uses the best corks, which he examines individually, even deciding which way up they are to go. After various experiments the first vintage he was satisfied with was 2001. In that year he made a white wine called Gallocanto for the first time, using Viura, Malvasía, and Garnacha Blanca in roughly equal amounts. His best reds are varietal Tempranillos, La Viña de Andrés and, at the top, Contador. They are indescribably glorious.

VIÑA SALCEDA

Ctra de Cenicero km 3, 01340 Elciego, Alava. Tel: +34 945 60 61 25; Fax: +34 945 60 60 69; Email: info@vinasalceda.com; Website: www.vinasalceda.com

Vines have been grown here by the family of the Conde de la Salceda for a very long time, and in 1969 a group of friends decided to establish a bodega, which was built in a delightful position just above the river Ebro near Elciego, in 1974. It produces only red wines and only *crianzas* and above. It took a great step forward in 1998, when it was bought by the family firm Chivite, of Navarra, which invested in all the things necessary for making fine wine. It owns forty hectares of vineyards and controls a further 100 hectares, growing mostly Tempranillo and some Mazuelo. One vineyard, on sandy soil, is ungrafted. The usual grape mix is 85–90 per cent Tempranillo and 10–15 per cent Mazuelo and Graciano, matured in American oak, but the top of the range Conde de la Salceda has five per cent Graciano and is matured in new Allier oak. These are excellent wines, especially the *reservas*, and mature notably well. What is more they are good value.

BODEGAS SAN PEDRO

Camino de la Hoya s/n, 01300 Laguardia, Alava. Tel: +34 945 62 12 04; Fax: +34 945 60 00 40; Email: comercial@vallobera.com

The San Pedro family have been growing grapes in the Rioja Alavesa for a very long time. Initially they sold them, and then started to make wine out of them to sell in bulk. Then they started to bottle some wine and sell it locally. In 2000 the younger generation, the brothers Javier and Carlos, inherited the eighty hectares of vineyard, which include some of the highest in Rioja, and decided to produce serious Riojas, backed by stocks that go back to 1996. The wines are sold under the name Vallobera. The 1996 Vallobera Cazador Reserva 1996, made with ten per cent Garnacha and given twenty-one months in French oak, is magnificent. The range now includes Pago Malarina (named after one of their vineyards), a Tempranillo made by carbonic maceration, through varietal Tempranillo *crianzas* and *reservas*. The *crianzas* and *reservas* all have the structure to age well.

SENORIO DE SAN VICENTE
See Sierra Cantabria.

BODEGAS CARLOS SERRES
Avda Santa Domingo 40, 26200 Haro, La Rioja. Tel: +34 941 31 02 79; Fax: +34 941 31 04 18; Email: info@carlosserres.com; Website: www.carlosserres.com
Founded in 1896 by a Frenchman who had come to the Rioja eleven years earlier to export to wine-starved France, this bodega in Haro produces a complete range. It has recently been bought by the Vivanco family that formerly traded as merchants and had a shareholding in Bodegas y Bebidas. It is noted for its Carlos Serres *gran reservas* and its *reserva* and *gran reserva* sold under the brand Onomástica. The Onomástica Reserva 1991 was mainly Tempranillo and Garnacha but with a little Macabeo, while the 1995 was ninety per cent Tempranillo and ten per cent Graciano.

SIERRA CANTABRIA/SENORIO DE SAN VICENTE
Amorebieta 3, 28338 San Vicente de la Sonsierra, La Rioja. Tel: +34 902 334 080; Fax: +34 941 600885; Email: info@eguren.com; Website: www.eguren.com
The Eguren family has been growing wine since 1870, though the date of foundation of the bodega is given as 1958, and it began to bottle wine in 1974. It has seventy hectares of vineyard. It also owns Señorio de San Vicente, set up in the same village in 1991 to exploit its eighteen-hectare San Vicente vineyard, and also Viñedos de Páganos in the village of that name. All three operate separately, fermenting in oak *tinas* and making wines of exceptional quality in the new high expression style. Sierra Cantabria has broken new ground with a white wine, Organza, made from forty-eight per cent Viura, thirty per cent Malvasía, and twenty-two per cent Garnacha Blanca. Its good red *joven*, made by carbonic maceration and sold under the name Murmuron, used to be made from ninety per cent Tempranillo and ten per cent Viura, but in the

2003 vintage was a varietal Tempranillo. Its best wines are the reds from *crianza* upward, and they are quite exceptionally good. At the top of the range are Finca El Bosque and, the show wine, Amancio, made in 500-litre casks followed by two years in new French oak. San Vicente produces a varietal Tempranillo Paludo of great quality. Viñedos de Páganos launched its outstanding wine with the 2001 vintage, a varietal Tempranillo. It is impossible to imagine a wine from this family that is not very good indeed.

BODEGAS TOBIA

Ctra Nacional 232 km 438, 26340 San Asensio, La Rioja.

Tel: +34 941 45 74 25; Fax: +34 941 45 74 01;

Email: tobia@bodegastobia.com; Website: www.bodegastobia.com

The Tobía family has long been growing grapes at San Asensio. In 1994 one of its members, Oscar Tobía, set up a boutique bodega to make high quality wine. The white *crianza* 2000 is unusual in being made from equal parts of Malvasía and Viura. The red *crianzas* and *reservas* are varietal Tempranillo and are good, if with rather a lot of oak. The very good top wine, Alma de Tobía, has ten per cent each of Mazuelo and Garnacha. It will repay keeping.

HEREDAD UGARTE

Carretera Vitoria–Logroño km 61, 01300 Laguardia, Alava.

Tel: +34 945 28 28 44; Fax: +34 945 27 13 19;

Email: info@heredadugarte.com; Website: www.heredadugarte.com

Although this bodega was founded in 1989, the Ugarte family has been growing wine since 1870 and has 125 hectares. The cellars really are cellars, hollowed out of the rock. The cheaper wines are sound if unexciting, but the *reservas* are very good. Dominio de Ugarte 1999 had five per cent Graciano, while the top, and excellent, Martín Cendoya 1998 had fifteen per cent Graciano and five per cent Mazuelo, given twenty-four months in casks with American staves and French ends – a way of getting the best of both worlds.

BODEGAS VALDEMAR

Camino Viejo s/n, 01320 Oyón, Alava. Tel: +34 945 62 21 88; Fax: +34 945 62 21 11; Email: bujanda@bujanda.com; Website: www.martinezbujanda.com

Until 2003 this bodega was famous as Martínez Bujanda, but then, confusingly, it changed its name. Joaquín Martínez Bujanda was a wine-grower on a very modest scale with ten hectares of vines in the Rioja Alavesa. In 1889 he set up a small winery built into a cave near Oyón. Those were modest beginnings, but the business expanded, steadily buying more vineyards. The wine, however, was sold in bulk to other bodegas and it was not until 1966 that the name appeared on a label. It is still a family-owned company, now in the fourth generation, and among the largest. A new, completely modern winery was opened in 1984. It is now run by Jesús Martínez Bujanda, whose father, also called Jesús, had a philosophy for making good wine: "A clean cellar, a clean cellar, a clean cellar!" And how he has followed his father's precept. He even goes to the length of softening the water to make cleaning easier.

Another unusual feature is that it is entirely self-sufficient for grapes, owning four vineyards in the Rioja Alta, one in the Rioja Baja, and twenty-three in the Rioja Alavesa, making 400 hectares in all. The Rioja Baja vineyard, Finca La Esperilla, has a rare microclimate on a relatively cool hillside, producing lighter wines with more finesse than is usual in the region. One of the best vineyards, Finca Valpiedra, was hived off in 1994 to form a separate entity (*see* above). Another unusual aspect is that Cabernet Sauvignon is grown, together with an unusually high proportion of Mazuelo. American oak is used for maturation, save for the Cabernet Sauvignon, which spends the first year in American oak and is then put into French; and the casks are kept in carefully temperature- and humidity-controlled conditions. There is a complete range of wines, the young sold under the name Valdemar and those with ageing under the name Conde de Valdemar. All are exceptionally good. (The *conde* himself is a benevolent bystander and takes no part in the business.) The barrel-fermented white avoids being over-oaked and shows that fine wines can be made from Viura. The *rosado* is a varietal Garnacha.

Of the red wines, the *crianzas* and *reservas* have about fifteen per cent Mazuelo. The very elegant *reserva* 1990 was the beginning of a new departure, being made of equal parts Tempranillo and Cabernet Sauvignon. The Finca Valpiedra wines, made with five per cent Cabernet Sauvignon, three per cent Graciano, and two per cent Mazuelo, are excellent and well structured. There is also a varietal Garnacha *reserva*, which shows how a well-balanced and carefully made Rioja Garnacha can have the ageing qualities and powerful style of wines made from this grape in Priorato. The top range is called Inspiración and includes a superb varietal Graciano. All the mature reds are notable for their ageing potential, helped perhaps by the unusually generous use of Mazuelo or Cabernet Sauvignon, which blend very well with the softer, fruity Tempranillo.

COMPANIA BODEGUERA DE VALENCISO

Apartado 227, 26200 Haro, La Rioja. Tel: +34 941 30 47 24; Fax: 941 30 47 28; Email: valenciso@valenciso.com; Website: www.valenciso.com

Founded in 1998 by two enthusiasts who had worked for Palacio, this is a boutique bodega indeed. In fact there was no bodega at all until 2005, when they built one at Ollauri. Before that they rented space. They make just one wine, but it is a very good wine – a varietal Tempranillo *reserva* matured in French oak. They own three hectares of vineyard and rent fifteen more.

BODEGAS VALSACRO

Ctra N 232 km 364, 26510 Pradejón, La Rioja. Tel: +34 941 39 80 08; Fax: +34 941 39 80 70; Email: ventas@valsacro.com; Website: www.valsacro.com

A boutique bodega founded in 1998 by the Escudero family. As it is in the Rioja Baja, the emphasis for red wines shifts to Garnacha, but it is not shy of experiment, growing Chardonnay and Cabernet Sauvignon. It also has old vines of a rare variety called Vidau, which it describes as "a mixture of Tempranillo and Garnacha with a predominance of Garnacha". There is a white Viura *crianza* but another made with sixty per cent Chardonnay. The 1999 red was fifty per cent Tempranillo, forty per cent Vidau, and ten per cent Mazuelo. These are early days and the winemaking is still evolving, but this is certainly one to watch and try.

VINA REAL

Ctra Logroño–Laguardia km 4.8, 01300 Laguardia, Alava. Tel: +34 945 62 52 10; Fax: +34 945 62 52 09; Email: laguardia@cune.com; Website: www.cune.com

Viña Real was once a brand owned by Cune (*see* above) – a good one, used for wines at the top of its range. But whereas the Cune wines were made from Rioja Alta grapes, the Viña Real wines were made with grapes from the Rioja Alavesa. In 2004 it was hived off.

When a Rioja shipper builds a new bodega he nearly always goes out of his way to beat his rivals in originality, and this is no exception. It is circular, and designed by French architect Philippe Mazières. On top of a hill, it can be seen for miles. What is more to the point, it is superbly equipped. The wines are soft, accessible, and very good. The grapes come mostly from 102 hectares of family-owned vineyards. There is a white, barrel-fermented Viura, but the red wines are the ones to look for, and they are likely to be even better in the future than they are now. The *reservas* have five per cent each of Mazuelo, Garnacha, and Graciano and go into new oak, mostly French with some American, while the *gran reservas* have five per cent

Graciano and go almost entirely into new French oak. The bodega is also experimenting with oak from Hungary and Romania. In 1993, a good year for Graciano, it made a varietal from the grape.

VINEDOS DEL PAGANOS
See Sierra Cantabria.

BODEGAS YSIOS
Camino de la Hoya s/n, 01300 Laguardia, Alava.

Tel: +34 945 60 06 40; Fax: +34 945 60 05 20;

Email: serdozai@adwes.com; Website: www.bodegasysios.com

There is no problem in locating this bodega; if you stand on the edge of the old town of Laguardia looking north towards the mountains, you will see a vast modern building, designed by Santiago Calatreva, with aluminium roofs that look like the waves of the sea. It is surrounded by its vineyards on a plateau 480 metres (1,574 feet) above sea level. It takes its name from the Egyptian goddess Isis. It was founded as recently as 1998 as part of the Iverus group, itself part of Bodegas y Bebidas (*see* Age, above), and the wines are made according to its philosophy, which it describes as "minimalist". The idea is to bring out the quality of the earth. Nothing could be more modern. It is built so that all the wine can be moved by gravity. It makes only *reservas* and is just beginning to get into its stride. This is one to watch.

5

The Centre North

NAVARRA

Geography

Navarra is a single autonomous province stretching up into the foothills of the Pyrenees and adjoining Rioja. Its capital is Pamplona, which lies to the north of the main wine-growing areas. A small part of Navarra is included within the Rioja DO. Apart from that, wine is grown in five areas: Tierra de Estella, the most westerly sub-zone, with 15.5 per cent of the vineyards; Valdizarbe, in the middle, with 7.9 per cent; Baja Montaña, to the north-east, with sixteen per cent; Ribera Alta, adjoining Valdizarbe to the south, with twenty-nine per cent; and Ribera Baja, at the south around Tudela, with 31.6 per cent. Ribera Alta is further sub-divided into three regions: Olite; Larín; and Marcilla.

Climate

There is not much difference between the first three sub-zones. All are described as dry, sub-humid, far enough from the sea to be essentially continental, yet far enough north to avoid being too hot in the summer. The summer high is 28°C (82°F) and the winter low is -2°C (28.4°F). In the Baja Montaña the rainfall is 683 millimetres (26.8 inches) and the mean temperature 12°C (53.6°F). The northern part of Ribera Alta is warmer and drier, with an average temperature of 13°C (55.4°F) and a rainfall of 525 millimetres (20.7 inches); but the southern part, the sub-divisions of Larín and Marcilla, is drier to the point of being classed as semi-arid, with a rainfall of 472 and 444 millimetres (18.6 and 17.5 inches) respectively and a mean

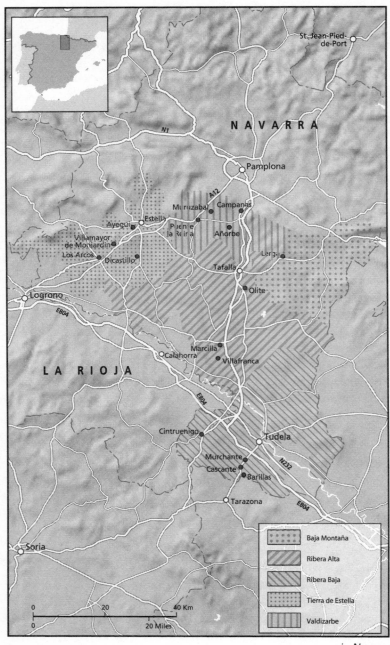

vi Navarra

temperature of 13.6°C (56.5°F). Ribera Baja is yet drier and hotter, with a rainfall of 448 millimetres and a mean temperature of 14°C (57.2°F). The vineyards in the pleasant rolling countryside vary between 250–650 metres (820–2,132 feet) in altitude. Throughout most of the area there are 2,200 hours of sunshine, but as many as 2,500 in the Ebro Valley.

Soils

Generally rather light brown with plenty of calcium and fairly fertile, beneath which is gravel sub-soil above chalk, though parts of the Ribera Baja are sand.

Grapes

Red varieties: Tempranillo; Mazuelo; Graciano; Garnacha; Cabernet Sauvignon; and Merlot. Many experimental varieties including: Monastrell; Ruby Cabernet; Cinsault; Bolicaire; Alicante; Gamay; Royalty; Tinta de Toro (another clone of Tempranillo); Cabernet Franc; Malbec; Pinot Noir; Sangiovese; Syrah; and Barbera.

White varieties: Macabeo; Chardonnay; Garnacha Blanca; Malvasía; and Moscatel de Grano Menudo. Again there are many experimental white varieties including: Xarel.lo; Parellada; Colombard; Sémillon; Chenin Blanc; Airén; Verdejo; Palomino; Syrah Blanc; Pinot Blanc; Riesling; Barbera; Gewürztraminer; and even Thompson Seedless.

Garnacha, which used to be predominant, still occupies thirty-two per cent of the vineyard, but is declining and has been overtaken by Tempranillo with thirty-six per cent.

Planting

Traditionally vineyards were planted in the square Marco Real pattern with 1.6 metres (5.2 feet) spacing, but some were on a wider pattern known as Ancho with up to 3 metres (9.8 feet) between rows. The vines were pruned *en vaso*, but recently there has been a lot of experimenting, using Guyot in the cooler regions, Geneva Double Curtain in the warmer ones, and Gobelet for the hottest sites. Growers are being encouraged to use wires, and about forty per cent of the vineyards are already being harvested mechanically, which has the advantage, particularly for white wines, that it can be done in the cool of night. There are about 2,400 vines per hectare.

Vineyard area

18,387 hectares.

Authorized yield

Ribera Baja: white 56hl/ha; red 42ha/ha. Other zones: white 42hl/ha; red 35hl/ha. In practice the average production is 35–40hl/ha.

Wines

Traditionally Navarra is noted for its *rosados*, which may be between 11–13.5% ABV. There is an increasing production of whites, between 10.5–12.5% ABV, though barrel-fermented Chardonnays may be one per cent higher, and reds between 11.5–14% ABV. There are also some white *vinos de licor* Moscatel, from 15–18% ABV, which must contain not less than four per cent unfermented sugar. In the past the emphasis was on *jóvenes*, but is now moving more and more to *crianzas, reservas,* and *gran reservas*. Moscatel *vino de licor* must be aged for at least two years with at least eighteen months in oak, but for these there is no limit on the size of casks.

Production

722,852 hectolitres (2003).

Vintages

1990 (3); 1991 (3); 1992 (3); 1993 (4); 1994 (4); 1995 (5); 1996 (4); 1997 (3); 1998 (4); 1999 (4); 2000 (4); 2001 (5); 2002 (4); 2003 (4); 2004 (5).

With so many zones and microclimates, these figures act only as a rough guide.

As Navarra lies next to Rioja (part of which lies within the province of Navarra), it might be assumed to have had the same history, but this is not so. Wine-growing is inevitably traced back to the Romans, and the Moors did not put an end to it. In the Middle Ages, like Rioja, it benefited from the steady passage of pilgrims along the route to Santiago de Compostela. As Navarre it was one of the most powerful kingdoms, stretching right into what is now France. It became part of the new kingdom of Spain when Ferdinand the Catholic seized all the land south of the Pyrenees in 1512. It was not until 1791 that Louis XVI renounced his title as King of France and Navarre to become King of the French. But the more recent history is what matters. Traditionally the leading grape of the area was Garnacha, which can produce very good wines, especially *rosados*; and modern viticulture gives much longer-lived wines, here as in Rioja and Priorato, whereas the old ones tended to be short lived. Nevertheless the wines historically were held in high regard. Samuel Pepys, in his diary for February 10, 1669, recorded: "And then [the Duke of York] did now mightily commend some new sort of wine lately found out, called Navarr wine; which I tasted, and is I think good wine." The editor's footnote suggests that it may have been Jurançon, but this is manifest nonsense. The Spanish ambassador had recently given the duke a recipe for a sauce and probably gave the wine as well.

The wines of Navarra were highly esteemed in Spain. They also were exported to England from San Sebastián. The trade was described in a book published in London in 1700 titled, *A description of San Sebastián by one who has been there*. The author described how "the late war with France, from which we received those excellent Graves Médoc and wines from Pontacq, was the reason for which our Parliament placed such high custom taxes on French wines and other liquors from that nation, so that the merchants, in order to pay fewer taxes, looked for a way to supply themselves elsewhere... fortunately they found within Spain a region called Navarra... which supplies us with wine as good as any which comes from France..." But although they were exported to England and to Ireland at the end of the seventeenth century, and continued to be exported until the end of the eighteenth century, they made little mark here until recent years. Production was large. At the beginning of the nineteenth century there were 30,000 hectares of vineyards, a good deal more than there are today, though they were probably less productive, and by the time of phylloxera the figure had increased to 49,213 hectares. The French arrived and traded in the wines as they had in Rioja, but with less impact and left no permanent legacy. Navarra was overshadowed by its neighbour; the relatively greater difficulties of transport and communication no doubt played their part, as did the predominance of Garnacha.

Phylloxera arrived in 1892 and, as has been seen, the French vineyards were re-established and France went protectionist. Phylloxera wiped out nearly all the vineyards, but these were gradually replanted, rising from practically nothing to 11,350 hectares in 1906 and to 26,330 in 1920. The growers were mostly smallholders and the history of this time is very much that of the cooperative movement, largely thanks to the leadership of the Catholic Agrarian Co-Operative Movement with its motto "*Unos por Otros, Dios por Todos*" (Some for others, God for all). Ninety per cent of all the wine produced came from the cooperatives, and it was not very good: massive "jug" wines for immediate drinking. The regular creation and occasional failures of these co-ops makes a fascinating story, but it falls within the sphere of economic history rather than this book. The area under vines steadily increased until in 1935 it was 30,000 hectares, though this includes the vineyards within the province of Navarra that were, and still are, included in the Rioja DO. Although there were eventually some sixty-nine cooperatives (and there are still about fifty), the area never quite got back to what it had been before phylloxera, and eventually started to decline, so that in 1980 there were 28,000 hectares and no new cooperatives were being founded. At that time the cooperatives were producing ninety-three per cent of the wine.

The great increase in the quality and prestige of Navarra wines was led by the merchant houses, some of which are of considerable age. The first moves to create a DO date as far back as 1933, but everything got stifled by the Civil War and then by the economic consequences of the World War II, so that the regulations were not finally approved until 1975. Soon afterwards there was a very important development: the establishment of a viticulture and oenology centre, at first a company called EVENSA and subsequently EVENA (*Estación de Viticulture y Enología de Navarra*), with the aid of funds provided by the provincial government and enthusiastically supported by the wine-growers. It is an extremely impressive place, with vine nurseries to produce virus-free plants of many varieties, experimental vineyards in all the sub-zones, and microvinifications to test grape varieties and techniques: 250 a year. Experiments are now being carried out by maturing wines in different kinds of oak, and comparing those from hand-picked vineyards with those that are machine picked. The great thing achieved initially, though, was simply to clean up the bodegas: old casks that harboured all manner of false flavours were burnt and stainless steel came in. Bodegas that had been producing filthy wines began to make clean, good ones that showed the great potential of the district. Now everyone has stainless steel and temperature control. While Rioja chose to stick to its very successful traditions, Navarra could and did branch out, aiming away from the production of Rioja lookalikes to create new, highly attractive wines. In this they were helped by the very liberal attitude taken by the authorities to the introduction of foreign grape varieties. There is a strong school of thought that favours sticking to Spanish varieties and developing them, but Navarra was effectively starting in the quality wine markets from scratch, and some of the new varieties, notably Chardonnay, Merlot, and Cabernet Sauvignon, have proved very successful. Viura is still substantially used for making white wines, but has been joined and enhanced by Chardonnay; some excellent wines are now being produced from each and often from blends of the two, sometimes barrel fermented. The traditional Graciano is now little grown. Garnacha is still used on a large scale for the excellent *rosados* and *jóvenes*, but has been joined by Tempranillo and the French varieties. New vineyards have been planted and others replanted, so the proportion made by cooperatives has declined. And the proportion of wine sold in bottle has gone up from fifteen per cent in 1970 to almost 100 per cent today.

Unfortunately, though, some of the smaller growers still go in for quantity rather than quality and cannot be persuaded to reduce their yields. Moreover, when planting the new varieties they have done so with insufficient expertise, planting them in areas where they will not ripen. The burden of this is borne by the cooperatives. Navarra is still lurking beneath the shadow of Rioja and generally has to charge less, but it has emerged as a grower of world class wines which, although they may contain varying quantities of foreign varieties, are proudly Spanish and do not attempt to be anything else, even though critics occasionally say that Navarra is an outpost of the New World. Things really started to take off in the 1970s and 1980s. With the aid of EVENA, Navarra is still developing. It would do well to concentrate on its traditional varieties and to use the foreign ones to give new dimensions rather than to rely on them too much, but it cannot be gainsaid that some of the best are made from the foreign varieties. It is an exciting place to be.

Some leading bodegas

BODEGAS Y VINEDOS ARTAZU
Mayor 3, 31195 Artazu, Navarra.
Tel: +34 945 60 01 19; Fax: +34 945 60 08 50; Email: artazu@artadi.com
This boutique bodega was founded in 2000 and produced its first vintage in 2001. There is an old house in the village that in its time has been a school and a prison, and is going to be the Artazu commercial centre. It is an offshoot of Artadi, one of the best Rioja bodegas, and is unique in two ways. First, it produces only Garnachas – from low-yielding, close-planted vines. Secondly, it has nothing to do with *reservas*. The winemaker said: "Put a third-rate wine in a barrel and leave it there for three years and you get a *gran reserva*." Perfectly true, of course, but it does not have to be a third-rate wine. All the wines here are absolutely first rate. The grapes are carefully gone over and more than half are usually rejected, to be used for bulk wine. Under the name Artazuri there is a *rosado*, made from relatively young vines, and a red that spends four to five months in wood, all of which is French. The top wine, the big and beautiful Santa Cruz de Artazu, spends a time in wood, anything from eight months to

over a year, depending on the vintage, first in old wood then a proportion in new. It is superlative and will be even finer with a few years in bottle.

VINEDOS Y BODEGAS ASENSIO

Mayor 84, 31293 Sesma, Navarra. Tel: +34 948 69 80 40; Fax: +34 948 69 80 97; Email: info@bodegasasensio.com; Website: www.bodegasasensio.com

A family bodega founded in 1994. It has seventy-two hectares of vineyard and in a decade has established a formidable reputation for top-quality wines. In 2000 it made three *reservas*: varietals from Cabernet Sauvignon and Merlot, and a blend of fifty per cent Cabernet Sauvignon, thirty per cent Merlot; and twenty per cent Tempranillo. The varietals were matured in French oak; the blend in American, French, and Russian; all sold as Javier Asensio. Its top *reserva* is Brojal, which in 2000 had sixty-six per cent Cabernet Sauvignon and thirty-four per cent Merlot, matured in French oak.

CASTILLO DE MONJARDIN

Viña Rellanada s/n, 31242 Villamayor de Monjardín, Navarra. Tel: +34 948 53 74 12; Fax: +34 948 53 74 36; Email: cristina@monjardin.es; Website: www.monjardin.es

This family-owned bodega is in the valley of San Esteban within the Estella zone. The family has owned land on the Pilgrims' Way since the twelfth century, and the castle is a thousand years old, but not the bodega. It has 120 hectares of vineyard at an altitude of 345–570 metres (1,132–1,870 feet), that are cooled at night by the *cierzo* wind. They are planted with low-yielding clones, and pruned by the cordon royal method that allows mechanical harvesting, which is done at night for the Chardonnays. They were planted in 1986 and 1987, before the company itself was formed in 1988. Initially the grapes were all sold, but in 1992 the vines were considered old enough to make good wine and vinification started. It began to export in 1995. The whole winery is semi-underground, built into the side of a hill, and is completely modern. Its wines are very good, especially the Chardonnays, of which there are three, all single vineyard wines. The fresh *joven* is fermented in stainless steel, the *reserva* in new French oak, the barrel-fermented in French oak with three months in the same barrel. The *rosado* is a single-vineyard varietal Merlot, barrel fermented and left on its lees until February. There are two red varietal Merlots, the top one Deyo. The red *joven* is from Merlot and Tempranillo, given three months in American oak. The *crianza* is from forty per cent each of Cabernet Sauvignon and Merlot, plus twenty per cent Tempranillo. A similar grape mix is used for the *reserva*, which is matured in two- and three-year-old American and French casks, while the *gran reserva* has two years in new oak.

BODEGAS JULIAN CHIVITE

Ribera 34, 31592 Cintruénigo, Navarra. Tel: +34 948 81 10 00; Fax: +34 948 81 14 07; Email: info@bodegaschivite.com; Website: www.bodegaschivite.com
The date given for the foundation is 1860, when Claudio Chivite started taking his wines into France, but the Chivite family has been growing wine in Navarra for much longer than that. There is documentary evidence going back to 1633, and although there is no continuous record, the family credibly claims to be the eleventh generation of wine-growers. And not only was an ancestor the first named person to have exported wine, but Chivite has been doing so ever since, and is usually the largest exporter from Navarra. Success has been based on quality, but far from resting on laurels, it has kept completely up to date and the wines are among the very best. The bodega in Cintruénigo was built in 1872 and completely renovated in 1988, but it has steadily expanded and in 1988 bought a new estate, the Señorío de Arínzano in Estella. Architect Rafael Moneo was employed to build a fine new bodega there in one of the most beautiful valleys it is possible to imagine at 420–80 metres (1,378–1,575 feet) above sea level. The vineyard is cultivated organically, and part of the estate is given over to nature conservation. There are now 550 hectares of vineyard in all.

Most of the wines are sold under the mark Gran Feudo, but in 1985 it created the Colección 125 Aniversario, to celebrate 125 years from the official foundation, for their top wines made in the new bodega, which works entirely by gravity. The Gran Feudo white is from Chardonnay and is left on its lees until ready for bottling. The *rosado* is from Garnacha. There is a red *joven* from Garnacha, but the red *crianza* has seventy per cent Tempranillo, twenty-five per cent Garnacha, and five per cent Cabernet Sauvignon. The *reserva* is eighty per cent Tempranillo, the rest Cabernet Sauvignon and Merlot, aged in fifty-fifty Allier and American oak. The Viñas Viejas comes from very old vines, seventy-five per cent Tempranillo, twenty per cent Garnacha, the rest being Merlot and Cabernet Sauvignon, and is aged in French oak. There is also a Blanco de Moscatel made in new Allier oak. The Colección 125 Blanco 2002 was a Chardonnay, barrel-fermented in French oak and left on its lees until bottled in July 2003. The 1999 *reserva* was sixty-eight per cent Tempranillo, thirty per cent Merlot, and two per cent Cabernet Sauvignon, while the 2000 was sixty-six per cent, twenty per cent, and fourteen per cent, illustrating how the blends are varied to suit the grapes of the year. Finally there is the Vendímia Tardia, a natural sweet wine from botrytis-affected Moscatel de Grano Menudo, picked in five passes through the vineyard and fermented in new French oak. The Gran Feudo range is very good indeed, the Colección range simply glorious.

VINA MAGANA

San Miguel 9, 31523 Barillas, Navarra. Tel: +34 948 85 00 34; Fax: +34 948 85 15 36; Email: bodegas@vinamagana.com; Website: www.vinamagana.com

Situated in a remote little town, and not all that easy to find, this small bodega is something quite apart. It makes wines of the very highest class, all of which are red. It was founded in 1968 by three brothers who modelled themselves on a Bordeaux château and pioneered French vines, which they rear themselves in their own nurseries and train on wires, pruning them to give a low yield of forty hectolitres per hectare. It is self-sufficient in vines with, at the moment, 120 hectares of vineyard planted almost entirely with French varieties (there is a little Tempranillo), including a very large planting of Merlot, with Cabernet Sauvignon coming second. Only the best of the grapes are used, the rest being sold on. It claims to have made the first Spanish varietal Merlot, and that grape remains king. The range begins with Dignus, the 1998 being from sixty per cent Merlot and Tempranillo, thirty per cent Cabernet Sauvignon, and "other varieties", aged for three months in new Allier and Spanish oak, with a further nine in "semi-new" casks. The Baron de Magaña 1999 *crianza* was made in two forms, one a varietal Merlot, the other from fifty per cent Merlot, twenty per cent Cabernet Sauvignon, ten per cent Tempranillo, and "other contributory grapes"; both were given one year in new Allier oak. The Viña Magaña Merlot *reserva* was given a year in Allier oak and then no less than five in bottle before release. The Viña Magaña *reserva* 1994 was from sixty-five per cent Merlot, fifteen per cent Cabernet Sauvignon, twenty per cent Malbec and Syrah, with a year in semi-new French and American oak, while the *gran reserva* 1985 was seventy per cent Merlot, fifteen per cent Cabernet Sauvignon, ten per cent Cabernet Franc, and five per cent Malbec. Production is small and the wines hard to find, but very well worth seeking.

BODEGAS MARCO REAL

Carretera Pamplona–Zaragoza km 38, 31390 Olite, Navarra.
Tel: +34 948 71 21 93; Fax: +34 948 71 23 43;
Email: info@lanavarra.com; Website: www.bodegasmarcoreal.com

Founded in 1988, but not in production until 1991, it is now part of the Navarra distillery group and has 200 hectares of vineyard. In the Olite zone, it makes good wines under the mark Homenaje, with a subsidiary range under the mark Mirador de la Reina. There is a complete range of Homenaje wines with the reds the most notable, especially the Reserva de la Familia, which is unusual in containing a proportion of Graciano. Its finest wines, though, come from its associated company at the same address, Señorío de Andión, with its own holding of sixty hectares of low production vineyard. The acclaimed high expression *tinto* 2001 was made from Cabernet Sauvignon, Graciano, Merlot, and Tempranillo, matured in Allier oak.

BODEGAS Y VINEDOS NEKEAS

Las Huertas s/n, 31154 Añorbe, Navarra.

Tel: +34 948 35 02 96; Fax: +34 948 35 03 00; Email: nekeas@ibernet.com

Six families got together in 1987 and thought out this enterprise. Now there are eight and it dates its foundation officially from 1993. They run it as a sort of cooperative. It has 230 hectares of vineyards in the north of the DO, most still relatively young – planted around 1989 – but already producing good wines. The potential is enormous. It sells under the brands Nekeas and Vega Sindoa. The 1995 Vega Sindoa Tempranillo/Cabernet and the 1995 Merlot were in Robert Parker's 90+ class, and the 1997 barrel-fermented Garnacha, from 100-year-old vines, was extraordinarily good. El Chaparral 2001, from a vineyard of that name with Garnacha vines over sixty years old, given nine months in fifty per cent new oak and fifty per cent one-year-old American, is excellent, as is the varietal Merlot from the Marain vineyard. The *tinto crianza* 2001 was fifty-two per cent Cabernet Sauvignon, thirty-three per cent Tempranillo, and fifteen per cent Merlot. The same varieties were used in the 2000 *reserva*, but with the last two in equal amounts. Among the whites the Vega Sindoa Chardonnay Cuvée Allier is outstanding.

BODEGAS NUESTRA SRA DEL ROMERO S CO-OP

Ctra de Tarazona 33, 31520 Cascante, Navarra.

Tel: +34 948 85 14 11; Fax: +34 948 84 45 04;

Email: info@bodegasdelromero.com; Website: www.bodegasdelromero.com

The Cascante cooperative, founded in 1951 and since enlarged by amalgamation with those of Los Arcos and Sesma, is now the biggest in Navarra and one of the best, with a well-established export trade. Its 1,000 members have 1,100 hectares of vineyard in the zones Ribera Baja, Tierra de Estella, and Ribera Alta. If its wines do not rise to the heights, they are reliable and good value. They are sold under a bewildering number of names: Malon de Echaide; Torrecilla; Plandenas; Señor de Cascante; Señorío de Yaniz; and Viña Parot.

BODEGAS OCHOA

Alcalde Maillata 2, 31390 Olite, Navarra. Tel: +34 948 74 00 06; Fax: +34 948 74 00 48; Email: info@bodegasochoa.com; Website: www.bodegasochoa.com

This large family bodega in the beautiful old town of Olite was established in 1845, though the family can trace its wine-growing history back as far as the fourteenth century. Today it is one of the leaders for quality, indeed the head of the family, Javier Ochoa, led Navarra into quality wines and did much to establish EVENA. It has 143 hectares of vineyard at 400–450 metres (1,312–1,476 feet) above sea level, and there are seventy hectares of good vineyard soil waiting to be planted. Most of the grapes are machine picked, which it finds gives better quality, and every parcel is vinified separately, the larger ones being split up. It goes without saying that the wines are immaculately made. The oak used for ageing is seventy per cent American and thirty per cent French, the American oak found best for maturing Tempranillo. Most of the wines are red but there is a white from seventy per cent Viura and thirty per cent Chardonnay, and two *rosados*, one a varietal Garnacha and the other, Lágrima, from equal parts of Garnacha and Cabernet Sauvignon; it is remarkably aromatic. There are red varietals, which it pioneered, from Tempranillo, Merlot, and Cabernet Sauvignon. The *joven tinto* is sixty per cent Tempranillo and forty per cent Garnacha. Another red is from equal parts of Garnacha and Graciano. The *reservas* and *gran reservas* have fifty-five per cent Tempranillo, thirty per cent Cabernet Sauvignon, and fifteen per cent Merlot. They are delicious wines of impressive length. The excellent *gran reservas* are made from the same grape mix. The Vendímia Seleccionada wines are from equal parts of Merlot and Cabernet Sauvignon. All of these reds have real ageing potential. Finally there is a delicious, light, sweet Moscatel, not made like most are as a *mistela* by adding alcohol, but by late harvesting, chilling to cut off the fermentation, and then microfiltering.

SENORIO DE BODEGA OTAZU

Señorío de Otazu s/n, 31174 Echauri, Navarra. Tel: +34 948 32 92 00; Fax: +34 948 32 93 53; Email: admin@otazu.com; Website: www.otazu.com

This is the most northerly vineyard in Navarra and perhaps in Spain, planted in 1991 by Gabarbide. The bodega building is striking – indeed a palace. There is a 110-hectare vineyard growing Chardonnay, Cabernet Sauvignon, Tempranillo, and Merlot with eighteen clones. Its wines, sold as Palacio de Otazu, are very highly regarded. There are two Chardonnays, one barrel fermented. The *tinto crianza* 2000 was from seventy per cent Merlot, ten per cent Tempranillo, and twenty per cent Cabernet Sauvignon. The *reserva* 1999 was made from the same grape mix. The top Altar 1999 was from eighty per cent Cabernet Sauvignon and twenty per cent Merlot. They are matured in French oak. As the vineyard is still relatively young, the future looks very promising indeed.

PALACIO DE LA VEGA

Condesa de la Vega s/n, 31263 Dicastillo, Navarra. Tel: +34 948 52 70 09; Fax: +34 948 52 73 33; Website: www.palaciodelavega.com

Palacio de la Vega, set up in 1991, really is in a palace, albeit a twentieth century one. In 1995 it was acquired by the Pernod Ricard group. It has a call on 300 hectares of vineyard, all surrounding the castle in Tierra de Estella, but only owns thirty-three. They are harvested mostly mechanically, which is particularly helpful for the Chardonnay as it can be harvested by night. The barrel-fermented Chardonnay spends three months in new French oak. The *rosado* is eighty per cent Garnacha with twenty per cent Cabernet Sauvignon. The reds begin with a Tempranillo *joven,* but eighty per cent of the production is *crianza* and above. These include varietals from Tempranillo, Cabernet Sauvignon, and Merlot. The very good and complex Conde de la Vega is fermented in new Allier oak and is typically sixty per cent Cabernet Sauvignon and twenty per cent each of Tempranillo and Merlot from low yield vineyards.

PALACIO DE MURUZABAL

Calle La Cruz s/n, 31152 Muruzábal, Navarra.
Tel: +34 948 34 42 79; Fax: +34 948 34 43 25; Email: a.marino@eresmas.net

Established in 1991 under the name A & B Marino, in the north of the DO, it is surrounded by its thirty-four hectares of vineyard, but only uses part of the grapes for its own wines, the rest being sold on. Its barrel-fermented Chardonnay is one of the best, but it also makes excellent reds.

BODEGAS PIEDEMONTE, S CO-OP

Rúa Romana s/n, 31390 Olite, Navarra. Tel: +34 948 71 24 06; Fax: +34 948 74 00 90; Email: bodega@piedemonte.com; Website: www.piedemonte.com

One of the most recent and modern of the cooperatives, founded in 1992 by eighty-five growers with 450 hectares of vineyard who were disillusioned with extant cooperatives and wanted to make better wine. It makes a complete range of thoroughly reliable wines under the brands Piedemonte, Oligitum, Viña Egozcue, Memorandum, and Agnes de Cleves.

BODEGAS PRINCIPE DE VIANA

Mayor 191, 31521 Murchante, Navarra. Tel: +34 948 83 86 40; Fax: +34 948 81 85 74; Email: info@principedeviana.com; Website: www.principedeviana.com

Príncipe de Viana, named after a fifteenth-century prince, began life in 1983 as an official organization to improve the marketing of agrarian products, particularly wine produced by the cooperatives. It changed to its present name in 1992, became a private company, and totally changed direction. It rose to top the league of Navarra wine exporters in 1996 and built a fine new bodega in 1998. It now has its own 400 hectares of vineyard, with automated irrigation, that are harvested mechanically. Additional grapes are bought in. For ageing, mostly American oak is used. It produces a complete range of wines under three marks: Campo Nuevo for the basic range sold in Spain; Agramont, which is used only for export; and Principe de Viana, which is used for the top range in all markets. There is a fourth range, Pleno, for supermarkets. All are stabilized by ultra cooling. They are very good and good value. One gets the impression that a degree of inspiration has come from the wines of the New World; indeed they claim to have been the first to use barrel fermentation in Navarra, guided by the Australian winemaker Nick Butler. The white for England is made from eighty-five per cent Chardonnay and fifteen per cent Viura. For the Spanish market there is a varietal Chardonnay. There is also a varietal Chardonnay barrel-fermented in American oak. In *rosados* there are varietals from Garnacha and Cabernet Sauvignon. Red varietals include a Garnacha made from old vines and a Tempranillo, both *jóvenes*, with a Cabernet Sauvignon *crianza*. The blended reds include *crianzas*, typically from sixty per cent Cabernet Sauvignon and forty per cent Tempranillo; *reservas* from equal parts of Tempranillo, Cabernet Sauvignon, and Merlot; and the excellent top of the range 1423 (the year King Carlos III created the principality), made from fifty per cent Tempranillo, thirty per cent Cabernet Sauvignon, and twenty per cent Merlot, the Tempranillo coming from vines at least thirty years old, and fermented in French oak.

BODEGA DE SARRIA

Finca Señorío de Sarría, 31100 Puente La Reina, Navarra.
Tel: +34 948 20 22 00; Fax: +34 948 20 22 02;
Email: info@bodesa.net; Website: www.senioriasarria.com

Founded in 1954, this bodega owed its origin to an industrialist who bought 1,100 hectares of land on the Pilgrims' Way to Santiago de Compostela, which included vineyards, but was mostly forest, orchards, and farmland, and whose aim was to produce top-quality wine. It is a most beautiful place. In 1981 it was bought by a savings bank, La Caja de Ahorros de Navarra, which greatly expanded it. There are now 210 hectares of vineyard including outposts in Olite and Corella. The wines are sold under the mark Señorio de Sarria, the basic ones forming the Tradition range, which are sound and reliable without reaching the peaks, with a top Viñedo range of mostly varietal and single vineyard wines, all of which are very good. The whites are from Chardonnay, the top Viñedo No 3 a very good wine, being barrel-fermented in Nevers oak, yet not tasting over-oaked. The *rosados* are varietal Garnachas, the top being Viñedo No 5. Red wines in the Tradition range include a *crianza* from seventy per cent Tempranillo and thirty per cent Cabernet Sauvignon, a *reserva* from equal parts of Cabernet Sauvignon and Merlot, and a *gran reserva* being mainly Merlot with two years in French oak. The Viñedo reds are No 4, a Merlot with six months in Allier oak; No 7, a Graciano also with six months in Allier oak; No 8, a Mazuelo with eight months in American oak; and No 9, a Cabernet Sauvignon with six months oak ageing, first in French and later in American. Viñedo Sotes is blended from Tempranillo, Garnacha, Merlot, Cabernet Sauvignon, Graciano, and Mazuelo, with six months in Allier oak. Finally there is a Moscatel from vineyards in the dry climate of Corella.

BODEGAS VALCARLOS

Ctra Circunvalación s/n, 31210 Los Arcos, Navarra. Tel/Fax: +34 948 64 08 06; Email: info@bodegasvalcarlos.com; Website: www.bodegasvalcarlos.com

This was set up by the Bodegas Faustino group in 2000 with eighty hectares of vineyard bought ten years earlier. Everything is very modern, not least the bodega building, and it markets wines under the marks Marqués de Valcarlos and Fortius, the latter being more upmarket. In both ranges the whites are blends of Viura and Chardonnay, the *rosados* from Tempranillo and Merlot, and the reds from Tempranillo and Cabernet Sauvignon. In the Fortius range there are also varietals from Merlot, Cabernet Sauvignon, and Tempranillo, though the last has some Cabernet Sauvignon in it. Its top wine is Elite de Fortius, made from equal parts of Merlot and Cabernet Sauvignon.

FINCA ZUBASTIA/BODEGAS ADA

Extramuros s/n, 31494 Lerga, Navarra.
Tel: +34 948 19 97 33; Fax: +34 948 19 97 32.

A very young bodega, founded in 2000 with the aid of wine-growers who got fed up with the co-op. It has forty hectares in Lerga and Mendivil. All the Garnacha is over sixty years old and some over 100 years – vines that survived phylloxera – with new plantings of Cabernet Sauvignon, Tempranillo, and Merlot. All are grown *en vaso* and have to be hand harvested. Some Cabernet Sauvignon from old plantings is bought in. At the moment there are only two wines, both necessarily *jóvenes*, sold under the name Ada: a *rosado*, which is a varietal Garnacha, and a red from fifty-four per cent Tempranillo, twenty-two per cent Garnacha, thirteen per cent Cabernet Sauvignon, and eleven per cent Merlot. Both are good and promise well for the future. This is one to watch.

OTHER WINES

GUELBENZU

31520 Cascante, Navarra. Tel: +34 948 85 00 55; Fax: +34 948 85 00 98; Email: guelbenzu@masbytes.es; Website: www.guelbenzu.com

A family-owned bodega now in its fifth generation, it is situated firmly within the Navarra DO, but opted out in 2001, giving it a free hand with the grapes it grows and what it does with them. It is now in the VT Ribera del Queles, a new denomination that it virtually created. The ancient bodega is next to the pink, nineteenth-century family house, standing high on a hillside above its garden. There was a period of eclipse when the grapes were sold to a cooperative, but things got going again in 1980 and it has been making wines of excellent quality every since. All the grapes come from its small vineyards in the Queiles Valley between 360–480 metres (1,181–1,575 feet) above sea level, which are planted for low yields – although they are individually small, they make a total of ninety-two hectares. Only French Allier oak is used for the maturation. Some *jóvenes* are sold under the name Jardín. Then comes Vierlas, made from twenty-six per cent Cabernet Sauvignon, twenty-four per cent Syrah, twenty per cent Merlot, twenty per cent Garnacha, and ten per cent Tempranillo. The next up is Azul, typically from forty-six per cent Tempranillo, thirty per cent Cabernet Sauvignon, and twenty-four per cent Merlot, which ages for nine months in two-, three-, and four-year-old casks. The top is Evo, made from Cabernet Sauvignon, Merlot, and Tempranillo, and given twelve months in new oak. The grape mix varies from year to year, but in 2003 was sixty/twenty-five/fifteen. It recently introduced Lautus at the very top, made only in the best years from fifty per cent Tempranillo, twenty per cent Cabernet Sauvignon, twenty per cent Merlot, and ten per cent Garnacha. At whatever level, these are excellent wines and the best are superb.

6

Castilla y León

Castilla – or Old Castile – is the cradle of Spanish culture. The Spanish language is called Castillian and here it is spoken in its purest form. Castilla is rightly thought of as a country of castles, for the citizens were once armed to the teeth and needed to be. The Moorish occupation of Spain got as far as the Cordillera Cantábrica mountains. The Christians were on the other side in the Asturias, only a little kingdom; but they were to reconquer Spain and drive the Moors out. This was where it all began, and beneath the towns were mazes of secret passages for defence and escape – later they came in useful to winemakers and many still exist. Here, too, is the great medieval university of Salamanca and some of Spain's most wonderful cathedrals, such as Burgos and León.

In terms of wine, though, the past was not very illustrious until Vega Sicilia was established in the nineteenth century – the first Spanish "table wine" to be acknowledged as great by world standards. It led the way and is still in front. Today Castillian wines are exciting, but its four major districts have very different histories and make very different wines. There is a fifth, El Bierzo, that although a part of Castilla, is far apart in terms of both geography and the style of its wines, so it will be included in the next chapter. The four districts lie along or around the river Duero. What a river! You can follow its course past Ribera del Duero, then Cigales, Rueda, and Toro. If you go on further and cross the Portuguese frontier, you come to the home of port and then Vinho Verde. It is one of the great wine rivers of Europe.

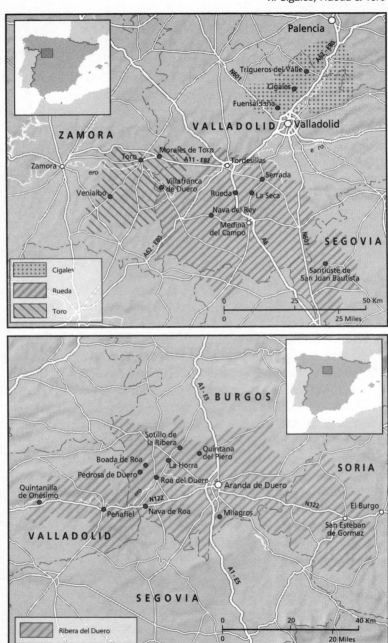

vii Cigales, Rueda & Toro

Cigales
Rueda
Toro

Ribera del Duero

viii Ribero del Duero

CIGALES

Geography

Cigales lies to the north of Valladolid and to the west of Ribera del Duero, in a fairly flat, infertile piece of countryside drained by the river Pisuerga, which flows into the Duero just southwest of Valladolid. The town of Cigales itself is a sleepy little place with a rather disproportionate Renaissance church; but the striking feature is the array of *luceras* (chimneys) rising from the earth and each showing the presence of an ancient cellar. The villages are even sleepier. Finding the bodegas is often difficult, as they revel in anonymity. It is high up in the central plain with the vineyards 700–800 metres (1,292–1,472 feet) above sea level, stretching from Dueñas almost to Valladolid.

Climate

The climate is said to be moderated by Atlantic influences, but if so, goodness only knows what it would be without them. It is continental, with summer temperatures rising to 40°C (104°F), and with very cold winters, the temperature going down to -6°C (21°F). There is frequent frost damage. The average temperature is 12.2°C (54°F), with 407 millimetres (16 inches) of rainfall, mostly in spring and autumn, and 2,616 hours of sunshine.

Soil

The typical, rather infertile soil of good vineyards usually looks light brown, sometimes with a touch of red, containing some limestone and lots of large stones, over a base of clay and marl.

Grapes

Red varieties: Tinto del País (the local name for Tempranillo); Garnacha Tinta; Garnacha Roja; Merlot; and Cabernet Sauvignon.
White varieties: Verdejo; Albillo; and Sauvignon Blanc.
The red varieties occupy eighty per cent of the vineyard area.

Planting

Traditionally this was in a square *marco real* pattern with three metres (10 feet) spacing, but recently planted vineyards are trained on wires.

Vineyard area

2,700 hectares.

Authorized yields
49hl/ha.

Wines

Rosado Cigales nuevo are *jóvenes* which must be labelled with the vintage year. Alcoholic strength 10.5–13% ABV. They must be made from at least sixty per cent Tinto del País and at least twenty per cent of the white varieties.

Rosado Cigales may not be sold until after December 31 of the year following the vintage. The minimum strength is 11% ABV, but otherwise the regulations are the same.

The *tintos* have an alcoholic strength 12–14% ABV. They must be at least eighty-five per cent Tinto del País. With suitable ageing there are *crianzas*, *reservas,* and *gran reservas*.

The traditional wines were *rosados,* but the production of reds is rising steadily, and these are seen as the wines of the future. There are no white wines within the DO, the grapes being used in the *rosados* or for making table wines.

Production
77,700 hectolitres (2003).

Vintages

1995 (3); 1996 (3); 1997 (3); 1998 (4); 1999 (4); 2000 (4); 2001 (4); 2002 (4 red/3 *rosado*); 2003 (5 red/4 *rosado*); 2004 (5 red/4 *rosado*).

Cigales makes unusually good *rosado* wines, which have been traditional here for centuries. There has always been a great demand for them in the north of Spain, but they are not much seen on the export markets thanks to their colour. Despite the versatility of *rosados*, they have never become universally popular; perhaps people think that they fall between two stools, and they are so easy to drink that there is a snob reaction against them. Since they're at their best on a hot summer's day, this does not help them in the frozen north; and while they can give great pleasure, no *rosado* can possibly be regarded as a great wine, and these would certainly make no such claim. They come in various colours: very pale; shading into a deeper pink; then into *clarete*; and then into red. The deeper *claretes* have always approximated to reds, but the real reds are new things dating from the 1990s, when bright young winemakers came in, encouraged by the creation of the DO in 1991. They planted vineyards, built bodegas, and brought their inevitable, and admirable, stainless steel. They also wanted a return on their capital and saw it in red wines. These are now well established and can be very good without rising to the heights. But their stainless steel has effected less of a revolution in quality here than it has in some other places. It enables good wines to be made above ground in bright new bodegas, but the local growers, thanks to the temperature control of their deep, cool cellars, have been making good *rosados* without it for years.

Some leading bodegas

CESAR PRINCIPE

Ronda, 47194 Fuensaladaña, Valladolid.

Tel: +34 629 77 92 82; Fax: +34 983 58 32 42

A family bodega founded in 1975 with forty hectares of vineyard, making some of the best varietal Tinta del País reds matured in eighty per cent French and twenty per cent American oak.

BODEGA COOPERATIVA DE CIGALES

Las Bodegas s/n, 47270 Cigales, Valladolid. Tel: +34 983 58 01 35;

Fax: +34 983 58 06 82; Email: bcc@bodegacooperativacigales.com;

Website: www.bodegacooperativacigales.com

Founded in 1956, this cooperative makes wine for 172 growers, whose grapes from 720 hectares of vineyard are mostly Tinta del País. It makes good wines, principally *rosados,* but an increasing number of reds, and sells them under the names Torondos, Viñatorondos, Villulas, and Viñavillulas. The Viñatorondos 2003 was from sixty per cent Tinta del País, twenty per cent Albillo, ten per cent Garnacha, and ten per cent Verdeja. Its best wines, though, are its reds and are varietal Tinta del País.

EMETERIO FERNANDEZ

Ctra Cigales 1, 47194 Fuensaladaña, Valladolid. Tel: +34 983 58 32 44;

Fax: +34 983 58 31 72; Email: Lalegua@lalegua.com; Website: www.lalegua.com

This very modern bodega, with its somewhat minimalist architecture, was established as a family concern in 1997, but the family had been working for the previous thirty years on seventy-two hectares of vines. Most of the wines are varietal Tinto del País, though there are minor proportions of Cabernet Sauvignon in the *crianzas* and above. In Spain they are sold under the names La Legua and Valdetan, but they are imported into Britain under the brand Aleno, and are good.

BODEGAS FRUTOS VILLAR

Carretera Burgos–Portugal km 115, 47170 Cigales, Valladolid.
Tel: +34 983 58 68 68; Fax: +34 983 58 01 80;
Email: exportacion.fvillar@cic.es; Website: www.bodegasfrutosvillar.com

This family-owned company began by establishing a bodega at Toro in 1920. In 1960 it started in Cigales, then bought a bodega in Ribera del Duero, and finally set up in Rueda. It also makes Vinos de la Tierra de Castilla y León. In Cigales it has 105 hectares of vineyard planted with Tinta del País and has an old, deep, cool cellar where it matures its wines in American and some French oak, but prefers American. It uses two brand names. Under Calderona it makes everything from *rosado* to a red *reserva*. The basic *rosado joven* is from seventy per cent Tinto del País, ten per cent Garnacha, the rest Verdejo and Albillo; but the lite is a varietal Tinta del País, as are all the red wines. The *crianza* has twelve months age in ninety-five per cent American and five per cent French oak, while the *reserva* has 18–24 months in eighty-five per cent American and fifteen per cent French. Perhaps its best wine of all is Elite, which falls between the *crianza* and *reserva* in ageing, with fourteen months in eighty-five per cent American and fifteen per cent French oak. The Conde Asurez range stops at *crianza*.

BODEGA LEZCANO LACALLE

Carretera de Valoria s/n, 47282 Trigueros del Valle, Valladolid.
Tel: +34 983 58 69 40; Fax: +34 983 58 66 97;
Email: oficina@bodegaslezcano.com; Website: www.bodegaslezcano.com

This family bodega was founded in 1991 with a twelve-hectare vineyard, planted *en vaso* on one of the highest sites, principally with Tinto del País, but with a small proportion of Cabernet Sauvignon and Merlot. Some of the vines were there when the vineyard was bought and are very old. It has now been expanded to sixteen hectares. The red wine bodega is very old and is dug into the hill, maintaining a temperature of 14°C (57°F). The wines are matured here in American Missouri oak coopered in Logroño. The *rosados* are sold under the name Docetañidos, the 2003 having eighty per cent Tinta del País and the rest Albillo, Verdejo, and Sauvignon Blanc. The reds are sold under the name Lezcano. It claims to have been the first to make Cigales *reservas*. The excellent 2000 was sixty per cent Tinto del País and forty per cent Cabernet Sauvignon.

FINCA MUSEUM

Carretera Cigales-Corcos km 3, 47270 Cigales, Valladolid. Tel: +34 983 58 10 29; Fax: +34 983 58 10 30; Email: fincamuseum@telefonica.net

The Cigales offshoot of the Rioja house Barón de Ley was established in 2000, and has 110 hectares of vineyard. It makes a good *crianza* matured for 13–16 months by giving it three month periods successively in French and American oak. It also makes some of the best *reservas*, which it matures in new French oak and sells with the name Museum Real. They are Tinto del País varietals.

BODEGA REMIGIO DE SALAS

Calle Puertecilla 21, 34210 Dueñas, Palencia.

This very old-established family bodega is something entirely apart. One gets used to the anonymity of bodegas in Cigales, but finding this one sets a challenge. Its entrance is a hole in a hillside, protected by rows of hanging beads, and nothing to suggest that it is a bodega at all. Inside there are groups of animated locals, each with a vessel to be filled up before they go home. That is the way the wine is sold. None is bottled, unless you ask for a bottle, when one is filled up and corked on the spot; there is no label. It has 100 hectares of vineyard and no grapes are bought in. The cellars are remarkable: a rabbit warren of tunnels, some very small and 1,000 years old, one made only a few years ago by hand, chipped out of the hillside, with the stone carried out in a barrow. The temperature changes not more than 1°C throughout the year. Here there is indeed no stainless steel. Apart from some resin-lined cement vats, it looks as if nothing has changed for 150 years, not even the presses. It makes only one style of wine, a dark *rosado* or *clarete*, which is sold with varying degrees of ageing. A sample was taken in a most unusual way: a ladder was placed by the side of an enormous barrel, a piece of rather dirty old carpet was removed from the top, a trap door opened, a jug lowered in and then raised – and then everything was put back into place. One might have expected the wine to be acetic or at least slightly tainted. Not a bit of it! The wine was clean and utterly delicious. But would it travel? It did! Several bottles were jogged all the way back to England in the far-from-ideal conditions of the boot of a car. Tasted several months later, they were even more delicious. It goes to show that a good winemaker can produce fine results using very old methods. It was well worth seeking out.

VALDELOSFRAILES

Carretera Cubillas s/n, 47359 Cubillas de Santa María, Valladolid.

Tel: +34 983 48 50 24; Fax: +34 983 10 71 04.

This is an offshoot of the Ribera del Duero Matarromera group and was founded in 1998 with fifty-one hectares of vineyard growing Tinta del País and Garnacha. It makes good wines, mostly Tinta del País varietals. The Vendimia Seleccionada 2001 oak-aged red is particularly highly praised.

RIBERA DEL DUERO

Geography

The wine-growing area of Ribera del Duero is centred around Roa de Duero, though the larger town of Aranda de Duero is its commercial capital. The vineyards occupy parts of four provinces: Burgos; Valladolid; Soria; and Segovia. The name means the bank of the river Duero, but very few of the vineyards are actually on the banks. Some of the best are high above it, with a cliff descending to the river, and although many are within three kilometres (1.8 miles) of the river, others are far away. The delimited area is 113 kilometres (70 miles) long, about fifty kilometres (31 miles) at its broadest width, and ten kilometres (6 miles) at its narrowest. It is high and hilly, with the vineyards at 700–1,000 metres (2,296–3,280 feet) above sea level. Most of the land is taken up with mixed farming, and the vineyards are scattered. The highest areas are generally too bleak, and right down by the river they are too damp.

Climate

Winters are cold, with many frosts. The temperature has been known to fall to as low as -20°C (-4°F), but temperatures below -5°C (23°F) are fortunately rare. There are fewer than 140 days in a year that are entirely free from frost, and frosts are the main problem; in one year out of three they halve the harvest. Preventive measures are being tried, and the most promising at the moment appears to be a spray of warm water. There is also a severe hail risk, one of the highest in Spain. Summers are warm with temperatures of 25–32°C (77–90°F), occasionally going as high as 42°C (107.6°F). However, owing to the altitude, nights are cool. There are great swings of temperature. The median is around 11°C (51.8°F). Rainfall is from 400–550 millimetres (15.7–21.6 inches), but there is little in summer, so irrigation has recently been legalized but is not widely used. There are 2,624 hours of sunshine.

Soils

In so large an area, and a hilly one at that, there are many kinds of soil, depending on altitude and whether one is east or west of Roa de Douro. The lower soils, down by the river bank, are alluvial with sand and clay. The gentle slopes on which the vineyards are generally planted are of clay, marl, and limestone to the east and limestone, marl, and gypsum to the west. The important factor is the limestone, which makes up a third of the soil to the west and half to the east.

Grapes

Red varieties: Tinto Fino, also known as Tinto del País, which is a clone of Tempranillo; Cabernet Sauvignon; Merlot; and Garnacha (also known as Tinto Aragonés). Tinto Fino is by far the most widely planted. A minimum of seventy-five per cent has to be used in the DO wines; and a minimum of ninety-five per cent of Tinto Fino, Cabernet Sauvignon, Merlot, and Malbec combined. The Garnacha does not ripen reliably here; it is used only for making *rosados* and may well be eliminated

White variety: Albillo. The French varieties are long established, having been brought in during the nineteenth century, but they may be replanted only in the villages where they already grow. There are no DO white wines; the Albillo is used for lightening *rosados*, is sometimes found (to the extent of about five per cent) in reds, and occasionally used for non-DO wines.

Planting

Traditionally in a rectangular pattern of 1.75 x 2 metres (5.7 x 6.5 feet) or a square pattern with 2.25 metres (7.3 feet) spacing, but new vineyards are planted with 1.5–2 metres (4.9–6.5 feet) between vines and three metres (9.8 feet) between rows, to make mechanical harvesting possible. The permitted density is not less than 2,000 or more than 4,000 per hectare. Traditional pruning was *en vaso* with a maximum of twelve buds per vine, but there is now a move towards *espaldera* trained in double cordon with a maximum of sixteen buds per vine. In either case there is a maximum of 40,000 buds per hectare.

Vineyard area

18,500 hectares.

Authorized yield

49hl/ha. The amount produced by small growers is carefully regulated by the *consejo regulador*. Each has a "smart card" that records his planting and yield, and this is processed when he delivers grapes to a bodega.

Wines

There are only reds and *rosados*, which must have a minimum strength of 11.5% ABV and 11% ABV respectively. The few white wines are not part of the DO. The regulations for the aged wines are the usual ones save that *crianzas* must have a minimum of one year in oak. Most of the *rosados* are sold as *jóvenes,* though there are some *crianzas*. Most growers are now concentrating on reds. Some reds are sold as *jóvenes,* and can be delicious, but others are disappointing. No doubt selling young wines helps the cash flow, but as the price of grapes goes up and up it becomes less economic to make them, and some bodegas are phasing them out. The great wines of this area are the *crianzas* and above. Some of the *crianzas* would be entitled to be sold as *reservas,* but growers keep the categories of *reserva* and *gran reserva* for their finest wines. A *gran reserva* must spend at least two years in oak. The best wines age very well. In the past there has been a tendency for wines to be over-oaked, but happily this fashion is receding.

Production

762,650 hectolitres (2003).

Vintages

1976 (4); 1977 (1); 1978 (2); 1979 (3); 1980 (3); 1981 (5); 1982 (4); 1983 (4); 1984 (2); 1985 (4); 1986 (5); 1987 (3); 1988 (3); 1989 (5); 1990 (3); 1991 (4); 1992 (3); 1993 (2); 1994 (4); 1995 (5); 1996 (5); 1997 (3); 1998 (4); 1999 (5); 2000 (4); 2001 (5); 2002 (4); 2003 (4); 2004 (4).

Although easily accessible from Madrid and from the ancient cities of Burgos and Valladolid, Ribera del Duero is off the beaten track. Tourists are refreshingly few and indeed no one in their right mind would go to winter there; while in summer they are drawn to the beaches, to the mountains, and to those many areas of Spain that are replete with ancient monuments. But nevertheless it is an enchanting countryside. In June the verges are red with poppies and wild flowers, and all around are hills remarkable for their striations, with some flat-topped like miniature table mountains. The river Duero flows through it from end to end and is joined by a network of tributaries, but the land is not very fertile even when irrigated. There are delightful places to visit and many good things to be seen: castles (notably at Peñafiel, which houses a wine museum); cloisters; unspoiled villages... It is a place where one always wants to return. For wine drinkers it is something else. For many years there was only one wine-grower of note – Vega Sicilia – and that was very notable indeed, producing one of the rarest, most sought after, and most expensive wines in the world. Now the whole area has sprung into life, growing great, world class wines. It is a very exciting place.

Inevitably wine-growing goes back to Roman times, but there is a difference: Roman cellars are still often in use. Around the towns and villages in this and neighbouring areas, notably Cigales, small towers or chimneys mysteriously rise from the ground, sometimes a profusion of them. They are the air vents and light shafts of cellars. Each house once had its own vineyard and its own *lago*, or wine press (*lagar* in most of Spain), where the grapes were trodden by foot. In the days when the Duero lay at the frontier between the Spanish and Moorish kingdoms, these cellars – some dating from Roman times but most from the fourteenth and fifteenth centuries – were also used as hide-outs and many are linked up, making subterranean networks and escape routes. There were 304 of them in 1752 and there are still 120. The history of winemaking here can be divided into three parts of very different durations: the old traditions; the time of the cooperatives; and the present day. The old peasant vineyards were very small – and most are still under one hectare. Families grew a variety of red and white grapes to produce rustic wines of the pale red colour known as *clarete*. They were drunk locally and never bottled, described as tannic, acid, and not more than 11% ABV. In the nineteenth century, the French influence was only indirect. Wine was taken into Rioja for blending and then sold on. Inevitably phylloxera arrived toward the end of the century and had its usual effect. The local authorities started to distribute American rootstocks in 1908, but growers found that the Tinto Fino did not do well on them, giving a much reduced yield, and this great variety largely gave way to the inferior ones. Apart from Vega Sicilia, no wine had any but a local reputation.

Although the first cooperative, the Cooperativa Ribera del Duero at Peñafiel, was founded by fifteen wine-growers and made its first wine in

1927, using the best techniques of the time, the movement took a long time to catch on. This cooperative and Vega Sicilia were the only two producers in the district to bottle their wines. Things might have got going sooner had it not been for the Civil War, but the disruption it caused, and the aftermath of starvation that moved resources into food growing, made the wine trade stagnate. In the 1950s and 1960s, though, the rapid expansion of industry in the towns brought an exodus from the countryside that made the old methods of winemaking practically unworkable. New cooperatives were founded. By 1976 there were thirty-two. At first the wines were little different from those made before, with the cooperatives paying by weight so that what mattered was a high yield. Initially the *rosados*, or *claretes*, were more highly prized than the reds, and only a few of the cooperatives made reds, but gradually good reds came into being.

The next development was the great one. The DO was created in 1982, and with it came the concept of Ribera del Duero wines. At first the change was gradual and got off to a rather sticky start, with problems of marketing and some growers gave up. But with the superb quality and high price of Vega Sicilia as the exemplar, it is not surprising that other growers, notably Alejandro Fernández, began to see that the future lay in quality. A new era of planting began in about 1984. The first thing was to plant more Tinto Fino. This happened and escalated. In 1987, 90.71 hectares were planted, but in 1988 the figure was 500 hectares and it has gone on at the same pace ever since. In 1990 about seventy-six per cent of the holdings were less than one hectare and only about four per cent were more than twenty-five hectares. Many large vineyards have been planted since, but there is still scope for consolidation.

In the 1980s, money started to pour in. Spain had become prosperous; restaurateurs and rich men wanted to boast of the quality of their own wines. Some of the cooperatives were bought up and others were rented, but most of the newcomers started from scratch with impressive buildings, state-of-the art equipment, and newly planted vineyards. And not all were newcomers. The message had been received by some families that had been making wine for generations and they suddenly brought themselves up to date. So despite the Roman cellars and the pioneering efforts of Vega Sicilia, the Ribera del Duero wines that we know today are among the most recent created in Spain. The descriptions of the bodegas that follow tell the story. There are now so many first-rate growers the problem has been which to leave out.

There is nothing unusual about the winemaking, which follows modern practice with lots of stainless steel and temperature-controlled fermentations. The wine is aged in oak and various cask sizes are used, up to 580 litres, but the traditional Bordelaise barrel of 225 litres is rapidly becoming universal, both American and French oak being used. The results are staggering. The *jóvenes* are fruity, fresh, and intended for early drinking. The *crianzas* are excellent and can go on improving for years in bottle. The best *reservas* and *gran reservas* are superb. Vega Sicilia can last and improve for decades, and some of its closest rivals may well match it. Indeed their growers claim that their *gran reservas* are Spain's most long-lived wines, and they may well be right. The best wines are big, dark, fruity, long, and impressively complex.

Some leading bodegas

BODEGAS Y VINEDOS AALTO

Carretera Peñafiel s/n, 09300 Roa de Duero, Burgos.

Tel/Fax: +34 947 54 07 81; Email: aalto@aalto.es; Website: www.aalto.es

This young bodega on the eastern edge of the district is hard to find, but enormously worth finding. It was started in 1999 by Mariano Garcia, who for thirty years was the legendary winemaker at Vega Sicilia, and Javier Zaccaguiri, who for six years had been head of the *consejo regulador*. It acquired thirty-two hectares of vineyard in three sub-districts, which it planted with old clone Tinto Fino; a further ten hectares of old vines in the village of Quemada; and it rents four vineyards, totalling fifty-two hectares of 45–100-year-old vines. The new bodega is built on several floors, so the whole winemaking process is gravity fed. The stainless-steel fermentation tanks are made to the bodega's own special design in a shape that it likens to Daleks, and it also has some new wooden ones. The wines are matured in French barriques, sixty per cent new each year, and are not filtered. They are not merely good, they are sensational. The top wine, Aalto PS (*Pagos Seleccionadas*), is made only in the best years.

BODEGAS ALION

Ctra N 122 km 312, 47300 Padilla de Duero, Valladolid. Tel/Fax: +34 983 88 12 36; Email: alion@bodegasalion.com; Website: www.bodegasalion.com

In 1986, the Alvarez family of Vega Sicilia decided to create a new, twenty-first century high expression wine. It was to be different from Vega Sicilia and complementary to it: not a second wine. In 1992 they bought the bodega of Liceo, conveniently next door at Peñafiel, and used it for the new wine. It has its own fifty-hectare-vineyard, some purchased and some created by extending those at Vega Sicilia, but the newly planted vineyards will not be used until they are ten years old; in the meantime grapes are bought from old vines in local vineyards. Eventually, like Vega Sicilia, it will be self-sufficient. It is run quite separately: Vega Sicilia has created a serious rival to itself. The first vintage was 1991, but the first put on the market was the 1992, a wine of great concentration, still dumb in 1998, and looking as if it will last for ever. And 1992 was not generally a very good vintage. In 2000 it took a step forward by moving backwards: it installed wooden fermentation tanks. Only Tinto Fino grapes are used, and in 2000 forty-five per cent of the crop was removed by green pruning. The wine of this vintage was given fifteen months ageing in new Nevers oak and marketed in 2004. These are great wines.

BODEGAS ARZUAGA-NAVARRO

Ctra N 122 Aranda–Valladolid km 325, 47350 Quintinilla de Onesimo, Valladolid. Tel: +34 983 68 11 46; Fax: +34 983 68 11 47; Email: bodega@arzuaganavarro.com; Website: www.arzuaganavarro.com

Founded in 1993 by the two families whose names it bears, its immense and impressive building also houses a luxury hotel and restaurant. Its 1,400-hectare estate includes 150 hectares of vineyard, principally planted with Tinto Fino, with small quantities of Cabernet Sauvignon and Merlot, which supplies seventy per cent of its needs. Eighty per cent of the vines are ten years old or more, but it has access to older ones; as the vineyard ages the wines should get better and better. Its *crianzas* are from Tinto Fino, with a small amount of Cabernet Sauvignon and Merlot, given 13–14 months in ninety per cent American oak (ten per cent of which is new) and ten per cent French. Its *reservas* are 85–97 per cent Tinto Fino with Cabernet Sauvignon and Merlot, given 16–21 months in American and French oak, the latter being seventy-five per cent in the 1998 vintage. Its *reserva especial* is a varietal Tinto Fino from eighty-year-old vines, given a year in new French oak and a further year in second-year oak, then bottled without fining or filtering. Its top wine is Gran Arzuega, made from Tinto Fino and aged half and half in American and French oak. A serious player, with very fine wines.

VINEDOS Y BODEGAS ASTER

Carretera Aranda-Palencia km 55, Término El Caño, 09312 Anguix, Burgos.
Tel: +34 947 52 27 00; Fax: +34 947 52 27 01;
Email: aster@riojalta.com; Website: www.riojalta.com

When La Rioja Alta decided to set up in this DO, it almost went without saying that its wines would be excellent. It bought an estate of ninety-five hectares in 1990, at an altitude of 830 metres (2,724 feet), and in the following year planted seventy-six of them with Tinto Fino. It made its first wine in 1999 and rejected it, selling it off in bulk. From 2000 onward things went right. Its barrels are half American and half French, renewed every eighteen months. The whole bodega is air conditioned at 14–15°C (57–59°F) and eighty-five per cent humidity. It concentrates on *reservas*.

DOMINIO DE ATAUTA
Carretera de Morcuera s/n, 42345 Atauta, Soria. Tel: +34 913 02 02 47;
Fax: +34 917 66 19 41; Email: dominiodeatauta.ribera@arrakis.es
A boutique bodega started in 2000 with a French winemaker from Chinon, it makes superb wines. It is built on a hillside in several stories so gravity can be used to move the wines, and is at an altitude of 1,000 metres (3,281 feet) with wonderful views. Its twelve hectares of vineyard is planted entirely with Tinto Fino and is divided into 116 parcels, putting one in mind of Burgundy. Some grapes from old vines with carefully supervised pruning are also bought in. The winemaker prefers concrete tanks and large wooden vats to stainless steel, but they are temperature controlled, and some stainless steel is used. Grapes from each terroir are given individual attention and fermented separately. Only French oak is used for ageing. La Mala and La Rosa are single-vineyard wines.

BODEGAS BALBAS
La Majada s/n, 09331 La Horra, Burgos.
Tel: +34 947 54 21 11; Fax: +34 947 54 21 12; Email: bodegas@balbas.es
The Balbás family can trace its history as wine-growers as far back as 1777, but it was reborn as a producer of fine bottled wines when the two brothers Juan José and Víctor founded the present bodega at La Horra in 1981. The modern bodega retains its ancient cellars. Its seventy-two hectares of vineyard provides it with sixty per cent of its requirements, and it buys the rest from local growers. Its very good red wines used to be varietal Tinto Fino, but now include Cabernet Sauvignon. Its top wine is Altius Reserva.

BODEGAS FELIX CALLEJO
Avenida del Cid km 16.4, 09441 Sotillo de la Ribera, Burgos.
Tel: +34 947 53 23 12; Fax: +34 983 53 23 04;
Email: callejo@bodegasfelixcallejo.com; Website: www.bodegasfelixcallejo.com
This family bodega was founded in 1989 and has sixty hectares of vineyard

including forty-year-old vines at 845 metres (2,772 feet). Most of its wines are varietal Tinto Fino, including the *rosado*, sold under the brand Viña Pilar. The reds are matured in new American and French oak. They include a four month oak-aged wine and progress from *crianza* to a *gran reserva*, Gran Callejo, made only in the best years. The exceptionally good Selección Viñedos de la Familia is top of the range.

CONDADO DE HAZA

Carretera de la Horra s/n, 09300 Roa, Burgos.
Tel: +34 947 52 52 54; Fax: +34 947 52 52 62;
Email: pesquera@pesqueraafernandez.com; Website: www.condadodehaza.com

In the 1980s, Alejandro Fernández of Pesquera fame (*see* below), spotted an abandoned hillside above the river at 950 metres (3,116 feet). After protracted negotiations he bought it. Some said he was mad, but he definitely was not. There are now 200 hectares of Tinto Fino, mostly planted in 1989. The new bodega buildings, between Roa and La Horra, were completed only in 1997 and are run as a separate enterprise. The wines are given fifteen months in American oak, and in exceptional years a top wine is produced – Alenza – which has twenty-four months' oak ageing. Although not quite up to the exceptionally high standards of Pesquera, the wines are very good. There is a parallel between Alejandro Fernández creating Condado de Haza and Vega Sicilia creating Alion: they have produced rivals to themselves. Anyone travelling along the Duero should make a small diversion to the irrelevant but delightful little town of Haza.

BODEGAS CONDE

Pizarro s/n, 09400 Aranda de Duero, Burgos.
Tel: +34 947 51 18 61; Fax: +34 947 51 18 61;
Email: info@bodegasconde.com; Website: www.bodegasconde.com

A boutique bodega founded by three enthusiastic young men in 2000. They have planted seven hectares of vineyard for the future, but at present buy Tinto Fino grapes from vines over fifty years old. The wines are matured in forty per cent Allier and sixty per cent American oak and are sold under the name Neo. The top wine, Neo Punta Esencia, is made only in very good years. The wines are highly praised.

BODEGAS MATARROMERA

Carretera Renedo-Pesquera km 30, 47359 Valbuena de Duero, Valladolid.
Tel: +34 983 10 71 00; Fax: +34 983 10 71 04.

The Matarromera group has bodegas in Cigales and in Castilla y Léon, in addition to no fewer than three in Ribera del Duero: Matarromera, founded in 1988; Emina, making *crianzas* and semi-*crianzas*; and, most recently, Renacimento. Matarromera has eighty hectares of vineyard and makes some very good *crianzas, reservas,* and *gran reservas,* but those most praised are Prestigio and Pago de las Solanas, both varietal Tinto Finos.

HACIENDA MONASTERIO

Carretera Pesquera-Valbuena s/n, 47315 Pesquera de Duero, Valladolid. Tel: +34 983 48 40 02; Fax: +34 983 10 71 04; Email: bmonasterio@vodafone.es

A modern bodega founded in 1991, it has sixty-eight hectares of vineyard planted with Tinto Fino, Cabernet Sauvignon, Merlot, and Malbec, and buys in a few grapes from local growers. It is run by the legendary Peter Sisseck (*see* Pingus, below). Its reds, matured in new Allier oak and sold under the bodega name, are very good indeed, with great ageing potential. They are typically made from seventy-five per cent Tinto Fino, fifteen per cent Cabernet Sauvignon, and ten per cent Merlot. The *reserva especial* wines are glorious. The second wine, La Granja de Monasterio, is almost as good.

EMILIO MORO

Carretera Peñafiel–Valoria s/n, 47315 Pesquera de Duero, Valladolid.
Tel: +34 983 87 84 00; Fax: +34 983 87 01 95;
Email: bodega@emiliomoro.com; Website: www.emiliomoro.com

Owned by a family with a long history of wine-growing and now in its third generation, this bodega decided to bottle its wine and built a modern winery in 1989. IiIt has seventy hectares of vineyard that have been planted with Tinto Fino, and uses no weed killers. The bodega was rebuilt between 1997–2001 on a slope that enables the wine to be moved almost entirely by gravity. It makes very good, well-balanced red wines entirely from Tinto Fino. Finca Resalso is a *roble* made from vines 5–15 years old and given four months in Allier oak. Emilio Moro comes from vines 15–25 and is given twelve months in oak, thirty per cent American and seventy per cent French. Malleolus is from 25–75-year-old vines and is given eighteen months in new Allier oak. The top wine is called Malleolus de Valderramiso, and is made from from vines over eighty years old, fermented in American oak, and aged for eighteen months in new Allier; it is superb and must be decanted. The top wines here are made for bottle-ageing.

PAGO DE LOS CAPELLANES

Camino de la Ampudia s/n, 09314 Pedrosa de Duero, Burgos.

Tel: +34 947 53 00 68; Fax: +34 947 53 01 11;

Email: bodega@pagodeloscapellanes.com; Website: www.pagodeloscapellanes.com

This bodega was established in 1996 with 100 hectares of old-vine vineyard owned by the Rodero family. Its wines are among the best. They are from 80–90 per cent Tinto Fino, the rest Cabernet Sauvignon, with some Merlot in the *joven*. Both American and French oak is used. Its top wine is the *crianza* Parcela el Picon, which is a varietal Tinto Fino.

PAGO DE CARRAOVEJAS

Camino de Carrovejas s/n, Peñafiel, Valladolid.

Tel: +34 983 87 80 20; Fax: +34 983 87 80 22.

Founded in 1988, this estate has eighty hectares of vineyard, formerly a joint enterprise of the local doctor and pharmacist. It is now owned by a syndicate of restaurateurs and wine men, planted with seventy per cent Tinto Fino and thirty per cent Cabernet Sauvignon, though the proportions used in its wines are somewhat different, with five per cent more Tinto Fino and less of Cabernet Sauvignon. It produces *crianza* and *reserva* reds of high quality, the *crianzas* matured in French and American oak, the *reservas* in French. Its top wine is Vendímia Seleccionada Cuesta De La Liebres.

BODEGAS HERMANOS PEREZ PASCUAS (VINA PEDROSA)

Carretera Pedrosa a Roa s/n, 09314 Pedrosa de Duero, Burgos.

Tel: +34 947 53 01 00; Fax: +34 947 53 00 02;

Email: vinapedrosa@perezpascuas.com; Website: www.perezpascuas.com

This is undoubtedly one of the most serious, quality bodegas. It was founded in 1980 by the three Pérez Pascuas brothers, but the date is misleading as the family had been established as wine-growers for a very long time and some of the vines they use today were planted by their great-grandfather. They gutted the local cooperative and started their own business. With 110 hectares of vineyard, 840 metres (2,756 feet) above sea level, planted in loose, friable soil with no clay, they are completely self-sufficient for grapes: ninety per cent Tinto Fino and ten per cent Cabernet Sauvignon, with the yield kept low. The wines are matured in American and French oak and most are varietal Tinto Fino. Cepa Gavilán is given twelve months in oak. The *crianzas*, *reservas,* and *gran reservas* are sold as Viña Pedrosa, the *reservas* and *gran reservas* having ten per cent Cabernet Sauvignon. The top wine is Tinto Gran Selección Pérez Pascuas, a varietal Tinto Fino from vines over forty years old.

DOMINIO DE PINGUS

Hospital s/n, 47350 Quintanilla de Onésimo, Valladolid.

Tel: +34 639 83 38 54; Fax: +34 983 48 40 20; Email: ps@pingus.es

This bodega was founded in 1995 by Peter Sisseck, the Danish winemaker and minority shareholder in Hacienda Monasterio, and is housed in an anonymous little building with vaulted cellars by the river. It is already legendary for the quality of its wines – and for their prices. Yields from its five hectares of organically farmed grapes are minuscule. The wines are made in small wooden vats without temperature control – but there are no problems. Only French oak is used and it is all new. Pingus is very concentrated and superb. None was made in 2003, as although officially classified as "very good", Sissack thought the weather too hot. The second wine, Flor de Pingus, is almost as good.

BODEGAS PROTOS

Bodegas Protos 24–8, 47300 Peñafiel, Valladolid.

Tel: +34 983 87 80 11; Fax: +34 983 87 80 12;

Email: bodega@bodegasprotos.com; Website: www.bodegasprotos.com

The Cooperativa Ribera Duero was founded in 1927, as mentioned above. Its wines were the first to bear the name of what is now the DO, and Protos is its descendant. It is still the largest producer and maintains the quality of its wines to a high standard. It is situated just beneath the magnificent castle at Peñafiel and its wines are matured in a medieval tunnel, two kilometres long (1.2 miles), in the castle mound. Soon there will be an additional bodega designed by Richard Rogers and linked to the old one by another tunnel. Today there are 240 partners who between them have 200 hectares of vineyard, growing almost entirely Tinto Fino. Another 200 hectares are cultivated under the bodega's supervision. It was the great pioneer, the first to go in for the fine bottled wines that are now produced by everyone, and it invented the brand Protos to help with its marketing. Apart from Vega Sicilia, which was a unique enterprise, these were the first wines from Ribera del Duero to become known outside Spain. The *rosado* is made from Tinto Fino, Garnacha, and Albillo, but all the reds are varietal Tinto Finos, matured in American and French oak, and going up to gran *reserva*, the *reservas* and *gran reservas* from old vines.

BODEGAS RESALTE DE PENAFIEL

Carretera N 122 km 312, 47300 Peñafiel, Valladolid. Tel: +34 983 87 81 60; Fax: +34 983 88 06 01; Email: info@resalte.com; Website: www.resalte.com

·Established in 2000, this bodega is owned by two wealthy businessmen and is already justly famous. There are no pumps or pipes. The wine is run into tanks that are then moved by cranes into positions where gravity takes it to where it is needed. At present it owns no vineyard, but gets good grapes from local growers with mature vineyards. All its wines are varietal Tinto del País. Seventy per cent French and thirty per cent American new oak is used for maturing its excellent *crianzas* and *reservas*.

BODEGAS RODERO

Carretera Boada s/n, 09314 Pedrosa de Duero, Burgos.

Tel: +34 947 53 00 46; Fax: +34 947 53 00 97;

Email: rodero@bodegasrodero.com; Website: www.bodegasrodero.com

The date given for the foundation of this bodega is 1989, but that is totally misleading, as the Rodero family has been growing vines here for many generations. They used to sell their grapes to Vega Sicilia, but in 1991 decided to start making wines themselves and have been expanding the vineyard; it is now eighty-one hectares, including an impressive ten hectares on crumbly, sandy soil with lots of stones at the top of a cliff 30–40 metres (98.5–131 feet) above the river. Carmelo Rodero's philosophy is that good wine begins in the vineyard: you should talk to it, and at vintage time select the bunches of grapes with great care. The grapes from each plot are then vinified separately. The bodega has been completely rebuilt and the wine is moved by gravity. The wines he makes are indeed good. The *jóvenes* are varietal Tinto Fino, but 3–10 per cent Cabernet Sauvignon is included in the *crianzas* and above. The *reservas* are made with grapes from the oldest vines. Vendímia Seleccionada has only three per cent Cabernet Sauvignon and is aged for twenty-four months in new Allier oak. Finally, and top of the range, is Valterraña, which has its malolactic fermentation in French oak and then spends at least thirty months in sixty per cent French and forty per cent American. The last two are made from vines not less than thirty-five years old. All the wines are sold under the grower's name, Carmelo Rodero, but he formerly used the marks Ribeño and Val Ribeño, which may still be found on old bottles.

TELMO RODRIGUEZ

Siete Infantes de Lara 5 Ofinina 1, 26006 Logroño, La Rioja.

Tel: +34 941 51 11 28; Fax: +34 941 51 11 31; Email: cia@fer.es

Yes, the office is in Rioja – and that is where Telmo Rodríguez hails from. His family owns the great estate of Remelluri (*see* Rioja), and he used to be the winemaker there, but left to establish his own brand, operating in several of the most noted regions, where his wines are made under his direction. They are very good, too, especially those from this area: Gazur, a young red, Matallana, oak aged and, the top wine, M2 de Matallana.

BODEGAS HERMANOS SASTRE

San Pedro s/n, 09311 La Horra, Burgos. Tel: +34 947 54 21 08; Fax: +34 947 54 21 08; Email: sastre@vinasastre.com; Website: www.vinasastre.com

The Sastre family has been growing grapes at La Horra, in a thirty-five-hectare vineyard of Tinto Fino, for three generations. Seventy per cent of their vines are over fifty years old. They used to sell the grapes, but in 1992 decided to make wine and installed a modern plant. The wines are sold as Viña Sastre and are absolutely first rate. They are varietal Tinto Finos. The top ones are Regina Vides and, at the very top, Pesus, which has a tiny amount of Merlot and Cabernet Sauvignon.

BODEGAS SENORIO DE NAVA

Carretera Valladolid–Soria s/n, 09813 Nava de Roa, Burgos.

Tel: +34 987 20 97 90; Fax: +34 987 20 98 00;

Email: snava@senoriodenava.es; Website: www.senoriodenava.es

A small and primitive cooperative, the Bodega Cooperativa de San Antolín, which had been founded in 1956, was bought by the Señorío de Nava company in 1986 and totally transformed. Impressive buildings were erected and all the new technology installed. It has 120 hectares of vineyard. Its wines are mostly varietals from Tinto Fino. It makes good *crianzas* and *reservas* but its top wine is Finca San Cobate Reserva, matured in American oak, a fine wine.

TINTO PESQUERA

Calle Real 2, 47315 Pesquera de Duero, Valladolid.

Tel: +34 983 87 00 37; Fax: +34 983 87 00 88;

Email: pesquera@pesqueraafernandez.com; Website: www.grupopesquera.com

Alejandro Fernández was put on the map when the American wine writer Robert Parker described his wine as Spain's Château Pétrus, and he was not exaggerating; but before Fernández received this accolade, his wines were already being sought out by those looking for something rare and superb. He founded his bodega in 1972, and until then was an engineer and inventor. He lives simply and works hard. Those who would disparage have been known to call him a peasant. But what a peasant! It would be more just to describe him as a genius. He did much to put Ribera del Duero on the map. His background contributed greatly to his success; all his equipment is immaculate and he knows about welding stainless steel, so there is not a crevice where bacteria can collect. He has 220 hectares of superbly kept vineyards, 800 metres (2,624 feet) above sea level, planted entirely with Tinto Fino, and is busy planting more on very fine sites. In addition, a small quantity of fruit is bought in some years. The wines are matured in oak, mostly American but with a small amount of Limousin, ten per cent of which are renewed every year. Only *crianzas*, *reservas,* and *gran reservas* are made. All the wines are first rate and the *gran reservas* are magnificent. In the very best years there is a special *gran reserva*, Janus, which is superb, combining the boldness of the old style with the fruit of the new: a wine that will mature for years in bottle. These are the wines that others seek to emulate.

VALBUENA

See Vega Sicilia.

BODEGAS VEGA SICILIA

Carretera N 122 km 323, 47359 Valbuena de Duero, Valladolid.

Tel: +34 983 68 01 47; Fax: +34 983 68 02 63;

Email: vegasicilia@vega-sicilia.com; Website: www.vega-sicilia.com

This bodega led the way, and has long been acknowledged as producing one of the world's best (and most expensive) wines, a wine that is almost mythical. It was not all plain sailing, though. The date of foundation is given as 1864, but the story begins in 1859, when Eloy Lecanda Chaves was given an estate by his rich father. This included two adjacent parcels of land, Vega Sicilia and Carrascal at Valbuena de Duero, following the course of the river Duero. In 1864 he went to Bordeaux and bought 18,000 vine shoots: Cabernet Sauvignon; Carmenère; Malbec; Merlot; and Pinot Noir, which he planted. The Carmenère and Pinot Noir have vanished, but descendants of the others still flourish and have adapted themselves to the alien soil and climate. The wine did not, however, achieve instant renown. He was principally interested in making brandy and *ratafia*. Antonio Herrero Vázquez was the next owner, acquiring a controlling interest in 1888 and ownership in 1890. From 1890–1903 the bodega was known as Bodegas de Lacanda, and then as

Hijos de Antonio Herrero, before becoming Vega Sicilia. In 1901, Cosme Palacios from Laguardia in the Rioja, whose vineyards had been devastated by phylloxera, leased the bodega and made the wines. In 1905, however, he stopped making them and did a most important thing: he hired Domingo Guarramiola, known as Txomin, who recognized the quality of the material with which he was working. Until 1915 the wines were sold as Rioja, but in that year the lease ran out. The first Vega Sicilia wine was then made, and under his management the great age began. Many prizes were won in the 1920s and the legend had been born. He died in 1933.

The bodega changed hands again in 1952 and in 1966 before falling into the safe hands of the Alvarez family in 1982. Unfortunately, under the previous ownership the winemaking had become suspect, and quite a lot of the bottles suffered from volatile acidity. When they were good they were very, very good, but when they were bad they were horrid. A bottle of the 1945 drunk in England in 1988 tasted like the wreckage of a great wine. I drank two bottles of the 1948, in 1977 and 1980, the first was superb but the second, though obviously great, was spoilt by volatility. The bodega had failed to keep up with the improvements in vinification that were taking place all over Spain, but the Alvarez family immediately changed all that, pressing on with renovation inside and out, and carefully tending the vineyards, which they were able to extend.

There are 270 hectares of vines, compared with the eighty it had when the family bought the estate, and since 1996 it has been self-sufficient. Some of the vineyard is used for Alión (*see* above). The care taken with the wine begins with a very careful selection of grapes. The vines are picked over four to six times and each lot is fermented separately. The aim is to bring out the individuality of each wine. The yield is not more than thirty-two hectolitres per hectare. The grapes are moved into the fermentation vessels by gravity. For fermentation there is a choice of stainless-steel or epoxy-lined cement vats that have now been supplemented by oak vats. It finds the former are better if the weather is hot and cooling may required, but the latter produce more interesting wines when the weather is cool. Both American and French oak is used for ageing, the French casks bought in France, but American wood is bought as planks, matured for three years on the premises, and made up into barrels, since 1987, by the bodega's own coopers. It chooses the casks to use according to the wine's personality. As used to be the practice in Rioja, the wine spends a very long time in the wood. It begins in new oak for four to eight months and then moves step by step into older and older wood. The top wine Unico generally spends up to ten years in cask and three in bottle before sale. Sometimes the maturation period can be very long indeed; for instance a magnificent 1970 tasted in 1995 had spent sixteen years in wood. It is never released less than ten years after the vintage. The most recent move toward self-sufficiency has been the planting of an oak forest from which corks will eventually be made; but that is a very long-term project.

The finest wines are made into Vega Sicilia Unico, which is never less than a *gran reserva*, and unless the year is very good indeed, none is made at all; for instance there was none in 1992, 1993, or 1997. Vega Sicilia Unico *reserva especial* is blended from several years and sold without a vintage. The second wine is Valbuena 5, a very fine *reserva*, aged long enough for it to be entitled to be called a *gran reserva,* though it is not; and again it is not made unless the wine is good. In 1963, 1971, and 1993, neither wine was made, with an enormous loss to the bodega. When this happens the wine is not sold on the market, but sent for distillation, as is any cask that falls below standard. The Unico is typically made from seventy per cent Tinto Fino, twenty per cent Cabernet Sauvignon, and five per cent each of Merlot and Malbec, the Valbuena from eighty to eighty-five per cent Tinto Fino and the rest Cabernet Sauvignon, Merlot, and sometimes a little Malbec. It is impossible to describe Vega Sicilia: one just has to taste it. It is on a Wagnerian scale with all that master's subtlety and complexity.

RUEDA

Geography

This is the most southerly DO in Castilla. The countryside is flat and there is little of interest except the wines, which are very interesting indeed; but there are some pleasant towns, including Medina del Campo and Tordesillas. Although flat, it is high, with the vineyards at 600–780 metres (1,969–2,559 feet) above sea level, mostly in the province of Valladolid, but some in Avila and Segovia. They are scattered among cornfields, centred on the town of Medina del Campo and bordered in the north by the river Duero.

Climate

Like the whole of the centre of Spain, this is continental, temperatures falling to -7°C (19.4°F) in winter and rising to 35.7°C (96.2°F) in summer, with an average of 12°C (53.6°F). There are 2,700 hours of sunshine. The average rainfall is 400 millimetres (15.7 inches), but this is highly irregular. Sometimes there are showers throughout the year and this produces the best conditions for a good vintage; but in other years there is little or no rainfall in the growing season. It is therefore not surprising that the most modern vineyards have provision for irrigation, which is used to secure quality, not to increase yield. It is also windswept.

Soils

There are some alluvial soils with limestone and clay near the river, but most are sandy and very stony, made up of sandstone and clay. All are poor in organic materials.

Grapes

White varieties: Verdejo; Sauvignon Blanc; Viura; and Palomino Fino.
Red varieties: Tempranillo; Cabernet Sauvignon; Merlot; and Garnacha.
Of these, by far the most important today is the Verdejo, which covers fifty-two per cent of the vineyard; it gives the wines their unique character and is on the increase. Palomino Fino used to be the most important variety, but is in steadily declining and no new planting is allowed. Viura is traditional here and covers 22.5 per cent of the vineyard. Sauvignon Blanc is a new-comer that is proving very successful and, although not widely planted at present, is increasing – it is the vine that everyone talks about and its wines are easy to sell. By far the most widely planted red variety is Tempranillo.

Planting

The traditional method of planting was the square *marco real* with 2.8 metres (9.2 feet) spacing and pruned in an unusual way: *en rastra*, which is similar to *en vaso,* but with five buds instead of three, as buds tend to be killed off by frosts. Traditionally the Verdejo vines used to trail along the ground to benefit from the heat of the soil. More modern vineyards are planted on *espaldera* wires, with 1.5 metres (4.9 feet) between the vines and three metres (9.8 feet) between the rows, or Guyot. The vine density is from 1,100–1,700 per hectare, the maximum being 5,000. Slightly more than half are mechanically harvested.

Vineyard area

7,336 hectares.

Authorized yield

Verdejo and Sauvignon trained *en rastra*: 49hl/ha. Verdejo and Sauvignon trained *en espaldera*, together with Viura and Palomino: 56hl/ha.

Wines

There are five kinds of whites. Rueda, which must have a minimum of fifty per cent Verdejo. Alcoholic strength 11–14% ABV. Rueda Verdejo, which must contain a minimum of eighty-five per cent Verdejo. Rueda Sauvignon Blanc must be varietal and 11–14.5% ABV. Rueda Espumoso, which is a sparkling wine made like cava, but with at least fifty per cent Verdejo grapes and eighty-five per cent if brut or brut *nature*. Alcoholic strength 11.5–13% ABV. Rueda Dorado, which is a dry *vino de licor* grown under flor, like sherry, and aged for at least three years in oak. The minimum strength is 15% ABV. A lesser *palido* is aged for one year less. These last two were traditional and still have a following in northern Spain, but are clearly in decline and not exported.

In 2001 the *rosados* and reds, which had long been grown here, were admitted to the DO. Rosado must have a minimum fifty per cent of the red varieties and a minimum 11% ABV. *Tinto* must not have more than fifty per cent combined of Merlot and Garnacha. *Crianzas, reservas,* and *gran reservas* must be made from Tempranillo and Cabernet Sauvignon. The minimum strength for the reds is 12% ABV.

Production

289,506 hectolitres (2003).

Vintages

Generally speaking the white wines are best drunk young, within two years of the vintage and the sooner the better, but some (especially if barrel-fermented) may be kept longer. Some of the reds have ageing potential.

1999 (4); 2000 (4); 2001 (3); 2002 (3); 2003 (4); 2004 (4).

As with almost everywhere in Spain, wine-growing in Rueda has a long history, but not as long as most places. There is no mention of the Romans, and for a substantial time it lay at the frontier of the Christians and the Moors; it was so often laid waste that it became known as the *Tierra de Nadie* (the Land of Nothing). But when the Christians finally conquered it, King Alfonso VI

(1040–1109) encouraged wine-growing by making gifts of land to those who planted vines. Like so much of Castilla, mazes of tunnels lie below its towns and villages, sometimes refuges and, in more peaceful times, wine cellars. So, although its history as a vineyard may be short by Spanish standards, it is long by almost anyone else's. Its wines were favoured at court, which sat originally at Valladolid, León, and Zamora, and remained in favour when it moved to Madrid, as all those places were relatively close. In those days they were strong wines, direct competitors with sherry. The growers were prosperous, and by the middle of the eighteenth century there were some 29,000 hectares of vineyard. By 1909 there were 45,541 hectares.

But then everything went wrong. The immediate cause was the arrival of phylloxera in that year. By then the big cities were linked by the railway network with areas like Valdepeñas and the sherry country, which could supply their needs. When these vineyards were reconstituted, the growers, tempted by the high yield, made the mistake of planting that negative vine (for table wine purposes), the Palomino. By 1922 only 13,637 hectares were left and much of the wine went for distillation. There was no driving force to bring about change, and there were inevitable periods of stagnation and decline during the Spanish Civil War and World War II, when the vineyard sunk further. Then the growers started to develop the district and obtained their DO in 1972. But this did not come from any sudden improvement. They were still making a vast number of wines: *generosos* that could not compete with Jerez or Montilla, whites largely from Palomino that could not hope for anything better than a local sale, and whites from Verdejo, but this variety, under the old methods of vinification, gave wines that oxidized very easily.

It needed someone with money, knowledge, and flair to create wines that could compete at the end of the twentieth century. In 1970 the great Rioja house Marqués de Riscal decided that it wanted a white wine that it could sell alongside its famous reds. Unlike practically all its competitors, it had never made a white Rioja and decided that the wine it was looking for could not be grown there. It looked at various other parts of Spain, but there were already too many vineyards in the northwest and northeast, many of them producing first-class wines. Assisted by Professor Peynaud of Bordeaux, it searched around Spain and found what it was looking for in Rueda. The professor recognized the enormous potential of Verdejo. The bodega was established there in 1972, coinciding with the creation of the DO. It also introduced Sauvignon. At that time it was criticized by its friends in Rioja for having moved elsewhere and by the growers in Rueda for producing uncharacteristic wines. But time soon proved the professor entirely right. Some old-established bodegas began to mend their ways and many others have jumped on the bandwagon.

The old style *generosos*, the *vinos de licor* listed above, are still made and are fascinating to try, as they show what Spanish wines used to be like; and if there is no future for them, they nevertheless retain an informed local following. But the new generation wines are a revelation. Verdejo is a very powerful grape that gives the wines an enormous flavour like a herb garden. In the past it was invariably spoiled because its wines oxidized so easily. When picked in the cool of the early hours, cold fermented in stainless steel, and kept away from oxygen by elaborate precautions that almost seem exaggerated, but which are essential, it can give big wines of ample acidity and great length. Complexity is added, and the tendency to oxidize further reduced, by blending in Sauvignon or Viura, which add a bite at the end. The Sauvignon grape has proved so adaptable that it now produces excellent wines all over the world, all with varietal characteristics, but no two tasting the same. The varietal Sauvignons made in Rueda are among the best. Some, however, are fermented in oak and take on so much oak flavour that their appeal is limited to those who have this particular taste; but their oakiness is now being moderated. The sparkling wines are very agreeable, but not, so far, much more. All these wines should be drunk as young as possible.

The next great development happened as recently as 2001 when red wines were added to the DO. They had long been made, but had to be sold simply as table wines, and many of them were very good. Now they can develop a place of their own and it remains to be seen whether they will rival those from Ribera del Duero and Toro, which they well might.

Some leading bodegas

AGRICOLA CASTELLANA
Carretera Rodilana s/n, 47491 La Seca, Valladolid.
Tel: +34 983 81 63 20; Fax: +34 983 81 65 62;
Email: ventas@agricolacastellana.com; Website: www.agricolacastellana.com
Founded in 1935, this old-established cooperative, with 350 members who cultivate 2,000 hectares of vineyard, has brought itself up to date. It makes wines of good quality and excellent value, selling them under a number of names: Azumbre is used for a varietal Verdejo from vines over thirty years old and for a varietal Sauvignon Blanc; Cuatro Reyas is a varietal Verdejo; Palacio

de Vivero and Valtierra are used for blends of Verdejo and Viura; Pámpano is a *semi-seco* from the same two grapes. Its *rosado* and its reds are varietal Tempranillo sold under the name Vacceos and include a *crianza* given ten months in American oak. Apart from its Rueda wines, it makes Vinos de la Tierra de Castilla, using the names Caballero de Castilla and Casa María. It also works with the Marqués de Griñon, who makes his excellent Rueda here using his own winemaker, and also uses it for his Durius non-DO wines.

ALVAREZ Y DIEZ

Juan Antonio Carmona 12, 28020 Nava del Rey, Valladolid.
Tel: +34 983 85 01 36; Fax: +34 983 85 07 61;
Email: comercial@alvarezydiez.com; Website: www.alvarezydiez.com

One of the older family bodegas, founded in 1941, it has seventy-five hectares of vineyard and has brought itself up to date. Since 1986 it has been growing its wines organically. They are good and are sold under the name Mantel. Mantel Blanco has a minor proportion of Viura. There is also a varietal barrel-fermented Verdejo and a varietal Sauvignon Blanc.

BODEGAS ANTANO

Arribas 7–9, 47490 Rueda, Valladolid. Tel: +34 983 86 85 33; Fax: +34 983 86 85 14; Email: info@bodegas-antano.com; Website: www.bodegas-antano.com

Although this is one of the new wave of bodegas, founded in 1989 by a prosperous Madrid restaurateur, its cellars are very old indeed – perhaps 500 years old – and very beautiful, dug down to three levels. It has 150 hectares of vineyard, trained on wires so that the grapes can be mechanically harvested in the cool of the night, and pruned short for low yields. Its white wines, sold as Viña Mocén, include a barrel-fermented Verdejo and a varietal Sauvignon Blanc. Outside the DO it also makes a Chardonnay. It went into red wines in a big way before they were admitted to the DO, and is now sitting pretty. Its reds include Vega Bravía and Viña Cobranza, both made from Tempranillo with fifteen per cent Cabernet Sauvignon, the latter going up to *reserva*, and Cobranza Vendímia Seleccionada, which is a varietal Tempranillo. In the last edition it was described as "one to watch" and it has been well worth watching.

AURA

Ctra Autovia del Noroeste km 175, 47790 Rueda, Valladolid.
Tel: +34 983 86 82 86; Fax: +34 983 86 81 68;
Email: mgonzalo@byb.es; Website: www.bodegasaura.com

Started in 1990, and part of the Bodegas y Bebidas empire, its ownership is now unclear. It has thirty-two hectares of vineyard, growing Verdejo and Sauvignon Blanc, and makes good wines in the modern Rueda style. Aura Verdejo is very nearly varietal but has two per cent Sauvignon Blanc. The Vendímia Seleccionada is a barrel-fermented Sauvignon Blanc.

BODEGAS CERROSOL
Camino Villagonzalo s/n, 40460 Santituste de San Juan Bautista, Segovia.
Tel: +34 921 59 60 02; Fax: +34 921 59 60 35;
Email: fernandovegas@avelinovegas.com; Website: www.avelinovegas.com

This is a modern bodega, founded in 1998, and part of the Avelino Vegas group, which has other bodegas in Rioja, Ribera del Duero, and Rías Bajas, as well as being strong in Vinos de la Tierra de Castilla y León. It is now one of the biggest players in Rueda, controlling multiple small plots making a grant total of 400 hectares, many of them with vines over thirty years old. Its wines are reliable and good value. The best are sold under the name Doña Beatriz, which include varietals from Verdejo and Sauvignon together with fifty-fifty Verdejo/Viura blends. It also sells wines under the marks Valle de la Vega, Cerrasol, and Viña Ivín.

BODEGAS DE CRIANZA DE CASTILLA LA VIEJA
Carretera Madrid–Coruña km 170.6, 47490 Rueda, Valladolid.
Tel: +34 983 86 81 16; Fax: +34 983 86 84 32;
Email: claire@bodegasdecastilla.com; Website: www.bodegasdecastilla.com

Various dates are given for the foundation of this bodega, but 1973 is about right. It was one of the earliest of the new bodegas, but its founder, Antonio Sanz, was a fourth generation wine-grower with a fine reputation. The family is ubiquitous in Rueda and has other bodegas in Ribera del Duero and Toro. It is now run by Ricardo and Antonio Sanz, who have some 200 hectares of vineyard with another 200 under long-term contracts. They produce some of the very best wines in the region under the marks Bornos and Palacio de Bornos. They are consistently excellent. The Palacio de Bornos Verdejo has a minor proportion of ten per cent Viura, but there is a varietal version barrel-fermented in French oak from vines over fifty years old. The barrel-fermented Bornos Verdejo-Sauvignon is a fifty-fifty blend. There is also a varietal Sauvignon. Reds include Señorío de Illescas, a varietal Tempranillo *crianza*. Outside the DO there is Exxencia, a sweet wine from the Verdejo, Palacio de Almirante, a barrel-fermented Chardonnay; and a whole range of sparkling wines, which they pioneered.

CUEVAS DE CASTILLA

For contact details, *see* Bodegas de Crianza de Castilla la Vieja, above.

This small bodega was founded in 1988 and used to be called Bodegas Con Class. It was run by Antonio Sanz of the sixth generation of family wine-makers, but it has now gone in with the interest described above, though it makes a separate range of wines that are also very good indeed. The name Con Class has been kept and is used for a wine with sixty per cent Verdejo and forty per cent Viura. Palacio de Menada is the mark used for its other wines, a Rueda Superior from ninety per cent Verdejo, eight per cent Viura, and two per cent Cabernet Sauvignon; a varietal Sauvignon Blanc; and a varietal Verdejo fermented in seventy-five per cent American and twenty-five per cent French oak.

VINOS BLANCOS DE CASTILLA

Carretera de la Coruña km 172, 47490 Rueda, Valladolid.

Tel: +34 983 86 80 29; Fax: +34 983 86 85 63;

Email: comercial@marquesderiscal.com; Website: www.marquesderiscal.com

Alphabetical order brings this bodega almost to the bottom of the list, but any other consideration would put it right at the top, for it is the Rueda arm of the Marqués de Riscal; it pioneered the development of the new style Ruedas and its wines are second to none. The earliest part of its history has already been given. In 1988 it started to plant vineyards and now has 195 hectares. At the beginning, the Spanish market was looking for oak and the wines were finished in barrels, but now the market seeks young, fresh, fruity wines and oak is not used save for wine is that is barrel-fermented. The Rueda Verdejo has eighty-five per cent Verdejo and fifteen per cent Viura. There is a varietal Sauvignon and a barrel-fermented Limousin, a varietal Verdejo fermented in oak and given eleven months in Allier, not Limousin, oak casks. From this great Rioja house you would expect some fine reds and indeed there is one, Riscal 1860, a varietal Tinto de Toro given five months' ageing in American oak, made outside the DO.

BODEGAS Y VINAS DOS VICTORIAS

Ctra Juan Mora s/n, 47530 San Román de Hornija, Valladolid. Tel/Fax: +34 983 78 40 29; Email: info@dosvictorias.com; Website: www.dosvictorias.com

The two Victorias, Victoria Pariente and Victoria Benavides, met as students. The Pariente family already had vineyards in Rueda, so they decided to set up in business in 1998 and made a sensational success of it. They are also active in Toro, where they make reds. They have sixteen hectares of vineyard. The

Ruedas are José Pariente Verdejo and a barrel-fermented version, fermented in eighty per cent Allier and twenty per cent American oak, both varietals.

TELMO RODRIGUEZ
See Ribera del Duero.

His local offering is Basa, a very successful blend of eighty per cent Verdejo, fifteen per cent Viura, and five per cent Sauvignon Blanc.

VINOS SANZ
Ctra Madrid-La Coruña km 171, 47490 Rueda, Valladolid.
Tel: +34 983 86 81 00; Fax: +34 983 86 81 00;
Email: vinossanz@vinossanz.com; Website: www.vinossanz.com

This family bodega is one of the oldest in the area, dating from 1870. It has 100 hectares of vineyard and has moved with the times, run by another member of the ubiquitous Sanz family, Juan Carlos Ayala Sanz, the sixth generation of wine-growers. In 2002 it had an injection of outside capital that enabled it to modernize completely. It produces Clásico from equal parts of Verdejo and Viura, a Verdejo that has fifteen per cent Viura, and two varietal Sauvignons, the top one called Finca La Collina. The *rosado* and the red Campo Sanz are varietal Tempranillos.

BODEGAS VERACRUZ
Juan A Carmona 1, 47500 Nava del Rey, Valladolid. Tel: +34 630 10 73 00;
Fax: +34 983 85 07 61; Email: b.veracruz@terra.es

A boutique bodega established in 2003. Its varietal Verdejo, Ermita Veracruz, is very good indeed. This is one to watch.

HERMANOS DEL VILLAR
Zarcillo s/n, 47490 Rueda, Valladolid. Tel: +34 983 86 89 04;
Fax: +34 983 86 89 05; Email: hvillar@infonegocio.com

Founded in 1995, it has seventy hectares of vineyard growing Verdejo, Sauvignon, and Tempranillo. The oenologist, Pablo de Villar, has isolated his own strain of Veredejo yeast and uses micro-oxygenation to bring forward the development of his wines. They are sold under the brand Oro de Castilla: varietals from Verdejo and Sauvignon, with an elegant barrique-fermented Verdejo.

TORO

Geography

The Toro vineyards extend west from those of Rueda and east of Zamora. The district takes its name from the agreeable little town of Toro, with its wonderful Romanesque Colegiata (collegiate church), on the river Duero, though most of the vineyards lie to its south and west. The little river Guareña passes through them and flows into the Duero just south of Toro. It is on Spain's central plateau and the vineyards are from 620–800 metres (2,034–2,625 feet) above sea level.

Climate
The climate is continental with very cold winters and long, hot summers. The maximum temperature is 40°C (104°F), the minimum -10°C (14°F), and the average 12.5°C (54.5°F). There is very little rain, 300–400 millimetres (11.8–15.7 inches) a year, most of which falls in the spring, and it is very sunny, with 2,600–3,000 hours of sunshine.

Soils
The alluvial soil down by the river is not much used for vineyards, which instead are planted on sandy, well drained, infertile soil with large pebbles and some calcium, at higher levels.

Grapes
Red varieties: Tinto de Toro and Garnacha. The leading red variety, Tinto de Toro, is a long-established clone of Tempranillo, though it has taken on a character of its own to such an extent that some authorities deny that it is Tempranillo at all. Its planting increased from sixty per cent of the vineyard in 1996 to seventy-five per cent in 2001. The Garnacha is known locally as Tinto Aragonés.
White varieties: Malvasía and Verdejo. Palomino used to be widely planted, but was banned in 1990.

Planting
En vaso with 900–2,700 vines per hectare. A lot of consolidation and replanting is in progress.

Vineyard area
5,507 hectares.

Authorized yields

Tinto de Toro: 42hl/ha. Those for the other varieties vary according to district: Garnacha and Malvasía 49–63hl/ha; Verdejo 28–49hl/ha.

Wines

Reds from 12.5–15% ABV, the minimum figure being the highest in Spain. All categories up to *gran reserva* are available and the standard rules apply. They must be made from not less than seventy-five per cent Tinto de Toro (alias Tempranillo), and while some bodegas use a little Garnacha, or even the white varieties, the best reds are 100 per cent Tinto de Toro. *Rosados* from 11–14% ABV. Whites from 11–13.5% ABV.

Production

75,000 hectolitres (2003).

Vintages

There is very little difference from one year to another, so much so that all between 1999–2003 were classified as "excellent" (5).

Toro has long been known for its wines, and its name has given rise to many jokes about bulls' blood, especially as its red wines used to be very dark (indeed, they are still dark) and dauntingly alcoholic, sometimes rising to as much as 17% ABV. They were aimed at the cheap end of the market and were often sent to other parts of Spain for blending with weaker wines, so a very old Toro should be approached with circumspection. The great change came in the 1980s. The better growers had long known they could produce fine wines, and in 1987 they got their DO. Now everything is very different. Modern winemaking moved in and the area took off. The best shippers are making very good wines that are generally affordable, for unlike those of Ribera del Duero, they have not yet become fashionable. How long will this last? Prices for the best ones are already rising rapidly. The whites and *rosados* are crisp and dry, with plenty of acid and good length: wines that would have been inconceivable in such a hot climate in the old days. But it is the reds that are really worth seeking. They are still splendid, strong stuff, but no longer dauntingly so, the usual strength being 13.5–14% ABV. They have plenty of tannin, but are well balanced. The *jóvenes* are meant to be drunk young, but the *crianzas* are aimed at five to eight years old, and it is likely that the *gran reservas* will last for twenty, though all can be drunk with great pleasure a good deal younger. There is the usual mushroom growth of boutique bodegas and most are good. In the last edition of this book only five bodegas were mentioned. With this one the problem is which to leave out.

Some leading bodegas

BODEGAS Y VINAS DOS VICTORIAS
For address and history *see* Rueda, above.

In Toro the two Victorias produce very good varietal Tinto de Toros under the mark Elias Mora. The Viña Elias Mora is given six months in American and French oak, the *crianza* has twelve months, and Gran Elias Mora is made only in the best vintages from vines over fifty years old and given seventeen months in French oak.

ESTANCIA PIEDRA
Carretera Toro-Salamanca km 8, Apartado de Correos 77, 49800 Toro, Zamora.
Tel: +34 980 69 39 00; Fax: +34 980 69 39 01;
Email: info@estanciapiedra.com; Website: www.estanciapiedra.com

This is one of the shining lights amongst the new bodegas, founded in 1999 and owned by an American family called Stein who have Scottish connections, but live in the Cayman Islands. *Stein* is German for stone, hence *Piedra*. It has sixty hectares of vineyard that include some very old Tinto de Toro vines, and there are two experimental three-hectare plots of Cabernet Sauvignon and Merlot. The *roble* is from ninety per cent Tinto and ten per cent Garnacha, aged in twenty per cent American and eighty per cent French oak. The Selección and the top Paredinas are both varietals from Tinto de Toro, the former given twelve and the latter eighteen months in new French oak and unfiltered. A very highly praised wine is La Gerona from seventy-five per cent Tinto de Toro and twenty-five per cent Garnacha, matured in eighty-five per cent French and fifteen per cent American oak.

BODEGAS FARINA
Camino del Palo s/n, 49800 Toro, Zamora.
Tel: +34 980 57 76 73; Fax: +34 980 57 77 20;
Email: comercial@bodegasfarina.com; Website: www.bodegasfarina.com

A family bodega founded in 1942 by the present owner's father, this was the first estate whose wines made a real impact. The standard has been maintained: all the wines are good and thoroughly reliable. It has two totally separate bodegas, a new one in Toro built in 1987 and since enlarged for DO wines, and the other, to make its very agreeable table wines. It has 250 hectares of vineyard. In the new bodega everything is stainless steel, from the reception of the grapes onward. The whites and *jóvenes* are sold under the name Colegiata, the *crianzas* and above under the name Gran Colegiata, the labels illustrated by a picture of the Colegiata in Toro. The whites are varietals from Malvasía, the *rosados* and reds are varietals from Tinto de Toro. There is a red *joven* called Primero made by carbonic maceration. The Colegiata *joven* has no oak ageing, but the Gran Colegiata *crianza* is given eight months in American and French oak, the *crianza* Roble Francés has eleven months in French oak, and the *reserva* has eighteen months in American oak. The top of the range, Campus, comes from vines 100–140 years old and is aged for fifteen months in fifty-fifty American and French oak.

J & F LURTON
Mostenses 4, 47400 Medina del Campo, Valladolid. Tel/Fax: +34 983 85 00 25; Email: jflurton@jflurton.com; Website: www.jflurton.com

The brothers Jacques and François Lurton, sons of a Bordeaux château owner, are famous as consultants and set up their own company in 1988. They have vineyards all over the world: Argentina; Australia; Chile; Uruguay; even France. They epitomize "flying winemakers". In Spain they have properties in Rueda and, since 1998, in Toro. In Toro they make very good wines under the mark El Albar, as varietals from the Tinto de Toro: the Clasico is given one year in French and American oak, and the Excelencia eighteen months in eighty per cent French and twenty per cent American. A recent and notable addition is Campo Elisio, also given eighteen months.

MARQUES DE IRUN
Nueva 7–9, 47491 La Seca, Valladolid.
Tel: +34 956 85 17 11; Fax: +34 956 85 34 62

A small bodega founded in 1990, it is part of the Luis Caballero group, a major sherry shipper in El Puerto de Santa María and a great wine enthusiast. The Toro wines are varietal Tinto de Toro sold under the mark Santuario.

BODEGAS Y VINEDOS MAURODOS
Carretera N 122 km 412 Villaester, 47112 Pedrosa del Rey, Valladolid.
Tel: +34 983 78 41 18; Fax: +34 983 78 40 18;
Email: info@bodegasmauro.com

Established in 1998, this is an enterprise of the Mauro family, long renowned for its *vinos de la tierra*. It has thirty-five hectares of vineyard with an average age of thirty-five years. Sold under the name San Román, the varietal Tinto de Toros are hugely praised.

BODEGAS Y VINEDOS PINTIA

Carretera de Morales s/n, 47530 San Román de Hornija, Valladolid. Tel: +34 983 78 41 78; Email: vegasicilia@vega-sicilia.com; Website: www.vega-sicilia.com

The email and website addresses give the game away: this is an offshoot of the great Vega Sicilia (*see* Ribera del Duero) and its wines, of course, are superb. It was originally called Alquiriz. The company moved in and acquired forty-five hectares of old vines in 1997 (it now has eighty), but the first wine was not put on the market until the 2001 vintage. Pintia is a varietal Tinto de Toro with thirteen months in oak, seventy per cent French and thirty per cent American.

REJADORADA

Ctra Reja Dorada 11, 49800 Toro, Zamora. Tel/Fax: +34 980 69 30 89; Email: rejadorada@rejadorada.com; Website: www.rejadorada.com

The bodega was founded in 1999 by a small group of enthusiasts with premises in the fifteenth-century palace of Monroy. All the wines are varietal Tinto de Toro. The *roble* is given six months oak ageing and the *crianza* twelve months. The top wine is Sango de Rejadorada, given eighteen months in French oak. These are already good wines, and the owners are aiming high. One to watch.

TELMO RODRIGUEZ

See Ribera del Duero.

Toro seems natural country for Telmo Rodríguez – an up-and-coming place where he can make the sort of wines he likes. Gago, Dehesa Gago, and his top wine, Pago La Jara, are certainly impressive.

TORESANAS

Carretera N 122 s/n, Poligono Carabizal, 49800 Toro, Zamora.
Tel: +34 983 86 83 36; Fax: +34 983 86 84 32;
Email: bodegasbccv@interbrook.net; Website: www.bodegasdecastilla.com

Founded in 1997, this is a member of the Bodegas de Castilla group. It has twenty-five hectares of vineyard. Antonio Sanz makes a number of very sound wines, all of which are Tinto de Toro varietals. Amant Novello is made by carbonic maceration. Amant is twenty-five per cent carbonic maceration and seventy-five per cent traditional. Puerto Adelia had twelve months wood ageing and is suitable for further ageing in bottle. Orot is a *crianza* with fourteen months oak ageing.

BODEGAS VEGA SAUCO

Avenida Comuneros 108, 49810 Morales de Toro, Zamora. Tel/Fax: +34 980 69 82 94; Email: vegasauco@vegasauco.com; Website: www.vegasauco.com

This small family bodega, established in 1991, makes very reliable wines that are matured in fine old underground tunnels. The *joven* has three months in American oak, the *crianza* twelve months, and the *reserva* eighteen months in French and American oak. These are all varietal Tinto de Toros. The top wine, Tinto Wences, is eighty per cent Tinto de Toro and twenty per cent other varieties from an experimental vineyard. All are best with bottle-age, and 10–12 years is recommended for the Wences.

BODEGA VINA BAJOZ

Avenida de los Comuneros 90, 49810 Morales de Toro, Zamora.
Tel: +34 980 69 80 23; Fax: +34 980 69 80 20;
Email: info@vinabajoz.com; Website: www.vinabajoz.com

This is a cooperative, and an extraordinarily good one. Started in 1962 by eight growers, it is now owned by 142 who between them have 1,050 hectares of vineyard, getting on for twenty per cent of the total, which makes it the biggest operator in the DO. What is more, the vineyards are old; the average age of the vines is fifty and some are 100 years old, giving a low average yield of twenty-seven hectolitres per hectare and very concentrated wines. Its top wines are among the best. Sold under the name Bajoz they are nearly all varietal Tinto de Toro. The *joven* has a short time in oak, five per cent of it new American. The *roble* is from 30–40-year-old vines and has three months in new American oak. The *crianza* has six months and the *reserva*, from vines 70–100 years old, has twelve months, both in new American oak and with ageing potential. Caño is the exception: seventy-five per cent Tinto de Toro, from vines 30–80 years old, and twenty-five per cent Garnacha. The top red, Gran Bajoz, is a single-vineyard wine from sixty-year-old vines and has twelve months in American and French oak. The white is a varietal Malvasía from fifty-year-old vines, and the *rosado* is a varietal Garnacha from 30–80-year-old vines.

Other wines

There are vineyards almost everywhere in Castilla y León. Some may eventually reach DO status, others not, and some do not want it – including some of the best.

BODEGAS ALTA PAVINA

Camino de Santibáñez s/n, 47328 La Parrilla, Valladolid.

Tel: +34 983 68 15 21; Fax: +34 983 33 98 90

Isolated in a vast, dull plateau, this was set up in 1988 by a Valladolid businessman for his oenologist daughter. There are ten hectares of vineyard planted with Cabernet Sauvignon and Pinot Noir, for the most part bravely ungrafted. The wines can be good, but are very variable.

PEREZ CARAMES

Peña Picón s/n, 24500 Villafranca del Bierzo, León. Tel: +34 987 54 01 97;

Fax: +34 987 54 03 14; Email: 1018fp@teleline.es

Established in 1986 it has thirty-two hectares. The main bodega is in Bierzo, and this is a subsidiary operation that sells a wide range of well-liked wines, mostly from Mencía and French varieties, under the mark Casar de Santa.

VERMILION DE VALBUENA DE DUERO

For contact details, *see* Matarromera in Ribera del Duero.

Vermilión is a highly praised non-DO varietal Tinto Fino made by the noted Ribera del Duero grower Matarromera.

VdIT CASTILLA Y LEÓN

This covers the whole region and allows wines to be made from grapes disallowed for the DOs. They can be extremely good.

ABADIA RETUERTA

Abadía Santa María de Retuerta s/n, 47350 Sardón de Duero, Valladolid.

Tel: +34 983 68 03 17; Fax: +34 983 68 02 86;

Email: info@abadia-retuerta.es; Website: www.abadia-retuerta.com

This great estate has 204 hectares of vineyard surrounding the ancient, restored abbey of Santa María de Retuerta, founded in 1143. It is within a stone's throw of Ribera del Duero, just to the west on the road to Valladolid. It was owned by a Spanish seed company that grubbed up all the vines, but was acquired in 1988 by the Swiss chemical giant Sandoz, and the chairman of the Spanish subsidiary decided to replant the vines as the rights had not expired. In 1995 Pascal Delbeck of Château Belair in St-Emilion was brought in, and a fine new bodega was built the following year. He found an ideal site suitable for several vine varieties, and concentrated on Tempranillo, Cabernet Sauvignon, and Merlot, with small plots of Petit Verdot and Syrah, which set it apart from the Ribera del Duero DO. In the bodega everything is moved by gravity. It makes excellent wines. Primicia, a *joven*, has sixty per cent Tempranillo, twenty per cent Cabernet Sauvignon, and twenty per cent Merlot. Rívola is sixty per cent Tempranillo and forty per cent Cabernet Sauvignon, with twelve months' oak ageing. The Selección Especial is seventy-five per cent Tempranillo, twenty per cent Cabernet Sauvignon, and five per cent Merlot; it regards this as its most representative wine and recommends long cellaring. Viña Arnoldo is eighty-five per cent Cabernet Sauvignon, ten per cent Syrah, and five per cent Tempranillo and is aged in new American casks. Cuvée El Campenario is a varietal Tempranillo from four different soils, and Cuvée El Palomar is from equal parts of Tempranillo and Cabernet Sauvignon, both the Cuvée wines being unfiltered. The best wines of all are Pago Negralda, a varietal Tempranillo with twenty-four months in French oak; Pago Valdebellón, a varietal Cabernet Sauvignon; and Pago La Garduña, a varietal Syrah: all are unfiltered. The Pago and Cuvée wines are of limited production. PV is a varietal Petit Verdot in very limited production.

BODEGAS Y VINEDOS MAURODOS
Cervantes km12, 47320 Tudela de Duero, Valladolid.
Tel: +34 983 52 19 72; Fax: +34 983 52 19 73;
Email: info@bodegasmauro.com; Website: www.bodegasmauro.com

The excellent wines from this bodega, founded in 1980, have already been mentioned under Toro, but the non-DO Mauro wines, grown in a thirty-five-hectare vineyard, have also long been recognized as seriously good. Those sold under the mark Mauro are ninety per cent Tempranillo with Syrah and a little Garnacha, matured for fifteen months in French and American oak. Terreus is usually a varietal Tempranillo, but may contain a minor proportion of Garnacha and is matured in new French oak. Vendímia Seleccionada is a varietal Tempranillo with thirty months' ageing in French and American oak. They are made by the legendary Mariano Garcia, who also makes the superb Aalto in Ribera del Duero.

BODEGAS Y VINEDOS RIBERA DEL DURATON
Carretera Valtiendas-Aranda s/n, 40314 Valtiendas, Segovia.
Tel: +34 921 52 72 85; Fax: +34 921 52 70 49;
Email: sofia@riberadelduraton.com

This bodega produces a highly praised range of wines: Duratón from fifty per cent Tempranillo, thirty-five per cent Syrah, and fifteen per cent

Cabernet Sauvignon; Duratón Syrah (a varietal); and Pago de la Moravia, a varietal Tempranillo.

GRUPO YLLERA

Carretera Madrid Coruña km 173.5, 47490 Rueda, Valladolid.

Tel: +34 983 86 80 97; Fax: +34 983 86 81 77;

Email: grupoyllera@grupoyllera.com; Website: www.grupoyllera.com

The González family, now in its sixth generation, had grown wine for ages; then in 1973 a new generation led by Jesús González Yllera started to bottle wine and formed the present company, originally called Bodegas Los Curros. It is active in Ribera del Duero and Rueda, but its most popular wines are its non-DOs, and their popularity is well deserved. All of them are varietal Tinto Finos. There are two *rosados* sold under the marks CUVI and Almenada, which are not given any cask ageing. CUVI Roble and Almenada Roble have six months in American oak. Its most notable wines, though, are the Yllera reds. The *crianza* has fourteen months in eighty per cent American, twenty per cent Allier oak, while the *reserva* has eighteen months, the proportions of oak being eighty-five per cent and fifteen per cent. Gran Selección has thirty-six months in American oak, and Dominus has the unusually precise number of 671 days in Allier.

VdT LOS ARRIBES DE DUERO-FERMOSELLE

The first of these two areas is to the southeast of the province of Zamora, the second to the northeast of Salamanca. Red grapes: Juan García; Bobal; Rufete; Bruñal; Garnacha; and Tempranillo. White grapes: Malvasía; Verdejo; and Palomino. The local Juan García is said to have great potential, but this has not yet been realized. It is on the up, though, and may well become a DO.

HACIENDAS DURIUS

Carretera Zamora-Fernoselle km 56, 49220 Fermoselle, Zamora.

Tel: +34 980 61 31 63; Fax: +34 914 36 59 20;

Website: www.haciendas-espana.com

Carlos Falcó, Marqués de Griñon, misses few tricks, if any. He has his own wonderful estate at Dominio de Valdepusa and is a big operator in Rioja. It was here, though, in 1999 that he chose to establish the new headquarters for his Durius table wines, red and white, always thoroughly sound and very good value. The whites are from Verdejo and Viura, the reds from Tempranillo. There are thirty-one hectares of vineyard with plenty of land for expansion.

VdlT RIBERA DEL ARLANZA

In the province of Burgos and not far from the famous DOs of Ribera del Duero and Rioja, with vineyards rising from 700–1,000 metres (2,297–3,281 feet), it is not surprising that this area has potential. After a period of decline it is now waking up and aspires to become a DO. Red grapes: Tinto del País (Tempranillo); Mencía; and Garnacha. White grapes: Albillo; Macabeo; Palomino; Verdejo; and Cañarroyo.

VdlT TIERRA DE LEON

This VdlT also aspires to become a DO. It grows mostly light red wines and its particular vines are the indigenous Prieto Picudo and the Mencía, but Tempranillo and Garnacha are also grown for reds. Verdejo and Palomino are the leading whites.

VdlT TIERRA DEL VINO DE ZAMORA

The province of Zamora used to grow large quantities of wine, but this fell away as the recognized districts took over, and much of the soil was diverted to cereals. Wine-growing is now on the increase again. Red varieties: Tempranillo (Tinto del País); Garnacha; and Cabernet Sauvignon. White varieties: Malvasía; Moscatel; Albillo; Verdejo; and Palomino.

VdlT VALLE DE BENEVENTE

A large area of small plots, north of the Duero and in the northwest of the province of Zamora. The principal grapes are Tempranillo (here called Tinto Fino or Cencibel); Mencía; and Prieto Picudo. New bodegas are mushrooming up; this is a place to watch.

BODEGAS OTERO

Avda El Ferial 22, 49600 Benevente, Zamora. Tel: +34 980 63 16 00; Fax: +34 980 63 17 22; Email: info@bodegasotero.es; Website: www.bodegasotero.com
This family business was started in 1906 and is now in its third generation, but it took on a new shape in 1950 when the cellars were dug out. The first vintage was in 1952, but it was incorporated formally in 1965. It makes quaffing wines under the marks Petra Trevinca, Panduco, and El Cubeto. Its very sound young wines are sold as Pago de Valleoscuro, the red and *rosado* coming from Tempranillo and Prieto Picudo, the white from Malvasía and Verdejo. The Otero *crianzas* and *reservas* are made from Tempranillo, Mencía, and Prieto Picudo.

7

The North

People imagine Spain as a country shimmering under the hot sun. For much of the country, much of the time, this is true; but it is not at all true of the north. Here the weather is influenced by the Atlantic, and there is no Gulf Stream to warm the sea. It rains a great deal, though it is far enough south for the sun to be warm in summer. The result is a countryside as lusciously green as Ireland, full of exquisite scenery. But the map shows that much of it grows little or no wine. The wines that do grow here, apart from some in favoured places, are white and very light. They are very northern in style.

Someone suddenly transported to the Asturias might well guess himself to be in Wales, while in Bierzo they even have coal mines to add to the illusion. It is a rugged countryside, with people to match, and was never conquered by the Moors. What is more, it is a principality, and the Crown Prince of Spain always has the title of *Principe de Asturias* (Prince of the Asturias). There is some wine, even red wine, but more cider.

Cantabria, with Santander as its capital and the wonderfully wild and beautiful Picos de Europa as its greatest scenic feature, grows hardly any wine.

The País Vasco, or Basque country, has its own language of obscure origin and its own government in Bilbao, while the Galician language is full of Xs. Galicia extends right into the Rioja DOCa, but most of the rest of it does not grow wine, with the notable exception of the Chacolís, which are very light and are delightful with the local seafood.

Further to the south and west there is the DO of Bierzo, which is at the edge of Castilla y León and stands alone, well inland. To the north and north-west of El Bierzo there is little or no wine, and the weather can be very wet. But directly to the west and to the southwest there are the major regions of Valdeorras, Ribera Sacra, Ribeiro, and Rías Bajas. In these places the weather can still be

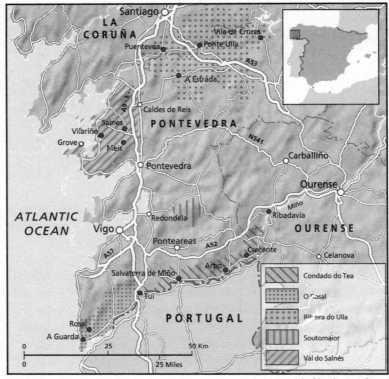

ix Northwest Coast

damp, though the climate is perhaps more kindly described as soft, and micro-climates provide warmth and shelter, to yield wines of great individuality and charm. The coastline is notable for its large inlets, or *rías*. Rías Bajas (Rías Baixas in Catalan) is the country of the lower or southern *rías*, and it still retains a good deal of its beauty despite some horrible "developments".

BIERZO

Geography

Although the DO is Bierzo, the region is El Bierzo. Looking on the map one might reasonably think it should be included with Galicia rather than the northwest; but it is in fact in Castilla y León, though it has grave doubts as to whether it should be. An old county, it has a degree of rugged independence.

The climate is Castillian, too, though that again is different. It is in a hollow surrounded by mountains. To the west and north there is the Cordillera Cantabrica, to the south the Sierra de Cabrera, and to the east the Montes de León. The principal town is Ponferrada – an agreeable old place that must once have been a gem, but which is now a mess surrounded by hideous development. Villafranca del Bierzo, in contrast, is a delightful little town.

Climate

Sheltered by the mountains yet influenced by the sea, El Bierzo is more temperate than the other wine districts of Castilla, despite the altitude of the vineyards at between 500–650 metres (1,640–2,133 feet). The temperature can rise to 32°C (89.6°F) in summer and fall to -1°C (30°F) in winter, though the range is generally 3.6–24°C (38.5–75°F) with an average of 13.1°C (55.5°F) and 2,150 hours of sunshine. The rainfall is 721 millimetres (28.3 inches). Severe damage can be caused, as in 1995, by frosts after an early flowering.

Soils

These are many and various: alluvial low down, sand and granite in the middle, and slate high up.

Grapes

Red varieties: Mencía; Garnacha Tintorera; Cabernet Sauvignon; Merlot; and Tempranillo. The first is the great grape of the area and the most encouraged. The last three are regarded as experimental.
White varieties: Godello; Doña Blanca; Malvasía; Palomino (here often called Jerez), Gewürztraminer; and Chardonnay. The first is the grape for the finest white wines, the second traditional, the last three experimental. The continued substantial presence of the Palomino can only be regretted.

Planting

Traditionally *marco real* with 1.6 metres (5.2 feet) spacing pruned *en vaso*, but more recent vineyards are trained on *espaldera*.

Vineyard area

3,853 hectares.

Authorized yield

Garnacha Tintorera and Palomino: 84hl/ha. All other varieties: 77hl/ha.

Wines

Reds must contain a minimum of seventy per cent Mencía and are 11–14% AB for *joven*, *crianza*, and *reserva*, with occasionally a *gran reserva*. *Rosados* are of the same strength and go up to *reservas*. The whites are all *jóvenes* and are 11–13% ABV in strength.

Production

210,000 hectolitres.

Vintages

1989 (3); 1990 (4); 1991 (4); 1992 (5); 1993 (2); 1994 (4); 1995 (3); 1996 (4); 1997 (3); 1998 (3); 1999 (3); 2000 (4); 2001 (4); 2002 (4); 2003 (4); 2004 (4).

The fact that this is a book about wine and not travel makes writing about El Bierzo rather exasperating. It is one of the most fascinating areas in Spain. It is a coal-mining district, but does not look like one, and also mines iron ore. The scenery on the way to Galicia is incredibly beautiful with dramatic, verdantly green mountains. The Romans flourished here and, helped by an army of slaves, made great water works with the unusual object of washing away mountains by hydraulic force; for the mountains were rich in gold. The mud carried in the water was filtered and the gold extracted. It also was one of the last stops on the pilgrim route to Santiago de Compostela. The superb monastery of San Nicolás el Real at Villafranca is one of its grandest relics, and the castle at Ponferrada was the headquarters of the Knights Templar. But it is the small towns and hermitages in the mountains, like Peñalba de Santiago, that are the most enchanting places, reached by narrow roads that are exciting to navigate. It also has some of the best fruit orchards in Spain.

But it does not have a long history as a source of fine wines. Galicia, lacking red wines of its own, was an easy market for indifferent reds from Mencía and Garnacha Tintorera grapes grown in over-fertile soils in the valleys. Even more indifferent whites from the high-yielding Palomino were apparently just as easy to sell. Decline had set in after 1882, when phylloxera arrived. The shy-bearing Godello grape practically disappeared and was replaced by more of the dim, high-yielding Palomino. When good wines came to be grown all over Spain, and transport became easy, the days of such wines were over. The immediate answer, as in so many parts of Spain, was the development of a cooperative movement, which brought about the establishment of the DO at the end of 1989, making it worthwhile to inject capital. The potential had always been there. The climate is very similar to that of the Rioja, the soils are excellent for growing vines, and the best local vine varieties were capable of producing highly individual wines. It is not yet one of Spain's leading districts, but is on the way up. Mencía is said to be related to the Cabernet Franc (research is continuing) and could well have been brought in by French monks in the high days of the pilgrimage to Santiago. Its best wines certainly have ageing capabilities and a delightful individuality. The Garnacha Tintorera, which has pink juice, is said by those who use it to add colour and complexity, but does not by itself produce very good wines. The *rosados* are unusually big in flavour, but the reds are more interesting. In the past they tended to be lusty, but lacking in subtlety and rather short. This cannot be said of the best wines made today. The Godello provides white wines of real fragrance and finesse. The best examples of all styles are now generally made by the independent boutique bodegas that have been springing up in the past decade. And some good non-DO wines are made from foreign varieties. It will be interesting to see what develops. There is still untapped potential.

Some leading bodegas

VINEDOS Y BODEGAS DOMINIO DE TARES
Los Barredos 4, Poligono Bierzo Alto, 24318 San Román de Bembribe, León.
Tel: +34 987 51 45 50; Fax: +34 987 51 45 70;
Email: info@dominiodetares.com; Website: www.dominiodetares.com
A leader among the new bodegas, it was founded in 2000 with twenty hectares of vineyard including some forty-year-old Mencía and ten-year-old Godello – the only vines from which it makes wine. There is a barrel-fermented Godello with three months in oak. The red *crianza corta* also has three months in oak. The very good Cepas Viejas has nine months in oak. The Bembibre *crianza* comes from six selected plots and is given fifteen months in oak; and the top Tares P3 from just one plot, is also given fifteen months in French oak.

ESTEFANIA
Ctra de Dehesas–Posada del Bierzo km 0.8, 24390 Ponferrada, León.
Tel/Fax: +34 987 42 00 15. Email: cascudo@tilenus.com; Website: www.tilenus.com
Another new arrival, founded in 1999, has thirty hectares of vineyard with 70–100-year-old Mencía vines. All its wines are varietal, beginning with a *joven*, then a *roble* with six months in eighty-five per cent French and fifteen per cent

American oak, and a *crianza* with twelve months in French oak, before coming to the top *reservas*, Pagos de Posada with fifteen months in French oak, and Pieros with seventeen months in new French oak.

BODEGAS Y VINEDOS LUNA BEBERIDE

Antigua Ctra Madrid a La Coruña km 402 Apdo 87, 24540 Cacabelos, León.
Tel: +34 987 54 90 02; Fax: +34 987 54 92 14;
Email: info@lunabeberide.com; Website: www.lunabeberide.com

Founded in 1986, this family bodega has eighty hectares of vineyard with one authorized variety, Mencía, and experimental plots of Cabernet Sauvignon, Gewürztraminer, and Chardonnay. The main production is varietal Mencía reds. The Gewürztraminer and a blend of equal parts of Gewürztraminer and Chardonnay, sold under the name Viña Arella, are very good.

DESCENDIENTES DE J PALACIOS

Calvo Sotelo 6, 24500 Villafranca del Bierzo, León. Tel: +34 987 54 08 21;
Fax: +34 987 54 08 51; Email: djpalacios@mail.ddnet.es

The Palacios family seems to breed gifted winemakers: *see* Rioja and Priorato. Here they have done it again. This bodega, with twenty-six hectares of vineyard, was founded in 1999 by the legendary Alvaro Palacios and his nephew, both descendants of J Palacios. They make varietal Mencías from old vines under the names Pétalos del Bierzo and Villa de Corullón, the former with four months' wood ageing and the latter with fourteen in new French oak.

PEREZ CARAMES

Peña Picón s/n, 24500 Villafranca del Bierzo, León.
Tel: +34 987 54 01 97; Fax: +34 987 54 03 14; Email: 1018fp@teleline.es

Founded in 1986, though members of the family had been growing vines in the district for forty years. The thirty hectares of vineyard, on remarkably stony soil near Villafranca, are cultivated organically and are exemplary. The vines are trained on *espalderas* – and the wires are stainless steel. They grow Mencía and Palomino, but also "experimentally" Cabernet Sauvignon, Merlot, Tempranillo, Pinot Noir, and Chardonnay. The oak used for ageing is entirely Allier. Varietal Mencía reds are sold under the name Casar de Valdaiga. These, especially the *crianzas*, are very good. Some of the most interesting wines, though, are those that are not DO and are sold under the name Casar de Santa Inés, including varietals from Merlot, Cabernet Sauvignon, Pinot Noir, and Chardonnay, with blends of Mencía/Cabernet Sauvignon and Pinot Noir/Tempranillo.

BODEGAS PEIQUE

Calle de Bierzo s/n, 24530 Valtuille de Abajo, León.

Tel/Fax: +34 987 56 20 44

A boutique bodega with ten hectares of vineyard established in 1999. Its varietal Mencías, matured in American, French, and Caucasian oak, are highly regarded, especially Peique Selección de Viñedos Viejos.

BODEGAS PRADA A TOPE

La Iglesia s/n, 24546 Cabedo, León. Tel: +34 902 40 01 01; Fax: +34 987 56 70 00; Email: info@pradaatope.es; Website: www.pradaatope.es

This is a most extraordinary place. "*A tope*" can loosely be translated as "flat out", and that is the way it is run. But is it a bodega at all? The answer is emphatically yes, and a very good one. But at first sight it is a shop selling most delectable foods of all kinds, including its own jams and bottled fruits, and quite different things like shoes. It is also a very good restaurant. This is how it all began, when in 1975 a cobbler began to bottle cherries in brandy. He started in wine the following year, and the creation of the DO in 1989 provided the incentive for expansion. It was clearly on the way up in 1988, and it was in that year he bought the ancient Canedo Palace to use as a bodega and planted vines; he now has twenty hectares, cultivated ecologically. He is an enchanting eccentric, rightly concerned with conservation. The bodega was established with state-of-the-art equipment in 1990. He makes some good wines. The white is Godello; the *rosado* eighty-five per cent Mencía and fifteen per cent Godello; the red *crianza* and *reserva* are never less than eighty-five per cent Mencía and usually 100 per cent; and there is a fresh and fragrant young red made from Mencía by carbonic maceration.

SOCIEDAD COOPERATIVA VINOS DEL BIERZO

Avenida de la Constitución 106, 24540 Cacabelos, León.

Tel: +34 987 54 61 50; Fax: +34 987 54 67 05

There are several cooperatives in Bierzo, but this was the first and is the biggest. It was founded in 1963 at Cacabelos with 600 members, and now has 2,000 and with over 1,000 hectares of vineyard. Ageing is in American oak. Wines of all colours are sold under various marks: Fontousal; Guerra; Señorío del Bierzo; Viña Oro; and Bocovi. The red Viña Oro is remarkably good value and shows the ageing potential of Mencía. Don Perejos is a sparkling wine. The reds and *rosados* are made from Mencía, the whites from Doña Blanca and Palomino.

THE CHACOLIS

There are three Chacolís: Arabako Txakolina or Chacolí de Alava; Bizkaiko Txakolina or Chacolí de Vizcaya; and Getariako Txakolina or Chacolí de Getaria. They have separate DOs, granted respectively in 2001, 1994, and 1990, but all come from the Basque country below the Bay of Biscay, and although separate have so much in common they will be described together.

Geography

The three are grown in different provinces: Alava inland in the province of Alava, toward Rioja; Vizcaya to the west; and Getaria to the east. Vizcaya is centred round Bilbao and stretches inland to beyond Durango, where there are three vineyards. The rest are very scattered; most are to the east of Bilbao, but all are very small. Nearly all are well inland on sites chosen for their sheltered locations and good microclimates. Getaria is to the west of San Sebastián, and again the vineyards are small and scattered. Most are near the sea and some are on beautiful terraces with marvellous views over the Bay of Biscay.

Climate

This is hardly propitious for grape growing. It is very damp and the summer has been described as "five days clear, five days cloud". The summer maximum temperature is 35°C (95°F) and the winter minimum 2°C (35.6°F), despite which there are frosts. The average is 13.5°C (56.3°F). The average rainfall is no less than 1,600 millimetres (63 inches), the sunshine 1,800 hours. Some of the inland vineyards, however, have a more continental climate with warmer summers, especially in Alava. Vineyards are between 10–100 metres (32.8–328 feet) above sea level.

Soils

With such a scattering of little vineyards, these are varied. Most, though, are on alluvial clay soil beneath a sandy topsoil.

Grapes

The most extraordinary thing about the vines is that they are on their own roots; phylloxera does not flourish here, so many are eighty years old.
White varieties: Hondarribi (or Ondarribi) Zuri, only in Vizcaya; Folle Blanc, known locally as Munemahatsa; and, only in Alava, Petit Manseng; Petit Corbu; and Gros Manseng. Some growers experiment with Riesling and Albariño.

Red variety: Hondarribi (or Ondarribi) Beltza; but not much is grown. It is said to be a relation of Cabernet Franc, but this is far from certain.

Planting

Traditionally the vines have been planted in the local *parral* style, which is a low pergola with the vines intertwined to provide protection against winds from the sea. The gaps are 1.8 metres (5.9 feet) between vines and two metres (6.6 feet) between rows. More modern vineyards, however, are planted in *espaldera* with the fruiting branches seventy centimetres (27.5 inches) above ground level to protect them from frosts. Maximum vine density is 2,500 per hectare for *parral* and 3,500 per hectare for *espaldera*.

Vineyard area

This is almost startlingly small, but growing. In Vizcaya it is 56 hectares, and in Getaria it is 17 hectares.

Authorized yield

63–97hl/ha, depending on location, but in practice usually much less.

Wines

These are all *jóvenes* and should be drunk very young. All three colours are produced and have a minimum alcohol level of 9.5% ABV and a maximum of 11.5% ABV, but those that are bottled generally work out at about 10.5–11% ABV. Almost all are whites and the other wines can be found only in local bars.

Production

Alava 1,502 hectolitres, Vizcaya 7,100 hectolitres, and Getaria 10,000 hectolitres (2003).

Vintages

Although these necessarily vary, as the wines should be drunk at no more than a year old there is no point in listing them.

That wine was grown here in the past can come as no surprise: at least since Roman times it has been grown all over Spain. But that it should still be grown commercially, albeit on a minuscule scale, is a triumph of enthusiasm over climate; and it is steadily growing, despite EU regulations that make it difficult to plant new vineyards.

The provinces are part of the País Vasco or Basque country. Although everyone can speak Castillian, it also has its own Basque language and more than its share of local patriotism, combining the national culture of Wales with the violence of Northern Ireland. And as in Wales (where wine is also grown), official names on signposts are often painted out and local ones substituted. The language appears to bear no resemblance to any other in the world and makes much use of the letter x. Thanks to the heavy rainfall the country is wonderfully green and beautiful, with a fine coastline.

In the Royal Historical Archives there is a mention of Chacolín [sic] in 1622, but the origin of the name is obscure. In the middle of the nineteenth century there were as many as 250 hectares of vineyard, but wine-growing went through a crisis brought on by a number of factors. Improved transport and the removal of restrictions on the movement of wine brought competition from Rioja and Navarra. Then there were the plagues from America: oïdium in 1860, mildew in 1885, and then phylloxera, which attacked the bulk of the vineyards, but mysteriously left some untouched, and these are the ones that flourish today. Mildew was a particular problem in the damp climate. The vineyards practically disappeared; then the wars of the twentieth century caused them to stagnate. By the 1980s there were only twenty-five hectares. Then there was a revival spurred by local pride and an increasing interest in local gastronomy. All the vineyards and bodegas are privately owned: there are no cooperatives.

The wines are made in an unusual way. They are left on their lees in tightly sealed containers so that some of the carbon dioxide from the fermentation gets dissolved and gives them their characteristic prickle. In a decent year they attain about 11% ABV without chaptalization, but they are light and very acid. This can be accentuated by a tendency to pick too early to avoid some of the hazards of the climate, together with insects and birds; but conversely some fruity and especially delicious wines can be produced by careful grape selection. Malolactic fermentation is not usual. The production, however, is minute and the wines are not cheap. The reds and *rosados* have a very small production indeed and are found only in local bars, but there are enough whites for there to be some exports, and in the summer they are delicious to drink in the fish restaurants from Bilbao to San Sebastián: light, refreshing, and perfect with the local seafood. The locals often pour them into tumblers, a little at a time, to be drunk while the sparkle lasts. They are well worth seeking.

Some leading bodegas

In Alava

ARABAKO TXAKOLINA

Maskuribal s/n, Edificio El Salvador, 01470 Amurrio, Alava. Tel: +34 945 89 12 11

Yes, this bodega, established in 1992 with twenty-six hectares of vines, has the same name as the DO. It is by far the biggest and the best in it.

In Vizcaya

DONIENE-GORRONDONA

Tel: +34 946 19 47 95; Fax: +34 946 19 58 31;

Email: gorrondona@euskalnet.net

It has twelve hectares of vineyard that produce good wines, the white sold as Doniene and the red as Gorrondona.

BODEGA ITSASMENDI

Barrio Arane s/n, 48300 Gernika, Vizcaya. Tel: +34 677 58 03 62;

Fax: +34 946 27 03 16; Email: bitsasmendi@euskalnet.net

This boutique bodega, founded in 1994, produces notably good whites.

BODEGAS VIRGEN DE LOREA

Barrio de Lorea, 48860 Otxaran-Zalla, Vizcaya.

Tel: +34 946 39 02 96; Fax: +34 946 67 05 21

Although old-established, with its first vintage in 1929, this bodega was bought by a millionaire in 1990, was totally modernized and is a showplace. It makes a first-class white wine under the name Señorío de Otxaran, and also a red.

In Getaria

AMEZTOI

Barrio Eitzaga 10, 20808 Getaria, Guipúzcoa.

Tel/Fax: +34 943 14 09 18; Email: amestoycb@euskalnet.net

A family-owned bodega producing good wine from eighteen hectares.

TXAKOLI GAINTZA

Caserío Gaintza, 20808 Getaria, Guipúzcoa.

Tel: +34 943 14 00 32; Fax: +34 943 89 60 38

One of the oldest established bodegas, dating from 1923, it produces good wines on a modest scale from its ten hectares.

TXOMIN ETANIZ

Finca Ametzmendl, 20808 Getaria, Guipúzcoa. Tel/Fax: +34 943 14 07 02.

A grower dating from 1930 making some of the best whites in the DO in a fine old cellar on a promontory with the steeply sloping vineyards behind it.

GALICIA

With Monterrei we enter Galicia in the northwest corner of Spain, an utonomy of four provinces: Coruña, Lugo, Ourense, and Pontevedra. In the distant past it was Celtic, but very few traces of that civilization remain. Its northern and western coastlines are Atlantic, while in the south it borders Portugal. In the east it is separated from the rest of Spain by the mountains of the Cordillera Cantabrica. The Atlantic weather gives its special verdant character. Over most of it there is a lot of rain, but in such a large area there are also many microclimates. The inhabitants of Pontevedra claim theirs to be the best climate in Europe. It is also remarkably beautiful. The coastlines are notable for their huge inlets, called *rías*; but alas they have been all but ruined by uncontrolled development. It is a country of unspoiled villages, exquisite mountains, and noble cities, the finest of which is Santiago de Compostela. Medieval pilgrims came here from all over Europe to visit the tomb of St James, and there seem to be just as many today, many of whom still walk. Lugo retains its Roman walls. It is a marvellous area of Spain to visit for those who seek art and beauty.

As expected, there are not many vineyards in such a damp and temperate area. Those producing quality wines are in the southern half, mostly in the valleys of the rivers Miño and Sil, which provide a dramatic landscape of almost vertical gorges. Others are found by smaller rivers that flow into the Atlantic.

MONTERREI

Geography

The Val de Monterrei borders Portugal. Monterrei itself is a fortified town with a castle and a thirteenth-century church. Verín, small as it is, is the commercial centre. The vineyards are 400–450 metres (1,312–1,476 feet) above sea level. It has two sub-zones: Val de Monterrei, the valleys of tributaries of the river Támega; and Ladeiro de Monterrei, the hillsides.

Climate

Being far inland, this is essentially continental. It is said to be the warmest place in Galicia with summers up to 35°C (95°F), but down to -5°C (23°F) in winter and an average of 12.6°C (54.7°F). Rainfall is 680 millimetres (26.8 inches).

Soil

Reddish, alluvial clay with a fertile topsoil.

Grapes

Red varieties: Mencía and Merenzao are preferred; with Alicante; Gran Negro; Tempranillo (Arauxa); Bastardo (María Ardoña); and Mouratón.
White varieties (which predominate): Treixadura (Verdello Louro); Verdello (Godello); Doña Blanca (Dona Branca); and Palomino (Jerez).

Planting

En vaso. The density must be between 3,700–5,000 vines per hectare.

Vineyard area

500 hectares, though other figures are published.

Authorized yield

5hl/ha.

Wines

Red, *rosado*, and white are produced. To carry the DO they need to have at least sixty-five per cent of the preferred varieties, and to be labelled Monterrei *superior* they need to have at least eighty-five per cent. The whites have a minimum 10% ABV, and if Monterrei *superior* 11% ABV. Reds a minimum 10% ABV, and if Monterrei *superior* 10.5% ABV.

Production

80,000 hectolitres (2003), but only a minority with the DO.

Vintages

1999 (4); 2000 (4); 2001 (5); 2002 (4); 2003 (4); 2004 (5).

Monterrei or Valle de Monterrei was granted DO status in 1996, but it is only slowly beginning to attract the investment that may make it a serious DO. It is at present perhaps the most obscure in Spain. The emphasis is on white wines, but a major presence is still the ubiquitous and wholly undistinguished Palomino. Most of the wines are made in two cooperatives and sold in bulk.

Some leading bodegas

GARGALO
Rúa de Castelo 59, 32619 Verín, Ourense. Tel: +34 988 59 02 03;
Fax: +34 988 59 02 95; Email: gargalo@verino.es; Website: www.verino.es
A family bodega founded in 1997, but with older origins. The wines are sold under the mark Terra do Gargalo. The agreeable young whites have sixty per cent Treixadura, thirty per cent Godello, and ten per cent Doña Blanca. The reds are made from Arauxa, Mencía, and Bastardo. The *roble* is given six months in new Allier oak.

BODEGAS BERNABE JIMENEZ
Rua Laureano Peláez 25, 32600 Verín, Ourense.
Tel: +34 988 41 03 14; Fax: 988 41 03 50
Very good wines, particularly the red Mencías.

ADEGAS LADAIRO
Lg O'Rosal s/n, 32613 Oimbra, Ourense. Tel: +34 988 42 27 57
A private grower consistently producing good wines.

RIAS BAJAS (RIAS BAIXAS)

Geography

This Galician DO dates from 1988 and used to have three distinct sub-zones; now it has five. Val do Salnés (the Salnés Valley) is the most northerly and is on the west coast, where the river Ulla flows into the Ría de Arousa and is centred on Cambados; El (or O) Rosal extends from the west coast along the right bank of the river Miño, which divides Spain from Portugal; Condado do Tea (*condado* means county) extends along the river further inland; Soutomaior, which was added in 1996, is inland southeast of Pontevedra; and Ribera de Ulla, which was added in 2000, is also inland to the northeast of Pontevedra and extending almost as far as Santiago de Compostela. This last is in the province of La (or A) Coruña; all the others in that of Pontevedra. Val de Salés is easily the biggest with almost 1,600 hectares; El Rosal comes next and then Condado de Tea, both with over 600 hectares. The other two at present are very small. Some of the westerly vineyards are almost at sea level, but go up to 300 metres (984 feet). In El Rosal the up-river vineyards are terraced on the steep slopes of the mountains that rise above the river and its tributaries.

Climate

This is dominated by the Atlantic. The Salnés Valley is the coolest of the sub-zones with an average temperature of 13°C (55.4°F) and few extremes. The summers can be dry and pleasant, but the proximity of the Atlantic gives a rain-fall of 1,500 millimetres (59 inches). El Rosal has a slightly higher average temperature of 14°C (57°F), but also a higher rainfall of 1,400–2,000 millimetres (55–78.7 inches). In either place the summer temperature does not rise above 30°C (86°F). Condado del Tea is less influenced by the Atlantic and has more extremes, freezing in winter and going up to 40°C (104°F) in summer, with an average of 13–15°C (55.4–59°F). It is generally wetter, with an average rainfall of 1,300–2,000 millimetres (51–78.7 inches). By comparison the average for all of England is 838 millimetres (33 inches). Sunshine averages 2,200 hours per year. The new sub-zones are more continental but still very wet.

Soils

The Salnés Valley and El Rosal are alluvial over the local pinkish granite. In the Condado do Tea granite and slate appear on the surface with light, granitic soils. Sautomaior has light sandy soils and Ribera de Ulla mostly alluvial ones.

Grapes

White varieties: Albariño (ninety per cent); Loureira Blanca (Marqués); Treixadura; Caiño Blanco; Torrontés; and Godello. Albariño grapes are the most expensive in Spain and are most dominant in Val de Salnés, which has little Loureira and no Treixadura. In Ribera de Ulla there is no Loureira, which is most widely planted in El Rosal. Godello is a new arrival.

Red varieties: Caiño Tinto; Espadeiro; Loureira Tinta; Sousón; Mencía; and Brancellao.

Planting

Traditionally on pergolas with the vines widely spaced: three metres (9.8 feet) apart and four metres (thirteen feet) between rows. They are pruned long, with seven *brazos* (arms) per vine and with one *pulgar* (pruning bud) and ten *yemas* (fruiting buds) per *brazo*. There can be as many as seventy bunches of grapes on a vine. There is now, however, a move to use a modification of the Geneva Double Curtain method of training, known as *Silvo*, and other pruning methods are being tried experimentally. This may eventually make mechanical harvesting possible in the flatter vineyards. There are 600–1,600 vines per hectare depending on the size and steepness of the site. The damp climate gives rise to fungal problems, but the local authorities give every assistance in monitoring so that treatments are kept to a minimum. There is a move toward organic viticulture, and already more than 500 hectares are grown in that way.

Vineyard area

2,643 hectares, but increasing within the limits of what the EU allows.

Authorized yield

Albariño: 71.5hl/ha. Others: 87.5hl/ha. In practice, however, the yield is usually 50–60hl/ha.

Wines

Although some red wines are made (with the abnormally low minimum alcohol level of 10% ABV), all the important wines are white and account for more than ninety-nine per cent of the total. The Albariño whites are 100 per cent varietal with a minimum strength of 11.3% ABV. Others sold as varietals must have at least eighty-five per cent of the named variety. Val do Salnés must be at least seventy per cent Albariño. Condado de Tea must have a minimum of seventy per cent Albariño or Treixadura vines, or of the two combined, and the rest authorized varieties. El Rosal must have the same combination of grapes. All the whites other than Albariño must have a minimum of 11% ABV; but they usually work out at 11–12.5% ABV, the Albariño 11.3% ABV and barrel-fermented ones 11.5% ABV. *Rosados* do not fall within the DO, but some good ones are made. The wines may be labelled with the names of the sub-zones where they are grown with the exception of Sautomaior, which is deemed too small.

Production

107,889 hectolitres (2003).

Vintages

Every vintage from 1991 has been officially classified as "good" (3).

Galicia is the wettest, coolest part of Spain where vines are grown, and it is near the limit of where they can be grown. It is so green, fertile, and beautiful in the Miño Valley (on both sides of the border, though in Portugal it is called Minho) that it looks like a vision of the Garden of Eden. The fresh, slightly sparkling Vinhos Verdes from Portugal became well known in the 1960s, though many that were exported were prepared specially for foreign markets and were very different from those sold in Portugal. The best were made from Alvarinho and Loureiro grapes, especially the former. In Spain these are the Albariño and Loureira Blanca. There were stories that Galicia produced fresh, light, acid wines like Vinhos Verdes, but these were never seen in the rest of Spain, not even in the north, though this can partly be accounted for by the famous Galician thirst. Perhaps the stories had been handed on by word of mouth from generation to generation, for there had indeed been a flourishing wine trade. But this began to collapse with the arrival of oïdium in 1851, when the vineyard area went down from 13,398 to 4,079 hectares, and much of the population left. Then mildew came in 1885 and phylloxera in 1899, so that in 100 years the vineyards were reduced to little more than a third of what they had been. By the 1970s these two varieties had almost died out. It was the old story: such vineyards as remained grew quaffing wines of no quality produced from high yielders like Palomino and Alicante. Then a revolution happened. Spain at that time had plenty of good red wines, and a few good white ones, but there were no fresh, light, delicate whites. The technology to produce them, even in a hot climate, was available and people started to use it. In the quest for light wines, someone happily thought of Rías Bajas. In the late 1970s and 1980s, leading bodegas from other parts of Spain such as Rioja and Penedès started to move in. Then came the smart money. Restaurateurs from Madrid and local businessmen who had made fortunes wanted vineyards. By 1988 the wines were good enough for a DO to be created, and the growers aspired to produce Spain's leading white wine. They may well have done so, though other districts would no doubt hotly dispute it. They have certainly produced something unique that has caught on to such an extent that it is Spain's most admired and most expensive white wine. The rate of expansion can be seen from the fact that in 1989 there were forty-three *adegas* (Gallego for a bodega) and 873 hectares of vineyard. In 2003, the numbers were 179 and 2,643.

The Albariño vine is by far the most important. The traditional way of growing it is on *parrales*, attractive pergolas with granite uprights and a canopy of wires. It produces varietal wines that are light and fragrant, but are sometimes so acid and astringent that they can be mouth-searing, especially when very young – though this is much less so today than it was in the past. It is a style that is sought after, though, and many growers retain the acidity by avoiding a malolactic fermentation altogether or by using it only on a proportion of the crop, as they find that it reduces not only acid, but also aroma and flavour. In the absence of a malolactic fermentation, the malic acid of the grapes often gives a rather apply element to the nose and flavour. Although it is generally recommended that these wines be drunk within the year, as they spend time in bottle the cutting edge becomes more blunted and some would say that they are at their most attractive after a year or two years in bottle. Nowadays some of the wines are specifically made for bottle-ageing, especially those that have oak. Some people prefer blended wines, and if they lack the unique penetration of the Albariño, they have layers of complexity. In El Rosal, which is the smallest of the original areas, but the one with the oldest tradition of wine-growing, Loureiro is a popular grape and gives a herbal element to the scent. In Condado del Tea, the Treixadura gives a flowery element, but the Torrontés by itself can make for rather bitter wines.

With bodegas springing up and new vineyards coming into production, it is not surprising that a lot of experiments are going on. No two winemakers do exactly the same thing. But one thing they all have in common is a wish to keep everything cool. The grapes are moved quickly into the press houses to avoid heating by the sun, and one extreme measure is to use cold water instead of air in the inflatable bags of the horizontal wine presses. Cold maceration is typical, and after fermentation the wines are often left on their lees. It goes without saying that fermentation is in temperature-controlled stainless steel. Then comes the question of oak. Very often there is none, but some have a few months in oak, usually American, with some Galician and French. Whether oakiness is or is not attractive in Albariño wines can only be a matter of opinion, but it certainly has its attractions.

"*Pazo*", which appears in many of the names, is best translated as "grange".

Some leading bodegas

BODEGAS AGNUSDEI
Bouza 19, Besoñaño, 36968 Axix-Simes-Meaño, Pontevedra.
Tel: +34 609 14 97 16; Fax: +34 986 71 08 27
Founded in 2002 in the sub-zone Val de Salnés, it has eighteen hectares of vine-

yard, some of which is very young. Its varietal Albariños are already good, though, and it is safe to say there are even better things to come.

AGRO DE BAZAN

Tremoedo 46, 36628 Vilanova de Arousa, Pontevedra.

Tel: +34 986 55 55 62; Fax: +34 986 55 57 99;

Email: agrodebazan@agrodebazansa.es; Website: www.agrodebazansa.es

It is not easy to pin down an exact date for the foundation of this bodega. Feasibility studies started in 1979 and work on the estate began in 1980, when trees were felled to make room for the vineyard, which was planted in 1981. The bodega was built in 1988, just in time for the vintage, and the first wines were sold in the following year. It is all very new and completely up to date, the creation of a Galician entrepreneur whose fortune is based on tinned fish. He set up the winery in a most beautiful position at Tremoedo in the Salnés Valley; and he did so with immense enthusiasm, which is justified by the quality of the wines. There are fifteen hectares of Albariño vines and no other variety is used. There is no malolactic fermentation, giving wines of great fragrance, the acidity being controlled by maceration and tank ageing. The wines (and also the tinned fish) are sold under the name Granbazán. The standard wine is Granbazán Verde, so called because it comes in a green bottle of a Rhenish shape. Granbazán Ambar comes in a brown bottle and is made from free-run juice, giving it an unusually generous flavour behind great freshness. Granbazán Limousin is likewise made from free-run juice, but only in the best years, and spends a year in Limousin oak followed by six months in tanks before bottling as a *crianza*. It is intended for ageing. At the opposite end of the range is Contrapunto, released early, just before Christmas. There is also a brandy, and the company has wine interests in Chile.

PAZO DE BARRANTES

Bodegas Pazo de Barrantes, Barrantes 36636, Ribadumia, Pontevedra.

Tel: +34 986 71 82 11; Email: bodega@pazodebarrantes.com;

Website: www.marquesdemurrieta.com

There can be few estates more beautiful than this one, which has been in family ownership for generations, passing to the Conde de Creixell through his mother in 1982. It now forms part of Dominios de Creixell, the other part being the great Rioja house Marqués de Murrieta. The ancient *pazo* in the Salnés Valley has been beautifully restored and is also the headquarters of the Fundacion Creixell which, among other things, has a considerable Graham Greene archive; he used to stay here. But although the estate has existed for centuries, it has entered the commercial production of Rías Bajas wines much more recently. There is a twelve-hectare vineyard of Albariño vines giving the first vintage in 1991. About half the wine is subjected to a malolactic fermentation, but there is still plenty of acidity. The wines are excellent and there is sometimes a very good, semi-sweet, late harvest one.

BODEGAS CASTRO MARTIN

Puxafeita 3, 36636 Ribadumia, Pontevedra.

Tel: +34 986 71 02 02; Fax: +34 986 71 06 07;

Email: info@bodegascastromartin.com; Website: www.bodegascastromartin.com

This family-owned bodega was founded in 1981, and built on three levels to allow the wine to be moved mostly by gravity. It has a ten hectares of vineyard of old vine Albariño in the Salnés Valley, and sells excellent varietal wines under the name Casal Caeiro, including a *barrica* version that has 6–8 months in Allier oak and is then blended with unoaked wine to get the balance right. This wine and Bodega Castro Martín are made from its own grapes, but a third label, Avian, introduced in 2002, is made from bought-in grapes. The bodega also make spirits and liqueurs.

PALACIO DE FEFINANES

Pza de Fefiñanes s/n, 36630 Cambados, Pontevedra.

Tel: +34 986 54 22 04; Fax: +34 986 52 45 12

Founded in 1904, this bodega in a sixteenth-century palace at Cambados in the extreme northwest of the area is the oldest in the DO and pioneered Albariño grapes. Starting first, it remains well up in the field. Its three wines are varietal Alberiños: a *joven*; Fefiñanes Fermentado en Barrica, which is given five months in American and French oak; and Fefiñanes III Año, given twenty-seven months in tanks and intended for further bottle ageing.

BODEGAS FILLABOA

Lugar de Fillaboa s/n, 36459 Salvaterra de Miño, Pontevedra.

Tel: +34 986 65 81 32; Fax: +34 986 66 42 12;

Email: info@bodegasfillaboa.com; Website: www.bodegasfillaboa.com

Originally a family bodega founded in 1986, in 2000 it was bought by the Masaveu group, which also owns the Murúa bodegas in Rioja. It now has sixty-eight hectares of Albariño vines in the sub-zone Condado del Tea. Its wines are among the very best: a *joven*; Selección Finca Monte Alto, from a selected part of the vineyard and matured on its lees in tanks for nine months; and Vino

Fermentado en Barrica, which spends 6–8 months in French and some Caucasian oak, which ages well.

LAGAR DE FORNELOS

Bario de Cruces Fornelos, 36870 O'Rosal, Pontevedra. Tel: +34 986 62 58 75; Fax: +34 986 62 50 11; Email: lagar@riojalta.com; Website: www.riojaalta.com

Founded in 1982 in El Rosal as Fernádez Cervera Hermanos by a shipbuilding family, it was bought by La Rioja Alta in 1988, which changed its name. It began with seven hectares of Albariño vineyard, but there were massive level-lings and plantings, with the vines trained on *espaldera*, so that now there are seventy-two hectares of Albariño. While most of the land nearby is granite, here there is an outcrop of slate and mineral-rich sand. There is only one wine, and it is very good indeed, the *joven* Lagar de Cervera, about seventy per cent of which is put through a malolactic fermentation. It also makes brandy.

ADEGAS GALEGAS

Meder s/n, 36457 Salvaterra edo Miño, Pontevedra.
Tel: +34 986 65 74 00; Fax: +34 986 65 73 71;
Email: galiciano@galiciano.com; Website: www.galiciano.com

Formed in the Condado del Tea in 1995 by twelve growers who between them have forty-seven hectares of Albariño, Treixadura, and Loureiro situated in var-ious areas of the DO. Its wines are among the best. Don Pedro de Soutomaior, Dionisios, and Rubines (a single-vineyard wine of limited production from old vines in the Condado del Tea) are varietal Albariño *jóvenes*. Bouza Grande Condado is seventy-five per cent Albariño, twenty per cent Treixadura, and five per cent Loureira. Veigadares is eighty-five per cent Albariño, ten per cent Treixadera, and five per cent Loureira, while Gran Veigadares and Don Pedro de Soutomaior Tiempo are varietal Albariños, all cask-fermented. It is unusual in producing a red, Señorío de Rubios, which is also cask-fermented and made from equal parts of Espadeiro, Brancellao, Mencía, and Caiño.

LUSCO DO MINO

Alxen, 36459 Salvaterra do Miño, Pontevedra.
Tel: +34 986 65 85 19; Fax: +34 985 24 41 13; Email: luscodominho@yahoo.es

This boutique bodega in Condado del Tea, with five hectares of vineyard, has won very high praise from Spanish critics ever since its foundation in 1996 with its *alta expresión* Lusco and Diversus varietal Albariños.

MARTIN CODAX

Burgans 91, 36663 Vilariño-Cambados, Pontevedra.

Tel: +34 986 52 60 40; Fax: +34 986 52 69 01;

Email: comercial@martincodax.com; Website: www.martincodax.com

Founded in 1986 by 280 Albariño wine-growers in the Salnés Valley under the name Bodegas de Vilariño-Cambados, some years ago it would no doubt have been a cooperative, but nowadays prefers to be described as a company with the growers as shareholders. Between them they have 215 hectares of vineyard. They keep themselves closely supervised, with a school for wine-growers, two agricultural engineers working in the vineyards, and five meteorological stations. Only the best grapes command the highest prices and all are Albariño. The bodega is built on a vertical plan so that the wine can be moved by gravity. In most years it is given a full malolactic fermentation, though this may be reduced to half in very good years. Its wines are among the best. About eighty per cent is sold as Martín Codax, the name of a thirteenth-century Galician poet and troubadour, and now the name of the bodega. The second wine (which is also good) is sold as Burgans. There is also a small production of Organistrum, named after an extinct medieval musical instrument depicted in stone on the portico of the Cathedral of Santiago de Compostela; it has its malolactic fermentation in Allier oak, which gives it complexity without making it too oaky, and is then returned to stainless steel for seven months. The bodega also make liqueurs.

PAZO DE SAN MAURO

Porto s/n, 36458 Salvaterra de Miño, Pontevedra.

Tel: +34 986 65 82 85; Fax: +34 986 66 42 08;

Email: info@pazosanmauro.com; Website: www.pazosanmauro.com

The bodega buildings date from 1591 and are among the oldest in Spain, and there is a fourteenth-century chapel. Not surprisingly it has a vineyard with old vines. It was founded in its present form in 1988 and made very good wines, in the Condado del Tea sub-zone, but things took a sharp turn upward in 2003 when this thirty-hectare estate was bought by Marqués de Vargas of Rioja fame. The vineyard is mostly old vine Albariño with small percentages of Loureiro, Treixadura, and Torrontes. There are two wines: the varietal Albariño Pazo San Mauro and Sanamaro, both made from ninety-five per cent Albariño and five per cent Loureiro from the oldest vines, which give great complexity.

SANTIAGO RUIZ

Rua do Vinicultur Santiago Ruiz, 36760 San Migule de Tabagón-O'Rosal,
Pontevedra. Tel: +34 986 61 40 83; Fax: +34 986 61 41 42;
Email: info@bodegaslan.com; Website: www.bodegaslan.com

It is a pleasant change to find a bodega that has been going for years and years, so as to have become legendary. The buildings themselves date from the seventeenth century. It was run by the founding family for over 100 years until the last died at the end of the 1990s, when it was acquired by the great Lan bodegas of Rioja. It owned only a very small vineyard, but this has been expanded to thirty-eight hectares. The wine is made typically from seventy per cent Albariño, twenty per cent Loureira, and ten per cent Treixadura, and is unusually fruity and complex, with a good balance of acidity well removed from the searing character of some of its rivals. It also produces a most agreeable *rosado*.

PAZO DE SENORANS

Vilanoviña, 36616 Meis, Pontevedra. Tel: +34 986 71 53 73; Fax: +34 986 71 55
69; Email: info@pazosenorans.com; Website: www.pazodesenorans.com

This delightful bodega was founded in 1989 by the woman who is now president of the *consejo regulador*. It has an eight-hectare Albariño vineyard. Its varietal Albariños are very good: Pazo de Señorans and Pazo de Señorans Selección de Añada, which is beautifully complex. It also makes brandy.

PAZO DE VILLAREI

Via Rápida del Sainés km 5, 36637 San Mariño de Meis, Pontevedra. Tel: +34 986
71 08 27; Fax: +34 986 71 08 27; Email: villarei@byb.es; Website: www.byb.es

Founded in 1993, this bodega is a member of the great Bodegas & Bebidas group. It has eighty-one hectares of vineyard. It makes very good varietal Albariños: Pago de Villarei and Terra Douro.

TERRAS GAUDA

Carretera Tui-A Guarda km 46, 36760 O'Rosal, Pontevedra.
Tel: +34 986 62 10 01; Fax: +34 986 62 10 84;
Email: terrasgauda@terrasgauda.com; Website: www.terrasgauda.com

This modern bodega, founded in 1990, exemplifies the influx of capital and winemaking skills. In its present form it is an amalgamation of two bodegas: Viñedos de Rosal and Adegas das Eiras, taking on the name of its most famous wine. It appeared in the last edition under the latter name. Its eighty-two-hectare vineyard enjoys an unusually warm microclimate with an average temperature of 15°C (59°F). It makes very good wines that are not exclusively monovarietal. Abadía de San Campo, however, is a varietal Albariño, but the exceptionally good flagship wine, Terras Gauda, is seventy per cent Albariño, twenty per cent Loureira, and ten per cent Caiño. The Etiqueta Negra (Black Label) has the same grape mix, but is fermented in French oak and left on its lees for twelve months; its high price is justified by extra dimensions of flavour.

VINA NORA

Bruñeiras 7, 36440 As Neves, Pontevedra.
Tel: +34 986 66 72 1; Fax: +34 916 16 02 46; Email: victorre@telefonica.net
This young boutique bodega has fifteen hectares of vineyard and has been acclaimed for the quality of its Albariño Nora.

RIBEIRA SACRA

Geography

Ribeira Sacra means "sacred riverbank". It is a staggeringly beautiful country of Romanesque monasteries, clearly divided into five sub-regions. Listed in the order of the official regulations, these are: Amandi, on the right bank of the river Sil and stretching inland toward Monforte de Lemos; Chantada, on the right bank of the river Miño; Quiroga, on the right bank of the river Sil toward Ribeiro; Ribeiras do Miño, on the left bank of the river Miño opposite Chantada; and Ribeira do Sil, on the left bank of the river Sil. The best vineyards are on the south-facing slopes – or a better word for some of them would be precipices – at an altitude of 200–500 metres (656–1,640 feet). But the area is at the limit for cultivation of vines and none are found above 400 metres (1,312 feet) except in sites that enjoy special microclimates.

Climate

The picture is extremely complicated, with the rivers twisting to give many microclimates, depending on the exposure and altitude of the vineyards. In the valley of the Sil, rainfall is 700 millimetres (27.5 inches) and the mean temperature 13.2°C (55.7°F). In the valley of the Miño the rainfall is 800–900 millimetres (31.5–35.4 inches) and the mean temperature 13.9°C (57°F). High winds roar down the valleys.

Soils

There is again great variety, with plutonic acid rocks, Silurian slates, and schist. The bedrock is slate.

Grapes

Red varieties: Mencía; Brancellao; Caiño; Loureiro Tinto; Sousón; Merenzao; Ferrón; Espadeiro; Mouratón; Negreda; and Alicante. Tempranillo, although not on the official list, is also grown. Of these Mencía is much the most widely grown and then Brancellao.

White varieties: Albariño; Treixadura; Godello (Gobello); Loureira; Dona Branca (Doña Blanca); Torrontés; and Palomino. Albariño is on the up and up, followed by Godello.

Planting

It is very flexible, indeed the regulations say "do whatever works best", but usually Guyot or Double Cordon Royat at 2,500–4,000 vines per hectare.

Vineyard area

1,220 hectares.

Authorized yield

62hl/ha for Albariño and Godello. Other varieties: 77hl/ha.

Wines

Reds and whites. To be labelled as monovarietal they must be made from at least eighty-five per cent of one of the preferred varieties (the first six of each colour listed above), the remaining fifteen per cent to be of other preferred varieties, and have a strength of at least 11% ABV. There is an increasing practice to make them genuinely varietal, particularly Mencía, Albariño, and Godello. Generic (*xenérico*) wines must contain a minimum of sixty per cent preferred varieties and have a strength of at least 10% ABV. The bulk of production is red.

Production

4,698 hectolitres (2004).

Vintages

With so many microclimates, and with most of the wines intended to be drunk young, ratings are meaningless.

No one could exaggerate the beauty of this place. Many of the best, terraced slopes are very steep, so viticulture and vintaging are difficult; but they also have very fine exposures to the sun, which must make them potentially among the best vineyards in the world. They have not yet come anywhere near to realizing their potential, but smart money is pouring in. The figures speak for themselves. In 1992 there were thirty bodegas, in 2005, ninety-nine. In the same period the area under vine rose from 300 to 1,220 hectares, production from 350 to 4,698 hectolitres, and the number of growers from 550 to 2,845. White wines from Albariño show greater ripeness and less acidity than their neighbours in Rías Bajas, with real complexity and enormous length. The reds are rapidly improving and some are very good; on such sites it seems likely that really fine ones will emerge. At the moment not much is exported, but the local thirst is well quenched.

Some leading bodegas

ADEGAS MOURE

Buenos Aires 12, 27540 Escarión, Lugo. Tel: +34 982 45 20 31; Fax: +34 982 45 27 00; Email: abadiadacova@adegasmoure.com; Website: www.abadiadacova.com

This family bodega with ten hectares of vineyard was founded in 1984 and is one of the few to export. It makes very good varietal wines marketed as Abadía da Cova. The Albariño is blended with fifteen per cent Godello and the Godello with fifteen per cent Albariño; both qualify as varietals, but the blending brings complexity. They are excellent. The Barrica Tinto is a truly varietal Mencía, given ten months in eighty per cent French and twenty per cent American oak. Cimbro is a Mencía only part of which has a malolactic fermentation, which enhances its acidity. The Mencía Selección Especial has ten per cent Tempranillo. It was the first to make a Mencía *crianza* here.

REGINA VIARUM

Doade s/n, 27424 Sober, Lugo. Tel: +34 986 40 16 99; Fax: +34 986 40 99 45; Email: clientes@reginaviarum.es; Website: www.reginaviarum.es

Established as recently as 2002, this bodega with an impressive building and twenty hectares of vineyard has got off to a fine start with varietal Mencías that are among the best, sold as Via Imperial and Regina Viarum. The Regina Viarum Barrica has four months in new Allier oak.

ADEGAS SAN JOSE
Sta Mariña de Eiré, 27439 Pantón, Lugo. Tel/Fax: +34 982 45 65 45;
Email: adegas@infonegocio.com
Although it has only one hectare of vineyard, this bodega, founded in 1992, actually makes more wine than either of the other two. Ribera de Valboa is a varietal Godello, and the same name is used for a varietal Mencía.

RIBEIRO

Geography

Ribeiro adjoins the better known area of Rias Bajas, but is further inland to the east, in the beautiful valley of the river Miño above the point where it forms the border between Spain and Portugal. The commercial centre is the delightful little town of Ribadavia, where the river Avia flows into the Miño. The river Arnoia, flowing from the east, joins the Miño a little further down. The vineyards are in the river valleys and on the slopes above them, at altitudes varying between 100–350 metres (328–1,148 feet), and many are on terraces.

Climate

Humid and relatively cool, influenced by winds blowing along the valley and from Portugal. Temperatures rise to 38°C (100°F) in summer and fall as low as -4°C (24.8°F) in winter, with an average of 14.5°C (58°F). The rainfall is 800–1,000 millimetres (31.5–39.4 inches). There are 1,900 hours of sunshine.

Soils

Generally sandy and alluvial over granite. Soils for quality wines are found on the higher levels.

Grapes

Red varieties: Caiño; Ferrón; Sousón; Brancellao; Mencía; Garnacha; and Tempranillo. The last two, while permitted, are not characteristic.
White varieties: Treixadura; Albariño; Godello; Tarrontés; Loureira; Palomino (Jerez); Macabeo; Albillo; and Lado. Treixadura is the principal local grape, but Albariño is making headway. Lado is experimental. The continued presence of the Palomino is unfortunate.

Planting

Traditionally on pergolas, but most are now grown, pruned, and trained by the Guyot or Silvo/Espada methods. Generally 1.3 metres (4.3 feet) between vines and 1.8 metres (six feet) between rows. 7,000 vines per hectare.

Vineyard area
3,100 hectares.

Authorized yield
91hl/ha, though in practice 50hl/ha is more realistic.

Wines
Whites 10–13% ABV. Reds 10–12% ABV. There is also a special category unique to this area: *enverado*. This is a relic of the days when white grapes were picked in August, before they were ripe to get acidity, but such wines are now rarely made. Their strength is 8–9% ABV. Eighty per cent are white.

Production
10,5000 hectolitres (2003).

Vintages
The wines are generally drunk young and no assessment is available, nor does there seem much variation.

According to the fourteenth-century French chronicler Froissart, John of Gaunt's archers were put out of action for two days after drinking Ribeiro's "ardent wines", and it is said that the same fate befell the Napoleonic troops in the Peninsular War. But until recently the story became rather sad. There was the usual trouble with phylloxera and then the equally usual reaction: quantity instead of quality. Depressing white wines were made from Palomino and equally dim, or even worse, reds from Alicante. Such wines are still found and should be assiduously avoided. Although the DO was set up in 1952, the story continued as before, one of cheap bulk wines. Then, in the 1980s, things began to change. The neighbouring DO Rías Bajas was a success story, both in terms of quality and profitability. Anyone looking around could have seen that Ribeiro was capable of competing, and they looked. The bodega to show the way forward was the cooperative – most unusual. It produced some wines of real quality, and it still makes them. This showed what could be done and, as in so much of Spain at that time, capital was waiting to be poured in. The result was the arrival of new bodegas and new oenologists producing excellent wines from the best local varieties grown on the higher terraces. If the whites do not have the searing penetration or the finesse of their neighbours from Rías Bajas, they are nevertheless fresh, light, fragrant, and, at their best, delicious. The reds do not quite measure up to them, but nevertheless they are excellent to drink, with plenty of fruit and body rather than complexity or elegance. All should be drunk young.

Some leading bodegas

BODEGA ALANIS

Carretera de Vigo 22–24, 32450 Barbantes, Ourense. Tel: +34 988 28 04 05; Fax: +34 988 28 03 46; Email: alanis@byb.es; Website: www.byb.es

Founded as a family bodega in 1910, it started bottling in 1970. Since 1991 it has been part of Bodegas y Bebidas and specializes in white wines from local varieties. It is thoroughly modern and its wines are very well made. Gran Alanís is made from Treixadura, Torrontés, and some Palomino and is very good, but the San Trocado, which omits the Palomino, is better.

BODEGAS CAMPANTE

Finca Reboreda, 32941 Puga, Ourense. Tel: +34 988 26 12 12; Fax: +34 988 26 12 13; Email: info@campante.com; Website: www.campante.com

One of the new wave of bodegas, founded in 1988, but with origins in the 1940s, it owns twenty hectares and makes both whites and reds, buying grapes from local growers. Its wines are: Campante, Gran Reboreda, Viña Reboreda, Lauro, and Coto de Ibedo. The Viña Reboreda has thirty per cent Palomino; the Gran Reborado from Treixadura, Torrontes, and Godello is better.

PAZO CASANOVA

Camiño Souto do Río 1, 32593 Santa Cruz de Arrabaldo, Ourense. Tel/Fax: +34 988 38 41 96; Email: casanova@pazocasanova.com; Website: www.pazocasanova.com

Founded in 2000, this uses only grapes grown in its own fourteen hectares of vineyard. Its white wines based on Treixadura have a good reputation.

A PORTELA

Piñeiros s/n, 32431 Beada, Ourense. Tel: +34 988 48 00 50; Fax: +34 988 48 02 01; Email: beadeprimicia@airtel.net

Founded in 1987, this makes red and white wines under the name Señorio de Beade. Its best white wine is a varietal Treixadura, Beade Primicia.

EMILIO ROJO

Puente, 32333 Arnoia, Ourense. Tel: +34 988 48 80 50

Founded in 1987 with three hectares of vineyard, this boutique's eponymous white, made from Albariño, Loureiro Treixadura, and Lado, is much praised.

BODEGAS VILERMA

Vilerma-Gomariz, 32429 Leira, Ourense.

Tel: +34 988 22 87 02; Fax: +34 988 24 85 80

Founded in 1988, its grapes come from vines planted in 1978. Its good, light white is from Lado, Torrontés, Albariño, Loureiro, and Treixadura.

VINA MEIN

Mein s/n San Clodio, 32420 Leira, Ourense. Tel: +34 617 32 62 48; Fax: +34 915 76 10 19; Email: vinamein@wol.es; Website: www.vinamein.com

In 1987, a lawyer from Madrid founded this small bodega in a beautiful old farmhouse surrounded by two hectares of vines which hae grown to sixteen. It makes exceptionally good white from Treixadura (typically eighty per cent) with Godello, Albariño, Loureiro, and Torrontés, and carefully adjusts the proportions each year. Viña Mein is a wooded version fermented in 3,300-litre Allier oak *tinos*. Its Tinto Clásico is from Caíño, Mencía, and Ferrón.

VITIVINOCOLA DEL RIBEIRO, SOCIEDAD COOPERATIVA

Valdepereira, 32417 Ribadavia, Ourense.

Tel: +34 988 22 87 02; Fax: +34 988 47 03 30; Email: mcastro@pazoribeiro.com

Although most of its wines do not aspire to excellence, this cooperative was a pioneer when established in 1968 and began to bottle wines under the name Pazo in 1970. The largest bodega in the DO, its members now have 670 hectares. The grapes it can draw on vary in quality, but it is guiding members toward the best. It has modern equipment and its wines are well made.

VALDEORRAS

Geography

Although in Galicia, this area borders Castilla y León and has much in common with the latter. Its centre is the little town of Barco de Valdeorras (or O Barco, in the Galicians' own romance language) on the river Sil, which flows into the river Miño northeast of Ourense. The vineyards are in the river valley and on the hillsides on either side at an altitude of 240–320 metres (787–1,050 feet). The best wines are from the slopes, mostly between O Barco and A Rúa.

Climate

Well inland, it is influenced by both continental and Atlantic weather systems. It has a relatively high rainfall of 850–1,000 millimetres, but that is a good deal lower than in some places to the west; it is one of the drier parts of Galicia. Temperatures can reach 44°C (111°F) in the summer and go down to -4°C (24.8°F) in the winter, with an average of 11°C (51.8°F). There are 2,700 hours of sunshine a year.

Soils

In the river valley the soils are alluvial, but in some places there is limestone underneath. The hillsides contain a lot of slate, which makes cultivation difficult, as it is slippery, but gives excellent wines from Godello.

Grapes

Red varieties: Mencía; Garnacha Tintorera (Alicante); Gran Negro; María Ardoña (Merenzao); Cabernet Sauvignon; and Tempranillo. The last two are experimental and only the Mencía is encouraged.
White varieties: Godello; Palomino; Valenciana (Doña Blanca or Mozafres); Lado; Moscatel; and Riesling. The last two are experimental and it is Godello that is encouraged. Palomino and Valenciana happily are declining.

Planting

Generally *en vaso* on the slopes and *espaldera* on the plains, with a spacing of 1.5–1.8 metres (5–6 feet) between vines and 2.7 metres (8.8 feet) between rows. *Espaldera* is taking over in the modern commercial vineyards. Maximum density 4,000 vines per hectare.

Vineyard area

1,329 hectares.

Authorized yield

56hl/ha on the slopes and 70hl/ha on the plains.

Wines

Reds, whites, and *rosados* with a minimum strength of 9% ABV. Traditionally made as *jóvenes*, but there are some *crianzas* and the best reds are considerably stronger than the minimum, typically 11.5% ABV and going up to 12.5% ABV.

Production

27,925 hectolitres (2003)

Vintages

These wines are generally made to be drunk young, so an assessment of old vintages is irrelevant; and there is not a great variation.

1999 (4); 2000 (4); 2001 (3); 2002 (3); 2003 (3); 2004 (4).

This area has yet to come into its own, but it is on the way. It came to grief with phylloxera (before there were 8,000 hectares of vineyard), for which various dates are given ranging from 1882–1911. Whatever the date may have been, there can be no doubt about the result: that excellent local grape Godello all but disappeared, and growers went in for quantity rather than quality, planting lots of Palomino, with Garnacha Tintorera, Gran Negro (producing very dark wines of little quality), and even hybrids. The wines were drunk locally, but there was no national market, and certainly no export market. The DO was set up in 1957, but had no immediate effect. However the *consejo regulador* has since been at the forefront of experimentation to find the best varieties, methods of viticulture, and techniques of vinification. It is ruthless in eliminating wines that do not reach its standards. In the 1970s there was a hot dispute whether to still go for quantity or to look for quality. At that time the government was encouraging the planting of French varieties, but after much experiment the more enlightened growers decided to look for quality and to return Godello. The main snag was that there were practically no Godello vines, so cuttings had to be taken, then propagated, and good clones, chosen and propagated further. The results, to the amazement of those who deplored the whole exercise, have been completely successful, but it has taken time; and it has been complicated by the fact that there are few large-scale growers, most of the vineyards being very small and peasant-owned. They are deterred by the fact that Godello is a shy yielder and hard to harvest. Much the same can be said of the red Mencía, which is also a great success; so much so that Valdeorras looks as if it will soon be as well known for its red wines as for its whites – a very odd thing to happen in Galicia; and some bodegas are experimenting with *crianza*s. Happily the vineyards are moving from alluvial soils up to the slopes. The move toward quality and the higher prices that would come with it brought investment, and the major bodegas are now as well-equipped as any. It has also brought about a considerable rise in grape prices, so the peasant growers make a living. Before this, practically all the wines were made by cooperatives and sold locally in bulk. Now most are sold in bottle, but despite an increase in exports, the local market is still the most important.

No one would claim that Valdeorras makes world-class wines, but they are thoroughly good and their excellent value has led them onto the shelves of English supermarkets. Although *rosado* is permitted in the DO, very little is made. About eighty per cent of the production is white. The best wines are varietal Godellos, which are dry, fragrant, fresh, fruity, and can be delicious, with excellent length; and varietal Mencías, which though lightweight, are thoroughly sound table wines, to be drunk young with great pleasure. Good, cheaper red and whites are made by blending these grapes with others. Those that do not contain the noble grape varieties are unexciting and are sold locally and cheaply. Quality is going up more rapidly than marketing skills, and this is an area to watch.

Some leading bodegas

A TAPADA
Finca A Tapada, 32310 Rubiá, Ourense.
Tel: +34 988 32 41 95; Fax: +34 988 32 41 97
A family-owned bodega founded in 1989 with ten hectares, concentrating on a Godello called Guitian, which includes a barrel-fermented version.

ADEGAS DIA-NOITE
Carretera Carballal s/n, 32356 Petin de Valdeorras, Ourense. Tel/Fax: +34 988 31 14 62; Email: cmurgaliciano@yahoo.es; Website: www.galiciano.com
This is the Valdeorras offshoot of Adegas Galegas (*see* Rías Bajas). It makes classic wines from twelve-hectares and bought-in grapes. The varietals are Godello and Mencía, both sold as El Galiciano: Día is the Godello and Noite, Mencía.

BODEGAS GODEVAL SAT
Avenida de Galicia s/n, 32300 El Barco de Valdeorras, Ourense. Tel/Fax: +34 988 32 53 09; Email: godeval@godeval.com; Website: www.godeval.com
Founded in 1985, it moved in 1988 into a restored ninth-century monastery, formerly of the military order of the Knights of St John of Jerusalem, in an exquisite, tranquil valley. It makes wine from its own seventeen-hectares on a vineyard on a south-facing slope with slate soil, planted exclusively with

Godello and pruned for very low yield. Everything is current. The result is a modest production of just one excellent white wine: Viña Godeval.

JOAQUIN REBOLLEDO

San Roque s/n, 32350 A Rúa, Ourense.

Tel: +34 988 33 60 23; Fax: +34 988 33 60 89; Email: jrebolledo@teleline.es

A lawyer created this thirty hectare vineyard on his family estate. The wines are varietals from Godello and Mencía, including an oak-aged Mencía.

COOPERATIVA SANTA MARIA DE LOS REMEDIOS

Langullo 11, 32358 Larouco, Ourense. Tel/Fax: +34 988 34 80 43.

Although sales are mostly local, it makes some good wines. Started in 1959, its members own some 250 hectares. Its best white is Arume Godello and its best red is sold under the name Medulio. The name Silviño is also used.

SANTA MARTA

Córgomo, 32340 Villamartin de Valdeorras, Ourense. Tel/Fax: +34 988 32 45 59

Founded in 1998 it has fourteen hectares and makes good varietal Godellos.

TELMO RODRIGUEZ

See Ribera del Duero.

Here he makes a good varietal Godello, Gaba do Xil.

BODEGAS VALDERROA

Córgamo s/n, 32348 Villamartin de Valdeorras, Ourense.

Tel: +34 988 33 79 00; Fax: +34 98833 79 01;

Email: valderroa@valderroa.com; Website: www.valderroa.com

A most impressive bodega founded in 1988 by a group of professionals whose goal was to produce first-class wine by controlling the winemaking from vineyard to bottle. Originally called Bodegas Señorio, and a SAT, it is now run by one family. It has twenty-five hectares of vineyard planted with the classic varieties on *espaldera*, save for one experimental hectare planted with all sorts of things. Grapes are also bought from local growers supervised by the oenologist. Winemaking is exemplary. It makes a complete range of wines including a tiny amount of *rosado*, but for practical purposes the production is eighty per cent white and twenty per cent red. There are three ranges. The top white is Valdesil (or VALdeSIL), a varietal Godello; and the top red is Valdeorroa, a varietal Mencía. Both are very good indeed. On the next level are the cheaper Montenovo red, from equal parts Mencía and Garnacha; and Montenovo white, from equal parts Godello and Palomino. The noble varieties dominate

8

The Levant

Wine has been grown here, as in most of Spain, at least as far back as Roman times. The old kingdom of Valencia covered the areas that were to become the provinces of Valencia, Alicante, and Castellón, and here grew "Vinos Valencianos". They have long had a flourishing export trade, and at the end of the nineteenth century benefited, as did so much of Spain, from the phylloxera catastrophe in France. In 1889 there were 247,423 hectares of vineyard. But phylloxera duly found its way here, and by 1922 there were only 152,841 hectares. The position of the vineyards changed too, and for the better. Before phylloxera vines flourished in the fertile soil of the coastal plain, but these were turned over to more profitable uses, notably orange groves and orchards of almonds, while the vineyards were replanted in the hills, where they still are.

Most of the vineyards in the Levant today are in the *autonomias* of Valencia and Murcia, but one – Almansa – is at the east of Castilla La Mancha. It makes more sense, though, to consider it as part of the Levant than as part of La Mancha. As many holiday-makers and colonies of foreign residents have found, the Levant is a most agreeable part of Spain. The coast is washed by the warm Mediterranean Sea and there is lots of sunshine. But for wine-growers this is a mixed blessing as it is too hot to make world-class table wines. Yet the holiday-makers have rightly enjoyed the sound, good value local wines and the bodegas here became pioneers in the export trade, which they have retained and expanded. This is the second-largest vineyard in Spain and third in the world; the ports of Valencia and Alicante handle forty-five per cent of Spain's wine exports, though these, of course, include wines grown elsewhere. And apart from wine there is a very large trade in table grapes and raisins. But even if no really great wines are grown here, it does not mean that this part of Spain has missed out on the wine revolution. Far from it, the best bodegas were

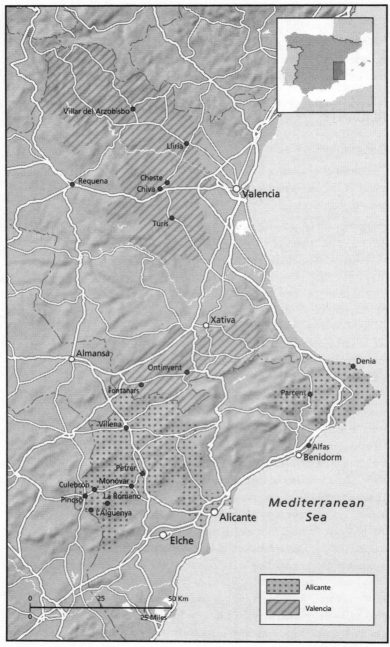

x Alicante & Valencia

among the first to install modern technology. They are as well equipped as those anywhere and their wines are just as well made; but modern oenology has not yet spread to all the bodegas, so it is easier to buy a disappointing bottle here than it is in most places. There are plenty of good wines, though, and the best from this region are undoubtedly the sweet Moscatels.

ALICANTE

Geography

The province of Alicante (or, to please the local nationalists, Alacant) lies at the south of the *autonomia* of Valencia. The city itself is a flourishing port and industrial centre dominated by the remains of two Moorish castles, but there is not much of the old town left. It has a long tradition of wine-growing and, like Valencia, grows many other things as well. The DO vineyards are separated into two distinct sub-zones. The northernmost sub-zone, La Marina, stretches inland from the coast around Denia. The southern sub-zone, Clásico, includes the city itself, though part of the old vineyard area, in what was once described as "the garden of Spain", has been swallowed up by development; then it stretches north and west as far as the foothills of the central Meseta and crosses the border of the province of Murcia, though the wines grown there are made and matured in the province of Alicante. It has borders with the DOs of Valencia, Yecla, Almansa, and Jumilla. The lowest vineyards are just above sea level, the highest, around Albanilla in Murcia, go up to 400 metres (1,312 feet).

Climate

Vineyards by the coast enjoy a Mediterranean climate, but this gets more continental inland. In the northern sub-zone the average temperature is 15.3°C (59.5°F), but in the south it is 18°C (64.4°F). Rain is unpredictable. Throughout most of the year there is no rain at all, and when it does come it is generally heavy, varying between the wide limits of 200–500 millimetres (7.9–19.7 inches), the latter in La Marina. The average annual sunshine is 2,500 hours. This climate makes it a wonderful place to winter IN, but in summer it can be very hot; grapes can easily become raisins.

Soils

There are some alluvial soils by the coast but for the most part they are stony, dry, and chalky, with some clay in places.

Grapes

Red varieties: Monastrell; Garnacha Tinta; Garnacha Tintorera; Tempranillo; Bobal; Cabernet Sauvignon; Merlot; Syrah; and Pinot Noir.

White varieties: Moscatel de Alexandría; Merseguera; Macabeo; Planta Fina; Airén; Riesling; Chardonnay; Verdil; and Sauvignon Blanc.

Monastrell is the classic and most widely planted red variety. Of the white varieties, Planta Fina is beginning to disappear and Airén to take its place. There is a lot of experimenting.

Planting

Pruned *en vaso* in cooler districts and *en cabeza* in hotter ones. Both square and rectangular patterns are used. Trained low to reduce the effect of heat.

Vineyard area

14,252 hectares.

Authorized yield

Reds: 35hl/hectares. Whites: 49hl/hectares.

Wines

Most are sold as *jóvenes,* but there are some reds up to *reserva.* The minimum strength for reds is 12% ABV, for *rosados* 11% ABV, and for whites 10% ABV. But there are also some special wines. Red *doble pasta* is made as in Valencia (*see* below) with a minimum strength of 12% ABV. White *licor Moscatel* must be made from 100 per cent Moscatel and have a minimum strength of 15% ABV. The unique Fondillón (*see* below) must be made from 100 per cent Monastrell, have a minimum strength of 16% ABV, and be aged for at least eight years.

Production

169,220 hectolitres (2003).

Vintages

1999 (4); 2000 (4); 2001 (4); 2002 (3); 2003 (3); 2004 (4).

Alicante used to be associated with rather dim table wines that were pleasant enough to drink but little more; there were rumours of a legendary wine called

Fondillón, which could never be found, and there also were sweet Moscatels that were out of fashion. But there have been great changes here as in the rest of Spain. The dim wines can still be found, but modern winemaking, though not universal, is now firmly in place. Cold-fermented white wines are much fresher and more fragrant than those of the past, and the sweet white wines, made from the Moscatel grape, are among the best anywhere. However, the real revolution has happened with the reds. Modern winemaking has shown how very good the local Monastrell can be, and imported varieties have made great headway. Some of the best reds today are those in which a proportion of these imports adds backbone and structure. They can be excellent. *Doble pasta* wines are still made and are exported in bulk for blending, as they always have been.

Alicante's unique wine, though, was and is Fondillón. It is made exclusively from the Monastrell grape, in the Valle de Vinalopó to the north-west of the city. From the sixteenth century until well into the nineteenth it was regarded as one of Europe's great wines, served at the tables of the aristocracy. It was certainly well known in England, though imports were not large. In the seventeenth century it was generally priced above sherry and was one of the most expensive wines imported. In his play, *The Honest Whore* (1604), Thomas Dekker made one of his characters say, "You'll bleed three pottles of Alicant, by this light, if you follow 'em." And William Salmon in his *Compleat English Physician* (1693), wrote: "Alicant. It is a delicate red, Stomach Wine, strengthens the Tone of the Stomach, stops Vomiting, causes a good Appetite, stops Fluxes of all sorts, restores the tone of the Bowels, and is excellent against a Tabes, Phthisick and spitting of Blood." A remarkable wine indeed. And in the same century the English fleet bought it in Alicante to ward off the scurvy.

These, and descriptions elsewhere, suggest the references were to Fondillón. One shipper, who opened a London office in 1876, listed seventeen qualities, nine dry and eight sweet, the oldest coming from a *solera* laid down in 1811. It disappeared at the end of the century and was not seen for fifty years. A few casks were preserved, though, in private bodegas. Then, at the end of the 1940s, Salvador Poveda Luz, whose family had a bodega in Monóvar, set about recreating it, guided by local traditions and the wines that were still to be found. It is now made by many of the leading shippers. But it is an expensive wine to make well, and its eclipse may well have been a result of the booming trade with the French, in which the Alicante growers fully joined, following the phylloxera disaster in that country. French families came in and settled, everyone grew rich, and exports from Valencia increased from half a million hectolitres in 1877 to eight million in 1882. But Fondillón was not what the French were looking for.

Traditionally it was made by selecting the best and ripest grapes and then drying them in the sun, further increasing the concentration of sugar; they sometimes lost as much as half their weight. Then they were pressed and put with their skins into oak vats where a tumultuous fermentation was followed by a slow one. The whole, including the skin contact, lasted thirty days and produced a deeply coloured, very alcoholic wine of 16–18% ABV, astringent with tannin and with 6–8 degrees Beaumé of sugar. The wine was then aged, usually using the *solera* system (*see* sherry). Old barrels, covered in cobwebs, were kept in the *sacristía* to be tapped only on special occasions.

Nowadays things are slightly different. The best grapes are selected to give the greatest strength, and they are either left for a long time on the vine (left too long in this climate they can become raisins) or occasionally are sunned. The wine is made with only a brief period of skin contact, to produce a *clarete*, avoiding the old astringency, and is then aged, sometimes in exceptionally good years as vintage wine, but usually in *soleras*. As it ages it oxidizes, the redness replaced by a pleasant amber. It must be aged for at least eight years and peaks at about twenty – or the equivalent produced by a carefully regulated *solera* in which never more than twenty per cent is withdrawn from the oldest scale in a year. The alcoholic strength is 16–18% ABV. The sweetness depends on the initial sweetness of the grapes, and some wines can be completely dry, others moderately sweet, 0–4 degrees Beaumé. They have an agreeable oxidized nose rather like a light oloroso sherry. The dry versions make good apéritifs, the sweeter kinds being "dessert wines" that, both in colour and in style, call to mind old, browning tawny ports.

Some leading bodegas

BODEGAS COOPERATIVAS DE ALICANTE/BOCOPA

Alicante-Madrid km 39, Paraje Les Pedreres, 03610 Petrer, Alicante. Tel: +34 966 95 04 89; Fax: +34 966 95 04 06; Email: info@bocopa.com; Website: www.bocopa.com
This macro cooperative was founded in 1987 to bring together eleven Alicante cooperatives which, between them, account for over half of the DO wine, grown by 1,800 members. It introduced modern winemaking and its well-made wines are very good value. Some are much more than that. It uses the trade names Marina Alta, Viña Alcanta, Viña Alone (*Alone* is Greek for Alicante), Marqués de Alicante, Terreta, Castillo de Alicante, Laudum, and Sol

de Alicante. The Viña Alone red *joven* is made from Monastrell, Merlot, and Tempranillo. The white version is Macabeo and Mersegueta. The red Marqués de Alicante is a *crianza* from Cabernet Sauvignon, Tempranillo, Monastrell, and Merlot; it is very well balanced and worth seeking out. The top red, Laudum, is from Cabernet Sauvignon, Merlot, and Monastrell, with sixteen months in American and French oak. The Moscatel Sol de Alicante is a good, luscious example, while the Alone comes in a very fancy bottle. Fondillón Alone 1970, despite apparently bearing a vintage year, is made from a *solera* laid down in 1970. It also makes an ecological red from Tempranillo, Cabernet Sauvignon, and Monastrell. Dulce Negre is a sweet red from Monastrell.

BODEGAS GUTIERREZ DE LA VEGA

Canelajas 4, 03792 Parcent, Alicante. Tel: +34 966 40 52 66; Fax: +34 966 40 52 57; Email: gutivega@arrakis.es

Founded in the late 1970s, this bodega operates only on a small scale with ten hectares of vineyard, but is a master of the Moscatel grape. The Moscatels are sold under the name Casta Diva. These include a dry one that actually is dry, and some excellent sweet ones including Cosecha Miel, which lives up to its name by really tasting honeyed. It also makes good reds, the top being Casta Diva Rojo y Negro from forty per cent each of Monastrell and Merlot with ten per cent each of Cariñena and Cabernet Sauvignon. Its Fondillóns are very good, particularly Casta Diva Fondillón 15 Años.

LADERA DE PINOSO

Paraje El Sequé 59, 03650 Pinoso, Alicante. Tel: +34 945 60 01 19; Fax: +34 945 60 08 50; Email: elseque@artadi.com

Artadi makes some of the best wine in Rioja and has now shown it can do the same in Alicante. This modest-sized bodega with forty hectares of well established vineyard was founded in 1999. The red wines are based on the local Monastrell, but it is blended with French varieties Cabernet Sauvignon and Syrah to give fine results. The top El Sequé is given twelve months in French oak. The second wine Laderas de El Sequé is also very good.

BODEGAS ENRIQUE MENDOZA

Partida El Romeral s/n, 03580 Alfáz del Pi, Alicante. Tel/Fax: +34 965 88 86 39; Email: bodegas-mendoza@bodegasmendoza.com; Website: www.bodegasmendoza.com

Founded in 1989, it has eighty hectares of vineyard and makes fine wines mostly from French varieties: Chardonnay; Cabernet Sauvignon; Merlot; Pinot

Noir; and Syrah. Other wines are made by blending with Spanish varieties including Tempranillo and are sold as Enrique Mendoza, Viña Alfas, and Savia Nova. The varietals are all worth seeking out, as are blends such as Enrique Mendoza Santa Rosa Reserva, from seventy per cent Cabernet Sauvignon and fifteen per cent each of Merlot and Syrah, matured in Allier oak. Peñón de Ifach is made from sixty per cent Cabernet Sauvignon, twenty per cent Merlot, and twenty per cent Pinot Noir, given eighteen months in American and French oak. Dolç de Mendoza is an acclaimed sweet red from sixty per cent Merlot, the rest being equal amounts of Cabernet Sauvignon, Syrah, Pinot Noir, and Monastrell. There are also very good Moscatels.

SALVADOR POVEDA

Benjamín Palencia 19, 03640 Monóvar, Alicante. Tel: +34 966 96 01 80; Fax: +34 965 947 33 89;

Email: salvadorpoveda@salvadorpoveda.com; Website: www.salvadorpoveda.com

This is a completely up-to-date family bodega, founded in 1919 and now in its third generation, with 150 hectares of vineyard. It has three white wines: Cantaluz from Macabeo, Aitana, a semi-sweet wine from the same grape, and, rather improbably, a Riesling. Its red Viña Vermeta wines, a *crianza* and a *reserva*, are varietal Monastrells. Toscar is a Monastrell from old vines and is given no filtration. Borrasca is similar but given twenty months in French oak. There is a sixty-forty Cabernet Sauvignon/Merlot blend and a varietal Tempranillo. It is particularly noted for its vintage Fondillón.

PRIMITIVO QUILES

Mayor 4, 03640 Monóvar, Alicante. Tel: +34 965 47 00 99; Fax: +34 966 96 02 35; Email: info@primitivoquiles.com; Website: www.primitivoquiles.com

A family bodega with deep roots in the district, the Quiles family has been growing grapes since 1780, so it knows all about Monastrell vines, which it cultivates to give a low yield. Tinto Cono 4 is a *joven,* but there is also a *crianza* matured in eighty per cent American and twenty per cent French oak, and Raspay, a *reserva.* There is a varietal *rosado,* Virgen. It makes a very good Moscatel, but is principally noted for its Fondillón, matured in *soleras* that go back to 1892. The Fondillón *gran reserva solera* 1948 is particularly good.

ALMANSA

Geography

Almansa is at the extreme eastern corner of La Mancha and should therefore strictly be considered in the context of that province, but in terms of
wine and scenery it has much more in common with the Levant, bordering
Alicante and the Murcian DOs Jumilla and Yecla. It is not contiguous with
the La Mancha DO and is a long way from its centre. It is a countryside of
small hills, like its neighbours, and totally unlike the vast plain of La
Mancha. The vineyards lie at altitudes between 700–1,100 metres
(2,296–3,609 feet), but many are in the flat land at the bottom of the hills.

Climate

Continental semi-arid, with summer highs of 40°C (104°F), winter lows of
-8°C (17.6°F), and an average of 13°C (55.4°F). The rainfall is between
300–400 millimetres (11.8–15.7 inches) mostly falling as heavy showers in
spring and autumn. There are 2,800 hours of sunshine.

Soils

Permeable, infertile, and with a high chalk content.

Grapes

Red varieties: Monastrell; Cencibel (Tempranillo); Garnacha Tintorera;
Cabernet Sauvignon; Merlot; and Syrah. The last three are officially experimental. The vast majority of grapes are red, with Monastrell in the lead, producing the best wines. The Garnacha Tintorera comes a close second in
quantity and used to be a poor third in quality but modern techniques of
vinification are making some very good wines from it. Cencibel is increasing
and now covers fifteen per cent of the vineyard.
White varieties: Merseguera; Verdejo; Chardonnay; and Sauvignon Blanc.

Planting

Vines are trained *en vaso* and planted in the *marco real* or *tres bolillos* patterns, with a maximum density of 1,600 per hectare.

Vineyard area

7,600 hectares

Authorized yield

Monastrell 21hl/ha. Garnacha Tintorera 35hl/ha. Merseguera 38.5hl/ha.

Production

254,000 hectolitres (2003).

Vintages

2000 (3); 2001 (3); 2002 (4); 2003 (3); 2004 (5).

The town of Almansa is surmounted by an impressive castle, one of the last to be built in the reconquest. Indeed the place has spent rather too much of its history as a battle ground, including a major battle in the War of the Spanish Succession. Some of the wines here are still made with rather primitive equipment and taste like it, yet there is something rather special about the place. Stainless steel has moved in, new vineyards have been planted, and in the last ten years production of bottled wines has enormously increased. The best reds are unusually well balanced and can even be elegant. The Monastrell, in particular, is a vine that holds out great promise. Its traditional trade has been in blending wines, sent to the coast and shipped from Alicante. But even though nothing as yet suggests that it is ever likely to move into the top league, its potential for producing very attractive wines is manifest. Its emergence into the export market was entirely thanks to one shipper: Bodegas Piqueras.

Some leading bodegas

BODEGAS PIQUERAS

Zapateros 11, 02640 Almansa, Albacete. Tel: +34 967 34 14 82; Fax: +34 967 34 54 80; Email: bodpiqueras@almansa.org; Website: www.bodegaspiqueras.es
This family bodega dating from 1915 was the first to export wines from the DO, in 1987, and has been going from strength to strength. It used to have no vineyards of its own but bought 190 hectares of farmland on a perfect (and beautiful) site for growing vines in 2000. It has Cabernet Sauvignon, Syrah, Merlot, Verdejo, and Sauvignon Blanc that are just beginning to produce and bode well for the future. Meanwhile it relies on 500 hectares it has under contract. In 2002 it opened a new bodega with air conditioning for maturing its wines, and was the first in the area to buy oak casks, both American and French. Its wines, sold as Castillo de Almansa, include an attractive white *joven* from Verdejo and Sauvignon, a *rosado* from Syrah, and a complete range of reds. The *crianza* is from Monastrell, Cencibel, and Cabernet Sauvignon with six months in new oak, while the *reserva* has Garnacha Tintorera in place of Cabernet Sauvignon.

The top wines are Marius Reserva from Monastrell and Garnacha Tintorera, and Terra Grande which also has Syrah; both are oak aged for twelve months, the former in American oak, the latter half in American oak and half in French.

BULLAS

Geography

The southernmost of the Mediterranean areas for DO table wines, in the province of Murcia, Bullas actually reaches the Mediterranean coast for a short distance just north of Aguilas and stretches inland into the hills, with its northern border joining Jumilla. It is thinly populated but includes two charming little towns: Bullas itself and Lorca. It is sparsely planted with vines, too, and most of the vineyards are well into the hills. There are three sub-zones: the northwestern rising from 500–810 metres (1,640–2,657 feet) and producing fifty-two per cent of the wine; the central sub-zone, round Bullas, at a height of 500–600 metres (1,640–1,968 feet) and producing forty per cent; and the northeastern sub-zone at 400–500 metres (1,312–1,640 feet) producing eight per cent. Bullas has an extremely good wine museum made out of an old bodega in the middle of the town.

Climate

From Mediterranean to continental as one travels north and west, it is semi-arid with summers going up to 40°C (104°F) and winter down to -4°C (24.8°F). The average temperature is 15.6°C (60°F), with 300 millimetres (11.8 inches) of rainfall, mostly as storms in September and October, and 2,900 hours of sunshine. In winter there are high winds.

Soils

On the hills it is brown and so hard it has to be broken up, but is well drained with plenty of chalk. In the valleys the vineyards are mostly between the rivers in sandy and sometimes alluvial soil with some chalk.

Grapes

Red varieties: Monastrell; Tempranillo; Cabernet Sauvignon; Garnacha; Merlot; and Syrah. The Monastrell is the traditional vine and is hugely predominant, occupying ninety per cent of the vineyard.
White varieties: Macabeo and Airén.

Planting

Density is 900–2,200 vines per hectare.

Vineyard area

2,800 hectares.

Authorized yield

49hl/ha for reds and 56hl/ha for whites, but in practice much less. In the northwest 45hl/ha, in the centre 13–25hl/ha, and in the northeast 5–13hl/ha.

Wines

Whites 10–12% ABV, *rosados* 11–12.5% ABV, and reds 12–14% ABV. *Rosados* and reds must contain a minimum sixty per cent of Monastrell.

Production

15,093 hectolitres (2003).

Vintages

1999 (4); 2000 (4); 2001 (4); 2002 (3); 2003 (3); 2004 (4).

Although wines have been grown here since Roman times, they are only just emerging from total obscurity. They used to be of the usual Mediterranean type: late picked; alcoholic; heady; flabby, and mostly sold in bulk. A provisional DO was granted in 1982 and the full DO in 1994, but despite the enthusiasm of some local wine-growers things were slow to get going. Until recently the DO wines were difficult to find if you were there and impossible anywhere else. Nevertheless it has real potential that is now being realized. In the past it produced mostly *rosados*, but has been moving rapidly over to reds. Winemakers are learning how well the Monastrell grape can perform in the hills behind the Mediterranean. Exports began in 1999. At the time of the last edition of this book, only two bodegas were bottling DO wines, now there are ten. This is certainly an area to watch.

Some leading bodegas

BODEGA BALCONA

Ctra de Avilés, Paraje "El Aceniche", 30180 Bullas, Murcia. Tel: +34 968 65 28 91; Fax: +34 968 65 26 66; Email: bodegabalcona@larural.es

A boutique bodega owned by a long established family of wine-growers with 100 hectares of vineyard at 825 metres (2,706 feet), of which it sets aside twelve hectares with vines 25–50 years old for its own wines. It started to make them in 1998 with the aid of the oenologist of Mas Martinet in Priorato. They are based on at least sixty per cent Monastrell and are aged in seventy per cent French Allier oak, the rest American. The Selección 37 has fifteen per cent Syrah with ten per cent each Cabernet Sauvignon and Tempranillo, given six months in oak. The *crianza* has fifteen per cent each of Cabernet Sauvignon and Syrah and ten per cent Tempranillo. The *reserva* has twenty per cent Tempranillo, fifteen per cent Cabernet Sauvignon, and five per cent Syrah. The proportions of course vary from year to year, but the results are uniformly excellent and the wines have ageing potential. They are the best in the DO.

COOPERATIVA AGROVINICOLA NUESTRA SENORA DEL ROSARIO

Avenida de la Libertad s/n, 30180 Bullas, Murcia. Tel: +34 968 65 20 75; Fax: +34 968 65 37 65; Email: cnsrosario@bullas.net; Website: www.bullas.net

This cooperative was established in 1950 by 1,200 members with an equivalent number of hectares of vines, so it controls almost half the production of the DO. It makes a complete range of wines, including varietal Monastrells, sold under the name Las Reñas. The top wines are a *crianza* made from eighty per cent Monastrell and twenty per cent Syrah, aged for twelve months in American and French oak; Señorío de Bullas Reserva, a varietal Monastrell with eighteen months in American oak; and Las Reñas Selección from eighty per cent Monastrell, from vines over forty-five years old, and twenty per cent Syrah. An unusual one is Monastrell Dulce, a sweet, late-harvest wine from vines over forty years old.

JUMILLA

Geography

Jumilla is bordered to the north by Almansa and to the east by Yecla and Alicante. Although most of the DO lies within the province of Murcia, it extends westward into Albacete, which forms part of Castilla La Mancha. It is also high, with the vineyards at between 400–800 metres (1,312–2,624 feet) above sea level. There are no trees, other than some olives and nuts, and very little wildlife.

Climate

This is continental and southern. In winter the temperatures fall below zero, but the summers are hot, sunny, and arid, with temperatures rising to 40°C (104°F) and sometimes more, with a yearly average of 16°C (60.8°F). The rainfall is very low at 300 millimetres (11.8 inches) and generally comes as heavy storms in late spring and late autumn. There are 3,000 hours of sunshine.

Soils

Permeable, grey-brown, infertile soil with sand, a high chalk content, and large stones.

Grapes

Red varieties: Monastrell; Garnacha Tintorera; Garnacha Tinta; Tempranillo (Cencibel); Cabernet Sauvignon; Merlot; Syrah; and Petit Verdot. The most important variety by far is the red Monastrell, which occupies eighty-five per cent of the vineyard.
White varieties: Airén; Macabeo; Pedro Ximénez; Malvasía; Chardonnay; Sauvignon Blanc; and Moscatel de Grano Menudo. The most important white variety is Airén, but this occupies only eight per cent.

Planting

Grown as bushes *en vaso*, trained low, and planted in the *marco real*, but new vineyards are often planted *en espaldera*. Two densities of planting are permitted: *cultivo extensivo* with 1,100–1,600 vines per hectare and *cultivo intensivo* with 1,600–3,200 vines per hectare. Irrigation of the vineyards is forbidden except in emergencies; there are many emergencies.

Vineyard area

41,279 hectares.

Authorized yield

For vines grown *extensivo* 31.5hl/ha for whites and 28hl/ha for reds; for those grown *intensivo* 49hl/ha; but, through drought and replanting, the actual yield is generally a good deal less.

Wines

Minimums: whites 11% ABV; *rosados* 11.5% ABV; reds 13% ABV.

Wines sold as Jumilla-Monastrell must contain at least eighty-five per cent Monastrell. The latest regulations of the *consejo regulador* lay down only minimum strengths; but this is traditionally an area of strong or even massive wines, and although they are now being made lighter than they once were, whites can still go up to 15% ABV, *rosados* and reds to 17% ABV. *Doble pasta* wines are no longer dealt with in the DO regulations, but are still made.

Production

235,030 hectolitres (2003).

Vintages

1990 (4); 1991 (4); 1992 (3); 1993 (4); 1994 (4); 1995 (3); 1996 (4); 1997 (3); 1998 (5); 1999 (4); 2000 (4); 2001 (3); 2002 (3); 2003 (4); 2004 (5).

The hills here are not very high or remote, and the soil, although rather sandy, is far from being the pure sand that phylloxera cannot get through, yet the aphid took a remarkably long time to arrive. The vineyards were free of it until 1989; and although 100 years overdue, it wrought its usual havoc, even though some of the old vineyards had been replanted with grafted vines to increase yields. The figures speak for themselves. In 1989, 673,792 hectolitres of wine were sold. By 2003 it had fallen to 287,825 hectolitres. But disastrous as this was, Spain was prosperous by then, giving Jumilla the chance of a fresh start. Wisely the growers decided to concentrate on the Monastrell vine, which can produce remarkably good results here, but the addition of French varieties has worked well. Fresh capital was attracted and new bodegas established, completely up to date. The traditional trade was largely in massive blending wines sold in bulk, many of them made by the *doble pasta* method, but the demand for these has greatly declined and the bodegas took the opportunity to make lighter wines with more finesse. Bulk wines, rather oddly, have found a market in Italy. Many are still powerful and heady and they have long had a devoted following in Spain. Tasting them, one can well see why. Jumilla is now an exciting place to be, like Ribera del Duero and Priorato in the recent past, and although its wines get nowhere near the peaks of quality those districts can produce, the bodegas have got their acts together and are making seriously good ones. It is an area, too, that can offer tremendous value for money, and the supermarkets have been quick to recognize this. A rather odd wine, found only locally, is a sweet red from the Monastrell. It is a pleasant place to visit, if you do not mind the heat. Jumilla is a most agreeable little town and the mountain views from the vineyards are spectacular.

Some leading bodegas

BODEGAS Y VINEDOS AGAPITO RICO
Casas de la Hoya s/n, El Carche, 30520 Jumilla, Murcia.
Tel: +34 968 43 51 37; Fax: +34 968 43 55 09

Founded in 1989 by two growers, this is one of the leading quality bodegas in Jumilla. It makes only red wines and is entirely self-sufficient for grapes, having 100 hectares of vineyard at an altitude of 700 metres (2,296 feet). The first were planted in 1983-4, before the bodega itself was founded, after careful study of the soil and microclimates. They are irrigated by night, when necessary, using water from a reservoir fed principally from wells in the higher mountains and also by catching rainwater – when there is any. Everything is completely up to date. Some of the wines are made by carbonic maceration and others tradition-ally, the *crianzas* and above being matured principally in French oak from Limousin and Allier, with a little American. The brand name is Carchelo, named after Monte Carche, which rises above the vineyards. The very good *joven* is made from fifty per cent Monastrell, thirty per cent Syrah, and twenty per cent Merlot – as was the *crianza* 2000, then matured in French oak, though both the grapes and proportions change from year to year. There are also *joven* varietals from Merlot and Syrah and a varietal Syrah *crianza*.

BLEDA
Avenida de Yecla 26, 30520 Jumilla, Murcia. Tel: +34 968 78 00 12;
Fax: +34 968 78 26 99; Email: wines@bodegasbleda.com

Established in 1935 this is an old bodega that is advancing with the times, and a major grower with 220 hectares of vineyard. It makes three ranges of wine, the simplest being sold as Montesinos, then Castillo de Jumilla and, for the top wines, Divus. The Divus red *crianza* 2002 was ninety-five per cent Monastrell and five per cent Merlot, given nine months in Allier oak.

BODEGAS 1890
Ctra Venta del Olivo km 2.5, 30520 Jumilla, Murcia. Tel/Fax: +34 968 75 70 99

This is one of the bodegas in the García Carrión group that has interests in

Rueda, La Mancha, Penedès, and Rioja. As its name suggests, it dates from 1890 and is a family company now in its fifth generation. Here it has seventy-eight hectares of vineyard and sells the wines under the name Mayoral. They are very sound and, apart from varietals from Syrah and Cabernet Sauvignon, are made from various combinations of Monastrell, Tempranillo, and Cabernet Sauvignon. They go up to a *reserva* from seventy per cent Monastrell and thirty per cent Tempranillo aged in American and French oak.

BODEGAS Y VINEDOS CASA DE LA ERMITA
Avenida de la Asunción 42 Bajo, 30520 Jumilla, Murcia. Tel: +34 968 78 30 35; Fax: +34 968 71 60 63; Email: bodega@casadelaermita.com; Website: www.casadelaermita.com

Established in 1999, this estate has spent vast amounts of money building a bodega where all the wine can be moved by gravity and establishing a 150-hectare vineyard, including old vines. This must be one of the most remarkable in Spain, for apart from forty-seven hectares of Monastrell and the other authorized varieties, it has 20.5 hectares of Petit Verdot and, more improbably, two hectares of Viognier grown at 700 metres (2,296 feet). There is also an experimental vineyard growing thirty-two varieties from all over the world. The wines are very good, including varietals from Viognier, Cabernet Sauvignon, Syrah, Monastrell, and Petit Verdot. The last has been highly praised and is a *crianza* with twelve months in eighty per cent American and twenty per cent French oak. Blended reds are made from combinations of Monastrell, Tempranillo, Cabernet Sauvignon, Merlot, and Syrah. There is also a sweet Monastrell. Monasterio de Santa Ana is a slightly cheaper range.

FINCA LUZON
Ctra Jumilla–Ontur km 17, Apto 45, 30520 Jumilla, Murcia. Tel/Fax: +34 968 78 41 35; Email: info@fincaluzon.com; Website: www.fincaluzon.com

This estate was founded in 1999 by three families that have been growing vines since 1916. Between them they own two farms at 500 and 700 metres (1,640 and 2,296 feet) with scope for expansion. Both American and French oak is used for ageing, and it makes thoroughly good wines. The range of red, *rosado,* and white *jóvenes* is sold as Finca Luzón. A very good range is sold as Castillo de Luzón. The red *crianza* typically has fifty per cent Monastrell, thirty per cent Cabernet Sauvignon, and twenty per cent Merlot. The top red Altos de Luzón is fifty per cent fifty-year-old Monastrell with equal parts of Tempranillo and Cabernet Sauvignon; it is very well structured with clear ageing potential.

JULIA ROCH E HIJOS

Finca Casa Castillo, Carretera Jumilla–Hellín km 15.7, 30520 Jumilla, Murcia.

Tel: +34 968 78 16 91; Fax: +34 968 71 62 38; Email: juliaroch@interbook.net

Founded officially in 1991, this bodega has a much longer history, back to 1870. It has 197 hectares of vineyard and its wines have been going up and up in quality – they are excellent. The standard range is sold under the name Casa Castillo and includes a varietal Monastrell. The top wines are Valtosca, a varietal Syrah with twelve months in new French oak, and the *crianza* Las Gravas, made from fifty per cent Monastrell, thirty per cent Syrah, and twenty per cent Cabernet Sauvignon from a single vineyard, given sixteen months in 500-litre French oak barrels. These are well worth seeking out.

BODEGA SENORIO DEL CONDESTABLE

Avenida de los Reyes Católicos s/n, 30520 Jumilla, Murcia.

Tel/Fax: +34 968 78 01 11; Website: www.byb.es

Founded by the great Bodegas y Bebidas empire in 1968, when it took over a vast bodega then known as SAVIN, the biggest supplier of bulk wines. It operates on a grand scale as Señorio del Condestable and Señorío de Robles. It has raised the quality enormously, concentrating on varietal Monastrells.

UTIEL-REQUENA

Geography

This area lies inland to the west of Valencia around the two towns of its name. Its vineyards are 600–900 metres (1,968–2,952 feet) above sea level, averaging 720 metres (2,362 feet), on an undulating plain surrounded by mountains.

Climate

Although influenced by the Mediterranean, the climate is essentially continental and very harsh, with a maximum temperature of 40°C (104°F) and a minimum of -15°C (5°F). The average is 13.9°C (57°F) and, to put these extremes into perspective, the average for the hottest month, July, is 23.2°C (73.7°F) and for the coldest, December, it is 5.9°C (42.6°F). The winters are long and cold, the summers relatively short and very hot. A few years ago a spring frost destroyed forty per cent of the grapes. Rain falls mostly in spring and autumn, 400–450 millimetres (15.7–17.7 inches), and there are 2,800 hours of sunshine.

Soils

These are very mixed, with the alluvial soils of the Magro Valley in the north and with sandstone, marl, and clay in the south, but there are also outcrops of limestone and the best vineyards are found here.

Grapes

Red varieties: Bobal; Tempranillo; Garnacha Tinta; Cabernet Sauvignon; Merlot; and Syrah. Bobal is the traditional variety and still occupies seventy-eight per cent of the vineyard, but the *consejo regulador* has been doing its best to get it replaced with Tempranillo. Bobal is therefore slowly decreasing, although it is now producing better wines than ever before.
White varieties: Macabeo; Merseguera; Planta Nova (Tardana); Chardonnay; and Sauvignon Blanc.

Planting

The square *marco real* pattern is used with 2.5 metres (8.2 feet) spacing, and pruning is *en vaso*, with a density of 1,600–2,500 vines per hectare.

Vineyard area

41,000 hectares

Authorized yield

For reds, 55.5hl/ha if grown in the traditional way, 67.3hl/ha on wires. For whites, 59hl/ha and 71.5hl/ha.

Wines

The lusty *doble pastas* are not quite extinct, though they form no part of modern thinking. To make them the must is run off after about twelve hours' maceration and fermented as *rosado*. The lees are left in the vat, which is then topped up with more grape pulp that is fermented. This results in very full-bodied wines that can go up to 18% ABV.

For modern wines the rules are rather complicated. They come in three kinds: the simple DO wines; those classed as *superior*; and a new kind, *vendimia inicial*, introduced in the 1990s to be used on young wines for immediate drinking. Minimum strength for the DO whites is 10% ABV, for the *superior* and for the *vendimia inicial* 11% ABV. A red Bobal must have at least 11% ABV, if *superior* 11.5% ABV. A wine labelled "*tradición*" must have at least seventy per cent Bobal and 12% ABV. *Vendímia inicial* reds must have 11% ABV. These *superior* reds may be aged as *crianzas* or *reservas* with a few *gran reservas*. There are also sparkling wines with a minimum strength of 10% ABV if made as a slightly sparkling *agujas*, and 11% ABV if made by the traditional method. A *licor* wine must be made from Planta Nova or Bobal and have a minimum strength of 15% ABV. Yet a further category is planned: *vinos de heredad* from selected plots.

Production

478,251 hectolitres (2003).

Vintages

1999 (4); 2000 (4); 2001 (5); 2002 (5); 2003 (4); 2004 (4).

Utiel-Requena is the largest of the three DO areas in Valencia. It has a long winemaking history and there are medieval cellars in the old part of Requena, which is a most enchanting little town; indeed, like some of the towns in the north, the whole place seems built above cellars carved out of sandstone. It also has an admirable little wine museum in a nineteenth-century, round bodega.

In the eighteenth century many of its wines were distilled, which made for easier transport, as the area was rather cut off from its principal market in Castilla and from the coast. Communications improved in 1847 with a new road, now the N111, linking Valencia to Madrid; and the railway line to Valencia opened in 1887. All of this came in time for it to benefit from the French wine crisis brought on by oïdium and phylloxera. New bodegas sprang up around the railway station. Between 1850–1890, 15,000 hectares of vineyard were planted. The trade was not destroyed by the revival of the French vineyards, and phylloxera did not get here until 1912 – it progressed relatively slowly, in part owing to the resistance of the local Bobal vines. The vineyards continued to expand while they were being replanted, and by 1950 there were 40,000 hectares, about the same amount as today. Vineyards are everywhere.

The Bobal vine, which is not grown in many other places, is at once the region's strength and its weakness. It does well in the higher vineyards where the summers are short and dry, and it is still by far the most widely planted variety, producing attractive and successful *rosados* and, with the aid of the *doble pasta* method of vinification, it used to give massive reds. This method has long been declared to be in its death throes, but it is still alive – it provides bulk wines that are popular for blending, finding an improbable market in what used to be the east European Soviet bloc, and a more likely one in Valencia, into which DO they are admitted by special dispensation to beef up the thin local reds. Vinified in the ordinary way, its red wines used to be astringent, tannic, and lacking in finesse, but had the advantage of being cheap. Careful viticulture and vinification has brought about an enormous improvement, giving very attractive wines that mature relatively quickly. though and some age well in the medium term.

Some leading bodegas

BODEGAS CASA DEL PINAR

Carretera Isidros–Venta del Moro, 46310 Venta del Moro, Valencia.
Tel/Fax: +34 962 13 91 21
A boutique bodega established in 2000 with two hectares of vineyard, it makes seriously good wine under the name Sanfir. Its *crianza* 2001, from thirty-four per cent Bobal, thirty-three per cent Tempranillo, twenty-three per cent Cabernet Sauvignon, five per cent Merlot, and five per cent Syrah, was perfectly balanced and delicious.

COVIÑAS SOCIEDAD COOPERATIVA

Rafael Duyos s/n, 46340 Requena, Valencia. Tel: +34 962 30 0680; Fax: +34 962 30 26 51; Email: covinas@covinas.com; Website: www.covinas.com
This enormous cooperative was formed in 1965 by amalgamating fourteen cooperatives in a modern building. Its 500 members between them have 11,000 hectares. It makes a very full range of wines sold as Peña Tejo, Enterizo, Viña Enterizo, and Requevin. There is a white from Macabeo, a *rosado* from Bobal, and reds made from Tempranillo, with some Garnacha and Bobal. They go up to varietal Garnacha *reserva* and *gran reserva*.

VICENTE GANDÍA PLA

Ctra Cheste-Godellata s/n, 46370 Chiva, Valencia. Tel: +34 962 52 42 42; Fax: +34 962 52 42 43; Email: gandia@gandiawines.com; Website: www.gandiawines.com
A quality, family producer, now in its fourth generation, it has a fine 200-hectare vineyard, Finca Hoya de Cadenas, on the best ground in an estate with almond and olive trees, and a delightful house dating from 1820. Its very good wines are sold as Hoya de Cadenas, Castillo de Liria, Fusta Nova, Mil Aromas, Cremonia, and Generación 1. For supermarkets it uses the mark Marqués de Chivé. The highly successful Hoya de Cadenas range has a white from forty per

cent Chardonnay, thirty per cent Sauvignon Blanc, and thirty per cent Macabeo; a *rosado* from Bobal; a *reserva* from ninety per cent Tempranillo and ten per cent Garnacha; and Reserva Privada from eighty-five per cent Tempranillo and fifteen per cent Cabernet Sauvignon. It also makes varietals from Chardonnay, Moscatel, Garnacha, Tempranillo, Merlot, and Cabernet Sauvignon. The top wine is the very good Vicente Gandía Generación 1 from fifty per cent Bobal, twenty per cent Garnacha, and fifteen per cent each of Merlot and Cabernet Sauvignon. *See* the section on Valencia, below.

BODEGAS SCHENK/CAVAS MURVIEDRO
Ampliación Poligono El Romeral s/n, 46340 Requena, Valencia. Tel: +34 962 32 90 03; Fax: +34 962 32 90 02; Email: murviedro@murviedro.es

It has built a fine new winery here and has a close relationship with the Cooperativa Valenciana de Viticultores, with 350 members. When it persuaded the local growers to prune short in the interests of quality, the strength of the wine went up by half a degree. Its wines are sold under the names Santerra and Coronilla, up to *crianza* level. The varietal Tempranillo *crianzas* are very good and the varietal Bobal *crianzas* are even better. *See* Valencia, below.

VALENCIA

Geography

Valencia is a thriving, modern city, the third-largest in Spain, and the biggest wine port. The vineyards are divided into four sub-zones: Valentino, to the west of the city, which includes Cheste and Marquesado (formerly a separate DO); Alto Turia to the northwest of the city; Clariano, which is quite separate, in the extreme south of the province, bordering on Alicante; and Moscatel de Valencia, to the southwest of the city. Each of these sub-zones, however, can be further sub-divided. Valentino is the biggest with about sixty per cent of the vineyards planted on slopes 100–550 metres (328–1,804 feet) above sea level. Sub-divisions include Campos de Liria at 260 metres (853 feet) and Serrania at 550 metres. Alto Turia, at 400–700 metres (1,312–2,296 feet), is hilly and has some ten per cent of the vineyard. Clariano can be divided into two parts: the eastern and the western, the vines being planted on terraces 160–650 metres (525–2,132 feet) above sea level with an average of 350 metres (1,148 feet). Moscatel de Valencia to the southwest of the city is rather scattered and only accounts for a small amount of the vineyard; it has outposts in Valentino and the altitude varies from sea level to 100 metres (328 feet). All these altitudes should be regarded as very approximate as no two sets of official figures agree.

Climate

Down by the coast it is Mediterranean and moderate, but with the odd local feature that it can be unexpectedly cold at night, even in summer, so temperature fluctuations of 30°C between day and night are not uncommon. Most of the vineyards are thirty kilometres (18.6 miles) or more inland, where the climate is more continental, rising to 35°C (95°F) in summer and going down to -5°C (23°F) in winter. In Valentino the mean temperature is 14°C (57°F), in Alto Turia it is 12.5°C (54.5°F), and in Clariano it is 15°C (59°F). The rainfall is least in Alto Turia, at 460 millimetres (18 inches) and highest in parts of Valentino, at 550 millimetres (21.6 inches), though it varies a lot between the various sub-zones, and Campos de Liria has only 280 millimetres (11 inches). There are some 2,700 hours of sunshine. The whole can be regarded as arid or semi-arid.

Soils

The lower parts of Valentino have brown or reddish-brown soils with limestone; higher up they are brown and contain limestone. Alta Turia has rather sandy soil but with some chalk. In Clariano the soils are rather similar to those of Valentino, but in the Valle de Albadia there is clay in the sub-soil.

Grapes

Red varieties: Monastrell; Garnacha Tinta; Garnacha Tintorera; Cabernet Sauvignon; Tempranillo; Forcayat (Clariano only); Bobal; Syrah; Cabernet Franc; Ruby Cabernet; and Mandó.
White varieties: Macabeo; Merseguera; Malvasía; Planta Fina de Pedralba; Pedro Ximénez; Moscatel de Alexandría; Planta Nova; Tortosí; Verdil; Sauvignon Blanc; and Sémillon.

Planting

In hot areas the vines are pruned *en vaso*, keeping the grapes close to the ground to protect them from the heat. The square *marco real* pattern is used, 2.5 metres (8.2 feet) apart where it is hottest and 2.25 metres (7.4 feet) where it is less hot. Where it is merely warm, they are pruned *en cordón* and planted in a rectangular pattern 3 x 1.75 metres (9.8 x 5.7 feet). The vine density is 2,500 per hectare in Clariano and 2,000 elsewhere. Drip-feed irrigation is allowed.

Vineyard area

17,500 hectares.

Authorized yield

Reds 59hl/ha. Whites 70hl/ha.

Wines

Whites must have a minimum strength of 10% ABV, *rosados* and reds 10.5% ABV. *Licoroso* and *rancio* wines are made from Moscatel and Pedro Ximénez and must have a minimum strength of 15% ABV. There are also some *espumosos* with a minimum strength of 11% ABV.

The whites, *rosados*, *claretes*, and many of the reds are made as *jóvenes*. Some of the reds are given ageing, but less is required than in any other Spanish region. A *crianza* need have only three months in oak, a *reserva* six, and a *gran reserva* nine. The move to make these wines came after the new plantings of Tempranillo and Cabernet Sauvignon. This style of wine has only just begun to develop. Generally the wines are light, to be drunk young. The very sweet *licorosos* and the *rancios* can be classified as *reservas* after twenty-four months in American oak and twelve months in bottle.

Up to thirty per cent of wines made from Bobal in neighbouring Utiel-Requena can be used in blending, adding body and fragrance. There are those who would simply combine the two DOs into one.

Production

704,334 hectolitres (2003).

Vintages

1999 (4); 2000 (5); 2001 (4); 2002 (4); 2003 (4); 2004 (4) ; 2005 (5).

Valencia is a delightful place to visit. It is a buzzing industrial city and the centre of the orange trade; but for the most part its wines are not distinguished. There are a few small bodegas, but the trade is mostly in the hands of big operators and cooperatives. They sell agreeable wines in enormous quantities at very attractive prices to fill the shelves of Spanish stores and supermarkets all over the world. Few of their DO wines rank highly by absolute standards but some of the Moscatels do. These come in all styles from light, sweet, and slight to massive and memorable. These companies were the pioneers of the export trade, efficient and commercial. They also sell table grapes, grape juice, and dry Moscatel to Italy for making *spumante*. In the old days the bodegas were around the port, but they have been displaced by development and are now mostly in the country.

Some leading bodegas

J BELDA

Salvaterra 54, 46635 Fontanars dels Alforins, Valencia. Tel: +34 608 96 23 65; Fax: +34 962 22 22 45; Email: daniel.belda@vinsbjb.com; Website: www.vinsbjb.com

A family-owned bodega run by Daniel Belda, whose name is used as the trademark and who has brought it completely up to date. It has 160 hectares of vineyard at an altitude of 600 metres (1,968 feet). Most of the wines are varietals: the whites Moscatel, Verdil, and Chardonnay; the reds Monastrell, Merlot, Tempranillo, Cabernet Sauvignon, Syrah, and Pinot Noir. Some, from Verdil, Chardonnay, and Pinot Noir, are barrel fermented. It is unusual in making wines up to *gran reserva* that are recommended for maturing in bottle. The Merlot, which has fourteen months oak ageing, has a suggested bottle age of fifteen years, and Cabernet Sauvignon *reserva* is recommended for 20–30 years bottle ageing. Selección is blended from Cabernet Sauvignon, Tempranillo, Monastrell, and Pinot Noir from a number of vintages.

ANECOOP

Monforte 1, 46010 Valencia, Valencia. Tel: +34 963 93 85 00; Fax: +34 963 93 85 10; Email: info@anecoop.com; Website: www.anecoop.com

Wine forms only part of the activities of this cooperative, which was established in 1975 as a cooperative of cooperatives, the wine department coming ten years later. It is a very large international concern mainly selling fruit and vegetables grown by members as far away as Sevilla and Navarra. Its wine side is a collective of six cooperatives, the total membership of which must be enormous. Although it does much to supervise how the wines are grown and made, results are somewhat variable. It is an enormous source of wines and some of them are good, especially the Moscatels.

HERETAT DE TAVERNERS

Ctra Moixent km 1.8, Fontanars, 46635 Valencia. Tel/Fax: +34 962 13 24 37; Email: info@heretatdetaverners.com; Website: www.heretatdetaverners.com

This boutique bodega, taking its name from a beautiful seventeenth-century *finca* that has been modernized, was founded in 1998 and has already established a fine reputation for its quality wines, which are made by Daniel Belda (*see* above). The wood used is eighty per cent American and twenty per cent French. The *crianza* red is from forty per cent Tempranillo, thirty per cent Monastrell, and thirty per cent Cabernet Sauvignon; the *reserva* is from fifty-five per cent Cabernet Sauvignon with fifteen per cent each of Monastrell, Merlot, and Tempranillo. There is also a varietal Graciano *reserva*, a grape that does not appear in the official list, but which clearly grows very well.

VICENTE GANDÍA PLA

Ctra Cheste-Godelleta s/n, 46370 Chiva, Valencia. Tel: +34 962 52 42 42; Fax: +34 962 52 42 43; Email: gandia@gandiawines.com; Website: www.gandiawines.com

This family bodega, now in its third generation with the fourth coming along, was founded in premises on the dockside at Valencia in 1895. In 1992 it moved into new premises at Chiva, which are an inspired piece of architecture, and everything is kept completely up to date. Its estate of 200 hectares at Finca Hoya de Cadena, in Utiel-Requena, is exemplary. But it also makes a very good value range of Valencian wines from Alto Turia, under the name Castillo de Liria, and is very big in the export markets. Its Moscatels are particularly good.

CELLER DEL ROURE

Carretera de Les Alcusses km 2.5, 46640 Moixent, Valencia. Tel: +34 962 29 50 20; Fax: +34 962 29 51 42; Email: cellerdelroure@hotmail.com

A boutique bodega established in 1995 whose wines are very highly rated.

BODEGAS SCHENK/CAVAS MURVIEDRO

Amplación Poligono El Romeral s/n, 46340 Requena, Valencia. Tel: +34 962 32 90 03; Fax: +34 962 32 90 02; Email: murviedro@murviedro.es

The Schenk empire is Swiss-owned with wine interests in Switzerland, France, Germany, and Italy, as well as Spain, and sells its wines internationally with offices in several countries. The Swiss company was founded in 1893 and created its Valencian bodegas in 1927. It is also active in Utiel-Requena and Alicante. Its wines are undoubtedly among the best and are sold under the names Cavas Murviedro, Los Monteros, Estrella, and Santerra.

YECLA

Geography

A small inland enclave around the town of Yecla in the province of Murcia, it is surrounded by the DOs of Alicante, Jumilla, and Almansa. It is the only DO in Spain to have the odd distinction of containing but a single municipality. The vineyards are on gentle hills at altitudes of 400–800 metres (1,312–2,624 feet), surrounded by higher hills and mountains, giving some most attractive views. It includes two small sub-zones: Campo Arriba, to the north, at 700–800 metres (2,296–2,624 feet), with deep limey soil, and which can have its name on the label and is noted for producing intense and alcoholic red wines; and Campo Abajo at 600–650 metres (1,968–2,132 feet) with more clay in the soil, where whites and lower strength reds are grown.

Climate

Southern continental. It is far enough inland to be hot in summer and cold in winter, but far enough south for the winters not to get too cold. The average temperature is 15°C (59°F) with a summer high of 35°C (95°F), though it can go up to 42°C (107.6°F). Winter lows are generally of 5°C (41°F), though it can go down to -10°C (14°F). The rainfall is 300–350 millimetres (11.8–13.7 inches) so it very rarely rains, but when it does, mostly in spring and autumn, it comes down in torrents. There are 3,000 hours of sunshine.

Soils

Mostly chalky over limestone with sandy topsoil and clay in some areas, particularly in the southeast. There are many big stones.

Grapes

Red varieties: Monastrell; Garnacha Tinto; Garnacha Tintorera; Tempranillo; Cabernet Sauvignon; Merlot; Syrah; and (experimentally) Petit Verdot.
White varieties: Merseguera; Macabeo; Airén; Malvasía; and Chardonnay.
Of all these, Monastrell is by far the most important, occupying eighty per cent of the vineyard.

Planting

Grown mostly *en cabeza*, but some of the newer vineyards are grown *en cordón*, planted in a rectangular pattern with 2.5 metres (8.2 feet) between vines and 3.5 metres (11.4 feet) between rows. Some of the newest vineyards of all, however, are being planted *en espaldera*. Density is 1,100–1,800 vines per hectare on dry sites, and 1,600–3,200 on irrigated land.

Vineyard area

4,500 hectares.

Authorized yield

52hl/ha, but generally much less, especially in the Campo Arriba sub-zone.

Wines

Minimum strengths: whites 10.5% ABV, *rosados* 11% ABV, reds and sparkling 11.5% ABV, *vinos de liquor* 15–22% ABV. In the Campo Arriba reds reach 14% ABV. Whites go up to *crianza* and reds to *gran reserva*. Only the reds are put through a full malolactic fermentation and some are made by carbonic maceration.

Production

45,100 hectolitres (2003).

Vintages

1999 (4); 2000 (5); 2001 (4); 2002 (4); 2003 (4); 2004 (4).

It may seem odd that the little enclave of Yecla has its own separate DO, but it is firmly based on history. The wine-growers have long had their own identity and they intend to keep it. For a long time the winemaking was in the hands of cooperatives making strong, heady wines sold in bulk for blending. The grapes were generally picked too late, giving wines of more than 13% ABV that oxidized very quickly. Now, like the other Levantine districts, they recognize that this trade has no future and that good wines, particularly from the local Monastrell, are the ones to make. The bodega that brought Yecla on to the international markets was Castaño. It was a remarkable solo pioneering effort. Others are following, and the potential of the district is starting to be realized. At present the best whites are remarkable achievements for wines grown so far south, fresh and with enough acidity. If the reds lack subtlety and complexity, they present an excellent initial impact, with lots of fruit, and are most enjoyable. The old fortified wines are fast disappearing.

Some leading bodegas

ANTONIO CANDELA E HIJOS

Avda de la Paz 58, 30510 Yecla, Murcia. Tel: +34 968 79 02 81; Fax: +34 968 79 23 51; Email: info@barahonda.com; Website: www.barahonda.com

A family bodega founded in 1925 and now in its third generation. It has 150 hectares of vineyard and started to bottle wine in 1999, which it sells under the mark Barahonda. It makes a varietal Monastrell and in 2001 introduced a varietal Cabernet Sauvignon. The Tinto Barrica is seventy per cent Monastrell and thirty per cent Cabernet Sauvignon with 4–5 months in American and French oak. The *rosado* is a varietal Monastrell and the white ten per cent Macabeo and ninety per cent Airén. It also sells bag-in-box wines under the name Los Toneles de Recuerdo (Old Vats to Remember). Its most highly praised wine is the sweet Monastrell Bellum El Remate.

BODEGAS CASTAÑO

Ctra Fuentealamo 3, 30510 Yecla, Murcia. Tel: +34 968 79 11 15; Fax: +34 968 79 19 00; Email: info@bodegascastano.com; Website: www.bodegascastano.com

Generations of the Castaño family have been respected wine-growers. In 1985 the present generation took a great leap forward, built a fine new bodega, and equipped it with the latest technology. It has four beautifully maintained vineyards with 400 hectares. The *jóvenes* are sold under the name Dominio Espinol, the *rosado* a varietal Monastrell, the red 2003 made from eighty-five per cent Monastrell and fifteen per cent Tempranillo, while the Selección 2002 was from eighty per cent Monastrell with ten per cent each of Tempranillo and Cabernet Sauvignon. Using the name Varietales it makes varietals from Monastrell, Cabernet Sauvignon, Merlot, and Syrah, with a white from equal parts of Macabeo and Chardonnay. Hécula is the best varietal Monastrell. The red *crianzas* and *reservas* are sold under the name Pozuelo, the name of one of the vineyards. The *crianza* 2002 was made from eighty per cent Monastrell, ten per cent Cabernet Sauvignon, and five per cent each of Tempranillo and Syrah, with ten months in American oak. The *reserva* 2001 was from eighty per cent Monastrell with ten per cent each of Tempranillo and Cabernet Sauvignon, given twenty months in American oak. Collección 2003 and Casa Cisca both came from low-yielding unirrigated vineyards, the latter a varietal Monastrell coming in at a resounding 15% ABV.

COOPERATIVA DEL VINO DE YECLA LA PURISIMA

Carretera de Pinoso 3, 30510 Yecla, Murcia. Tel: +34 968 75 12 57; Fax: +34 968 79 51 16; Email: info@calpyecla.com; Website: www.calpyecla.com

Founded in 1945 with twenty-six members, it now has 1,300 and is one of the biggest cooperatives in Spain with 2,100 hectares of vineyard. It has brought itself up to date and is making good wines. Its *jóvenes* and oak-aged wines are sold under the names Estío and Valcorso, the *crianzas* and *reservas* under the name Iglesia Vieja. It makes varietals from Cabernet Sauvignon, Syrah, Monastrell (including an ecological wine), and Tempranillo. The Iglesia Vieja 2001 *crianza* was made from seventy per cent Monastrell and fifteen per cent each of Tempranillo and Cabernet Sauvignon.

OTHER LEVANTINE WINES

VdlT Campo de Cartagena

SERRANO

Finca La Cabaña 30, 30594 Pozo Estrecho, Murcia. Tel: +34 968 55 62 98; Fax: +34 968 55 62 98; Email: vinos@bodegaserrano.com; Website: www.bodegaserrano.com

A family bodega founded in 1940 with fifteen hectares. This used just to make bulk wines from Meseguera, but in 1991 changed direction, growing a wide range of vines and specializing in semi-sweet wines. The Viña Galtea range has no oak and the Darimus range is given eight weeks ageing in French oak.

VdlT El Terrerazo

MUSTIGUILLO

Carretera N-330 km 195, 46300 Las Cuevas de Utiel, Valencia.
Tel: +34 620 21 62 27; Fax: +34 618 30 82 88

A family bodega founded in 1999 that has ninety hectares, but has chosen to stay out of the DO Utiel-Requena and is making very highly praised wines based on Bobal, especially Finca Terrerazo. The 2002 was made from sixty-five per cent Bobal, twenty per cent Tempranillo, and fifteen per cent Cabernet Sauvignon, given seventeen months in French oak.

9

The Centre

Much of the centre of Spain is flat: the Meseta is a dull plain. The forests that filled it centuries ago have long since been cut down, creating something of a desert: broiling hot in summer and desperately cold in winter. Until the 1970s the only wines of any note grown here were those of Valdepeñas, which were very agreeable, but they were wines people drank when they could not afford Rioja. Most of the vines in the central plain produced large quantities of thin white wines, that were distilled for brandy. Modern wine-making has changed all that. Good quality and very good value wines are now grown all over the place. The transformation has been remarkable, and many wines are now well worth seeking out. This applies especially to the modern wines of Valdepeñas, much better than their predecessors, largely thanks to being able to control the temperature of fermentation.

VINOS DE MADRID

Geography

The area is divided into three sub-zones: San Martín de Valdeiglesias (thirty-five per cent of the vineyard); Navalcarnero (fourteen per cent); and Arganda (fifty-one per cent). San Martín de Valdeiglesias is to the west of the city of Madrid and slightly south, joining the DO of Méntrida, a landscape of gentle hills that rise into the Sierra de Gredos. Navalcarnero is on the Meseta, also to the west and nearer the city, likewise joining the DO of Méntrida. Arganda is southeast of the city, joining the DO of La Mancha and many of the best wines come from here. The vineyards vary in altitude from 522–800 metres (1,713–2,624 feet). Wines from different sub-zones cannot be mixed.

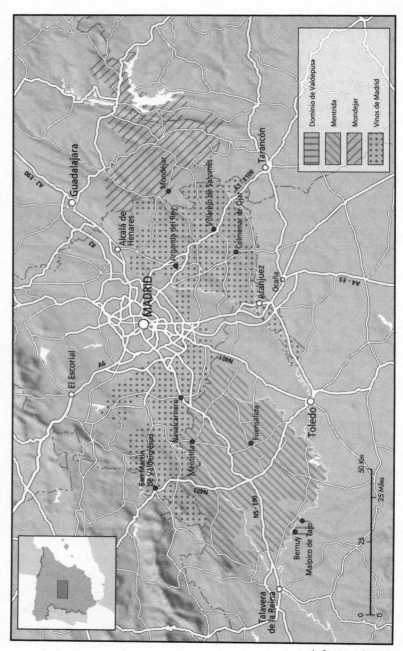

Legend:
- Dominio de Valdepusa
- Mentrida
- Mondéjar
- Vinos de Madrid

Guadalajara

Tarancón

Mondéjar

Villarejo de Salvanés

Alcalá de Henares

Arganda del Rey

Colmenar de Oreja

A3·E109

Aranjuez

Ocaña

A2·E90

R2

MADRID

N401

A4·E5

El Escorial

A6

Navalcarnero

Fuensalida

Toledo

San Martín de Valdeiglesias

Méntrida

N403

N401

N5·E90

50 Km

25 Miles

25

Bernuy

Malpica de Tajo

Talavera de la Reina

0

0

xi Centre of Spain

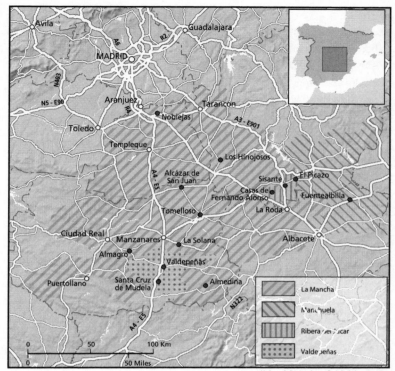

xii La Mancha & Valdepenas

Climate

This is continental and given to extremes, rising to 40.7°C (105°F). in summer and falling to -8°C (17.6°F). in winter, with an average of 13.7°C (56.6°F) and 2,800 hours of sunshine. The differences between the three sub-zones are illustrated by their rainfalls: 461 millimetres (18.1 inches) in Arganda; 529 millimetres (20.8 inches) in Navalcarnero, and 658 millimetres (26 inches) in San Martín de Valdeiglesias.

Soils

Again there are substantial differences between the sub-zones. In San Martín de Valdeiglesias it is brown, slightly acid clay/marl over granite. In Navalcarnero it is poorer in quality, covering a sub-soil of sand and clay. In Arganda it is richer, with clay/marl over granite, and there is limestone in some places.

Grapes

Red varieties: Tinto Fino (Tempranillo or Cencibel); Garnacha; Merlot; Cabernet Sauvignon; and Syrah.

White varieties: Malvar; Albillo; Airén; Parellada; Torrontés; Moscatel Gran Menudo; and Viura (Macabeo).

In San Martín de Valdeiglesias the principal grapes are Garnacha and Albillo; in Navalcarnero, Garnacha and Malvar; and in Arganda, Tinto Fino and Malvar, though there is also a good deal of Airén.

Planting

Most of the vineyards are planted in the *tres bolillo* pattern, though others are used. The vines are generally pruned *en vaso*, though there is some use of Guyot and *doble cordón*. The density varies widely: 900–4,000 vines per hectare. Organic viticulture is increasing.

Vineyard area

10,561 hectares.

Authorized yield

Reds 56hl/ha, whites 49hl/ha.

Wines

Reds, *rosados*, and whites. The minimum strengths are: reds 11.5% ABV in Arganda, 12% ABV in the other sub-zones; *rosados* 11% ABV in Arganda, 11.5% ABV in the other sub-zones; whites 10% ABV in Arganda, 11% ABV in the other sub-zones; sparkling 11.5% ABV. All can go up to a heady 15% ABV. Some of the reds are *claretes* and contain a proportion of wine from white grapes. Practically all the wines are *jóvenes*, but the first *crianza* red was released in 1992. Whites now go up to *crianza* and reds to *gran reserva*.

Production

40,060 hectolitres (2002).

Vintages

1987 (4); 1988 (3); 1989 (5); 1990 (5); 1991 (5); 1992 (5); 1993 (4); 1994 (4); 1995 (4); 1996 (3); 1997 (3); 1998 (4); 1999 (4); 2000 (4); 2001 (5); 2002 (5); 2003 (3); 2004 (4).

Madrid was chosen to be the capital of Spain in 1561 by King Philip II. At 646 metres (2,119 feet) above sea level it is the highest capital in Europe and as far from the sea as it is possible to be in Spain. Of all Spanish cities it suffers from one of the nastiest climates. It had the inestimable advantage, though, that it was small, unknown, and not associated with any of the old kingdoms that were united to form the modern Spain. It was not chosen for the excellence of its wines. The bars of Madrid provided a captive market and the vineyards around the city produced large quantities of cheap wines for them. In the nineteenth century, however, the railways brought competition. Nevertheless, at the beginning of the twentieth century there were 30,000 hectares of vineyard. Then the story developed as in so many parts of Spain, save that here phylloxera arrived late. It reached San Martín de Valdeiglesias in 1914 and then wrought its inevitable devastation, with the usual result that the vineyards were replanted with varieties calculated to give large yields, notably Garnacha and Airén. Tempranillo was brought in, though, by a native of the Rioja in 1930 and showed that the vineyards were capable of producing much better wines.

The transition from bulk wines to good bottled ones started in the 1970s. Spain's increasing prosperity meant that the market was shifting toward quality and the demand for bulk wines fell. In 1981 a movement was started to create a DO, which finally came about in 1990. At that time there were only two or three bodegas bottling wine, and the new *consejo regulador* had to create a quality wine region virtually from scratch. There was very careful selection of the wines that were allowed to carry the DO label and the majority were rejected. Those that did qualify began to show that good quality wines could indeed be produced, especially reds from Tempranillo. Bodegas started to use modern methods and production rose from 72,000 bottles in 1986 to 2,000,000 in 1995 and 5,000,000 in 2002. It has been going from strength to strength and produces good wines, some of them now very good indeed, at attractive prices, the reds better than the whites.

Some leading bodegas

BODEGAS RICARDO BENITO

Las Eras 5, 28600 Navalcarnero, Madrid. Tel: +34 918 11 00 97; Fax: +34 918 11 26 63; Email: bodega@ricardobenito.com; Website: www.ricardobenito.com
Founded by Felipe Benito Alvarez in 1940, this bodega, with fifty hectares

of vineyard, was developed by his son Ricardo Benito Lucas and is now in the third generation. It makes some of the finest wines in the region and is one of the most active in the export markets. Its marks include Tapón de Oro and Señorio de Medina Sidonia, and its reds go right up to *gran reserva*. Its Asido Vino de Guarda is from equal parts of Tinto Fino and Merlot, while its top wine, Divo Gran Vino de Guarda, is a varietal Tinto Fino.

BODEGAS FRANCISCO CASAS

San Cosme 6, 28600 Navalcarnero, Madrid. Tel: +34 918 11 02 07; Fax: +34 918 11 07 98; Email: f.casas@bodegascasas.com; Website: www.bodegascasas.com

This bodega was founded in 1940 and is active in the export markets. Its wines are sold under the names Tochuelo, Pintón, and Los Caminillos.

BODEGAS CASTEJON

Ronda de Watres 29, 28500 Arganda del Rey, Madrid.
Tel: +34 918 71 02 64; Fax: +34 918 71 33 43;
Email: castejon@bodegascastejon.com; Website: www.bodegascastejon.com

A family bodega founded in 1959, it has sixty-two hectares of vineyard in the Arganda sub-zone and long-term contracts with local growers covering a further 300. Its reds and *rosado* are varietal Tempranillos. The *jóvenes* are sold under the name Viña Rey, as is 70 Barricas, which has six months' oak. The name Viñadul is used for *crianzas* and *reservas*, given twelve months in American oak – the *gran reserva* is given twice as much.

BODEGAS Y VINEDOS GOSALBEZ ORTI

Real 14, 28813 Pozuelo del Rey, Madrid.
Tel: +34 918 72 53 99; Fax: +34 918 72 52 02;
Email: bodega@bodegagosalbezorzti.com; Website: www.bodegagosalbezorti.com

A boutique bodega founded in 2000 with ten hectares of vineyard that is unusual in being cultivated ecologically. The wines, sold under the name Québel, are generally ninety per cent Tempranillo and ten per cent Cabernet Sauvignon, though in the 2000 ten per cent of the Tempranillo was replaced with Syrah. This is certainly one of the top quality growers.

VINOS JEROMÍN

San José 8, 28590 Villarejo de Salvanés, Madrid.
Tel: +34 918 74 20 30; Fax: +34 918 74 41 39;
Email: vinosjeromin@vinosjeromin.com; Website: www.vinosjeromin.com

Founded in 1954, this family bodega with fifty hectares of vineyard in the Arganda sub-zone has expanded rapidly and moved with the times. It sells a wide range of wines under the names Vega Madroño, Puerto de Alcalá, and Puerta del Sol. These include varietal Tempranillo *crianzas* and *reservas*. Its top wines are given individual names. Grego is a *crianza* mainly from Syrah and Tempranillo. Félix Martínez Cepas Viejas 1999 *reserva* was from ninety per cent Tempranillo with Merlot and Cabernet Sauvignon. Manu Vino de Autor 2001 *crianza* was forty-five per cent Syrah, forty per cent Tempranillo, ten per cent Cabernet Sauvignon, with minor parts of Garnacha and Merlot, matured for twelve months in eighty per cent French and twenty per cent American oak. These top wines are among the best of the district.

BODEGAS ORUSCO
Alcalá 54, 28511 Valdilecha, Madrid.
Tel: +34 918 73 80 06; Fax: +34 918 73 83 36
This family bodega in Valdilecha, in the Arganda sub-zone, was founded in 1896, which makes it one of the oldest established. It has ten hectares of vineyard, planted with Tempranillo and Malvar. It sells a complete range of wines under the names Maín and Viña Maín.

VINAS DE EL REGAJAL
Antique Ctra de Andalucia, km 50.5, 28300, Aranjuez, Madrid.
Tel: +34 651 52 21 98; Fax: +34 913 07 96 36; Email: dgpita@terra.es
In 1998 a small vineyard of ten hectares was planted in a large estate with the object of growing fine wines. It has certainly succeeded with its El Regajal Selección Especial 2002 from forty-five per cent Cabernet Sauvignon, thirty per cent Syrah, seventeen per cent Merlot, five per cent Tempranillo, and three per cent Petit Verdot. The vineyard is still young and future wines may be stunning.

BODEGAS TAGONIUS
Carretera Ambite km 44, 28550 Tielmes, Madrid. Tel/Fax: +34 918 74 45 97.
Established as recently as 2000, its Tagonius wines from Tempranillo, Cabernet Sauvignon, Merlot, and Syrah have been acclaimed.

DOMINIO DE VALDEPUSA

Climate
This is continental at 550 metres (1,804 feet) above sea level, averaging 26°C (78.8°F) in summer and 5°C (41°F) in winter, with 400 millimetres (16 inches) of rain.

Soil

Clay on limestone.

Grapes

Red varieties: Syrah; Cabernet Sauvignon; Petit Verdot; Merlot; and Graciano.
White varieties: Verdejo; Chardonnay; and Viura. The white varieties are minimal.

Vineyard area

40 hectares.

Wines

Red and mostly varietal. 13.5–15% ABV.

Production

880 hectolitres (2002).

FINCA DOMINIO DE VALDEPUSA

Ctra San Marín de Pusa km 6, 500, Finca Casadevacas, 45692 Malpica de Tajo,
Toledo. Tel: +34 925 59 72 22; Fax: +34 925 78 94 16;
Email: mcarmen@pagosdefamilia.com

At first sight the Finca Dominio de Valdepusa does not seem very promising for making fine wines: a charming eighteenth century house on flat land that looks slightly too fertile. But when Carlos Falcó, Marqués de Griñón, has a hand in anything one may be sure the results will be good and usually outstanding. In 1982 he decided to grow wine seriously – very seriously – on a small part of the 3,000-hectare estate that his family has owned since the thirteenth century. Geographically it falls within the DO of Méntrida, but its aims are far different and never joined the DO. It is in rather dull countryside at Malpica de Tejo, between Toledo and Talavera de la Reina, with the river Tajo flowing through it, but is named after the river Pusa, a small tributary. It goes to show that not all of Spain's best wines are grown in beautiful places. On the way down into the air-conditioned cellar there is a sort of subterranean window, a sheet of glass through which you can see the striations of the land: clay on top of limestone. The vineyard is beautifully kept with hedges of lavender; it was the first in Europe to be drip-irrigated, and the technique of canopy management was imported from the New World with Richard Smart's advice.

In 1991 Falcó made the first Spanish varietal Syrah, and he also made the inspired choice of Petit Verdot, a grape that attains a maturity here that it seldom achieves in its native Bordeaux. He led the way with these varieties, and a great number of growers are following. In 2003 he received the singular recognition of being the first Spanish single estate (*pago*) to be made a DO in its own right, following years of superb wines.

The principal wines are varietals from Cabernet Sauvignon, given eighteen months to two years in wood; Syrah, given eleven months; and Petit Verdot, given eight months. The top wine is Emeritus, blended from fifty per cent Syrah with Cabernet Sauvignon and Petit Verdot, given thirteen months in oak. French Nevers and Allier casks are used and there is minimal filtration.

Apart from these single-vineyard wines, Falcó has a flourishing business producing blends under the name Marqués de Griñón Durius, Durius being the Latin name of the River Duero.

FINCA ELEZ

Geography
A *pago* within the Sierra de Alcaraz in the province of Albacete, 1,000 metres (3,280 feet) above sea level, one of the highest vineyards in Spain.

Climate
Continental, being within La Mancha, but cooler at night owing to its altitude.

Soil
Sandy clay sediment on chalk.

Grapes
Red varieties: Cabernet Sauvignon; Tempranillo; Merlot; and Syrah.
White varieties: Chardonnay and Viognier.

Vineyard area
40 hectares.

Wines
Reds and whites, but predominantly the former.

Production

250,000 bottles.

Manuel Manzanique is a man of many parts. Originally he was an actor and then a director, but above all a wine enthusiast. In 1993 he founded his own vineyard and bodega, his wines soon being acknowledged as among Spain's best. At a time when few good Spanish Chardonnays were made, his was exemplary; but the emphasis is now mainly on the very good reds. In 2003 the estate was made a *pago* with its own DO, a well-deserved distinction. Before then the wines were labelled Manuel Manzanique, but now they are Finca Elez. French oak is used for ageing.

FINCA ELEZ

Carretera Ossa de Montiel a El Bonillo, 02610 El Bonillo, Albacete. Tel: +34 967 58 50 03; Fax: +34 967 58 50 03; Email: manuelmanzanique@wanadoo.es

The Chardonnay may be varietal, but it sometimes has a small addition of Viognier. Other varietals include Tempranillo and Syrah. Finca Elez 1995 was made from seventy-five per cent Cabernet Sauvignon, fifteen per cent Tempranillo, and ten per cent Merlot, while in 2001 the proportions were sixty-five per cent, fifteen per cent, and twenty per cent.

LA MANCHA
Geography

La Mancha is a huge, slightly sloping plain in the middle of Spain. It is in the southern part of the Meseta, a high plateau between the Sierra Morena and the river Tajo (Tagus), and is the largest DO, stretching from the DO of Madrid in the north to Valdepeñas in the south, which it practically surrounds. The slope is invisible to the eye, but the altitude is 489 metres (1,604 feet) in the north and 645 metres (2,116 feet) in the south though it is not quite flat and parts are higher. At the moment this parched plain is the world's largest wine-producing area. There is talk of sub-dividing it, but so far nothing has happened save for cutting off an edge to create the new DO of Ribera del Júcar in 2001. It is in four provinces: Albacete; Ciudad Real; Cuenca; and Toledo.

Climate

This is continental. It is very hot indeed in the summer (it has reached

45°C/113°F) and very cold in the winter (the lowest recorded temperature is -22°C/-7.6°F), but the average is more reasonable at 13.5–14.8°C (56–58.6°F). The rainfall is 300–400 millimetres (11.8–15.7 inches), with rain falling mostly in the winter. There are 3,000 hours of sunshine and 200 cloudless days. It has been sensibly described as high and dry. The hot dry climate over the grape-growing season results in the vines being remarkably healthy and needing minimum attention.

Soils

Mostly red-brown sandy clay, but with some limestone and chalk.

Grapes

Red varieties: Cencibel (Tempranillo); Moravia; Garnacha; Cabernet Sauvignon; Merlot; and Syrah.
White varieties: Airén; Macabeo; Chardonnay; and Sauvignon Blanc.
Airén is the traditional white variety, producing wines for distillation into brandy, though with modern cold fermentation it has shown itself capable of giving good table wines; it occupies 63 per cent of the vineyard. Cencibel is the leading red, occupying 14.6 per cent of the vineyard and increasing.

Planting

The density varies between 1,200–1,600 per hectare, depending on available water. They are planted in a square, or *marco real* pattern, with 2.5 metres (8.2 feet) spacing, and are pruned *en cabeza* to keep them close to the ground, avoiding evaporation and limiting the penetration of sunshine.

Vineyard area

191,699 hectares.

Authorized yield

Whites 85hl/ha, reds 75hl/ha. But in practice the yields are a good deal less: in 1993, 17hl/ha.

Wines

Many are *jóvenes* but the reds go up to *gran reservas*. Whites 10–14% ABV, but are tending toward the former and come in all degrees of sweetness from very dry to very sweet. *Rosados* 10–14% ABV, reds 11–15% ABV. Some sparkling whites from Airén and Macabeo have been made since 1995.

Production

1,170,000 hectolitres (2003).

Vintages

1990 (3); 1991 (3); 1992 (4); 1993 (5); 1994 (4); 1995 (3); 1996 (4); 1997 (4);
1998 (5); 1999 (4); 2000 (4); 2001 (4); 2002 (4); 2003 (4); 2004 (5).

The most famous native of La Mancha is undoubtedly Don Quixote. His ghost haunts the place and there are still plenty of windmills. Some were there in his day, though the more affected have been created in his memory, and nowadays many of the windmills a traveller sees are wind farms. But in the days when he took his tilts, it was rather different. There were many fields of grain to feed the windmills, and there were far more trees. Now there are very few trees and they get fewer every year as water is pumped out of the sub-soil, starving them of nourishment, to cultivate crops that would be better grown elsewhere. Happily, though, this does not apply to vines, which are famous for being able to flourish in impossible places. Scenically it is a very dull plain, an area to hurry through. But those who do so miss some charming towns and villages. Almagro, for instance, is a delightful town with a Parador built in an old monastery and two enchanting theatres, one of which dates from the sixteenth century, while the other is a little early nineteenth-century gem. Also Tembleque, with wooden galleries around its *plaza mayor*, has not changed for hundreds of years.

Forty-three per cent of the surface area of La Mancha is vineyard, and if Spain has seventeen per cent of the world's vineyards, La Mancha itself has eight per cent. In sheer quantity it is very important, but not all the grapes go into making wine. Some are eaten; others – quite a high proportion – go to make wine that is distilled to make *holandas*, which are matured in the sherry bodegas and elsewhere to provide Spain's justly popular brandies. Nevertheless there is a lot of wine, and in the past much went into the "wine lake", while the local growers tried to dissuade EU bureaucrats from pulling up their vineyards. The wine used to be dreadful, but that is no longer so. And perhaps it was not always so; when Captain George Carleton published his memoirs in 1728 he was strong in praise of Manchegan "Vino Sainte Clemente".

In 1966 a *consejo regulador* was appointed to look after La Mancha,

Almansa, and Méntrida, but that did not work as there were obvious conflicts of interests. In 1970 they were split up, and at much the same time big money started to flow in. La Mancha is so dry that the vines are unusually healthy, calling for remarkably little work in the vineyards. The large corporations saw that this was the place where bulk wine could be made economically, and they made it well, led by RUMASA, then the largest quality wine producer in Spain. All this came as a revelation to the locals, mostly cooperatives. The secrets, of course, were early picking and cold fermentation. The Airén grape, in particular, was transformed. It had been regarded as a bulk producer for distillation, giving flat, unattractive wines. With the yield limited, the grapes picked earlier, kept cool, lightly pressed, and the fermentation temperature controlled, it proved capable of giving rather attractive wines. The malolactic fermentation is usually avoided to retain acidity. And newcomers brought in French varieties that gave backbone and structure to the reds, which are becoming increasingly important. No one would suggest that this is a district for great wines, though some of them can be very attractive. What it does brilliantly is to produce decent, agreeable wines in large quantities that can be sold at affordable prices.

Some leading bodegas

BODEGAS AYUSO

Miguel Caro 6, 02600 Vilarrobledo, Albacete. Tel: +34 967 14 04 58; Fax: +34 967 14 49 25; Email: comercialayuoso@telefonica.net; Website: www.bodegasayuso.com

This large family-owned bodega was founded in 1947, started selling bottled wines in 1961, and introduced its Estola brand in 1965, which included the first *reserva* in the DO. Its whites are made mostly from Airén, its reds and *rosados* from Cencibel. It has large vineyard holdings and produces ranges of wines under the marks Abadia del Roble, Viña Q, Castillo de Benizar, and Estola. Its white wines include the unusual semi-sweet, late-harvested Armiño, from Airén. It is particularly noted for its Estola range, the reds going up to *gran reserva*.

BODEGAS CENTRO ESPAÑOLAS

Carretera Alcázar km 1, 13700 Tomelloso, Ciudad Real. Tel: +34 926 50 56 53; Fax: +34 926 59 56 52; Email: allozo@allozo.com; Website: www.allozo.com

A fine bodega founded in 1991 by fourteen shareholders. It has 243 hectares of vineyard at 650 metres (2,132 feet), most of which was planted in 1986 before the company itself was formed. Eighty-five per cent of its wines are red. The wines are good, consistent, and excellent value. Its principal trade name is Allozo, under which it produces a complete range, including Selección from sixty per cent Cencibel and twenty per cent each Merlot and Cabernet Sauvignon. The *crianza* and the *gran reserva* are varietal Cencibels, the former aged in American oak, the latter in fifty-fifty American and French. The Cencibel/Cabernet Sauvignon and Cencibel/Merlot are both fifty-fifty. Rama Corta is seventy-five per cent Cencibel and twenty-five per cent Cabernet Sauvignon. Fueste del Ritmo is a varietal Cencibel. Other names used for ranges of wines are Ladero and Aldoba.

EL VINCULO

Avenida Juan Carlos 1 s/n, 13610 Campo de Criptana, Ciudad Real.
Tel: +34 926 56 37 09; Fax: +34 926 56 37 09.
Alejandro Fernández set up this enterprise in 1999. For further details, *see* Ribera del Duero, where he is legendary. A master of the Tempranillo (or here the Cencibel), he brought his genius with him and is making world class wines, the best in the DO.

FINCA ANTIGUA

Carretera Quintanar-Los Hinojosos km 11.5, 16417 Los Hinojosos, Cuenca.
Tel: +34 969 12 97 00; Fax: +34 969 12 94 96;
Email: info@fincaantigua.com; Website: www.bujanda.com
Again this is new blood from elsewhere, this time Rioja. After completing its new Finca Valpiedra there, Martínez Bujanda looked for new worlds to conquer and after a long quest bought this 976-hectare estate, with 283 hectares of fifteen-year-old vineyards planted with noble varieties at an altitude of 840–880 metres (2,756–2,887 feet). It made its first wine in 1999 and, finding it good, built a spectacular new bodega in 2003. The wines are among the very best in the DO. Varietals from Cabernet Sauvignon and Cencibel are given six months in new American oak. The *crianza*, made from sixty per cent Cencibel and twenty per cent each of Cabernet Sauvignon and Merlot, is given twelve months in half American and half Allier oak. The *reserva* is seventy-five per cent Merlot, twenty per cent Cabernet Sauvignon, and five per cent Syrah.

FONTANA

Extramuros s/n, 16411 Fuente de Pedro Naharro, Cuenca.
Tel: +34 969 12 54 33; Fax: +34 969 12 53 87;
Email: bf@bodegasfontana.com; Website: www.bodegasfontana.com

Founded in 1997, this is a family bodega aiming high. It has no fewer than 500 hectares of vineyard, 230 of them in scattered small plots and 270 in a single holding. New American oak is generally used for the malolactic and for maturation. Most of the wines are sold under the name of Fontal. The *roble*, given six months in oak, is from 90 per cent Cencibel with five per cent each Cabernet Sauvignon and Merlot, while the *crianza* is from 85 per cent Cencibel and 15 per cent Cabernet Sauvignon. Gran Fontal is a varietal Cencibel from forty-year-old vines, as is the top Quercus, which is not a DO wine, but sold as VdlT de Castilla, which looks odd unless it has its sights on the higher rank of a *gran pago*. Pago el Púlpito is a sweet red made from late gathered Cencibel.

FREEWINE

Castilla La Mancha 4, 16670 El Provencio, Cuenca.
Tel: +34 609 11 92 48; Fax: +34 916 16 02 46; Email: victorre@telefonica.net
Founded as recently as 2003, with ten hectares of vineyard, this bodega has established a fine reputation with its high expression Mano a Mano *roble*, a varietal Cencibel.

COOPERATIVA JESÚS DEL PERDÓN

Poligono Industrial s/n, 13200 Manzanares, Ciudad Real. Tel: +34 926 61 03 09;
Fax: +34 926 61 05 16; Email: yuntero@yuntero.com; Website: www.yuntero.com
This is a fine, up-to-date cooperative, founded by a group of local wine-growers in 1954 and since expanded by amalgamation with the other Manzanares cooperatives: San Isidoro Labrador in 1996, and El Porvenir and El Progreso in 2000. It now has 700 wine-growers with 3,525 hectares of vineyard giving an average yield of forty hectolitres per hectare. It is planning to expand the reds. Its principal mark for DO wines is Yuntero with two additional ranges: Casa la Teja and Viña Tomar. All go up to *gran reserva* reds. It sells certified organic wines under the mark Mundo de Yuntera, VdlT wines under the mark Lazarillo, and non DO under the mark Viña Altair.

VINEDOS Y BODEGAS MUNOZ

Carretera Villarrubia 11, 45350 Noblejas, Toledo.
Tel: +34 925 14 00 70; Fax: +34 925 14 13 34; Email: vibomu@teleline.es
A family bodega established in 1940 with forty-five hectares of vineyard. It sells very good wines under the mark Artero, which includes varietals from Macabeo, Cencibel, and Merlot, including a Merlot *reserva*. Artero *crianza* is fifty-fifty Cencibel and Merlot. One of its most highly praised wines is the barrel-fermented Chardonnay, Blas Muñoz.

NUESTRA SEÑORA DE LA CABEZA

Topias 8, 16708 Pozoamargo, Cuenca. Tel: +34 969 38 71 73; Fax: +34 969 38 72 02; Email: info@casagualda.com; Website: www.casagualda.com

Founded in 1958, this is the best cooperative for quality wines, which are right up at the top, sold under the mark Casa Gualda. Its members have 900 hectares of vineyard. Its Allier-fermented white is made from eighty per cent Macabeo with twenty per cent Sauvignon Blanc. Its *joven* reds are mostly Cencibel, with small proportions of Merlot and Cabernet Sauvignon. For *crianzas* there is also a little Merlot, and there is a *crianza* fifty-fifty Cencibel/Cabernet Sauvignon. Its top wines are Selección C&J, a varietal Cencibel, and Singular, from Cencibel, Bobal, and Syrah.

VINICOLA DE CASTILLA

Poligono Industrial Call 1, 13200 Manzanares, Ciudad Real.
Tel: +34 926 64 78 00; Fax: +34 926 61 04 66;
Email: nacional@vinicoladecastilla.com; Website: www.vinicoladecastilla.com

As modern as can be, including a Vinimatic installation for making reds, this model bodega was founded by the Ruiz-Mateos empire in 1976, when the latter was the largest producer of quality wines in Spain, and it led the way to the remarkable improvement of Manchegan wines. After Rumasa's dispossession by the state, the La Mancha operation was acquired by private shareholders. It has 250 hectares of vineyard. There are underground cellars for maturing the *crianzas* and above in American oak. It makes a huge, rather bewildering, range of wines and, apart from a considerable number of buyers' own brands for supermarkets, they are sold under a number of names. Sound wines offering good value are Finca Vieja (which now goes as high as a *gran reserva*), Viña del Castillo, and Gran Verdad. The varietal wines are sold under the name Castillo de Alhambra and include a red (made by carbonic maceration) from Cencibel, a *rosado* from Garnacha, and a white from Airén. The next, higher range is Señorío de Guadianeja, which includes varietals from Cencibel, Cabernet Sauvignon, and Syrah up to *gran reservas*. The Reserva Especial is made from fifty-year- old vines. Other wines at the top of the range are sold under the name Selección and are blended from a number of varieties: the white from fifty per cent Viura, thirty per cent Airén, and twenty per cent Chardonnay; the red from fifty per cent Cencibel, thirty per cent Cabernet Sauvignon, and twenty per cent Merlot. There is also a sparkling wine, Cantares, from ninety per cent Viura and ten per cent Airén.

VINÍCOLA DE TOMELLOSO

Carretera Toledo-Albacete km 130.8, 13700 Tomelloso, Ciudad Real.

Tel: +34 926 51 30 04; Fax: +34 926 53 80 01;

Email vincola@vinicolatomelloso.com; Website: www.vinicolatomelloso.com

This large cooperative was founded in 1986, its members providing 2,500 hectares of vineyard. It makes good wines, sold mostly under the name Torre de Gazete, but Añil is mostly of Macabeo, and remarkably good. Other whites are an Airén with ten per cent Macabeo and a varietal Sauvignon Blanc. The *rosado* is a varietal Cabernet Sauvignon. The red *crianza* is sixty per cent Cencibel and forty per cent Cabernet Sauvignon, while the *reserva* is fifty-fifty. The *gran reserva* is a varietal Cabernet Sauvignon. Another mark is Finca Cerrada, a very good *crianza* made from eighty per cent Cencibel, fifteen per cent Cabernet Sauvignon, and five per cent Syrah. Alsur is a red *crianza* from eighty per cent Cencibel and fifteen per cent Cabernet Sauvignon. A sparkling wine called Mantolan is a varietal Macabeo.

MANCHUELA

Geography

In the provinces of Cuenca and Albacete, it is surrounded by the DOs of La Mancha, Almansa, Jumilla, and Utiel-Requena. The vineyards are at 600–700 metres (1,968–2,296 feet).

Climate

Although its position would suggest a continental climate, it is in fact remarkably temperate. It is high and cooled by fresh, humid winds, with the temperature normally reaching a maximum of 25°C (77°F) and a minimum of 4°C (39.2°F). The rainfall is 463 millimetres (18.2 inches) with practically none between May and September.

Soils

Mostly clay over limestone.

Grapes

Red varieties: Bobal; Cabernet Sauvignon; Tempranillo; Garnacha; Merlot; Monastrell; Moravia Dulce; Syrah; and (experimental) Touriga Nacional.

White varieties: Albillo; Chardonnay; Macabeo; Sauvignon Blanc; and Verdejo.

The traditional varieties were Macabeo and Bobal – the latter still covers seventy per cent of the vineyard. New plantings, however, are principally French varieties.

Planting

Old vineyards *en vaso*, new ones *en espaldera*. Controlled irrigation is practised.

Vineyard area

10,000 hectares. Only about 4,000 are planted, but it goes up every year.

Authorized yield

55–70hl/ha for reds, 24–80hl/ha for whites.

Wines

Reds are a minimum 12% ABV, *rosados* 11.5% ABV, and whites 11% ABV. Reds go up to *gran reservas*, the *crianzas* and above are made from Tempranillo, Cabernet Sauvignon, and Bobal. Traditionally many of the reds were made by the *doble pasta* method, which still accounts for about thirty per cent of the production. Of the rest there are thirty per cent each of red and *rosado*, with ten per cent white. Some are barrel fermented and some of the young reds are made by carbonic maceration.

Production

2,000,000 hectolitres.

This considerable area used to form part of a vast DO that included Almansa, La Mancha, and Méntrida. When this was reorganized to give separate DOs to those three areas, Manchuela was left out as its wines did not rate highly: most were sold in bulk and many distilled. After various negotiations and preliminary stages it eventually got its own DO in 2004. While ninety per cent of the wines are still sold in bulk, including *doble pasta* wines for blending, more and more are being bottled, so the figure is likely to be very different in a few years' time. There can be no doubt that this district is capable of producing very good wines, indeed it is already doing so. In particular the Bobal, with modern vinification, can make wines very much better than those of the past. Most are still made by cooperatives, but these are bringing themselves up to date and will no doubt compete in the quality market when the price is right and they can. There is already one very good *pago* and now that the DO is functioning it will be in a position to attract new capital and talent, as has happened elsewhere.

Some leading bodegas

FINCA SANDOVÁL

CM-3222 km 26,800, Ledaña, Cuenca.

Tel: +34 616 44 48 05; Fax: +34 915 86 48 48; Email: consulto@terra.es

This boutique bodega, founded in 2001 by leading Spanish wine writer, Victor de la Serna, with two friends, and housed in an old grain store, leads the way with quality and shows what can be done. It is one of the *pagos* and makes only *crianzas*. Its eleven hectares of vineyard, which is semi-ecological, includes Syrah. Its two main wines are Finca Sandovál, from ninety-one per cent Syrah and nine per cent Monastrell, and Salia, from fifty-five per cent Syrah and forty-five per cent Monastrell. Both are very good, the first superlative. There is also a very small production of a top wine, Cuvée TNS. The wines are matured mostly in French oak with some American.

COOPERATIVA UNIÓN CAMPESINA INIESTENSE

San Idefonso 1, 16235 Iniesta, Cuenca. Tel: +34 967 49 01 20;

Fax: +34 967 49 07 77

A large cooperative, founded in 1944 with thirty-four members. It now has 1,200 and can draw on 7,000 hectares of vineyard, but some grow only VdlT wines. It has invested heavily in modernization. It sells good wines under the marks Realce (for DO wines), Señorio de Iniesta, and Mirabueno (both for VdlT wines including bag in box). The Realce range includes a varietal Tempranillo and varietal Bobals that go up to *reserva*.

VITIVINOS ANUNCACIÓN

Camino de Cabezuelas s/n, 02270 Villamalea, Albacete. Tel: +34 967 48 31 14;

Fax: +34 967 48 39 64; Email: vitivinos@wanadoo.es

The 183 members of this cooperative, founded in 1969, cultivate 1,166 hectares of vineyard. Its wines are sold under the marks Azua and Viña Albaba. Its white Viña Albaba comes from ninety per cent Macabeo and ten per cent Albillo. Its *rosado* is a varietal Bobal. Its best wines are the red varietal Bobals, *crianza* and *reserva*. It pioneered good winemaking with this variety and produced the first *reserva* in 1998. These are matured in mostly

French with some American oak. The Azua Selección Bobal Viejo, from thirty-year-old vines, is especially good.

MENTRIDA

Geography

Near the great city of Toledo, Mentrida adjoins the DO Vinos de Madrid. Part of it is in the province of Madrid, but most is in that of Toledo. There are some hills to the northwest but most of the area is dull and flat. The altitude of the vineyards is 200–500 metres (656–1,640 feet).

Climate

Right in the middle of Spain, it is continental and given to extremes: 40°C (104°F) in the summer and -4°C (24.8°F) in the winter, with many frosts and an average of 15°C (59°F). There is rainfall of 300 millimetres (11.8 inches), mostly in the autumn and winter, and 2,800 hours of sunshine.

Soils

Some sandy, some clay, and a little limestone.

Grapes

Red varieties: Tempranillo; Cabernet Sauvignon; Merlot; Syrah; and Garnacha. Although the Garnacha is listed last, it is still predominant, occupying eighty per cent of the vineyard; but it is now "permitted" rather than "authorized", as the official line is to replace it.
White varieties: Albillo; Macabeo; Sauvignon Blanc; and Chardonnay. This is a new development, as white wines are now permitted in the DO, but they are not yet widely planted.

Planting

Generally rectangular and pruned *en vaso*, but new vineyards are being planted on *espaldera*. 1,100–2,500 vines per hectare.

Vineyard area

13,000 hectares.

Authorized yield

96hl/ha for whites and 89hl/ha for reds, but these colossal yields are seldom achieved and are assiduously avoided by the better growers.

Wines

Reds have a minimum 12% ABV, *rosados* 11.5% ABV, and whites 11% ABV. Most of the wines are *jóvenes*, but there are reds up to *reserva*.

Production

245,200 hectolitres (2003).

Vintages

1999 (4); 2000 (4); 2001 (4); 2002 (3); 2003 (3); 2004 (3).

By no stretch of the imagination was Méntrida, ever a fine wine area, though the potential was always there, as the Marqués de Griñón has shown – his vineyards (*see* p. 268) are on the edge of it, but he understandably would have nothing to do with the DO and now has his own. Traditionally the wines were enormous and heady, the *rosados* 13–18% ABV and the reds 14–18% ABV. They were made from overripe grapes (the growers paid according to sugar) by the method of *doble pasta*, where the skins from one fermentation were left in for another. The market for these heavy wines has gone, and in 1991 new, low levels of acceptable strength were introduced. But it was a vicious circle: the wines were bad so they fetched very low prices, and the prices were so low that no one could afford to modernize and produce good wines. Moreover the locals had developed a taste for oxidized Garnacha and continued to be willing to buy it. Now things are changing fast with modern winemaking and the arrival of new talent, though many old-style wines still persist. The permitted vineyard area has increased, but the amount in cultivation has not, showing a welcome selectivity. There were no exports at all until 2000, now they are substantial, a measure of the improvement.

Some leading bodegas

DELISPAIN

Fray Pedro Payo Piñeño 17 bajo, 15009 A Coruña, A Coruña. Tel: +34 670 52 25 77; Fax: +34 881 92 44 92; Email: delispain@delispain.com www.delispain.com
No, the address is not a mistake. This company is interested in a whole

range of gastronomic products, including wines from Rías Bajas, and has its headquarters in Coruña. But the wines it sells from Méntrida, under the name Vega Gitania, are good ones. The red *joven* is a varietal Garnacha; the Premium Red is sixty per cent Tempranillo, the rest Garnacha; and the *rosado* is ninety per cent Garnacha, the rest Tempranillo.

LA CASA DE LAS CUATRO RAYAS
Finca La Verdosa, 45513 Santa Cruz del Retamar, Toledo.
Tel: +34 647 34 20 97; Fax: +34 916 63 27 96;
Email: comercial@arrayan-laverdosa.com; Website: www.arrayan-laverdosa.com

A newcomer and at present easily the best winemaker in the DO, this bodega was set up in 1999 with twenty-six hectares of vineyard and advised by Richard Smart. The wines are modern and ambitious. Sold as Arrayán, there are varietals from Petit Verdot, Merlot, Cabernet Sauvignon, and Syrah, all given twelve months in Allier oak, and a notable blended wine, Arrayán Premium, from fifty-five per cent Syrah, twenty per cent Merlot, fifteen per cent Cabernet Sauvignon, and ten per cent Petit Verdot, given 12–14 months in Allier oak.

SOCIEDAD COOPERATIVA COMARCAL VITIVINÍCOLA SAN ISIDRO
Carretera Toledo-Valmojado km 24, 45180 Camarena, Toledo. Tel: +34 918 17 43 47; Fax: +34 918 17 46 32; Email: cosanisidro@hotmail.com

Founded in 1972, this is not the biggest cooperative in the DO, but is the best. It members have 780 hectares of vineyard. The wines are sold under the marks Bastión de Camarena and Campo de Camarena.

MONDEJAR

Geography

This is the only significant wine-growing area in the province of Guadalajara, and lies to the southeast of the town. There are two parts, one centred around Mondéjar and the other around Sacerdón. Until it received DO status in 1997 it was known as VdlT Sacerdón-Mondéjar or Mondéjar-Sacerdón. It is contiguous with Vinos de Madrid and just touches La Mancha. It is gently undulating.

Climate

Continental, but tempered by the Mediterranean. The extremes of the temperature range of -8–39.5°C (17.6–103°F) are rare. The average temperature is 18°C (64.4°F) and the rainfall 500 millimetres (19.7 inches).

Soils

In the north, red over lime and clay. In the south, brown and chalky. Neither sort is very fertile.

Grapes

Red varieties: Cencibel; Cabernet Sauvignon; and Syrah.
White varieties: Malvar; Macabeo; and Torrontés.

Planting

Maximum density 1,200 per hectare with an average of 1,100.

Vineyard area

2,100 hectares.

Authorized yield

In terms of grape production, 6,000kg/ha for white varieties and 5,000kg/ha for reds.

Wines

Mostly reds but with some whites, including sweet ones. Most are sold as *jóvenes*, but reds go up to *reserva* and there is provision for *gran reserva*. Minimum strengths 11% ABV for whites and *rosados*, 12% ABV for reds.

Production

2,000 hectolitres (2003).

Vintages

1999 (3); 2000 (5); 2001 (4); 2002 (4); 2003 (3); 2004 (3).

This area has never been noted for fine wines, most being sold in bulk to the bars of Madrid or drunk locally, where there was a high demand as historically it was a staging post between Valencia and Madrid. It is still early days for the

DO, but there are signs that much better wines are being made. Out of the five bodegas, three are cooperatives, which are getting their acts together.

Leading bodega

MARISCAL
Carretera de Perales km 71, 19110 Mondejar, Guadalajar.
Tel: +34 949 38 51 38; Fax: +34 949 38 77 40.
Founded in 1913, it was active in getting the DO established. It sells wines under the names Vega Tajuña, Pago de Aris, Señorío de Mariscal (a red *crianza*), Cueva de los Judíos (a red *reserva*), and Tierra Rubia (a varietal Syrah that has been praised). Some of the reds are made by carbonic maceration.

RIBERA DEL JÚCAR

Geography
This rolling plain between La Mancha, of which it was formerly a part, and Méntrida has its vineyards at an altitude of 750 metres (2,460 feet).

Climate
Essentially continental, but with a substantial Mediterranean influence. Maxima and minima are not available, but the average temperature is 24°C (75°F) in summer and 5.1°C (42°F) in winter. It has a special microclimate, warmer in winter and cooler in summer than its neighbours.

Soils
Covered with pebbles left by the river Júcar, but deep, fertile, and water retentive. The pebbles are part of the microclimate, heating up by day and radiating the heat by night. Under them the soil looks sandy brown and phylloxera finds it hard to penetrate, so many vines are direct producers.

Grapes
Red varieties: Cencibel (Tempranillo); Bobal; Cabernet Sauvignon; Merlot; and Syrah.

Planting

Minimum density 1,200 vines per hectare. Traditionally *en cabeza* with 3 x 3 metres (9.8 x 9.8 feet) spacing.

Vineyard area

9,141 hectares.

Authorized yield

70hl/ha for vines grown *en espaldera* and 63hl/ha for vines grown *en vaso*.

Wines

All DO wines are red, 12–14.5% ABV, and go up to *crianza*. There is a special category of Vino Tradicion Júcar that is given four months in oak.

Production

10,000 hectolitres (2003).

Vintages

All since the creation of the DO have been good, but it is still early days and it will be some years before proper assessments can be made.

It has long been realized that the DO of La Mancha is too big, so it is not surprising that growers in some parts have been seeking separate identities. The creation of sub-zones, though much mooted, has been fraught with difficulties and disagreements; so although some think this would have been better as a recognized sub-zone, it has been hived off and a new DO was created in 2003. The wines, like most from La Mancha, tend to be big, powerful, and quaffable rather than subtle; but they have a character of their own, with fragrance and even complexity, so it is not surprising that the growers wanted to go their own way. It remains to be seen what they make of their new independence but things look promising. Nearly all the wines are made by cooperatives, and it is they that moved for the creation of the DO. They have installed modern plants, even air-conditioned cellars, and are moving forward rapidly. It would not be surprising to find fresh talent and capital coming in, but at present the wines are only able to command low prices, which will limit the amount that is likely to be invested – though this may not deter the far-sighted. The bright side is that they represent remarkable value and production is rising rapidly.

Some leading bodegas

NUESTRA SENORA DE LA CABEZA

Tapias 8, 16708 Pozoamargo, Cuenca. Tel: +34 969 38 71 73; Fax: +34 969
38 72 02; Email: info@casagualda.com; Website: www.casagualda.com

A large cooperative active principally in La Mancha (*see* above). Here it uses
the mark Casarriba.

SOCIEDAD COOPERATIVA PURISIMA CONCEPCIÓN

Carretera Minaya-San Clemente s/n, 16610 Casas de Fernando Alonso, Cuenca.
Tel: +34 969 38 30 43; Fax: +34 969 38 31 53; Email: purisima@ucaman.es

Opened in 1958, this cooperative has 400 members, of which 310 grow
wine, the rest produce mainly cereals. Its winemaking is completely up to
date, has an air-conditioned cask cellar with some French but mostly
American oak, and is experimenting with different degrees of toast, all of
which bodes well. Its members have old vineyards of Cencibel and Bobal,
younger ones of Cabernet Sauvignon, and younger still of Merlot. There
are fifty-year-old Bobal vines growing next to the bodega. The French varieties are at present used only for making *jóvenes*. It sells its wine under the
mark Tiatinos, and they are good, especially the Cencibels (Tempranillos).

SOCIEDAD COOPERATIVA SAN GINÉS

Virgen del Carmen 6, 16707 Casas de Benitez, Cuenca.
Tel: +34 969 38 20 37; Fax: +34 969 38 24 49;
Email: cincoalmudes@cincoalmudes.es; Website: www.cincoalmudes.es

A cooperative dating from 1956, with 350 members, it sells wines under the
names Almudes and Cinco Almudes. The Almudes 5 Décadas is a varietal
Cencibel *crianza* with two years in American oak. Its wines are good and
include varietals from Cencibel (Tempranillo), Cabernet Sauvignon, Merlot,
Syrah, and Bobal. Non-DO wines are sold under the marks Campo de
Benitez and Torre de Benitez.

VALDEPEÑAS

Geography

The DO of Valdepeñas is almost entirely surrounded by that of La Mancha.
It is a plain with small hills, 650–820 metres (2,132–2,690 feet) above sea

level. The best vineyards are in the western area of Los Llanos (The Plains) and in the northern area of Las Aberturas (The Openings).

Climate

This is continental. It is very hot during the long summer, reaching up to 42°C (107.6°F). In winter to -10°C (14°F), and even less. The vines are sometimes damaged by frost. The average temperature is 16°C (60.8°F). The rainfall is 200–400 millimetres (7.9–15.7 inches), mostly in the spring and autumn, but sometimes there is a deluge and floods, as in 1979. The average annual sunshine is 2,500 hours and on eighty per cent of the days there are clear skies. Over the grape growing season the weather is hot and dry, making the vines easy to tend, with cold nights.

Soils

Valdepeñas means "valley of stones", and to look at the soil it is indeed stony, light in colour from almost white to faintly red light brown, and shallow; but the sub-soil is chalky and retains moisture well, deep down. There is little or no clay.

Grapes

Red varieties: Cencibel (Tempranillo); Garnacha; Cabernet Sauvignon; Merlot; Syrah; and Petit Verdot. Cencibel occupies eighty per cent and is going up as it is the recommended variety for replanting.
White varieties: Airén (Valdepeñera); Macabeo; Chardonnay; Verdejo; Sauvignon Blanc; and Moscatel Grano Menudo. Airén, which withstands the cold winters, is sixty-five per cent but going down.

Planting

The vineyards are planted in the square, or *marco real*, pattern with 2.5 metres (8.2 feet) spacing and normally 1,600 vines per hectare, the limits being 1,400–2,300. The Airén vines are pruned *en cabeza* and the Cencibel *en vaso*.

Vineyard area

29,616 hectares.

Authorized yield

Whites 52.5hl/ha and reds 42hl/ha, but the better growers work with a much lower yield of some 22hl/ha.

Wines

Whites must be 11–12.5% ABV. *Rosados*, which must contain at least twenty-five per cent of the red varieties, are 11.5–13% ABV. Reds must contain at least eighty-five per cent of the red varieties and at least twenty-five per cent Cencibel, though most have more, and are 12–14% ABV. *Reservas* and *gran reservas* are supposed to be varietal Cencibel, though in practice minor proportions of other varieties are often included.

Production

552,637 hectolitres (2003).

Vintages

1989 (5); 1990 (4); 1991 (4); 1992 (3); 1994 (5); 1995 (4); 1996 (4); 1997 (3); 1998 (4); 1999 (3); 2000 (4); 2001 (4); 2002 (4); 2003 (4); 2004 (5).

Valdepeñas, like so many Spanish vineyards, traces its history back to the Romans. In the remote past it grew white wines, but the reds started as long ago as the twelfth century, when black grapes were introduced by monks from Burgundy. This may help to reinforce the theory that Cencibel is remotely related to Pinot Noir. By the end of the eighteenth century, Valdepeñas was on the Royal Road between Madrid and Andalucía, and its wines regularly travelled in both directions, as they still do. They were highly regarded in Madrid and production was as high as 4,000,000 litres. The area got a fillip in 1861, when the railway arrived and provided easy transport not only to Madrid but to the ports. It was one of the last districts to be hit by phylloxera, which did not come until 1911, when it had its usual devastating results. By then the remedy was well established and the vineyards soon recovered, but the region succumbed to the temptation to go in for quantity rather than quality.

Valdepeñas has long had a reputation for making good wines that offer excellent value. Forty years ago, if you were giving a party you had Rioja if you could afford it and Valdepeñas if you had to set your sights a little lower. They were the two wines distributed nationally. In those days, though, the town of Valdepeñas was rather a rundown place producing wines that were agreeable and easy to drink, but noticeably lacking in aroma. Now, with the introduction of modern techniques and cool fermentation, the aroma is there and the wines are notably better. The reds are robust and can be positively heady, but the best are excellent and can achieve real complexity of flavour, while the light reds (*claretes*), made with a mixture of red and white grapes, have a very pleasant fragrance and an agreeable balance. There are good *rosados*, too. If the white wines are overshadowed by the reds, they are nevertheless fruity and sound, if sometimes rather lacking in acidity, but in this aspect they are rapidly improving. If the wines no longer have the special position they once had, it is simply because so many world class wines have emerged in the rest of Spain – wines that often did not exist twenty or thirty years ago. Valdepeñas wines are not world class, but they are nevertheless very sound and remain excellent value. The rundown town has become prosperous.

Some leading bodegas

ARÚSPIDE

Francisco Morales 102, 13300 Valdepeñas, Ciudad Real. Tel: +34 926 34 70 75
Fax: 926 34 78 75; Email: info@aruspide.com; Website: www.aruspide.com

A promising young bodega established in 1999 with seventy hectares of vineyard. Although it grows other varieties, at present its reds are from Cencibel, its whites (some of which are made by carbonic maceration) from Airén. Its main trade mark is Agora, though it also uses Odre and, for ecological wines, Ardales. It also makes *vinos de la tierra* under the mark Codal.

CASA DE LA VIÑA

Carretera de la Solana a Infantes km 15, 13248 Alhambra, Ciudad Real.
Tel: +34 926 69 60 44; Fax: +34 926 69 60 68;
Email: casadelavina@byb.es; Website: www.byb.es

Remote in the countryside, this great estate of 2,850 hectares was bought by the Bodegas y Bebidas group in 1987, and its history as a major winemaker dates only from then. The buildings used to be a farm and stockyard and are deceptive – from the outside everything looks ancient, but once you are inside you see the plant is as modern as can be. The vineyards are remarkable. From the bodega they extend for six kilometres (3.7 miles), making a total of 980 hectares. Not surprisingly, it is completely self-sufficient for grapes. The "cellar" is above ground, but it is impressively cool and there is plenty of new American oak, with twenty per cent replaced each year. It claims to press the grapes within ten minutes of picking. Its red, *rosado*, and white wines are all first class. It makes an excellent red *joven*. The *crianzas* and above are given plenty of ageing – well above the legal minimum. The wines are sold under the bodega name.

MIGUEL CALATAYUD

Postas 20, 13300 Valdepeñas, Ciudad Real. Tel: +34 926 34 80 70; Fax: +34 926 32 21 50; Email: vegaval@vegaval.com; Website: www.vegaval.com

To make wine in Valdepeñas with a surname that is the name of a major and totally different wine-growing area might invite confusion, but there seem to be no problems. Miguel Calatayud set up his business in 1940 and moved into his present premises, in the middle of the town of Valdepeñas, ten years later; it remains a family business, now run by his son. It has fifty hectares of vineyard, thirty-five of Cencibel and fifteen of Airén. Walking into the bodega gives the impression of stepping into the past, as it retains a massive installation of earthenware *tinajas*, which are temperature controlled by heat exchangers, but there is plenty of stainless steel as well. The wines, red, *rosado*, and white, sold under the name Vegaval Plata, are good and go up to *gran reservas*; the *crianzas* and above are matured in American oak.

BODEGA LOS LLANOS/COSECHEROS ABASTECEDORES

Ctra N-IV km 200.5, 13300 Valdepeñas, Ciudad Real. Tel: +34 926 32 03 00; Fax: +34 926 32 27 42; Email: losllanos@coabsa.com; Website: www.coabsa.com

Bodegas Los Llanos was founded by the Caravantes family in 1875. In 1971 they sold it to Cosecheros Abastecedores, a large company with wine interests in other parts of Spain, which in turn became part of the Bodegas Vinartis group and is now controlled by a Spanish venture capital fund. In 1979 it moved to a new, completely modern bodega in the country, the old premises becoming a museum. It has 350 hectares of vineyard. The oak used for ageing the *crianzas* and above is mostly American, but there is some French. New casks are bought every year and the old ones are thrown away when they are twelve years old, giving an average cask age of six years. The wines are divided between casks of different ages and blended together before bottling. This is one of the most active Valdepeñas bodegas in the export market; its wines are well known and appreciated in the UK. Sound *jóvenes* are sold under the names Armonioso, Don Opas, and Torneo. *Crianzas* and above, going up to *gran reservas*, are sold under the names Señorio de Los Llanos and Pata Negra. The Pata Negra *gran reserva*, a varietal Cencibel, is very good and has considerable ageing potential, with qualities of aroma and flavour that show how good a Valdepeñas can be. The Torneo *reservas* are also very good. A varietal Cabernet Sauvignon is sold under the name Loma de la Gloria.

BODEGAS JA MEGÍA E HIJOS

Magdalena 33, 13300 Valdepeñas, Ciudad Real. Tel: +34 926 34 78 28; Fax: +34 926 34 78 29; Website: www.corcovo.com

In 1994 five members of an old-established wine-growing family with ninety hectares of vineyard bought an old bodega and restored it. They now make a wide range of excellent wines sold mostly under the mark Corcovo, but also Carril de Faracho. The whites are varietal Airén, the reds varietal Cencibel, with the exception of a second year wine that is made in the old way with seventy per cent Cencibel and thirty per cent Airén. The very good *media crianza* has three months, the *crianza* eight, magnum twelve, and the *reserva* fifteen months in new American oak.

BODEGAS NAVARRO LOPEZ

Autovia Madrid-Cádiz km 193, 13300 Valdepeñas, Ciudad Real. Tel: +34 902 19 34 31; Fax: +34 902 19 34 32; Email: laboratorio@navarrolopez.com

Founded in 1904 by Doroteo Navarro, this remains a family bodega with about 150 hectares of vineyard. It has been moving with the times and its wines are steadily on the up. It has invested in modern equipment and has new American and French Allier barrels – seventy per cent and thirty per cent. It goes for varietal wines that include a Macabeo and a range of Cencibels up to *gran reserva*, which is matured in sixty per cent French and forty per cent American oak. In Spain they are sold under the mark Don Aurelio, but in the UK as Laguna de la Nava.

BODEGAS REAL

Finca Marisánchez, Carretera a Cózar km 12,800, 13300 Valdepeñas, Ciudad Real. Tel: +34 914 57 75 88; Fax: +34 914 57 72 10; Email: communicacion@bodegas-real.com; Website: www.bodegas-real.com

This beautiful *finca*, which practices general farming, not just wine-growing, was bought by the Barroso family from Cataluña in 1984 and is now in the second generation. The winery was not established until 1989 and made its first vintage in 1990 from the unusually large vineyard holding of 280 hectares, eighty per cent of which is Cencibel grown on *espalier* with royal double cordon cultivation, at 650 metres (2,132 feet) above sea level. It makes the wines it wants to make, and if they fall foul of the DO regulations it makes them outside it. The Chardonnay, for instance, is a VdlT Castilla, as is the red Vega Ibor *crianza*, a varietal Cencibel. Palacio Ibor Reserva is a DO Valdepeñas from 80–85 per cent Cencibel, the rest Cabernet Sauvignon, matured in 225-litre French Allier casks. The Finca Marisánchez *roble* is from Cencibel, Cabernet Sauvignon, and Merlot, given six months in American and French oak. These are among the best wines of the district.

FÉLIX SOLÍS

Autovía de Andalusía km 199, 13300 Valdepeñas, Ciudad Real. Tel: +34 926 32 24 00; Fax: +34 926 32 24 17; Email: bsf@felixsolis.com www.felixsolis.com

This is one of the largest family-owned bodega in Spain. It was founded in the 1940s but its real growth started some twenty years later with the introduction of oak ageing and development of the export markets. It is very strong in the UK, where it supplies large quantities of supermarket wines. It owns 500 hectares of vineyard in two large estates: Viña Albali and Los Molinos. It makes several complete ranges of good wines. Two are named after the estates. Others include Diego de Almagro, Soldepeñas, and Castillo de Soldepeñas. The Viña Albali wines are perhaps the best of all, the reds being varietal Cencibels going up to *gran reserva*. It is exceptionally reliable. It also makes VdlT wines under the names Sendas del Rey and Pañasol.

OTHER WINES

In 2002 an organization was set up by a group of individualists who wanted to make wines their own way in their own place. Others joined the following year. There are six in Castilla La Mancha: Dehesa del Carrizal; Dominio del Valdepusa; Finca Elez; Finca Sandoval (*see* p.278); Pago de Vallegarcía; and Uribes Madero. Two of these have already been awarded with DOs of their own, and as such have their own entries: Dominio del Valdepusa (*see* p.268) and Finca Elez (*see* p.270). No doubt others will be similarly honoured.

Vinos de la Tierra de Castilla

DEHESA DEL CARRIZAL

13140 Retuerta del Bullaque, Ciudad Real. Tel: +34 914 84 13 85; Fax: +34 916 62 42 09; Email: jalcubilla@investblue.es; Website: www.dehesadelcarrizal.com

Marcial Gómez Sequeira, a doctor, impresario, and above all a wine connoisseur, set up this bodega in 1987 with the advice of his friend Carlos Falcó (Marqués de Griñón), in the valley of the Guadiana, seventy kilometres (forty-three miles) from Toledo and eighty-five from Ciudad Real. It is a VdlT de Castilla, Montes de Toledo. In the twenty-two hectares of vineyard he grows Cabernet Sauvignon, Syrah, Tempranillo, Merlot, and Chardonnay. The wines, matured in French oak, are among the best in Spain. Varietals are made from Cabernet Sauvignon, Syrah, and Chardonnay, the blended reds from varying proportions of Cabernet Sauvignon, Syrah, and Merlot.

PAGO DE VALLEGARCÍA

Finca Vallegarcia, 13194 Retuerta de Bullaque, Ciudad Real.
Tel/Fax: +34 915 74 55 34; Email: fvallegarcia@terra.es

Next door to Dehesa del Carrizal (*see* above), this estate was founded in 1999 by wine-loving industrialist Alfonso Cortina de Alcocer, with advice from Carlos Falcó and Richard Smart. It has twenty-four hectares and grows Viognier, Cabernet Sauvignon, Merlot, and Syrah. Like those of its neighbour, its wines are rated among Spain's best, but there the resemblance ends, for the most renowned is the barrel-fermented Viognier. There is a varietal Syrah and fine blended wine from Cabernet Sauvignon and Merlot.

VIÑEDOS CIGARRAL SANTA MARÍA

Cerro del Emperador s/n, 45001 Toledo. Tel: +34 925 25 29 91; Fax: +34 925 25 31 98; Email: adolfo-toledo@adolfo-toledo.com; Website: www.adolfo-toledo.com

Anyone who has visited the Restaurante Adolfo in Toledo will have enjoyed a memorable meal. They also will have chosen from one of the best wine lists in Spain, fed from vast cellars. It includes wines from the restaurant's own modest five hectares of vines. Small it may be, but what wonderful wines it produces! They are sold under as Pago del Ama: a varietal Syrah and a Colleción wine made from Merlot, Syrah, and Tempranillo.

FINCA LA ESTACADA

Carretera N-400 km 103, 16400 Tarancón, Cuenca.
Tel: +34 902 10 19 25; Fax: +34 969 32 71 99;
Email: fincalaestacada@fincalaestacada.com; Website: www.fincalaestacada.com

Although founded in 2001 and still very young, this bodega bought established vineyards that gave it a head start, and its wines were highly praised from the beginning. It sells young reds and whites, respectively varietal

Tempranillo and Airén, under the mark Laman, and a Tempranillo/Cabernet Sauvignon blend as Viñasar but its leading wines are sold under the bodega name. There is a white from Chardonnay, Macabeo, and Sauvignon Blanc; two varietal Tempranillos given six months and twelve months ageing in American and French oak; and a varietal Syrah has also recently been introduced. Selección Varietales is a blend of five varieties; 45 per cent Tempranillo; 20 per cent Cabernet Sauvignon; 15 per cent Syrah; 15 per cent Merlot; and 5 per cent Mazuelo, given eighteen months in new American oak.

ANTONIO GALLEGO HERREROS, BODEGAS BRUJIDERO
Calle Mayor 75, 45810 Villanueva de Alcardete, Toledo.
Tel: +34 925 16 60 92; Fax: +34 925 16 66 49
This bodega: is absolutely unique. It is also hard to find, preferring anonymity. Inside, the rows of old-fashioned concrete *tinajas* make it look like Ali Baba's cave; but closer examination shows they are fitted with heat exchangers for cold fermentation. The eye soon wanders to other things. There are cabalistic signs, strange arrangements of obscure artifacts, and patterns of evident but enigmatic symbolism. The proprietor claims to be an alchemist and probably is. The bodega was set up in 1790 by Antonio Herreros Duclos, of Roman descent on his father's side and French on his mother's, and has been in the family ever since. Some of the wines are excellent; most are good, or at the very least interesting; they are certainly unlike anyone else's. They surprisingly include a *flor* wine that is not at all bad and certainly unique. Beneath the bodega, built in 1921, is a cellar of very old wines. The best are made from the Brujidero grape and sold under the Brujidero name. He claims they come from ungrafted vines that phylloxera missed and that no one else has. He tried vinifying in an old-fashioned clay *tinaja*, but this was not a success as it burst in sunder, taking its support with it. Vinified in the comparatively new, temperature-controlled cement *tinajas*, it is one to seek out.

FONTANA
Extramuros s/n, 16411 Fuente de Pedro Naharro, Cuenca.
Tel: +34 969 12 54 33; Fax: +34 969 12 53 87;
Email: bf@bodegasfontana.com; Website: www.bodegasfontana.com
Founded in 1997, this family-owned bodega has unusually large vineyard holdings of 500 hectares in the provinces of Toledo and Cuenca, at 750–800 metres (2,460–2,624 feet) altitude. Some are small and scattered, but one major plantation is of 230 hectares. Its wines are unusually good and it is

clearly aiming to be a *gran pago*. Its *jóvenes*, of which the best is a varietal Tempranillo, are sold under the Mesta mark. A *crianza*, from eighty-five per cent Tempranillo and fifteen per cent Cabernet Sauvignon, and a *roble* from ninety per cent Tempranillo and five per cent each of Cabernet Sauvignon and Merlot, are given twelve months and six months respectively in American oak and sold under the mark Fontal. Dueto is a very successful fifty-fifty blend of Cabernet Sauvignon and Merlot, with three months in new and six months in third year American oak. Quercus and Gran Fontal are both varietals from forty-year-old Tempranillo vines. Pago el Púlpito is a slightly sweet red from late-gathered Tempranillo with three months in new French oak and twenty-one in third year American.

OSBORNE MALPICA

Finca El Jaral, Carretera Malpica-Pueblanueva km 6, 45692 Malpica de Tajo, Toledo. Tel: +34 925 14 07 70; Fax: +34 925 86 09 05;
Email: comunicaciones@osborne.es; Website: www.osborne.es
The sherry bodega Osborne, having already acquired interests in Rioja, decided to go into table wines in La Mancha. And how! It bought a large estate that now includes 600 hectares of vineyard near Dominio de Valdepusa. Its first wine, Solaz, from Tempranillo and Cabernet Sauvignon, given four months in new American oak, was launched in 2001 along with by Dominio de Malpica, a varietal Cabernet Sauvignon with at least twelve months in American oak. The most recent addition is Solaz Shiraz-Tempranillo (for Shiraz read Syrah). These are good wines and it is early days yet: clearly one to watch.

PAGO DEL VICARIO

Juan II 7, 3 Planta, 13001 Ciudad Real.
Tel: +34 926 66 60 27; Fax: +34 926 66 60 29;
Email: susana@pagodelvicario.com; Website: www.pagodelvicario.com
Two brothers bought a beautiful estate on the banks of the river Guadiana, crossed by a Roman bridge, nine kilometres (5.6 miles) from Ciudad Real at 600 metres (1,968 feet) altitude, in 2000, and started this bodega from scratch. It is a grand enterprise with a modern luxury hotel and restaurant. There are 130 hectares divided into twenty-five lots on different types of soil, growing Chardonnay, Sauvignon Blanc, Airén, Macabeo, Tempranillo, Garnacha, Graciano, Merlot, Syrah, Cabernet Sauvignon, and Petit Verdot. The two whites are: Talva, from all four white varieties fermented in new French casks; and Corte Dulce, a sweet wine with a dry finish from Chardonnay and Sauvignon Blanc, the fermentation arrested by cooling.

The deep-coloured, strong-flavoured *rosado* is from Petit Verdot. The reds are: Monagós, from eighty per cent Syrah and twenty per cent Garnacha; 50-50, from equal parts of Tempranillo and Cabernet Sauvignon with twelve months in mostly French with some American and Caucasian oak; and the top Agios (Greek for saint), from eighty per cent Tempranillo and twenty per cent Garnacha, both low yielding and given ten months in French oak. These are good wines, particularly the reds, and fascinatingly different. These are early days and the future looks very promising.

URIBES MADERO

Carretera Huerte – Cuenca km 3.2, 16500 Huete, Cuenca. Tel: +34 969 14 30 20; Fax: +34 969 14 70 47; Website: www.pagodecalzadilla.net

Uribes is the landowner and Madero the oenologist, making a conspicuously successful team. They started to plant the fourteen-hectare vineyard in 1980 and established the bodega in 1995. Their Calzadilla wine range includes a varietal Syrah and a *reserva* from sixty per cent Tempranillo, thirty per cent Cabernet Sauvignon, and ten per cent Garnacha. Their top Gran Calzadilla Reserva is from sixty per cent Tempranillo and forty per cent Cabernet Sauvignon, with eighteen months in French and American oak.

CASTILLA Y LEON

DEHESA LA GRANJA

Finca La Granja, 49420 Vadillo de la Guareña, Zamora.
Tel/Fax: +34 980 56 60 09; Email: lagranja@dehesalagranja.com Website: www.dehesalagranja.com

Better known by the name of its wine, Dehesa La Granja, this is another enterprise of the redoubtable Alejandro Fernández. When he bought the 800-hectare estate on the banks of the river Guareña in 1998, it was a run-down bull farm that had once grown vines. Impressed by the wines of Toro, he thought the DO might be extended, but it was not and he makes a VdlT. He planted 125 hectares of Tempranillo, which has since been doubled, and kept the bulls for two years, by which time they had taken part in thirty bull-fights, but that was not his scene. The rest of the estate is now devoted to organic animal farming. The principal wine spends two years in new American oak – and it is very good indeed. It would not be legal to make a *reserva*, but with thirty months in French oak, the Cosecha de 1999 Roble Francés is one in all but label.

10

Extremadura

Extremadura (or Estremadura) is in the middle of that enchanting part of Spain that runs along the north/south border with Portugal. A lot of it is hilly or even mountainous, some of it flat, and all of it full of farming. The name means "the limit of the land beyond the Duero". In Spain the limit is the Portuguese border, but there is a similarly named part of Portugal that stops at the Atlantic. The city of Mérida was once the capital of the Roman province of Lusitania, and the Roman remains there are wonderful. Some of the vineyards are in the province of Badajoz, others in that of Cáceres. There is some beautiful countryside and some enchanting little towns, such as Jerez de los Caballeros.

The Romans, of course, planted vines here and the area went on growing large quantities of very sound table wines. In recent years they have flowed steadily into UK supermarkets, yet until 1997 there were no DO wines. There were six VdlTs, though: Tierra de Barros; Cañamero; Matanegra; Montánchez; Ribera Alta del Guadiana; and Ribera Baja del Guadiana. These have now all been combined into a single DO: Ribera del Guadiana.

RIBERA DEL GUADIANA

Geography

Despite their combination into a single DO, the six areas must be considered separately. Tierra de Barros (much the most important) is in the middle of the provice of Badajoz, most of the vineyards being on either side of the river Guadiana in the direction of the Portuguese border. The countryside here is fairly flat and 300–350 metres (984–1,148 feet) above sea level. Cañamero is far away to the east, in the province of Cáceres, and up in the hills of the Sierra de Guadalupe at an average altitude of 521 metres (1,709 feet). Matanegra is further south and centred around the town of Zafra, with an average altitude of 638 metres (2,093 feet). Montánchez is in the Sierra de Montánchez, in the province of Cáceres, northeast of Badajoz and southeast of Cáceres, also with an average altitude of 638 metres. Ribera Alta del Guadiana, with an average altitude of 427 metres (1,400 feet), and Ribera Baja del Guadiana, with an average altitude of 286 metres (938 feet), are both in the province of Badajoz, the former upstream on the river Guadiana and to the east of Mérida, by the city of Badajoz by the Portuguese frontier. Thus the area as a whole covers a lot of ground, and joining the six original sub-divisions into a single DO may be regarded as a matter of administrative convenience rather than of geographical logic, though all the areas run into one another with the exception of Cañamero.

Climate

Such a wide area brings many variations. Tierra de Barros is very hot in summer and fairly dry, with a rainfall of 350–450 millimetres (13.7–17.7 inches). Cañamero has a generally rather temperate climate but is rather wet, with annual rainfall of 750–800 millimetres (29.5–31.5 inches). Matanegra is likewise temperate, but no statistics are available. Montánchez has a more continental climate, hot in summer and cold in winter, but with a smaller rainfall of 500–600 millimetres (19.7–23.6 inches). No statistics are available for the two Riberas. The annual rainfall for the whole area is 400–500 millimetres (15.7–19.7 inches).

Soils

Barros means clay, and the vineyards of Tierra de Barros are on fairly flat, fertile ground. In Cañamero they are on slatey hillsides. In Matanegra the soil is similar to that in Tierra de Barros. In Montánchez it is dark and acid. In Ribera Alta it is very sandy. In Ribera Baja it is muddy clay, but the best vineyards are in rather shallow, not very fertile, soil.

Grapes

Red varieties: Tempranillo; Garnacha; Bobal; Cabernet Sauvignon; Graciano; Mazuelo; Merlot; Monastrell; Syrah; Garnacha Tintorera; Jaén; and Pinot Noir.

White varieties: Pardina; Alarije; Borba; Cayetana Blanca; Macabeo; Chardonnay; Chelva; Montúa (or Mantúa); Malvar; Parellada; Pedro Ximénez; Verdejo; Eva; Cigüente; Moscatel de Alejandría; Moscatel de Grano Menudo; Perruno; and Sauvignon Blanc.

These many varieties include some found nowhere else in Spain. The most widely planted is Tempranillo followed by Pardina.

Planting

Either *en vaso*, spaced 2.75 metres (9 feet) in *marco real*, or *espaldera* spaced 2.75 x 1.5 metres (9 x 5 feet), but densities may in fact vary from 1,000–4,000 vines per hectare.

Vineyard area

21,290 hectares and rising steadily.

Authorized yield

84hl/ha for whites and 70hl/ha for reds.

Wines

Whites were traditional, but now there are reds, whites, and *rosados* in that order of importance. Sparkling wines are also made, including a DO cava, but that is considered separately. Minimum strengths: 11% ABV for reds, 10% ABV for whites and *rosados*.

Production

61,127 hectolitres (2004).

Vintages

From 1999 to 2002 all were rated four. In 2004 the rating was three.

Several years must pass before this new DO begins to show its potential and there will have to be a good deal of replanting with approved varieties and experimentation to see what can be made. The principal area is Tierra de Barros, with Bodegas Inviosa leading the way and a prominent exporter. There are now some very good wines, with the grapes picked early enough for there to be ample acid, and vinified in the modern way. That being said, most wines produced are not within the DO at all, as yet, and many are rustic: bulk wines for drinking locally or distilling. Some are also distinctly odd; for instance Montánchez used to produce a heavyweight red that actually grew some *flor*. Some white wines are matured in the sherry style, using *criaderas* and *soleras*. It would be a pity to lose such curiosities, but there is no immediate sign of their demise. The bodegas see the future, though, in producing wines with an appeal that enables them to compete nationally and internationally. It is hoped that they will not be overly tempted by international vine varieties and manage to produce good and interesting wines from some of the unique local vines. Such wines do exist.

Apart from the DO itself there is the VdlT Extremadura. Most of the bodegas have their buildings within the DO area, but some make VdlT wines as well, and this is indicated in the relevant entries.

Some leading bodegas

LAR DE BARROS/INVIOSA

La Fuente 8-A, 06200 Almendralejo, Badajoz. Tel: +34 924 67 12 35; Fax: +34 924 66 59 32; Email: info@lardebarros.com; Website: www.lardebarros.com
Established as long ago as 1931, this family-owned bodega was the first to move with the times, making wines that have earned a safe place in the export markets as well as in Spain. It is in the leading area of Tierra de Barros, where it has 400 hectares of vineyard at 500 metres (1,640 feet), the largest plantings being Tempranillo, Cabernet Sauvignon, and Macabeo. It is unique in Extremadura in producing an excellent cava, but that belongs to another chapter. Its wines are sold under the name Lar de Barros, Lar de Lares, Lar de Oro, Valle de la Mina, and Viña Adelaida. The Lar de Barros reds are varietal Tempranillos up to *gran reserva*, matured in American oak with some French for the *crianza*. The white has seventy per cent Macabeo, twenty per cent Chardonnay, and ten per cent Sauvignon Blanc. Lar de Oro (VdlT) is used for varietal wines, Chardonnay and Cabernet Sauvignon, with a red *joven* from sixty per cent Cabernet Sauvignon and forty per cent Tempranillo.

MARCELINO DÍAZ

López de Ayala 13, 06200 Almendralejo, Badajoz. Tel: +34 924 67 75 48; Fax: +34 924 66 09 77; Email: bodega@madiaz.com; Website: www.madiaz.com This claims to be a family-owned bodega founded in 1931 by Marcelino Díaz and now run by his son, but it traces this ancestry through Lar de Barros (*see* above). Marcelino Díaz split it off to make a separate range of modern high expression wines. It has 100 hectares of vineyard at 500 metres (1,640 feet) and sells under the mark Puerta Palma. New American oak is used for ageing the reds. The white is seventy-five per cent Macabeo and twenty-five per cent Sauvignon Blanc. The red *roble* is eighty per cent Tempranillo, fifteen per cent Cabernet Sauvignon, and five per cent Graciano. Finca Las Tenderas, from ninety per cent Tempranillo and ten per cent Cabernet Sauvignon is given one year in oak, as is the single vineyard Finca El Campillo, from eighty per cent Tempranillo and twenty per cent Graciano.

RUIZ TORRES

Cañadahonda 61, 10136 Cañamero, Cáceres. Tel: +34 927 36 90 24; Fax: +34 927 36 93 02; Email: info@ruiztorres.com; Website: www.ruiztorres.com One of the oldest family bodegas, founded in 1870, this is a considerable enterprise producing everything from bag in the box to a fine *reserva*, VdlT, and table wines, as well as DO wines. It has eighty-six hectares of vineyard in the sub-zone of Cañamero growing Cabernet Sauvignon, Petit Verdot, Tempranillo, Monastrel, Garnacha, Syrah, and Macabeo in sandy soil. Apart from Ruiz Torres it uses the names Trampal (VdlT), Attelea, Cepa, and, for non-DO made largely from the rare local varieties, Ribera Del Rucas. Its *crianza* and *reserva* reds are made by the unusual method of giving them a substantial time in stainless steel before completing their maturation in American oak and bottle. Its top wine is Attelea, the *crianza* from Tempranillo and Cabernet Sauvignon, with eight months in new American oak after twelve in stainless steel. The *roble* is a varietal Tempranillo.

BODEGAS VENTURA DE VEGA

Badajoz 70, 06200 Almendralejo, Badajoz. Tel: +34 924 67 11 05; Fax: +34 924 67 72 05; Email: bodegas@vegaesteban.com; Website: www.vegaesteban.com A family bodega established in 1927 with 300 hectares of vineyard growing Tempranillo and Macabeo. The wines are varietals. Leyenda has nine months oak, and the unoaked Cadencia has part carbonic maceration.

VIÑA SANTA MARINA

Ctra N 630 km 634.5, 06800 Mérida, Badajoz. Tel: +34 902 50 63 64; Fax: +34 924 02 76 75; Email: export@vsantamarina.com; Website: www.vsantamarina.com

A young bodega, founded in 1999, it has fifty-eight hectares of vineyard soon to be extended to 110. A Roman village has been found on the site and includes a wine press. Viña Santa Marina (VdlT) is a *semi-crianza* from Cabernet Sauvignon and Syrah. The rest of the reds are varietal Tempranillos. Equus (VdlT) is from old vines. The name Torremayor is used for the *crianza*, given seven months in American and French oak, and the *reserva*, with fourteen months in French oak. Other VdlT wines include Altara, Celtus, and Miraculus, a *reserva* from fifty per cent Tempranillo, thirty per cent Cabernet Sauvignon, and twenty per cent Syrah.

VINAS DE ALANGE

Palomas km 6, 06840 Alange, Badajoz. Tel: +34 924 67 01 75; Fax: +34 924 66 09 89; Email: info@alvear.es; Website: www.alvear.es

These are early days as the bodega was not established until 2000, but it is owned by the famous Montilla house Alvear, which has planted 100 hectares with Tempranillo, Cabernet Sauvignon, Graciano, and Syrah. Its varietal Tempranillos, sold under the name Palacio Quemado, have been well received. This is one to watch.

11

Andalucía

Thanks perhaps to *Carmen*, the very name Andalucía conjures up romantic visions of wild gypsy girls with roses in their hair, bulls, and flamenco dancing. Oddly enough, there is an element of truth. It was here that the Moorish civilization in Spain reached its high point. It can be savoured in the exquisite buildings and gardens that survive in Granada, Cordoba, and Sevilla, in the houses with their patios, and in the *pueblos blancos* (the white villages) dotted throughout the countryside. The great river Guadalquivir, which is navigable all the way up to Sevilla, is a seam of history flowing through a lively world. Along it the conquistadors set sail to conquer the New World, taking the local wines with them, and along it they brought their treasures back. On the right bank of the estuary where it meets the Atlantic lie the *marismas*, with one of the world's greatest nature reserves, the Coto Doñana. At the other extreme there are the mountains of the Sierra Nevada. And there is still something Moorish about the people. I remember with joy walking by night through the streets of Sanlúcar de Barrameda when all my Spanish friends broke out spontaneously into singing and dancing flamenco. It is hard to imagine a more pleasant place to live.

Wine has been grown here since before the time of the Romans and, because the sea borders it on two sides, has been exported from time immemorial. One of its wines is among the first to be mentioned in English literature. Chaucer's father was a leading wine merchant in London, and when his son wrote of wine, he knew what he was talking about. In *The Pardoner's Tale* (c.1390), he wrote of the wine of Lepe, which lies within the area now defined as Condado de Huelva, but alas the vineyards have recently been grubbed up.

Although Andalucía has always grown table wines, which are now being

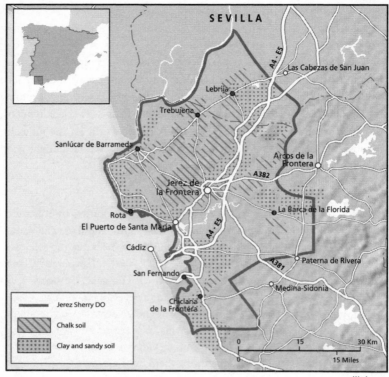

xiii Jerez

revived, its speciality has been the strong, usually fortified, wines that Chaucer knew. These are now known as *vinos generosos* and (for sweetened wines) *vinos generosos de licor*. They are grown principally in four *Denominaciones de Origen* from west to east, Condado de Huelva, Jerez, Xérès or Sherry, y Manzanilla de Sanlúcar de Barrameda, Montilla-Moriles,and Málaga. The first to receive the distinction of its own DO was Jerez, in 1933. Until then no very clear distinction was drawn between them. The prosperous merchants of Jerez used to bring in wine from their neighbours for blending with their own – even, in the more remote past, from Málaga. There was nothing in the least wrong about that. Unlike the notorious blending of Burgundy with Algerian wine, it was blending like with like, all grown in the same general area of Spain and according to a tradition dating back for centuries. However delimitation is now the thing, and the regulations have been tightened up over the years so that they are now very strict indeed. It is doubtful whether the consumer has either benefited or suffered; but it has certainly made life more difficult for the growers in Condado de Huelva and Montilla-Moriles.

These powerful wines have had their ups and downs in the scales of fashion, and at the moment it must be admitted they are having a down. The shippers brought this on themselves, at least to some extent, by becoming too commercial, which cost them their quality image. The fact remains, though, that the wines are among the finest in the world. At the moment, because the demand has been reduced, they are also astoundingly good value for money. They are due for a great revival.

JEREZ-XÉRÈS-SHERRY Y MANZANILLA DE SANLUCAR DE BARRAMEDA
Geography

The vineyards fall within a carefully defined area as shown on the map, but the best lie within a triangle formed by the towns of Jerez de la Frontera, El Puerto de Santa María, and Sanlúcar de Barrameda, on rolling downland at 20–100 metres (65.6–328 feet) above sea level. These names are generally shortened to Jerez, Puerto, and Sanlúcar. There are two sub-zones: Jerez Superior (the best) and Zona.

Climate

This is Atlantic, not Mediterranean, but being so far south is a law unto itself. Although it can be rather damp in winter and distinctly too hot for comfort at the height of summer, the sherry country has a very pleasant climate to live in and one that is excellent for growing vines. The average temperature is 17°C (62.6°F) with a maximum rising to 44°C (111°F) and a minimum as low as -5°C (23°F), but these extremes are very rare and there is no frost problem. The climate is moderated by the nearness of the sea. The mean maximum is 23°C (73.4°F) and the minimum 11°C (51.8°F). The total rainfall is about 650 millimetres (25.6 inches), but there are years of drought and periods of deluge. The mean humidity is surprisingly high at sixty-six per cent, but this varies considerably according to the two prevailing winds. The Poniente, from the west, is cool, not very strong, and humid: it can raise the humidity to ninety per cent. The Levante, from the southeast, is horrible, strong, and hot: it can reduce the humidity to thirty per cent.

These figures come from the meteorological station that is in the vineyards and rather more exposed to extremes than the towns. In particular El Puerto, near where the river Guadalete flows into the sea, is cooler, and Sanlúcar, on the estuary of the river Guadalquivir, is cooler still. These differences influence the development of the wines in the bodegas. It is very sunny, with some 3,000 hours of sunshine.

Soils

There are three kinds. The finest is *albariza*, so called because under the sun it looks almost as white as snow. It usually contains about sixty per cent chalk and can go up as high as eighty per cent. It acts like a sponge to water and can absorb as much as thirty-four per cent by weight, which it then retains under a surface that does not crack in the sun. The next quality is *barro*, which is found in the valleys and looks brown, or even reddish, owing to the presence of iron; it is only about ten per cent chalk. The third kind is *arena*, which is sandy with a more yellowish-red tinge, again brought about by iron. There are few vineyards on the second kind and practically none on the third.

Grapes

Once there were perhaps as many as 100 varieties, and a survey in 1868 listed forty-two, but now there are only three: Palomino Fino (Listán), which accounts for about ninety-five per cent; Pedro Ximénez; and Moscatel. The latter two are for sweet wines.

Planting

There are two traditional patterns for planting: *marco real*, which consists of squares, and *tresbolillo*, of equilateral triangles. From the 1960s, however, these patterns were abandoned and the vines planted in rows with about 1.1 metres (3.6 feet) between the vines and 2.3 metres (7.5 feet) between the rows, to allow for mechanical cultivating and harvesting. Traditionally the vines have been grown as bushes, but recently they have been cultivated on wires – *espalderas*. This makes life easier and allows canopy control in the interest of quality. The maximum density of planting allowed is 4,100 vines per hectare. The method of pruning for bush vines is to leave one long branch (the *vara* or stick) with 8–10 "eyes" to bear the crop and a stub (*pulgar* or thumb) with one or two eyes for the following year. Hence it is known as *vara y pulgar*.

Vineyard Area

10,372 hectares (2004).

Authorized Yield

80hl/ha, but this is liable to revision downward.

Wines

The *denominacion* covers two distinct styles: sherry and manzanilla (itself a sub-division of sherry) – hence its compound name. There are two basic classifications: *vino generoso* (15–22% ABV), where the wines are bone dry, and *vino generoso de licor* (17–22% ABV) for wines that are off-dry to sweet. In addition there is sweet *vino dulce natural* made by partial fermentation of Pedro Ximénez or Moscatel grapes. But each of these names encapsulates a bewildering variety of wines with many subtleties described in the main text. The basic categories are: fino (15–18% ABV); manzanilla (15–18% ABV); amontillado (16–22% ABV); palo cortado (17–22% ABV); and oloroso (17–22% ABV).

Production

628,643 hectolitres (2004).

Vintages

The production of vintage wines is minuscule and these are selected only from the best vintages. There tends to be little difference between vintages anyhow, and these are evened out by the method of maturation, so vintage years are irrelevant.

Sherry is beyond doubt one of the greatest wines in the world, and at the moment, because the pendulum of fashion has swung against it, it is remarkable value. If asked about Spanish wines, this is the one people always think of first, for it has a remarkable history and was the first Spanish wine to become established on the export markets. It has already been mentioned that the Andalusian wine of Lepe was well known in Chaucer's day, and sherry has a continuous history from that time to now. The origin of the name goes back to a much earlier period, though. In AD 711 the Moors won Andalucía by defeating the ruling Visigoths at the battle of Guadalete. Despite their religion, the Moors grew wine and Jerez became prosperous. It was called Seris, pronounced Sherish, a name later corrupted to Jerez by the Spanish and to Sherry by the English. In 1264 it was reconquered by the Christians under King Alfonso X, and its modern history dates from then. The suffix "de la Frontera" was added in 1380 by King Juan I in recognition of its services as one of the frontier towns between the two kingdoms. Old records show that sherry was being exported to England from the beginning of the fifteenth century, and one of the more specific ones records that in 1485 it was shipped from El Puerto de Santa María to Plemma, which is in the kingdom of England – presumably Plymouth.

English merchants have long travelled the world in search of trade. William Ostrych, from Bristol, was living in Sanlúcar as early as 1523, and in 1530 he and his fellow English merchants petitioned King Henry VIII to grant them a charter, which he did, with a detailed constitution. They had their own church of St George, which still stands in Sanlúcar. By Elizabeth I's reign sherry sack was established as a firm favourite. The word "sack" comes from the Spanish verb *sacar*, to draw out or export, and was used for Spanish wines generally. When Drake "singed the King of Spain's beard" by setting fire to the Spanish fleet as it lay at anchor in the bay of Cádiz in 1587, he remained for three days and made off with 2,900 casks of wine – though the figure may be slightly exaggerated. Perhaps he helped to make it popular in England, and if so his theft has been repaid many times over. In 1598 the wine received its most famous tribute from Shakespeare, through the mouth of Falstaff, who says it all:

> *A good sherris-sack hath a two-fold operation in it. It ascends me into the brain; dries me there all foolish and dull and crudy vapours which environ it; makes it apprehensive, quick, forgetive, full of nimble fiery and delectable shapes; which deliver'd o'er to the voice, the tongue, which is the birth, becomes excellent wit. The second property of your excellent sherris is, the warming of the blood; which, before cold and settled, left the liver white and pale, which is the badge of pusillanimity and cowardice: but the sherris warms it and makes it course from the inwards to the parts extreme. It illumineth the face, which, as a beacon, gives warning to all the rest of this little kingdom, man, to arm; and then the vital commoners and inland petty spirits muster me all to their captain, the heart, who, great and puffed up with this retinue, doth any deed of courage; and this valour comes of sherris. So that skill in the weapon is nothing without sack, for that sets it a-work; and learning, a mere hoard*

of gold kept by a devil till sack commences it and sets it in act and use...
If I had a thousand sons, the first human principle I would teach them
should be, to forswear thin potations and to addict themselves to sack.

Sherry has been with us ever since, but it has had its ups and downs. In the ups, when the sales are buoyant, the merchants have repeatedly become over- confident and the quality has suffered, with the inevitable consequence that a down has followed. One of these downs lasted practically throughout the eighteenth century, but toward the end of that century restrictive prac- tices that had lowered the quality were done away with and merchants flocked in from England, Scotland, Ireland, and France. Their descendants are still there and the families will be mentioned in the accounts of the lead- ing bodegas that trade today. In the nineteenth century, the trade reached a climax. In 1864, 43.41 per cent of the total wine imports to Great Britain were sherry, and sales peaked to 68,467 butts (each of 108 gallons) in 1873. But thereafter things went into a decline. There can be no doubt but that some awful wines were shipped, and to add to the miseries came the inevitable arrival of phylloxera in 1894. At that time sherry was largely taken as a wine with food and lighter wines were coming into vogue. The idea of taking an apéritif came on the scene surprisingly late. The days of high pros- perity had gone.

In 1910 the Sherry Shippers' Association was formed in London. The shippers pooled their resources and launched a generic advertising cam- paign, certainly one of the first if not the first. But perhaps the greatest fillip of all came in the 1920s when Carl Williams, of Williams & Humbert, gave the first sherry party, and the idea caught on. The craze for cocktail parties was just beginning, but the more discriminating began to take sherry instead. Eventually the ethos that had produced the cocktail vanished, but the taste for sherry remained and went from strength to strength. The Spanish Civil War had surprisingly little effect on the trade: things were quiet in the Sherry Country. But World War II made a big impact; little wine was exported in 1941, 1942, or 1943, and there was considerable hardship in a period where things were very grim throughout Europe. After the war trade steadily got better. One of the postwar phenomena has been the remarkable rise in the Netherlands market, which started to take off in the mid-1960s. It remains one of the largest. The graph of sales throughout the world went up and up, reaching a dramatic peak of 1,519,852 hectolitres in 1979. Then it started to go down, and although there were false dawns, the fall proved to be inexorable. In 1996 production was 741,934 hectolitres. The trade had been extremely prosperous when sales were a good deal lower, but when the graph was going up the shippers had projected it ever upward and had committed themselves to enormous expenditure, planting vineyards and buying expensive new premises and equipment. Many of the smaller ones went to the wall. The reasons for this fall are complicated. Who can analyze the caprices of fashion? But there can be no doubt that some atrocious sherries were being shipped at the height of the boom and that cannot have helped. There has been an elaborate reconstruction plan. Surplus wine has been disposed of and many hectares of vineyard have been grubbed up. The shippers must now look to the future. Happily they are doing so by making very fine wines.

The vinification of sherry has moved with the times. Not so very long ago the grapes were pressed by foot (though the feet were in specially designed boots) in wooden *lagares*, which were found in all the vineyards. From the *lagar* the must was run off into oak casks where it fermented so rapidly that this first stage was known as the tumultuous fermentation. The casks were then transported to the bodegas in the towns where the fermentation was completed and the wines matured.

The bodegas are remarkable and very beautiful buildings. Large and very high, they have often been described as "cathedrals of wine", and anyone who has seen them will know how just the description is. There is a very good reason why they are so high: to keep the temperature down in that very hot climate. Happily many of the traditional buildings remain and fine examples can be seen in Jerez at old established bodegas (the term is also used for the companies who own them) such as Domecq, Gonzalez Byass, Harveys, Sandeman, and Lustau; in El Puerto de Santa María at Osborne and Luis Caballero; and in Sanlúcar at Barbadillo, Hidalgo, Romero, and Argüeso. Alas, though, many in Jerez have been pulled down in the name of progress, to make way for high-rise blocks, and others will undoubtedly follow. They are being replaced by modern and not very beautiful buildings on the edge of the town, one of which is partially underground. This does not detract from the quality of the wine, though, as the new buildings are well insulated and the edge of the town is cooler.

Nowadays the grapes are pressed in modern horizontal presses and everything is computer controlled. Only the free-run must (*mosto yema*), is used for making sherry, with temperature-controlled fermentation in stainless steel, though some is still made in the traditional way. The first fermentation is rapid and is over in a couple of days, by which time ninety-five per cent of the sugar has been converted into alcohol. This is followed by a further slow fermentation in tanks or in American oak casks that lasts for forty or fifty days. So all sherry begins by being bone dry. This is only the beginning, though: its character and flavour are not yet at all developed and it is known as *mosto*, or must – a term that is also confusingly applied to the unfermented juice.

At this point the wine begins to develop. It is all put into American oak casks of 120 gallons' capacity, which are filled only about five-sixths so that there is a substantial air space over the surface of the wine, and very loose bungs are used, which keep dust out but allow air to circulate. Those wines that are destined to develop as finos start to develop *flor*, which is a thin layer of yeasts of the genus *saccharomyces*. It looks rather like a layer of cream cheese. These yeasts protect the wine from oxidation and profoundly affect the nature of its development, giving a form of biological maturation. These wines receive a light fortification with a mixture of equal parts wine and grape alcohol to bring their strength up to 15% ABV or so. Those that do not grow much *flor*, or any at all, are fortified to 17% ABV or so. The *flor* is very sensitive to the level of alcohol and this higher level kills it off, leaving the wines to develop by an oxidative maturation to become olorosos. It is also sensitive to temperature and grows best in spring, when the vines flower, and in autumn, when the vintage is gathered in – coincidences that led to a certain amount of mythology. It grows least abundantly in Jerez, the hottest of the sherry towns, and most abundantly in Sanlúcar, which is the coolest. Consequently the finos of Sanlúcar are the lightest and most pungent. They are known as manzanilla. Those from Jerez are the most robust.

Although a very small number of casks are matured apart as vintage wines – known as *añadas*, or wines of the year – sherry is almost entirely matured in an unusual way: the *solera* system, or fractional blending. This works by adding younger to older wine and leaving it for a while. If a shipper has a cask of mature wine of a style that he likes and he draws some of it off – typically a third – he then fills the void with a younger wine of the same style and leaves it for some time – typically six months – to return the cask back to where it started: the young wine has taken on the character of the older one and tastes exactly the same. Of course this is not done just with one cask. There may be perhaps a hundred in the *solera* (a term that is applied to the casks in the final stage of the process, as well as to the process as a whole) and these are fed by a similar number of casks of slightly younger wine. These constitute the last scale in the *criadera*, or nursery, of wines that is used to feed the solera. This in turn is fed by the wine in another scale of the *criadera*, which may have only two or three scales or as many as twenty. The exact number depends on the style being made and the speed it is moved from one scale to another: operating a *solera* properly is rather complicated and calls for considerable skill. When the wine made is a fino, growing *flor*, there is another aspect to it. *Flor*, being a yeast, requires nutrients. These are found in the young wine, and as some of it finds its way into the older wine, the *flor* is kept nourished and growing.

As a fino grows old, the nutrients are used up and so the *flor* grows weaker and eventually disappears. The biological ageing process is then replaced by an oxidative one. The wine grows darker in colour and begins to acquire a totally different aroma. It is then called an amontillado because it resembles the wine grown in Montilla-Moriles (*see* below), where wines of this kind originated. With great age, wines that are not growing under *flor* get stronger as the water evaporates more quickly than the alcohol in the cool, dry atmosphere of the bodega. An amontillado can grow to be as strong as 22% ABV and its flavour can become so strong that it is magnificent – but practically undrinkable. A little of such a wine in a blend, though, can result in something marvellous. Thus a true amontillado is the product of long, patient ageing. It must therefore necessarily be expensive. A cheap amontillado has to be a spoof. The word is much misused.

With olorosos there is no *flor,* but otherwise the effects of age are similar.

In between amontillado and oloroso there is another style known as palo cortado, meaning "cut stick", from the mark that the bodega foreman puts on the casks to identify it. It has the bouquet of an amontillado with the flavour of an oloroso. There is not very much of this as only a few casks develop in this special way, so again the real thing is necessarily expensive. It is a wine of great finesse, much sought by connoisseurs. It can be imitated, relatively cheaply and quite well, by blending amontillados with olorosos.

All sherries are therefore by nature completely dry. It has often been written that finos are dry, amontillados medium, and olorosos sweet. This is complete nonsense. If a sherry is sweet it is because it has been sweetened. It is a pity to sweeten a fino, as this robs it of its elegance and its tremendous impact. It must be admitted, though, that not all finos are elegant. Deficiencies are masked by sweetening and the result can be an acceptable wine that is easy to drink and less of an acquired taste than the real thing. Amontillados, palo cortados, and olorosos take to sweetening wines very well, though, and the results are those exquisite dessert sherries that are among the joys of wine drinking. Several wines are used for sweetening. The basic one nowadays is *mosto concentrado rectificado*, which is must concentrated under low pressure and treated to remove flavours other than sugar. Sweet and very light in colour, such preparations are used throughout the EU. The traditional sweetening wines have lots of flavour and impart something of their own to the blend. There are three of these and all are made in much the same sort of way. The great one is Pedro Ximénez (or PX), made from the grape of that name. Naturally sweet, the sweetness is concentrated by drying the grapes in the sun, then pressing them and running the must into casks containing some grape alcohol, so the yeasts stop working while there is still plenty of sugar left. A similar traditional wine is made from Moscatel grapes. A more recent innovation is a wine made from the usual Palomino Fino grapes in the same way. The first two are both very strong in flavour and are matured in *soleras*, gathering distinction as they age. They are regularly bottled as single varietals and the *soleras* of them are among the precious possessions of the bodegas. The dessert wines are made by blending these with dry wines, differing in style and age, to produce the kind required.

The wines from Sanlúcar de Barrameda are something slightly apart. As has been mentioned, *flor* grows there particularly abundantly, and as the climate is slightly cooler, it flourishes all the year round. As a result the finos have a character that is all their own and are given the name manzanilla, which means "camomile". Beware! If you ask for a manzanilla in northern Spain, where sherries are little understood, you are likely to be given a cup of camomile tea, which is said to be good for the digestion.

As the wine ages, in the same way as in the other sherry towns, it becomes a manzanilla pasada and then a manzanilla amontillada. Likewise there is manzanilla olorosa. These are usually simply labelled amontillado and oloroso. The local palo cortado is called jerez cortado. All have a typical manzanilla tang. Some people detect a certain saltiness and ascribe this to the nearness of the sea, but this is nonsense: there is no salt in them. It is a fair description, though.

Some sherries are straight *solera* wines, but others are blended and sold under fancy names. In addition there are a number of recognized descriptions. These are:

Abocado: sweetened.

Amontillado: true amontillados are as described above, but unfortunately the name has been widely bastardized by the trade, especially in the UK, and has come to signify simply a wine of reasonably full body and moderately sweet. If you buy a cheap amontillado it will be that sort. A young amontillado is amber or very light brown, becoming darker with age.

Amoroso: the name suggests "loving", but the origin is derived from the name of a vineyard. A soft, fairly sweet wine, usually based on oloroso.

Brown: brown sherries used to be very popular, especially in Scotland, owing to their warming nature. They are not often found nowadays as a result of the fashion for light wines. They are olorosos that are sweetened to a high degree and their colour often enhanced by the addition of specially prepared concentrated wines.

Cream: these popular wines are based largely on olorosos, blended to be sweet, but not to have too deep a colour.

Fino amontillado: a wine maturing from fino to amontillado. When a little older, the words may be written the other way round.

Manzanilla pasada: the manzanilla equivalent of fino amontillado.

Medium: moderately sweetened (15–22% ABV).

Milk: sweetened oloroso traditionally associated with merchants in Bristol.

Pale cream: based on fino, blended to be sweet, but very light in colour, a great marketing success but seldom found on the tables of sherry lovers. (15.5–22% ABV).

Solera: practically all sherry is made on the *solera* system, but the name has been usurped by merchants and applied to sweetened olorosos.

Vino de pasto: once quite popular, this name has largely fallen from use. In the days when most of the sherries exported were sweet, it was applied to a drier style of wine that nowadays would be sold as medium sherry.

Finally there are indications of age. In the past these were never given, as the *solera* system is one of continuous blending and the shippers were anxious to avoid false claims. Nevertheless many sherries were very old, and as other districts could use the terms *crianza*, *reserva*, and *gran reserva*, something had to be done, so a system was evolved. It is in fact not all that difficult to assess age: the palate tells you most and it can be confirmed by C14 testing. A wine aged 12–15 years can say it on the label, and there are two higher categories: VOS stands for *Vinum Optimum Signatum* (Very Old Sherry) with a minimum age of twenty years; and VORS stands for *Vinum Optimum Rare Signatum* (Very Old Rare Sherry) with a minimum age of thirty years. The age in years may also be put on the label. VORS wines are not necessarily better than VOS ones; they are simply older. Which to buy is simply a matter of taste. And some wines that could easily carry these designation do not, as the regulations are complicated, shipping quotas are limited, and they cost a lot of money to use, as the wines have to be tested and monitored. They cannot, of course, be applied to finos as after such ageing they will have turned into amontillados. A special designation for mature finos is being considered, but at the time of writing this is not yet in place.

Before bottling most sherries are further fortified to shipping strength if necessary, microfiltered, and ultra-cooled – their temperature reduced to a very low level and kept there for a period so that tartrate crystals are precipitated and do not appear in bottle. This process dates from the 1960s, when the markets demanded wines that threw no deposits, particularly the American market which thought that there was something wrong with a wine that had crystals in it. This is rather a pity, as some flavouring elements are lost at the same time. When sherry was generally shipped at high strength – 18% ABV and upward – there were no problems of stability, but with lighter wines becoming steadily more fashionable, the strength has gradually been reduced and the lowest now permitted is 15% ABV. These low-strength wines, particularly if sweetened, require very fine filtration and sterile bottling. Ultra-cooling is not, however, used with the finest dessert wines, which do tend to throw a deposit in bottle and can advantageously be decanted.

With other sherries decanting should be avoided though, unless they are going to be drunk right away, when a decanter can look attractive. The reason for this is that sherry, like all wines, oxidizes in contact with the air. Finos also tend to deteriorate in bottle. Modern methods of stock control have helped a lot, as merchants no longer keep them for months or even years. A fino should ideally be drunk within three months of bottling and definitely goes off after a year. After opening it is best to drink them within three days, though they last a week or more if kept cool in the door of a refrigerator. Sweet wines can be kept for several years and are all right for two or three weeks after opening. The finest dessert wines are actually worth laying down. They gradually become less sweet and acquire fascinating qualities of flavour and bouquet: a sort of agreeable mustiness. In the past the leading merchants used regularly to list old bottled sherries, but this practice has largely disappeared owing to the modern demand for cash flow. They can be laid down privately, but to be worth while they need to be laid down for ten years and upward. They should be cellared standing upright, as strong wines tend to attack the corks.

In Spain sherry is invariably served with *tapas*. These can be very simple: nuts, crisps, olives, slices of sausage, and so on, though the best bars vie with each other in the range of *tapas* they offer. The fact is that sherry tastes at its best if accompanied with a little food – and it need not be just a little. Fino is one of the few wines that will stand up to quite a vinegary hors d'oeuvre and tastes good with soup; but it is also good with fish, especially shell fish, chicken, salads, and so on. And of course it is superb as an apéritif. The other styles of sherry, when dry, make excellent apéritifs, too, and the added weight of a fine dry amontillado, palo cortado, or oloroso can be delightfully warming in a cool and damp northern climate. These wines can also be excellent with meats and other foods that are generally associated with red wines. The rich olorosos are best at the end of a meal, with cheese, a sweet course or dessert; they are marvellous with Stilton and with nuts.

Like every other good wine, an important part of the attraction of sherry is its bouquet. To smell this, it is essential to serve the wine in decent glasses. The so-called sherry glass, which looks like a thimble on a stem, is dreadful; and Elgin glasses, which go in toward the middle, are the worst of the lot. As with all other wines, the aromatic elements need to expand in the air space above the surface: there just has to be an air space. Tulip-shaped wine glasses are admirable and the Spanish *copita*, which is wide at the bottom and gradually tapers towards the top, is ideal. Glasses should not be filled to more than about a third of their capacity, so that the aroma can expand and concentrate in an enclosed space.

The labels of many fino bottles state that the wine should be served cool. This is important. A good test for a restaurant is to ask if they have chilled fino. If they have, and serve it in the right glasses, one has got off to a good start. But it should not be frozen stiff, as this kills the flavour entirely. The door space of a refrigerator is generally about right. The other styles can be served at room temperature, though many people like them very slightly cooled: cellar temperature of about 14°C (57°F) is ideal.

Some leading bodegas

HEREDEROS DE ARGÜESO
Mar 8, 11540 Sanlúcar de Barrameda, Cádiz. Tel: +34 956 38 51 16;
Fax: +34 956 36 81 69; Email: argueso@argueso.es; Website: www.argueso.es
Established in 1822, this is one of the oldest and best of the manzanilla bodegas. Family owned, its wines include Las Medallas manzanilla, San Léon manzanilla pasada, and older wines such as amontillado viejo.

ANTONIO BARBADILLO

Luís Eguilaz 11, 11540 Sanlúcar de Barrameda, Cádiz.

Tel: +34 956 38 55 00; Fax: +34 956 38 55 01;

Email: barbadillo@barbadillo.com; Website: www.barbadillo.com

An independent house in Sanlúcar, this is one of the leading shippers. Founded in 1821, its bodegas in the old bishop's palace are among the most beautiful in the whole of the sherry towns. It may well have been the first shipper to sell a wine as manzanilla. Nowadays it provides a very extensive range and all its wines are excellent. The best known are its Manzanilla de Sanlúcar and Manzanilla Pasada Solear, but it produces good wines of all styles, including a fino, Principe Amontillado (VOS), a superb Palo Cortado de Obispo Gascon (VORS), and Oloroso Seco Cuco (VORS). There is also a table wine (*see* below).

LUIS CABALLERO

San Francisco 24, 11500 El Puerto de Santa María, Cádiz. Tel: +34 956 85 17 51; Fax: +34 95686 92 04

This is still a completely independent family firm in Puerto de Santa María, dating from 1830 and known throughout Spain for its orange liqueur Ponche Caballero. The present Don Luis Caballero is a large and dynamic man who, among many other things, owns the local castle of San Marcos. His enthusiasm is for sherries of the very highest quality, and his aim is to produce them. He has invented his own way of making fino, which he markets under the name Puerto Fino. The idea is to keep it as fresh as possible. A mature *solera* fino is blended with a small proportion of young wine growing vigorous *flor*, under which it remains until it is ready for bottling. The results are impressive and he claims that it has a longer shelf life. In 1990 he took over the Jerez house of Emilio Lustau, which was noted for its fine wines, but which was too small really to be viable. With his enthusiasm and capital all went well. This name is now the one used on the export markets, and for the rest of the story, *see* below.

CROFT JEREZ

See Gonzalez Byass.

JOSÉ DE SOTO

See Garvey/Zoilo Ruiz-Mateos.

PEDRO DOMECQ/JOHN HARVEY

San Idefonso 3, 11403 Jerez de la Frontera, Cádiz. Fax: +34 956 33 40 11; Website: www.domecq.es

Domecq has such a long and complicated history that a whole book could be written. It was founded in 1730 by an Irishman called Patrick Murphy, a bachelor, one of whose kinsmen was Pedro Domecq, whose family came from the French side of the Pyrenees, but who had been born in Jerez. He took over the business in 1816 and appointed a brilliant agent in England: John Ruskin's father, John James Ruskin. From then onward the business expanded rapidly. Pedro Domecq died as a result of an accident in 1839 and 8,000 followed his funeral. The House of Domecq became pre-eminent in the sherry trade and was protected from its vicissitudes by a very healthy parallel trade in brandy. In 1984 it was taken over by Allied Lyons to form the giant corporation Allied Domecq, which has now changed hands. Harveys was a subsidiary of the same company and the two have now come together. Domecq wines include the renowned fino La Ina, but there is a complete range of very fine wines including amontillados Botaina, Bolivar, and 51–1 (VORS); palo cortados Nelson and Capuchino (VORS); olorosos Rio Viejo, MDV, and Sibarita (VORS); and Pedro Ximénez Venerable (VORS).

Turning now to Harveys, this was founded in 1796 in Bristol, and from the beginning concentrated on selling sherry and port. The last director with the name Harvey was Jack Harvey, who died in 1958. In the same year the business became a public company, and eventually part of Allied Domecq. Despite having acquired a great reputation for sherry it had no presence in Jerez until it bought the family bodega Mackenzie & Co, a name that has now disappeared. Today it has extensive bodegas there, separate from Domecq, in a beautiful garden. It is best known for its very popular dessert wine, Bristol Cream, which now comes in a blue bottle, reflecting the tradition of Bristol glass. Dune is a good fino. John Harvey Fine Old amontillado and palo cortado are both classics.

JOSÉ ESTÉVEZ/VALDESPINO

Ctra N-IV km 640, 11408 Jerez de la Frontera, Cádiz. Tel: +34 956 32 10 04; Fax: +34 956 34 08 29; Email: visitas@grupoestevez.com; Website: www.grupoestevez.com

This company, with bodegas on the edge of Jerez, was founded by José Estevez, a local businessman with a deep love of sherry, who began by acquiring the long established and respected Marqués del Réal Tesoro and then the *soleras* of the excellent fino, Tio Mateo. Its most recent acquisition, in 1999, was Valdespino, the oldest bodega in Jerez and one of the most respected. This brought the excellent fino Inocente, Deliciosa manzanilla, the amontillados Tio Diego and Coliseo (VORS), Cardenal palo cortado (VORS), the dry olorosos Don Gonzalo (VOS), Su Majestad (VORS), and Covadonga (VORS), the sweet oloroso Solera 1842 (VOS), and El Candado Pedro Ximénez. It has enthusiastically kept the quality up and makes a remarkable range of top-flight wines.

BODEGAS GARVEY/ZOILO RUIZ-MATEOS SL

R. Circunvalación-Bellavista, 11403 Jerez de la Frontera, Cádiz.

Tel: +34 956 31 96 50; Fax: +34 956 31 98 24

Zoilo Ruiz-Mateos was an *almacenista* in Jerez whose son, José María, had ambitions and built up an industrial and banking empire that included many of the most famous names in sherry. He was dispossessed by the state in 1983. Books could be written about that and indeed some have been, but the story cannot be told here. Predictably the Ruiz-Mateos family rose from the ashes and bought the famous if run-down bodega of Garvey in 1978, building fine new premises (part underground) on the bypass.

William Garvey came to Spain from Ireland in 1780, and by 1798 had established bodegas in Jerez that were destined to become among the greatest. His main bodega building, the Bodega de San Patricio, was in its time the largest of all: a truly magnificent building. Alas, gone is the glory! It was pulled down in 1997. The site in the middle of Jerez had become too valuable. Its wines have always been excellent and include the fino San Patricio, the amontillado Tio Guillermo, the palo cortado Special Reserve, and the dessert oloroso flor de Jerez. Other good wines are sold under the Don José María name. The group also includes José de Soto, noted for its *ponche* and selling a separate complete range of sherries.

The most recent and important development happened in 2005 when it acquired the great Sandeman vineyards and most of its wine. It now makes the Sandeman wines, but these are marketed separately (*see* below).

GONZALEZ BYASS

Manuel Ma Gonzalez 12, 11403 Jerez de la Frontera, Cádiz.

Tel: +34 956 35 70 60; Fax: +34 956 35 70 43;

Email: reservas@gonzalezbyass.es; Website: www.gonzalezbyass.es

This great bodega was founded in 1835 by Manuel María Gonzalez Angel and is still controlled and managed by his direct descendants. Robert Blake Byass was taken into partnership in 1855, and the Byass family retained its interest until 1988, when the Gonzalez family acquired it. The bodega buildings are among the finest in Jerez and include a remarkable, and not very practical, building designed by Eiffel, he of the tower. Queen Isabella II visited the bodegas in 1862, but unfortunately chose to arrive long after the vintage was over. Nevertheless Don Manuel acquired a large quantity of grapes that had been preserved for eating, so he could show her everything. From them he made a very fine wine and bought an enormous cask from Heidelberg to hold it – 3,500 gallons. Somewhat irreverently perhaps (because it contains thirty-three butts and Christ was thirty-three years old when he died) it was called El Cristo; but perhaps because the present generation is more wary of blasphemy than was its predecessor, it is now called El Maestro, as the apostles used to call Jesus. It now has twelve apostles, each filled with the best possible examples of different styles of sherry. (Though Judas does not appear: he is in the vinegar store). The superb Tio Pepe (which means Uncle Joe and was named after Don Manuel's uncle) is the most famous fino in the world. Other wines of impeccable quality are: Manzanilla El Rocío, Amontillado del Duque (VORS), Oloroso Seco Alfonso, Palo Cortado Apostoles (VORS), the beautiful, opulent dessert Oloroso Muy Viejo Matusalém (VORS), and the Pedro Ximénez Noé (VORS). It has also recently introduced some vintage (añada) wines, which cost the earth and are worth every penny.

In 2002 it took over Croft & Co, one of the oldest companies in the wine trade. It was founded in 1678, but the name Croft did not appear until 1736, when it was called Tilden, Thompson, and Croft. One of the partners, John Croft (1732–1820), somehow combined his activities in Oporto with being a wine merchant in York, of which he became sheriff. In 1727 he wrote an interesting little book on wines, and he was a notable antiquary. Early in the twentieth century the company was bought by Walter and Alfred Gilbey. They had strong links with the Gonzalez family who kept a bodega specially for them. In 1962 W & A Gilbey Ltd merged with two other companies to form International Distillers and Vintners, which eventually became part of Diageo. Croft Jerez was established in Jerez separately in 1970 and was able to take over the *soleras* of old wine then held for them by Gonzalez Byass. The new company achieved enormous commercial success with its Croft Original Pale Cream. One might say it is now back where it started.

Another subsidiary of long standing is Wisdom & Warter. It is said that if you repeat the name often enough you go mad, and in the nineteenth century Punch was pleased to say that Warter made the wine and Wisdom sold it –

which was true of the partners. Joseph Warter came to work for the Haurie bodegas in 1852, and two years later left to set up on his own taking Mr Wisdom into partnership. They prospered, though Mr Warter was a difficult man and made mistakes, the worst of which was to get rid of Alexander Williams, who left to found Williams & Humbert (*see* below). The bodega has long been a subsidiary of Gonzalez Byass, but has always been left to its own devices and operates independently under robust management.

JOHN HARVEY
See Domecq.

EMILIO HIDALGO
Clavel 29, 11402 Jerez de la Frontera, Cádiz.
Tel: +34 956 34 10 78; Fax: +34 956 32 09 22; Email: emidalgo@teleline.es
A small but well-established Jerez house whose main business is exporting cheap wines to the Netherlands, and is not to be confused with Hidalgo-La Gitana of Sanlúcar. It has some *soleras* of fine wines, which include Palo Cortado Privilegio (VORS) and Santa Ana Pedro Ximénez (VORS).

BODEGAS HIDALGO-LA GITANA
Banda de la Playa 42, 11540 Sanlúcar de Barrameda, Cádiz.
Tel: +34 956 38 53 04; Fax: +34 956 36 38 44;
Email: bodegashidalgo@lagitana.es.; Website: www.lagitana.es
One of the oldest-established bodegas in the sherry towns, now managed by the sixth generation of the family that has owned it since 1792. It produces wines of the highest quality notable for their finesse and lightness of touch. Going for quality rather than quantity, some of the vines in its extensive vineyards are eighty years old. La Gitana is a classic manzanilla. The mark Pastrana is used for single-vineyard wines, a manzanilla pasada, and an amontillado viejo (VOS). The mark Napoléon is used for some of the superior wines. VORS wines include Amontillado Solera Especial, Amontillado Vaedro, Palo Cortado Hidalgo, and Oloroso Vaedro – a remarkable range.

EMILIO LUSTAU
Calle Arcos 53, 11402 Jerez de la Frontera, Cádiz. Tel: +34 956 34 15 97; Fax: +34 956 34 77 89; Email: lustau2@a2000.es; Website: www.emilio-lustau.com
The Lustau family was French and founded the bodega in 1896. It operated on a small scale producing high-quality wines in historic bodegas on the city walls of Jerez. The great breakthrough came in 1981, when the late Rafael Balao, then manager, had the brilliant idea of introducing his *almacenista*

range. The word refers to the source of the wines, not to their style. An *almacenista* is a storekeeper or wholesaler. In all the sherry towns, some enthusiasts, often professional men such as doctors or lawyers, have had their own small bodegas with fine *soleras*. They never sold in bottle, but in bulk to the shippers, who bought them as required for their blends, some relying on them extensively. However, the shippers all had stocks of their own and, as demand fell, their requirements from the *almacenistas* grew less. The wines were still there and their quality first rate, but the quantity of each was quite small. Lustau bought, bottled, and put the wines on the market. The success was phenomenal, as connoisseurs came to realize how good sherry could be. Some of the other shippers then saw there was a special market for wines of this class and started to sell them too, to the benefit of all. It was clearly time for Lustau to expand, and it was sold to Luis Caballero in 1990 – he has the necessary capital – so it remains a family concern, but owned by a different family. There is now a range of fine quality sherries from the combined resources of the two companies. These include Jaranda Fino, Manzanilla Papirusa, Amontillado VOS, Oloroso VORS, the dessert wines East India Solera and Emperatriz Eugenia Solera, the Pedro Ximénez Solera Reserva San Emilio, and the Moscatel Solera Reserva Emilín. There are fewer *almacenista* sherries than there used to be, as some of the original suppliers have become shippers, but those remaining include: manzanilla amontillada (Jurado); Amontillado del Puerto (Obregon); palo cortado (Vides); Oloroso del Puerto (Obregon); and Oloroso de Jerez Pata de Gallina (Jarana). The names in brackets are those of the *almacenistas*. There are also some single-cask vintage wines of amontillado, palo cortado, Pedro Ximénez, and Moscatel.

PEDRO ROMERO

Trasbolsa 84, 11540 Sanlúcar de Barrameda, Cádiz.

Tel: +34 956 36 07 36; Fax: +34 956 36 10 27;

Email: pedroromero@pedroromero.es; Website: www.pedroromero.es

Founded in 1860, the present owners are the sixth generation. Once the bodega was on the seashore, but the sea has receded and it is now inland. Its excellent manzanilla is Aurora, and it has a fine range of VORS wines: Don Pedro Romero amontillado; Prestige Hijo de Pedro Romero Villareal palo cortado; and Don Pedro Romero oloroso.

PILAR ARANDA/BODEGAS DE A DOMECQ

Alamos 23, 11401 Jerez de la Frontera, Cádiz.

Tel: +34 956 33 96 34; Fax: +34 956 34 04 02;

Email: alvarodomecq@alvarodomecq.com; Website: www.alvarodomecq.com

Formerly an *almacenista* dating from 1730, this small bodega was bought in 1998 by Alvaro Domecq after his family firm went to Allied. At present it operates on a small scale, but with fine wines, notably fino La Janda; the 1730 range of amontillado, palo cortado, oloroso; and Pedro Ximénez, Amontillado AD (VORS), and Oloroso Alburejo (VORS).

HIJOS DE RAINERA PÉREZ MARÍN

Misericordia 1, 11540 Sanlúcar de Barrameda, Cádiz. Tel: +34 956 31 95 64;

Fax: +34 956 31 98 69; Email: laguita@laguita.com; Website: www.laguita.com

This bodega occupies a historic building that was once a hospital, and is noted for its manzanilla La Guita, the market leader in Spain. It owns the Bodegas M Gil Luque in Jerez, producing a notable range of VORS wines: Amontillado de Bandera; Palo Cortado de Bandera; Oloroso de Bandera; and Pedro Ximénez de Bandera.

BODEGAS OSBORNE

Fernán Caballero 7, 11500 El Puerto de Santa María, Cádiz.

Tel: +34 956 86 90 90; Fax: +34 956 86 90 78;

Email: comunicaciones@osborne.es; Website: www.osborne.es

This important bodega is another still family-owned. Best known for its range of brandies, its trade mark is the great black bull. Despite the ban on roadside advertising, the bulls are still seen adorning the hilltops of Spain; but the name Osborne has had to be painted out and the bulls are now classified as sculptures. Thomas Osborne arrived in Cádiz from Devon in 1781 to join a firm of merchants, Duff Gordon. Until 1890 all the wines were sold under the Duff Gordon name, but in that year they decided to enter into the Spanish market and to make brandy, which they did under their own name, as Duff Gordon is unpronounceable in Spanish and Osborne is easy – they just sound the last e. The Duff Gordon brand is now discontinued. Its wines have always been good, and a few years ago it introduced some very special ones. It ships an excellent manzanilla, Fino Quinta, Fino Amontillado Coquinero, Amontillado Seco Solera AOS, Oloroso Bailén, and four fine dessert wines: Premium Oloroso 10RF; Oloroso Solera India; Palo Cortado Abocado PdeltaP; and Pedro Ximénez Viejo (VORS).

MARQUÉS DEL REAL TESORO

See José Estévez, above.

REY FERNANDO DE CASTILLA

Jardinillo 7-11, 11404 Jerez de la Frontera, Cádiz. Tel: +34 956 18 24 54; Fax: +34 956 18 22 22; Email: bodegas@fernandodecastilla.com

A boutique bodega with excellent quality wines including Antique Amontillado, Antique Oloroso, and Antique Pedro Ximénez.

SÁNCHEZ ROMATE HERMANOS

Lealas 28, 11403 Jerez de la Frontera, Cádiz. Tel: +34 956 18 22 12; Fax: +34 956 18 52 76; Email: generencia@romate.com; Website: www.romate.com

With a history going back to 1781, this bodega is still happily independent. Although it is best known in Spain for its high-quality brandies, it has some excellent sherries. The very best are the Sacristía range including Amontillado La Sacrisía (VORS), Oloroso La Sacristía (VORS), and Pedro Ximénez La Sacristía (VOS); and the Reservas Especiales, including Amontillado NPU, Oloroso Don José, and Pedro Ximénez Cardenal Cisneros.

SANDEMAN JEREZ SL

Pizarro 10, 11403 Jerez de la Frontera, Cádiz. Tel: +34 956 15 17 00; Fax: +34 956 30 35 34; Email: the.don@sandeman.com; Website: www.sandeman.com

George Sandeman was a member of an old and prominent Scottish family. In 1790 he left for London with a £300 loan from his father and the affirmed intention of making his fortune, which he abundantly did. He hired a wine cellar, and it continued as a family firm for many years, then became a public company and, after having belonged to Seagram for a time, was bought by the Portuguese company Sogrape. For many years its wonderful trade mark, the *don* in the black cape, was seen all over Spain; but when poster advertising was banned, although Gonzalez Byass got its little *torero* and Osborne its great black bull classified as sculptures, which were allowed to stay, the *don* somehow got missed out, to the loss of all. In 2005 much of the old bodega was sold off and the winemaking passed to Ruiz-Mateos (*see* above), but it retained the *soleras* of old wine and kept a visitor centre. Amontillado Royal Esmeralda (VOS), Pedro Ximénez Royal Ambrosante (VOS), and the rich dessert wine Royal Corregidor (VOS) are excellent.

BODEGAS TRADICIÓN

Plaza Cordobeses 3, 11407 Jerez de la Frontera, Cádiz. Tel: +34 956 16 86 28; Fax: +34 956 33 19 63; Email: recarpet@arrakis.es

A fascinating creation set up by three members of old Jerez families who, in 1998, bought a derelict bodega in the oldest part of the city and completely renovated it, filling it with very old wines bought from bodegas that had been absorbed or ceased trading, and created their own top-quality *soleras*. The wines include Tradición Amontillado (VORS), Tradición Oloroso (VORS), and Tradición Pedro Ximénez (VOS).

BODEGAS WILLIAMS & HUMBERT SL

Carretera N-IV km 641.75, 11408 Jerez de la Frontera, Cádiz.

Tel: +34 956 35 34 00; Fax: +34 956 35 34 08;

Email: williams@williams-humbert.com; Website: www.williams-humbert.com

Alexander Williams was an ambitious clerk working for Wisdom & Warter. He was told that he would never be taken into the partnership, and so decided to start up on his own in 1877. He married Amy Humbert, and his father-in-law advanced the considerable sum of £1,000 on condition that his son should become a partner when he came of age. Mr Humbert wrote to his son "…if the firm fails I shall lose my £1,000 and as to Williams and Amy all will be destruction. You must, therefore succeed…" It did. It rose to be in the big league, just behind Domecq, Gonzalez Byass, and Osborne. Like so many English family companies, it had to go public to avoid the ruin of death duties and succumbed to a takeover bid by Ruiz-Mateos in 1972. Following the appropriation of the Ruiz-Mateos empire by the Spanish state in 1983, it endured a period of rudderless state management until it was bought by Barbadillo in 1988, which sold it on to become part of Grupo Medina started by two enterprising brothers in Sanlúcar in 1970. Alas it has had to move from its beautiful buildings in the centre of Jerez to a highly efficient concrete structure on the edge of the town. Historically its success was founded on the medium sherry Dry Sack, and this name has now become its principal mark. It has some excellent wines including Dry Sack Fino (formerly called Pando), Solera Especial Amontillado 30 Años, Jalifa (formerly Solera Especial Amontillado 20 Años) (VORS), palo cortado Dos Cortados, Solera Especial Palo Cortado 20 Años (VOS), oloroso Dry Sack Solera Especial 15 Años, and Don Guido (formerly Solera Especial Pedro Ximénez 20 Años) (VOS).

WISDOM & WARTER

See Gonzalez Byass.

MONTILLA-MORILES
Geography

The two towns of Montilla and Moriles lie in the province of Cordoba and are surrounded by low hills in the area shown on the map. The "superior" zone is in the middle. It is roughly a square of fifty kilometres (31 miles). The wine may also be aged and blended in the city of Cordoba, but few are. The vineyards are at an altitude of 125–690 metres (410–2,264 feet).

Climate

Being well inland, this is distinctly continental, with cold winters and long, hot summers. Temperatures can rise as high as 45°C (113°F) in summer and fall to -6°C (21°F) in winter, but the yearly average is a pleasant 17°C (62.6°F). It is also relatively high, so when the days are hot, the nights can be cool. The average rainfall is 625 millimetres (24.6 inches), most of which falls between November and April. There are some 2,900 hours of sunshine.

Soils

The best vineyards in the superior zone are *albariza*, similar to those of Jerez, white in appearance and high in chalk, though here they are called *albero*. Surrounding this zone there are the border areas, or Ruedos, where there is less calcium and more sand, giving a higher yield of less delicate wines, usually olorosos.

Grapes

The classic vine here is the Pedro Ximénez, which ripens fully and attains very high sugar levels for *vinos generosos*. For making table wines the grapes are picked earlier. The other variety for *vinos generosos* is the Moscatel. In addition, Lairén (Airén), Balardí, Montepila, Torrontés, Riesling, Chardonnay, and Sauvignon Blanc are grown for table wines.

Planting

The vines are grown as bushes, mostly in the *marco real* or square pattern, the old spacing being 1.67 metres (5.5 feet) but now usually two metres (6.5 feet). They are pruned *a la ciega*, with a fruiting top and buds at each end. The maximum density of planting allowed is 3,600 vines per hectare. Growing in bushes helps to protect the vines from the intense sun; if they were grown on wires it would be necessary to irrigate.

Vineyard Area

10,082 hectares.

Authorized Yield

60hl/ha in the superior zone and 80hl/ha elsewhere. In practice the yield is usually twenty per cent less.

Wines

There are three categories: *vinos jóvenes afrutados*, which are sold within a year of production at a strength of 10–12% ABV; *solera* (formerly called *crianza*) wines, sold as "pale dry", "medium dry", "pale cream", "cream", etc., at a strength of 13–15% ABV; and higher strength *solera* wines sold everywhere except in the UK (as explained later) as fino, amontillado, oloroso, and Moscatel, with a strength of over 15% ABV, classified as *vinos generosos*. The DO, however, unlike Jerez, has been broadened to include table wines, which will be described separately at the end of this section.

Production

193,365 hectolitres (2003).

Vintages

These influence the table wines, but there is not much difference between vintages, which are usually rated 4 or 5. For the *vinos generosos*, any differences are evened out by the method of maturation, so vintage years are irrelevant.

In a country of beautiful vineyards, those of Montilla-Moriles are among the most attractive. It is a landscape of low hills and wide, delightful views. Montilla is a charming old town on a hilltop, with fine old houses, impressive bodegas like those of the sherry towns, and vines growing right up to the town walls. Moriles, in contrast, is rather a dump. While the superior zone is largely planted with vineyards, in the rest of the area there is mixed farming, many olive trees, and hilltop villages, which add considerably to the enchantment of the place. Generally speaking the wines grown in the area of Montilla are light and of great finesse, while those grown near Moriles tend to be bigger. Some of the best wines are made by blending from the two styles and are very good indeed. The *jóvenes* are table wines.

It is the tragedy of Montilla-Moriles that it has always, metaphorically speaking, lain in the shadow of sherry. It is easy to see why. The sherry shippers had easy access to the sea; and until 1933 no distinction was drawn between the two districts, so that shippers in the sherry towns bought the wines and sold them throughout the world as sherry. The wines were Andalusian, very similar in style, and of equal quality. Some were used for feeding sherry *soleras* and others for making sherry blends. Either way they added nuances of their own and increased the range of styles available. In particular the Pedro Ximénez grapes attained a higher degree of ripeness in the warmer climate and were invaluable for the preparation of sweet wines. PX can still be brought into the sherry DO, and it is the best of its kind. The others, however, could no longer be sold as sherry. Montillas had to make their way in the export markets and it was an uphill task, made all the more difficult by that swing in the pendulum of fashion that, for the time being, has taken strong wines out of favour. This is a great pity, for the wines are very good and unjustly underrated. They deserve better.

The difference in style between Montilla and sherry is easy to detect, but hard to describe. The clue lies in the word amontillado. Sherries of this style were so named because they resembled Montilla, but in fact it went much further than that: many of them in the past actually came, wholly or in part, from Montilla-Moriles. But anyone who knows what amontillado tastes like will have some idea of the difference between Montilla and sherry. Even in Montilla finos it is easy to detect a touch of the amontillado character.

The preparation of Montilla is so similar to sherry that to set it out would be repetitive. There used to be one striking difference, but it is now at least partly historical. In the past the wine used always to be fermented in *tinajas*. These are huge vessels, originally made of earthenware, but for many years now made of concrete. At the time of the vintage they are a wonderful sight with the must fermenting and bubbles bursting from the brim. Today about half the wine is still fermented in this way, the other half being fermented in temperature-controlled stainless steel tanks like everywhere else. These are more prosaic, but the temperature control is a good deal better. But even after fermentation in stainless steel, the wine is passed into *tinajas* to complete its slow fermentation before being fed into the *criaderas*.

Apart from this difference, what has been written about sherry applies. The bodegas look very similar, though in the hotter climate some of the more modern ones are air-conditioned. They all contain impressive structures of oak butts containing the *soleras* and *criaderas* of the *generosos*, which work in exactly the same way. The finos grow under *flor*, and have a similar *flor* nose with that subtle difference mentioned above. The styles they develop are the same, too: fino (15–17% ABV); amontillado (16–22% ABV); palo cortado (16–20% ABV); and oloroso (16–20% ABV), which are blended in the same way to make creams and dessert wines. There are also varietal wines of excellent quality made from Pedro Ximénez and Moscatel grapes (15–18% ABV).

In the UK, though, there is a difference in the way they can be labelled and it is less than fair. The sherry shippers had long used those words, descriptive of the styles, to distinguish their own wines. When a Montilla shipper (now defunct) started to use them in England, the sherry shippers brought a passing-off action against him. It was never fought out. Lacking resources, he caved in and gave undertakings to desist. The Montilla shippers regard themselves as bound by this and anyhow do not want to invite devastatingly expensive litigation, so the words are not used. The sherry shippers tried a similar action in Spain, but there they failed as the Spanish courts held, on ample evidence, that the Montilla shippers had been using them for years. In the result, Montilla shippers cannot describe their wines on export markets as amontillado, though it was from them that the name was derived. It remains to be seen whether EU directives will alter things. In the meantime they will continue to be described simply as dry, medium, or cream, which is exasperating for the shippers and not very helpful to the drinkers.

There is another thing that differentiates them from sherry: with the exception of the varietal dessert wines, they are not usually fortified, as the very ripe Pedro Ximénez grapes are full of sugar, and give wines of 15% ABV when fermented. If the level of alcohol is too high, this can be corrected with wine from the other varieties. Finos are marketed with 15–17.5% ABV, and the amontillados and olorosos from 16–20% ABV. An old oloroso can even go up to 22% ABV.

Some leading bodegas

ALVEAR
María Auxiliadora 1, 14550 Montilla, Córdoba. Tel: +34 957 65 01 00;
Fax: +34 957 65 01 35; Email: info@alvear.es; Website: www.alvear.es
This is undoubtedly the leading bodega and easily the strongest in the export markets. It was founded in 1729 by Diego de Alvear y Escalera and is still owned by his descendants. His assistant was Carlos Bilanueva, who put his initials CB on the casks containing the choicest wines, and they are now immortalized as a brand name. Wines include Fino CB, Capataz Fino, Carlos VII Muy

Viejo Amontillado, Asunción Oloroso, Alvear PX Solera 1830 Reserva, and some vintage wines. It is also active in Extremadura and Argentina.

DELGADO
Cosano 2, 14500 Puente Genil, Córdoba. Tel: +34 957 60 00 85; Fax: +34 957 60 45 71; Email: fino@bodegasdelgado.com; Website: www.bodegasdelgado.com
Founded in 1874, its wines include Secunda Bota Fino, 1874 Amontillado Natural Muy Viejo, 1874 Oloroso Viejo, and 1874 Pedro Ximénez.

GRACIA HERMANOS
Avenida Marqués de la Vega de Armijo 103, 14550 Montilla, Córdoba.
Tel: +34 957 65 01 62; Fax: +34 957 65 23 35;
Email: comercial@bodegasgracia.com; Website: www.bodegasgracia.com
Founded in 1959, in the late 1980s it became a member of the same group as Perez Barquero (*see* below), but is run independently. It is the market leader in Spain. Its fino is María del Valle, an old amontillado, sold under the name Montearruit, and other mature wines under the mark Tauromaquia.

PEREZ BARQUERO
Avda Andalucía 27, 14550 Montilla, Córdoba. Tel: +34 957 65 05 00; Fax: +34 957 65 02 08; Email: export@perezbarquero.com; Website: www.perezbarquero.com
Founded in 1905, this is now part of a group that includes Gracia Hermanos (above). Although its bodegas are beautiful and old fashioned, it is right up with modern technology and does all its fermentations in temperature-controlled stainless steel. Its wines are very good indeed, notably the Gran Barquero range.

CONDADO DE HUELVA
Geography

Vines used to be the predominant crop throughout the whole of the area shown on the map, but the amount planted has been declining for many years and there are now only isolated vineyards, most of them near Bollullos del Condado, Manzanilla (not to be confused with the sherry), and Chucena. Lying in the province of Huelva, it extends down to the Atlantic and, at its eastern edge, just into the Parque Nacional de Doñana, where the marshes of the Marismas del Guadalquivir form one of the greatest nature reserves in Europe. The vineyards are from sea level to twenty-five metres (eighty-two feet). The sherry vineyards are on the other side of the estuary.

Climate

Being so far south, this is as much Mediterranean as it is Atlantic, but the Atlantic breezes and the proximity of the sea have a moderating influence. The average temperature is 18°C (64.4°F), with a maximum of 28°C (82.4°F) and a minimum of 9°C (48°F), though it sometimes falls lower and frosts are not unknown. Rainfall is 500–800 millimetres (19.7–31.5 inches) but is liable to Atlantic vagaries, with twice the annual average in 1996 after five years of drought. There are 3,000 hours of sunshine.

Soils

There is a certain amount of *albariza*, mostly around Manzanilla and Chucena, which gives the highest quality and lowest yield, but most of the soils are reddish in appearance, consisting of sand and clay, with some *barros*.

Grapes

The special local variety is the Zalema, whose high yield endears it to the growers, but which also results in rather neutral and diluted wines. They would be well advised to reduce the yield drastically, but are disinclined to do so. Despite the efforts of the *consejo regulador* to replace it, it still occupies some eighty-six per cent of the vineyards and is likely to stay that way. Next in importance are the authorized (and encouraged) varieties, the Palomino with its close relation the Listán, and the Garrido Fino. There is a very small amount of Moscatel and Pedro Ximénez.

Planting

The old vineyards are planted in a rectangular pattern with 0.6 metres (two feet) between the vines and 2.5 metres (8.2 feet) between the rows. They are pruned in the same way as the traditional sherry vineyards: *vara y pulgar*. This pattern makes mechanical cultivation, even with miniature tractors, difficult; it is one of the very few places where horses can still be seen in regular use. They are slow and the plough is easily controlled, as the ploughman walks behind it, allowing safe cultivation right up to the vines. More modern vineyards are planted in rectangles with wider spacing of 3.25 x 1.5 metres (10.6 x 5 feet) to allow for mechanical cultivation with possible mechanical picking in the future. A few are cultivated on wires. The maximum permitted densities are 2,500 per hectare for bushes and 3,000 per hectare for wires.

Vineyard Area

5,311 hectares (2003), a decline from a historic figure of 21,000.

Authorized Yield

60hl/ha for young whites, otherwise 70hl/ha, but it is typically rather less, about 50hl/ha.

Wines

Since 1984 the emphasis has been on *joven afrutado*, a light white "table wine". Traditionally, however, the district has grown *vinos generosos*. These are of two kinds: the Pálido, a fino style at 15.5% ABV and the Viejo, an oloroso style fortified to 17% ABV and which can go up as high as 24% ABV.

Production

113,286 hectolitres (2003).

Vintages

These are immaterial for the *vinos generosos*. For the table wines there is some variation from one year to another, but as they are intended to be drunk in the year they are made, there is no point in investigating the qualities of past vintages.

To visit the smaller bodegas in Condado de Huelva is to walk into a time warp. They are rather like the very smallest bodegas in Jerez forty years ago. Admittedly the larger ones have modern equipment, but it is used largely for the "table wine". The *vinos generosos* are made with loving care, as they have always been. They have a loyal local following, but it is clearly a trade in decline and one fears that it may be in terminal decline. It needs a vigorous enthusiast with a great deal of money and marketing skills to put it on its feet again. Such people do exist and they are active all over Spain, making the new generation of table wines, but there is none here. And such a person looking at *vinos generosos* would be more likely to look at sherry or Montilla. Many of the bodegas are in the enchanting little town Bollullos del Condado, but others are found throughout the area.

Wine has been grown here, as in almost all of Spain, from time immemorial. It had a rare moment of glory in the fifteenth century. The Monasterio de la Rábida lies near the coast at the western end of the delimited area. It was here that Christopher Columbus was sheltered and prayed before he set off from an island near Palos de la Frontera to discover the New World. His ships were provisioned with the local wine and so it is probably safe to say that Condado de Huelva was the first wine to be drunk in the New World, even before sherry; but no distinction was drawn between them in those days. Hence the badge of the modern *consejo regulador* bears the sail of a galleon and a bunch of grapes.

Condado de Huelva is suffering, like sherry and Montilla, from the decline in popularity of wines of this kind – but more so, as they have never had a serious export market nor have they been distributed nationally in Spain. Up to 1933, when the sherry district was delimited, their principal market was in the sherry towns, where they were blended in with the cheaper grades. Now they have lost even that market. *Condado* is derived from *conde*, or count, so it is the county of Huelva. To the west there is the Rio Tinto, with its minerals, to the east the Coto Doñana, and to the south there are magnificent Atlantic beaches, full of holidaymakers at weekends. It is an agreeable countryside of mixed agriculture, olive trees, pines, cork oaks, and above all, strawberries. It is the strawberries that make the money, and as the vineyards decline, the strawberry fields increase; but whether this will continue at the same giddy pace is doubtful, as there are now so many of them that the price has gone down. Lepe, mentioned by Chaucer, is vineless and surrounded by strawberries. There is hope, though. Some of the new vineyards are very serious and the Andrade bodega has a particularly fine one.

There are two traditional kinds of *vinos generosos*. *Condado pálido*, a fino style from Palomino and Garrido Fino grapes, generally fermented without temperature control either in vats or in *tinajas*, known locally as *conos*. They are then aged in American oak butts for a minimum of two years. They are frankly rather feeble things compared with the finos of Jerez or Montilla and have been likened to the *pálidos* of Rueda – themselves a dying species. They make a pleasant drink in the local bars, but not one to seek out. The other kind is *condado viejo*, usually from Zalema grapes. Fermented in the same way, they can attain a natural strength as high as 15% ABV. They are matured on ullage in oak casks for the same minimum time and are fortified to as much as 23% ABV. The best of them are much older. Matured on ullage by oxidation in the *solera* system, they resemble oloroso sherries and can be good, especially when slightly sweetened. Shippers usually have a cask or two of really old wines and these can be very good indeed, vast in flavour and with considerable depth. These really are worth seeking out but hard to find. There are also some good palo cortados. Although most of the olorosos are vinified from Zalema grapes, some of the best are from the other varieties. As with Montilla, however, and for the same reason, the terms fino, palo cortado, and oloroso cannot be used in export markets.

Some leading bodegas

Bodegas Andrade (look for the dry oloroso Doceñero), Iglesias, Jaime Oliveros, Privilegio del Condado (look for *fino* Mioro and *oloroso* Botarroble), and A Villarán (look for solera 1934).

MÁLAGA AND SIERRAS DE MÁLAGA

Geography

The city of Málaga is a port and a holiday centre. All Málaga wine is matured there, but the vineyards are split between two totally distinct areas. The smaller is on the coast, around and behind Estepona. It grows mostly Moscatel grapes. The second, which is much larger, includes Málaga itself and stretches to the east and north right up into the mountains. This is further sub-divided into three areas. Molina is to the northwest, around the town of that name, growing mostly Pedro Ximénez. Axarquía lies along the coast between Málaga and Nerja, stretching inland to the border of the province of Granada, where the vines are mostly Moscatel. The third, smallest and best, is Mountain, right up in the north around Cuevas de San Marcos, where the grapes are predominantly Pedro Ximénez. For Sierras de Málaga the principal area is Serranía de Ronda at an altitude of 500–1,000 metres (1,640–3,280 feet).

Climate

Down by the coast it is Mediterranean and most agreeable, with an average temperature of 18.5°C (65.3°F) and 3,000 hours of sunshine. But up in the mountains it is distinctly continental: hot in summer and bitterly cold with frosts in winter. The average rainfalls are 400 millimetres (15.7 inches) in Axarquía, 550 millimetres (21.6 inches) in Molina, and as much as 810 millimetres (31.8 feet) in the Mountain, where the average temperature is only 13.2°C (55.7°F); but the whole area has recently been experiencing droughts and deluges. In the mountains there are wide temperature variations between day and night. Some of the Axarquía vineyards are as high as 2,000 metres (6,562 feet).

Soils

In so large an area it is not surprising that these are bewildering in their variety. Around the coast it is alluvial, with clay, quartz, and mica. In Molina it is ferruginous clay with chalk. In Axarquía it is gravelly with chalk. In the Mountain it is mainly limestone with thin layers of sand and clay in the subsoil.

Grapes for Málaga

White varieties: The predominant, traditional grape is the Pedro Ximénez, here known as the Pedro Ximén. There is also Moscatel de Alejandría, Moscatel Morisco, Lairén, and Doradilla.

Grapes for Sierras de Málaga

White varieties: Pedro Ximénez; Moscatel; Chardonnay; Macabeo; Sauvignon Blanc; Lairén; Doradilla; and Colombard.
Red varieties: Romé; Cabernet Sauvignon; Merlot; Syrah; Tempranillo; Garnacha; Cabernet Franc; Pinot Noir; and Petit Verdot.

Planting

Grown mostly in squares (*marco real*) of 2.25 metres (7.4 feet) though more recent plantings have been 3 x 1.5 metres (9.8 x 4.9 feet) and some Pedro Ximénez is grown on wires.

Vineyard Area

1,172 hectares.

Authorized Yield

80hl/ha.

Wines for Málaga

Twelve types of wine and seven descriptive terms are recognized:
Lágrima: (literally "tears") wine traditionally made from free-run must, but nowadays coming from a first, very light pressing.
Pálido: wine from fully fermented grape juice.
Seco: wine that has been fermented out so that it contains less than five grams per litre of sugar. Wines of this kind are often referred to as olorosos, which is

a perfectly fair description, but is unofficial and cannot be used on the export markets for the usual reason. The strength varies from 15–23% ABV.

Abocado: fairly sweet with 5–50gms/l of sugar.

Añejo: 3–5 years in cask.

Trasañejo: more than five years in cask.

Semi-seco: the same as *abocado*.

Dulce: sweet wine with about 600 grams per litre of sugar.

Dulce Pedro Ximén and **Dulce Moscatel:** sweet varietal wines.

Dulce Lágrima: a *dulce* made from *lágrima* must.

Noble: must have spent 3–5 years in cask.

The descriptive terms are: *blanco* (white); *dorado* (golden); *rojo-dorado* (red-gold); *oscuro* (dark); *negro* (black – in fact very dark); *crema* (cream); *pajarete* (semi-sweet). They are 15–22% ABV in strength.

Wines for Sierras de Málaga

White 10–15% ABV, *rosado* 11–15% ABV, red 12–15% ABV. They can go up to *gran reservas*.

Production

50,000 hectolitres (2003).

Vintages

Because of the way the wine is matured, these do not matter for Málaga. They may well matter for Sierras de Málaga, but these are early days.

Málaga and Sierras de Málaga are two totally different things. The first dates back to the earliest days of Spanish wines, and the DO from 1933, with a long and fascinating history, but an unhappy recent past. The second is a new creation dating from 2001 and faces an interesting future that at the moment is a matter for hope and speculation. They must be considered together, though, as they both fall under the control of the same *consejo regulador* and share the same geographical area. First, Málaga.

Málaga is a sad story. Its wines were once very popular, but now they are sharing in the fate of all *vinos generosos*. Although sold throughout Spain they do not have much of a presence on the export markets, which is a pity, as they can be very good. In Elizabethan times they were known as Malaga- (or Maligo-) Sack and were rivals to Sherris-Sack. In the seventeenth century they were helped by having a customs rebate denied to wines shipped through Cádiz. When Sherry suffered a serious decline in the eighteenth century, Málaga flourished and enjoyed a golden age. The best wine was sold as Mountain, which is where it came from. Elegant silver decanter labels so inscribed are now, alas, seldom used for their original purpose. The decline set in during the nineteenth century and has gone on ever since. In 1876 Málaga had the very doubtful distinction of being the first Spanish vineyard to be invaded by phylloxera, and the destruction became almost total. From a production of 32.5 million litres in 1880, it had practically disappeared by 1886. But by then Málaga was already in a decline. In the hundred years from 1878–1978 the vineyard area decreased to one tenth. Most were not replanted and those that were had other calls on their fruit: raisins and table grapes, particularly the Moscatel. There were other catastrophes. One of the best export markets was Russia, and this collapsed with the Revolution. Then it suffered grievously in the Spanish Civil War, when nearly all the wine was taken by the troops, most of it stolen. Spain was bankrupt and potential export markets had, for the time being, gone. Málaga rose from its ashes but never really got going again and is now suffering the ravages of fashion. Many of the shippers went bankrupt, one of the greatest losses being the old-established house of Scholtz Hermanos, which made some of the finest wines and whose stocks were bought by Larios.

Most of the vineyards are small, though some of the shippers have substantial estates, notably Lopez Hermanos. Despite the wine's decline in popularity, there is a shortage of Pedro Ximénez and up to ten per cent of the total requirement is allowed to be brought in from Montilla-Moriles. To make the traditional sweet wines the grapes are dried on *esparto* grass mats in the sun. It is very labour-intensive, especially as they have to be covered over at night to avoid dilution by dew or rain, so that the practice has disappeared from the sherry vineyards; and the shrivelling of the grapes results in low yields. The sugar content is so high, though, that it does not all ferment out and gives a sweet wine called *vino maestro* (literally master wine). Though sweet wines are made mostly by stopping fermentation with alcohol and are called *vino tierno* (literally soft wine). *Dulce natural* is made from a fifty-fifty mixture of the two. Another agent used for blending is *arrope*: must boiled down to a third of its volume to make a dark syrup. The leading shippers, who aim at more subtle styles of wine, avoid using too much as it imparts a burnt taste.

All Málaga has to be matured in bodegas within the city. It can attain

15% ABV naturally, but is usually fortified to 18% ABV, using *vino borracho* (literally "drunken wine") made from a mixture of equal parts wine and alcohol, before maturation. They are matured for at least two years in oak casks, but these are generally full, so the oxidation is gradual. It is typical to draw out about a third of the wine at a time and to fill in the void, but a full *solera* system is used only for making the oldest and most expensive wines. The Sierras de Málaga wines are a recent development - still considered experimental table wines. Some may be good, as they are grown in high, relatively cool vineyards, but growers must find out which grapes work best.

Some leading bodegas

LARIOS

César Vallejos, 24 Poligono Industrial Guadalhorce, 29004 Málaga.
Tel: +34 952 24 70 56; Fax: +34 952 24 03 82; Email: asantana@priarios.es
This large concern, now a subsidiary of Pernod Ricard, is famous for its gin and other spirituous drinks, but also produces some excellent Málagas.

LOPEZ HERMANOS

Canadá 10 Poligono Industrial El Viso, 29006 Málaga. Tel: +34 952 31 94 54;
Fax: +34 952 35 98 19; Website: www.lopezhermanos.com
Owned by the de Burgos López family, this bodega was founded in either 1885 or 1896. Whichever is true, it is old established and successful. Among its fittings are two vast casks made of red pine from the Russian steppes, dating from when Russia was the principal export customer. Its fine *finca* is at 500 metres (1,640 feet). The Málaga Virgen has a very sweet impact, but enough acidity to give an unexpectedly dry aftertaste and prevent it from being cloying. For the beautifully fragrant Moscatel Reserva de la Familia the grapes are sunned for ten days and then gently pressed to give one litre of wine for every four kilos of grapes, the wine then given two years in Allier oak. There are also some very good table wines.

TELMO RODRÍGUEZ

See Ribera el Duero. This admirable peripatetic winemaker is active in Málaga to good effect, making delightful, light Moscatel wines labelled Molino Real, which he claims is what Málaga once was like and ought to be like again.

OTHER WINES

Most of Andalucía's table wines have no DO, but two of the DOs have expanded their definitions to include them: Montilla-Moriles and Condado de Huelva. Throughout Andalucía summers are hot, and only ten or twenty years ago one would have expected the wines to be of a very southern style: lacking in acidity, with little fragrance, flabby, and uninteresting. This is no longer so, thanks largely to the availability of temperature-controlled fermentation and the understanding that, to get the acidity that table wines require, the grapes have to be picked early. Although no great table wines have yet emerged, there are now plenty of very acceptable ones.

MONTILLA-MORILES

The DO regulations include white "table wines" and these are among the best grown in Andalucía. They were started in the late 1970s to mitigate the damage caused by the dwindling sales of *vinos generosos* and have been a great success. To make them, Pedro Ximénez grapes are picked early, in August, and the must is given a low-temperature fermentation to retain the fruitiness. The resulting wines are light, fragrant, and most agreeable. They are not wood aged and are intended to be drunk young.

CONDADO DE HUELVA

The white "table wine" (*blanco joven* or *blanco afrutado*) is a small part of the production, but is likely to become more important. The principal grape is the local Zalema. Some growers would experiment such classic European varieties as Chardonnay and Riesling, but say that everyone is growing them and that they want to retain their individuality. It is a pity the local grape is so disappointing. For table wines the grapes are picked in August and the must is cool fermented. They tend to resemble a very dilute fino, and although pleasant enough, are unexciting. There is not a lot of choice among the various shippers.

VdlT CÁDIZ

Owing to the decline in sherry sales, many of the good *albariza* vineyards are now used for table wine that, because it needs no maturation, is more profitable and therefore is here to stay. It has not, however, been incorporated into the sherry DO. Aside from these vineyards, where sherry could legally be produced, a wide variety of grapes are grown for table wine in the same general area, but outside the sherry zone. Although the Palomino vine produces glorious sherries, it makes rather poor, bland table wines. It can produce good, if unexciting, wines, as Antonio Barbadillo has proved with his Castillo de San Diego, successful in Spain and abroad. Other active sherry shippers include J Ferris, Osborne, and Hijos de Rainera Pérez Marín.

ANDALUCÍA

The exquisite little town Arcos de la Frontera is well outside the sherry area, but vines there produce wines that are very similar. One grower, Bodegas Paez Morilla, deserves special mention. Its small bodega in Jerez produces sherry (and some remarkably fine sherry vinegar), but its most interesting vineyard is in the hills outside Arcos. It started to produce white "table wine" in 1979 and, disappointed in the wine it got from Palomino, planted Riesling, which though hard to grow has certainly added another dimension to the wine it sells as *tierra blanca*. A large part of the vineyard is planted with red wine varieties, including Tempranillo, Garnacha, and Cabernet Sauvignon. Several other varieties, both red and white, are being tested. Sold as Viña Lucia, the red wine is agreeable, but lacks intensity. Young wines drawn from the oak tasted very promising and these should get better as the vines age and techniques are refined. It is worth keeping an eye on.

VdIT GRANADA SUROESTE

The mountains around Granada provide many microclimates suitable for vine growing, as they are cool by night with strong sun by day. This rapidly expanding area is attracting much investment and vast planting efforts.

Some leading bodegas

H CALVENTE

18699 Jete, Granada. Tel/Fax: +34 958 64 41 79; Email: bodegasmar@arrakis.es
Good sweet wines are made from old Moscatel vines that used to provide table grapes and are pruned right back for quality, just leaving a stump; but Cabernet Sauvignon, Syrah, Merlot, and Tempranillo have been planted recently, providing impressive reds that are clearly capable of ageing. The 2000 was from forty per cent Cabernet Sauvignon, thirty-five per cent Syrah, twenty per cent Merlot, and five per cent Tempranillo.

SEÑORÍO DE NEVADA

Carretera de Cónchar s/n, 18569 Villamena, Granada. Tel: +34 902 30 00 28; Fax: +34 958 77 70 62; Email: bodegas_nevada@teleline.es
This began as a family winery growing Tintilla de Granada, probably a clone of Tempranillo. The vineyard is at 600–700 metres (1,968–2,296 feet) and the beautiful *finca* has twenty-one hectares, mostly Merlot with Cabernet Sauvignon and Syrah. It produced no wine in its first five years but started to take off in 2000. These are big, opulent wines with ageing potential.

12

The Islands

The two groups of islands covered in this section – the Balearics and the Canaries – have almost nothing in common save that they are both Spanish. The former is in the Mediterranean, the latter in the Atlantic and much further south. Only one of the Balearics grows wines in commercial amounts: Mallorca. The Canary Islands have between them no fewer than ten DOs. But something else that they have in common is that they drink nearly all their wine themselves, assisted – if not overwhelmed – by the enormous number of tourists, for whom they cater. Mallorca exports only a very small amount and the Canary Islands export even less, though they are now making efforts to enter the export markets. However the many visitors who drink the wines on the spot find lots that are interesting and (especially in Mallorca) an increasing number that are very good. The Canary Islands are particularly strong in sweet wines. Exports are for two countries whose tourists have been introduced to the wine on their holidays: Britain and Germany.

MALLORCA

Mallorca was once a kingdom with territories that stretched as far as the south of France. Although it is now clearly a part of Spain, it has retained a proud independence despite historic links with Cataluña. The English used to spell its name with a j instead of ll, though no one seems to know why. The Mallorcan language (Mallorquín, which is widely and increasingly spoken) is very similar to Catalán, and the island has much in common with the neighbouring mainland; but the wines are very different, and the growers are emphasizing the individuality of their wines by concentrating on long-established local varieties: Manto Negro and Callet for reds, and Moll for whites. The great Spanish vine Tempranillo does well here, too, as in so many other places. International varieties are, of course, also grown. Cabernet Sauvignon and Merlot have shown their remarkable ability to adapt and add backbone to the blends that include them. They have recently been joined by Syrah, which promises well. Although the Burgundian varieties Pinot Noir and Chardonnay are also grown, the former cannot at the moment be recommended and the latter only with reservations. Pinot Noir is notoriously difficult both to grow and to vinify, while Chardonnay needs a long, slow period of ripening that the Mallorcan climate just does not provide. There are two DOs, Binisalem-Mallorca and Plá i Llevant de Mallorca, and another wine-growing area that is unclassified, near Andraitx. Local wines can be found on restaurant lists, but are not so easy to find in the shops, as most of them are sold direct, though serious wine shops have sprung up in the last few years and are well worth seeking, notably La Vinoteca (C/Padre Bartolomé Pou 29) in Palma. You get what you pay for, and on the whole the cheap local wines are best avoided. At the beginning of the nineteenth century there were 35,000 hectares of vines on the island. Late in the century they were wiped out by phylloxera and have never recovered. Today there are 2,000 hectares. The once famous vineyards, growing Malvasías on the west coast, have long since disappeared.

BINISALEM

Geography

The vineyards are in the middle of the island on a plain north of Palma at an altitude of 75–200 metres (246–656 feet), sheltered by the mountains from the northerly winds.

Climate

Mediterranean, with summer temperatures going up as high as 35°C (95°F) and fairly mild winters, though it can go down to freezing point. The average temperature is 16°C (60.8°F). There are 2,800 hours of sunshine and about 450 millimetres (17.7 inches) of rainfall, mainly in the autumn. The vineyards are sheltered from the north winds by mountains.

Soils

Not very fertile, with some limestone over clay, and rich in calcium.

Grapes

Red varieties: Manto Negro (of which DO red wines must contain at least fifty per cent); Callet; Tempranillo (Ull de Llebre); Monastrell; Cabernet Sauvignon; Syrah; and Merlot. The first two are the traditional grapes.

White varieties: Moll (Prensal Blanco); Parellada; Macabeo; Moscatel; and Chardonnay. Only the first is traditional.

To qualify for the DO, red wines must contain at least fifty per cent Manto Negro, with a maximum of thirty per cent for Cabernet Sauvignon, Syrah, and Merlot. Whites must have at least seventy per cent Moll. Moscatel wines must contain at least seventy per cent of the Moscatel varieties. There are some experiments with drip irrigation. Clonal selection is taking place to select the best strains of the native vines. As a general rule, Manto Negro (often written as one word) tends to produce wines that are low in acid, high in alcohol, and with a tendency to oxidize, while Callet give higher yields, less alcohol, and more colour.

Planting

Traditional vineyards are planted in a rectangular pattern 2.4 x 1.2 metres (7.9 x 4 feet), but some of the newer ones are on wires. There are 1,700–3,500 vines per hectare.

Vineyard area

Officially 419ha, with 384 registered as being in production, though there are 508 in all.

Authorized yield

Red varieties: 7,500kg/ha, except Callet, which is limited to 9,000, and Cabernet Sauvignon, which is limited to 6,500.

White varieties: 9,000kg/ha, except Parellada, which can go up to 10,000. Unfortunately the most recent regulations are expressed in this way. The amount of wine produced per kg varies but it takes roughly 140kg to produce one hectolitre, so 10,000kgs/ha corresponds roughly to 71hl/ha. Actual production is usually less.

Wines

Red *crianzas* must be matured for at least two years, of which at least six months must be in oak casks of less than 1,000 litres. They go up to *reservas*, which must have a year in wood with a total of three years' ageing, and *grandes reservas* require two years in wood and three in bottle, but they account only for one per cent of the production. The maximum strength is 14% ABV. White wines must have a minimum strength of 10.5% ABV and *rosados* 11% ABV, with maxima of 13% ABV and 13.5% ABV respectively. These are sold as *jóvenes* and are not given a malolactic fermentation.

Production

8,000 hectolitres.

Vintages

1990 (4); 1991 (3); 1992 (3); 1993 (3); 1994 (5); 1995 (4); 1996 (3); 1997 (4); 1998 (5); 1999 (4); 2000 (4); 2001 (4); 2002 (3).

Binisalem is the local spelling. In Castillian there is only one s, and going back to the Arabic root, this is probably right. Over the years, though, it can be found spelled in all sorts of ways. The wines were highly regarded in Roman days and kept their reputation, so that Al Henderson in his *History of Modern Wines* (1824), wrote:

> The island of Majorca furnishes several wines of sufficiently good quality to bear exportation; among which those made in the district of Benesale, three leagues from Palma, are accounted the best, at least of the red growths. The vintage, however, is not treated in the most judicious manner; the grapes being fermented for fifteen or twenty days in deep stone cisterns, into which they are introduced at repeated intervals, so that the operation is frequently checked in its progress, and is seldom fully completed. When it is thought to have ceased, the liquor is drawn off into large tuns, containing five or six pipes each; and there the secondary fermentation, as might be expected, is often so violent as to burst the vessels, though made of olive staves four inches in thickness, and bound with hoops proportionally strong.

Wine production reached its peak between 1866–1890, when vines were planted in quite unsuitable places to sell vast quantities of very poor wine to the phylloxera-stricken French. Then, in 1891, phylloxera came to Mallorca and wine production collapsed, but never disappeared. The vineyard area went down suddenly from 30,000 hectares to 5,000 in 1900. The wines of Binisalem retained a good reputation, but it was much abused. Unscrupulous merchants used to import wines from the mainland, which were of very mixed quality, and sell them as the real thing, to the intense indignation of the serious local growers. This state of things happily ceased with the creation of the DO in 1991, thanks largely to the efforts of the very reputable grower José Ferrer, who used to put "*autentica*" on his labels to distinguish his wines from the bogus ones.

Conditions nowadays are very different from those described by Henderson. The bodegas are full of gleaming stainless steel and the wines, which in the past were somewhat musty, are now completely clean. The whites and *rosados* are very acceptable and may well grow better as new techniques are mastered. In particular there are experiments with giving the whites wood contact and even wood fermentation. The best whites are unexpectedly light and have good acidity. The reds have long been worth looking for and might well have been sought out much more had people realized how well they age; though the quality of the corks used until quite recently did not encourage this. They are not wines that immediately call out for ageing, as some do; but given the chance to age they do so very gracefully and gain a lot in complexity. A 1959 Ferrer Reserva had developed beautifully by 1972, but by 1992 had been let down by its cork. Nowadays the corks are much better.

Some leading bodegas

JOSÉ L FERRER (FRANJA ROJA)

Conquistador 103, 07350 Binisalem, Balears. Tel: +34 971 51 10 50; Fax: +34 971 51 10 50; Email: info@vinosferrer.com; Website: www.vinosferrer.com

This bodega, which is by far the biggest, was founded in 1931 and for years was the only quality producer on the island. It is still family-owned. It has some seventy-eight hectares of vines and still makes some of the best wines. Modest quantities are exported. Its red wines are particularly good. They make sensible use of oak, rotating the barrels over five years and having a notable variety: Nevers; Tronçais; Romanian; Caucasian; and some from east and central Europe. The 2001 *crianza* was made from fifty-eight per cent Manto Negro, twenty-one per cent Cabernet Sauvignon, fifteen per cent Tempranillo, three per cent Callet, and three per cent "others". The Cabernet gives an extra dimension of backbone, and the oak, which was prominent when it was young, soon melded in, resulting in a delightfully balanced, relatively light wine. The 2000 *reserva* was made from sixty-two per cent Manto Negro, twenty-eight per cent Cabernet Sauvignon, eight per cent Tempranillo, and two per cent "others". Fermented for fifteen days at 32°C (89.6°F), it had its malolactic and maturation in American oak. It is good, well structured, and has considerable complexity. Its top wine is Reserva Desmil Especial, made from sixty-two per cent Manto Negro, twenty-eight per cent Cabernet Sauvignon, eight per cent Tempranillo, and two per cent Callet. Only the best grapes are used, fermented for eighteen days at 30°C (86°F), and aged for twenty-one months in American, French, and central European oak. It is bottled in immensely heavy bottles and the label is by the artist Luis Maraver. It is highly individualistic, undoubtedly fine, with complexity and considerable ageing potential. It sells a separate range under the name Veritas, which is only for restaurants. The barrel-fermented white Veritas 2002, made from ninety per cent Moll and ten per cent Parellada, is good, but the *reserva* 1999, made from sixty-five per cent Manto Negro with Tempranillo and Cabernet Sauvignon was outstanding, with remarkable complexity and length.

HEREUS DE HERMANOS RIBAS

Camí de Muntanya, s/n, 07222 Consell, Balears.

Tel: +34 971 62 26 73; Fax: +34 971 62 27 46; Email: hhribas@hotmail.com

This small bodega has a history going back to 1711, which makes it the oldest on the island, but the present family company dates from 1986. It used to be called *"Herederos"* (heirs), but everything is being translated nowadays. It has forty hectares of vineyards with 100 more under contract. It is notable for using exotic grape varieties and makes good wines. They include a good *rosado*, and some very agreeable whites, but perhaps the best are the reds. The Hereus de Ribo was made from fifty-seven per cent Manto Negro, twenty-seven per cent Cabernet Sauvignon, eleven per cent Syrah, and five per cent Merlot. The Sió Collita 2001 was made from fifty-five per cent Manto Negro, twenty-five per cent Cabernet Sauvignon, and twenty per cent Syrah. Many of the wines are sold under the trade mark Sió. It also makes some good wines outside the DO.

JAUME DE PUNTIRÓ

Plaza Nova 23, 07320 Santa María de Camí, Balears.

Tel: +34 971 62 00 23; Fax: +34 971 62 00 23.

Founded in 1981, this small, family-owned bodega with eleven hectares of vineyard consistently produces good quality wines.

MACIA BATLE

Camí de Coanegra s/n, 07320 Santa María del Camí, Balears. Tel: +34 971 14 00 14; Fax: +34 71 14 00 86; Email: correo@maciabatle.com; Website: www.maciabatle.com

Founded in 1998 by members of a family that had been making wine for 150 years, this well-run bodega has got into its stride producing individualistic wines with good ageing potential. It has forty hectares of vines with another 100 under contract. The *crianza* 2001 came from vines more than twenty-five years old, seventy per cent Manto Negro, with Callet and Cabernet Sauvignon, and matured for ten months in American and French oak. It was a great mouthful, with soft tannins and considerable length, needing a year or two in bottle to reach its peak. The Pagos de María 2001 came from vines more than fifty years old, fifty-nine per cent Manto Negro, twenty-one per cent Cabernet Sauvignon, sixteen per cent Syrah, and four per cent Merlot, was given thirteen months' wood ageing, almost entirely in French oak, and was 13.8% ABV. Tasted when newly bottled, it had great personality and needed to age for some years before reaching its peak. There is an excellent, crisp *rosado*.

PLÁ Y LLEVANT DE MALLORCA

Geography

The name means the plain and coast of Mallorca. It covers the plain in the centre and east of the island and includes an area once known as Felanitx. It used to be a catch all for interesting winemakers who lay outside the area of Binisalem, but in 2001 it was granted DO status.

Climate

As Binisalem.

Soils

A considerable variety, but they tend to be deep and reasonably fertile.

Grapes

Red varieties: Callet; Fogoneu; Tempranillo (Ull de Llebre); Manto Negro; Monastrell; Cabernet Sauvignon; Merlot; and Syrah. The Callet is more prominent in this area, whereas the Manto Negro predominates in Binisalem.

White varieties: Prensal Blanc (Moll); Moscatel; Macabeo; Parellada; and Chardonnay.

Vineyard area

276 hectares.

Authorized yield

Chardonnay: 7,000kg/ha. Other whites 11,000kg/ha. Indigenous reds 10,000kg/ha. Cabernet Sauvignon and Merlot 9,000kg/ha. Unfortunately the new regulations are expressed in this way. The amount of wine produced per kg varies, but it takes roughly 140kg to produce 1hl, so 10,000kg/ha corresponds to about 71hl/ha. In practice the yield is about 50hl/ha.

Wines

White, red, *rosado*, sparkling, and fortified.

Production

9,983 hectolitres.

Vintages

1998 (5); 1999 (4); 2000 (5); 2001 (4); 2002 (3).

This used to be a very vague area of about 1,000 hectares. Since the coming of the DO it is much smaller and more clearly defined. In the past, the red wines were the most highly rated and they can indeed be good, particularly blends containing Cabernet Sauvignon and Tempranillo or, more recently, Syrah. But Pinot Noir does not at present seem to come off; it is a difficult vine and very particular about where it is grown. The white wines can be good, too, notably dry Muscats. There are also some popular *rosados* and *agujas* (lightly sparkling white wines). Some growers are experimenting with sparkling wines.

Some leading bodegas

CAN MAJORAL

Carrer Campanar s/n, 07210 Algaida, Balears. Tel/Fax: +34 971 66 58 67;
Email: bodega@canmajoral.com; Website: www.canmajoral.com
A young but noted bodega dating from 1994, it goes for ecological viticulture. Its wines are sold mostly under the name Butíbalausí.

JAUME MESQUIDA

Calle Vileta 7, 07260 Porreres, Balears. Tel: +34 971 64 71 06; Fax: +34 971 16 82 05; Email: info@jaumemesquida.com; Website: www.jaumemesquida.com

Founded in 1945, this family bodega was the first to establish a reputation for imported varieties and to market monovarietal wines. It has twenty-five hectares of vineyards and produces a wide range that include a barrel-fermented Chardonnay, varietal Cabernet Sauvignons, both red and *rosado*, and a varietal Syrah, as well as sparkling wines.

MIQUEL GELABERT

Salas 50, 07500 Manacor, Balears. Tel/Fax: +34 971 82 14 44; Email: info@vinsmiquelgelabert.com; Website: www.vinsmiquelgelabert.com

A progressive family bodega established in 1985 that is justly proud of its Chardonnays. Blanc Sa Vall is an unusual white made from ninety per cent Riesling and ten per cent Gewürztraminer. Its two best reds are Gran Vinya San Caules, which in 2001 was made from seventy-five per cent Callet and five per cent each of Manto Negro, Cabernet Sauvignon, Merlot, Syrah, and Fogoneu, and Torrent Negre Barrica, which in the same year was made from forty per cent Cabernet Sauvignon, thirty-five per cent Syrah, and twenty-five per cent Merlot. It also makes a highly praised varietal Syrah and a good Muscat.

TONI GELABERT

Camí dels Horts de Londra km 1.3, Son Fangos, 07500 Menacor, Balears. Tel/Fax: +34 971 55 24 09; Website: www.vinstonigelabert.com

A small family bodega founded in 1979 with five hectares of Biodynamically cultivated vineyards. The red wines are matured for 12–15 months in French and American oak, while the Chardonnay is fermented and matured for three months in French oak. Torre d'es Canonge is similarly made, but using the rare Giro Blanc grape. Ses Peres is a varietal Riesling. There are also varietals of Cabernet Sauvignon, Merlot, and Syrah, while Torre d'es Canonge Negra is made from Pinot Noir, Merlot, and Syrah. The wines are highly praised.

MIQUEL OLIVER

Font 26, 07520 Petra, Balears. Tel/Fax: +34 971 56 11 17; Email: miqueloliver@miqueloliver.com; Website: www.miqueloliver.com

Founded in 1912, it has ten hectares, with twenty more under contract. It is semi-ecological (*i.e.* employs as little treatment as possible) and makes a wide range of wines. Mont Ferrutx Negra 2003 is very good value, made from Callet and Foganue. Its best red is Ses Ferritges, the 2001 made from thirty per cent each of Cabernet Sauvignon, Callet, and Merlot, and ten per cent Syrah, show-ing complexity and ageing potential. The Gran Chardonnay (made only in one year out of three) is one of the best of this variety grown on the island. Its best white is the dry Muscat, made from Moscatel de Alejandría and Moscatel de Grano Menudo; it is dry but has all the attractive nose and flavour of Moscatel. The San Caló 2003 is a varietal Prensal with a good nose, its somewhat south-ern bulk being well balanced with acid.

VINOS de la TIERRA

This vague denomination covers various areas that fall outside the two DOs and is also used by growers for wines that fall outside DO regulations in a catch-all *Vinos de la Tierra de Illes Balears*. There is one specific area in Mallorca.

Some of the best wines of this category are made by Bodegas Ribas (*see* above). Its Ribas de Cabrera 2000 was made from a number of unspecified varieties and was remarkably good; the 2001 was made from fifty per cent Syrah, forty per cent Manto Negro, and ten per cent Cabernet Sauvignon, matured in seventy per cent new and thirty per cent old French oak; again an excellent wine and one with ageing potential. It also makes a very suc-cessful Chenin Blanc. Wines from this bodega are well worth seeking out.

Some leading bodegas

AN NEGRA VITICULTORS
30 Volta 18, 07200 Felanitx, Balears.
Tel: +34 971 58 44 81; Fax: +34 971 58 44 82; Email: annegra@hotmail.com
A bodega of modest size with twenty-five hectares of vineyard that produces consistently good wines, mostly from Callet.

FINCA SON BORDILS
Carretera Inca-Sineu km 4, 07300 Inca, Balears. Tel: +34 971 18 22 00;
Fax: +34 971 18 22 02; Email: info@sonbordils.es; Website: www.sonbordils.es
This property claims to trace its history back to 1433. Some of its vines are clones selected from the south of France. The wines have a high reputation and the Syrah 2001 (with nine per cent Monastrell) is a splendid great thing.

SERRA DE TRAMUNTANA-COSTA NORD

This falls between Cape Formentor and Andratx and includes a number of microclimates comprising seventeen hectares that produce 688 hectolitres from the usual grape varieties.

ILLA DE MENORCA

This agreeable island is rather windswept and wetter than Mallorca with over 600 millimetres (23.6 inches) of rainfall and deep, brown, chalky soils. The usual vine varieties are grown, but the best reds are made from Merlot and Cabernet Sauvignon, while the best whites are the Moscatels.

IBIZA

Called Eivissa in Mallorquín, this island is much favoured by holidaymakers and is hotter and drier than Mallorca. Its twenty hectares of vineyards, producing sixty-nine hectolitres, are found in the valleys of the two small mountain ranges. The traditional grape for red wines is Monastrell, though there are now varietals from Cabernet Sauvignon, Merlot, and Syrah. The traditional grape for whites is the Macabeo, though there are now also Malvasía and Chardonnay.

FORMENTERA

The smallest of the Balearic islands has a sub-tropical climate with a rainfall of 450 millimetres (17.7 inches), falling to 300 millimetres (11.8 inches) in the north. The usual vine varieties are grown widely on sandy and clay soils.

THE CANARY ISLANDS

The early history of the Canary Islands is fascinating, stretching back to before the Christian era. Ptolemy put his meridian line through the isle of Hierro, at the edge of the known world in AD 150. The Romans paid a visit and found the island of Fuerteventura full of wild dogs, so they called it Insula Canum (Dog Island), later corrupted to Las Islas Canarias in Spanish and the Canary Islands in English. Descendants of the dogs are still there. They were also known as The Fortunate Isles. Thereafter they disappeared into the mists of mythology, and although expeditions reached them in the thirteenth and fourteenth centuries, the first serious expedition took place in 1402. They were coveted by various powers, but by 1496 were firmly Spanish and have been so ever since. It is at this time that the story of wine begins. It is said that the first vines came from Crete to produce the Malvasía of Lanzarote, known in England as Canary Sack. When Sir John Hawkins made his second voyage to the West Indies in 1564 he recorded that the wines were better than any in Spain; and when in 1583 Thomas Nicholas published, *A pleasant Description of the Fortunate llands called the llands of Canaria*, he wrote glowingly of the wines of Gran Canaria and Tenerife, but of Hierro he said, "...there is no wine.... but only one vineyard that an Englishman of Taunton in the West Countrie planted among rockes, his name was John Hill."

When Shakespeare wrote *The Merry Wives of Windsor* (c.1600), he knew Canary Sack as well as Sherris-Sack, for the Host of the Garter Inn was given the line, "Farewell, my hearts: I will to my honest knight Falstaff, and drink canary with him." By then it was so highly favoured that it became the usual *douceur* given by the Spanish to English officials from whom they expected a favour. In 1634 Lord Cottington and Sir Francis Windebank were each given a tun of Canary wine by the Spanish agent in London; and the Parliamentarians liked it as much as the Royalists, for Giles Greene, chairman of the Navy Committee, received two casks in 1644. Not surprisingly English merchants settled there, and in 1683 sought to ship wine direct to New England instead of via England as wines were being "clandestinely imported under the Notion of Madeira Wines". By 1687, 12,000 pipes were exported to England annually, but the trade had begun to decline. The wine was dear, it had fallen out of fashion, French wine had become the "modish liquor", and, not least:

> ...the much adulteration of it by the mystery of vintners and Coopers... having stoakt the cuntry with such trash brewed wines under the Notion of Canarys that the Gentry and others when [they] come to towne, come pre-possessed with a Prejudice against that noble liquor Canary.

How often has a like story been told! But unlike sherry, Canary disappeared for ever. When Cyrus Redding published his *History of Modern Wines* (1833), he wrote, "Canary was once much drunk in England, and was known only by that name. The writer of this tasted some which was 126 years old, it having been kept during all that period in the family cellars of a nobleman, with whom he happened to be dining, and who produced a bottle, its contents little more than a pint, as a *bonne bouche*. Its flavour was good, and it had ample body." It must originally have been sweet and strong. *Sic transit gloria.*

There have been great changes, and they have all happened recently. New winemakers have arrived and with modern equipment. Here, as all over Spain, there are stainless-steel tanks and temperature-controlled fermentations. So there is a new generation of light table wines of all colours that are delicious to drink locally. But some of the old pattern remains. The wines are generally expensive, so there is never likely to be much of an export market, and the most exciting are still the sweet Malvasías. But the islands have the great advantage that they are remarkably free from disease, and phylloxera has never struck. The result is that old varieties that have long since disappeared elsewhere are still to be found, and the visitor can find himself in a time warp, drinking wines that have not existed anywhere else for a couple of hundred years. Other varieties were kept out to avoid the importation of phylloxera, but they are now coming in after quarantine. It remains to be seen whether they will eventually supplant the old varieties or enhance them.

Situated so far south, seasonal differences are not as marked as they are in Europe, though they can be significant in the higher vineyards, and there are many microclimates; nor is there much variation in the daylight hours, which range from a minimum of ten hours eleven minutes to a maximum of thirteen hours forty-nine minutes, and the weather is less affected by dramatic changes than it is, for example, in Madeira. The environment for wine growing is therefore most unusual and vintage years largely irrelevant.

There are seven main islands in the archipelago and six small ones, but wine growing is only significant on Tenerife, El Hierro, Lanzarote, and La Palma.

TENERIFE

Vinously this is the most exciting island. It has six DO areas and also grows VdlT wines. They appear below in alphabetical order.

ABONA

Geography

This is in the extreme south of the island, the vineyards varying in altitude from 200–1,600 metres (656–5,249 feet), averaging 600 metres (1,968 feet) on the slopes of Spain's highest mountain, Mount Teide (3,715 metres/12,188 feet). The area of the zone is 1,936 hectares, but only 935 are planted.

Climate

Summer high 35°C (95°F), winter low -5°C (23°F). Average rainfall 400 millimetres (15.7 inches), but much less in some vineyards and up to 550 millimetres (21.6 inches) in others; irrigation is allowed. There are 2,500 hours of sunshine.

Soils

There are many. In the valleys there is clay, sand, limestone, marl, and volcanic ash. Over 600 metres (1,968 feet) they are volcanic, giving good wines but small yields.

Grapes

Red varieties: Bastardo Negro; Cabernet Sauvignon; Castellana Negra; Listán Negro; Listán Prieto; Malvasía Rosada; Moscatel Negro; Negramoll; Pinot Noir; Rubí Cabernet; Syrah; Tempranillo; Tintilla; and Vijariego Negro.

White varieties: Bastardo Blanco; Bermejuela; Forastera; Gúal; Malvasía; Listán Blanco; Moscatel; Pedro Ximénez; Sabro; Torrontés; Verdello; and Vijariego.

Listán Blanco accounts for about sixty per cent of the vines and Listán Negro for about thirty-five per cent.

Authorized yield

70hl/ha, but in practice much less.

Wines

Mostly white, but with some red and *rosado,* and a minute amount that are fortified. The minimum strength for white and *rosado* is 11.5% ABV, for red 12% ABV, and for *vinos de licor* 15% ABV. All are *jóvenes.*

Production

The average is said to be 5,000 hectolitres but this is probably an exaggeration.

Although first alphabetically, this area was the last to get official recognition and cannot as yet be regarded as of any great importance. It is really a combination of two quite distinct areas with the dividing line at 600 metres (1,968 feet) altitude. The best wines come from the highest vineyards, which go up to 1,700 metres (5,577 feet). Most are made in three cooperatives.

Some leading bodegas

VINICOLA CUMBRES DE ABONA
Camono del Viso s/n, 38589 Arico, Santa Cruz de Tenerife. Tel: +34 922 76 86 04; Fax: +34 922 76 82 34
The biggest cooperative, founded in 1989, whose members own 300 hectares. It makes only whites and *rosados*, and exports ecological wines to Germany and Switzerland.

EL TOPO
Finca Frontos, Lomo Grande 3, Los Blanquitos Ctra TF28 km 70.2, 38600 Granadilla de Abona, Santa Cruz de Tenerife. Tel/Fax: +34 922 77 72 53
Makes good white and red wines.

TACORONTE-ACENTEJO

Geography

The area is in the northwest of the island, twenty-three kilometres (14.3 miles) long. The main road from Santa Cruz de Tenerife to the tourist resort of Puerto de la Cruz passes through it. The vineyards are on north-northwest terraces facing the sea, 200–800 metres (656–2,624 feet) above sea level.

Climate

The Atlantic influence gives a humid and temperate climate, occasionally disturbed by hot winds from Africa; the average temperature is 16°C (60.8°F), rising to 30°C (86°F) in summer and falling to 12°C (53.6°F) in winter. The rainfall is low, at 200–300 millimetres (7.9–11.8 inches), but mists, light drizzle, and heavy dew ensure that the vineyards are adequately watered. The relative humidity is sixty per cent. The average sunshine is 2,500 hours.

Soil
Reddish, fertile loam with a little chalk over a volcanic sub-soil.

Grapes
Red varieties: Listán Negro; Negramoll; Malvasía Rosada; Moscatel Negro; Negra Común; and Tintilla.
White varieties: Gúal; Listán Blanco (which predominates); Malvasía; Marmajuelo; Forastera (Gomera Blanca); Moscatel; Pedro Ximénez; Verdello; Vijariego; and Torrontés.

Planting
There is a unique local practice of trailing the vines along the ground and providing supports where necessary. New vineyards, however, are being planted on the double cordon system. The maximum density is 3,000 per hectare.

Vineyard area
2,500 hectares.

Authorized yield
70hl/ha, but in practice much less.

Wines
Red, *rosado*, and white wines are produced, most of which are *jóvenes*, but there are now some *crianzas* and *reservas*. Some red wines are fermented in oak, some are made by carbonic maceration, and only the reds go through a complete malolactic fermentation. The most important production is of reds, accounting for about eighty-five per cent of the total, some of which have a little wine from white varieties blended in. The whites are between 10–13% ABV, but some old style whites are made between 12–14% ABV. The *rosados* are between 10.5–13% ABV. The reds are between 12–14% ABV. There are also some *vinos de licor* between 15–22% ABV. Wines sold as varietals have to be 100 per cent of the variety named.

Production
1,6500 hectolitres (2003).

This was the first district in the Canary Islands to get its own DO, and it remains both the most important and the most ambitious. All the wines are pleasant and some are more than that. The whites are easy to drink, the *rosados* can be excellent, and the reds range from the passable to the impressive. Apart from the DO wines there is a special local wine that I must confess I have never tasted but would like to: *vino de tea. Tea* is the local name for the Canary pine; it also means firebrand and is used idiomatically to indicate intoxication. These are vinified from the Albillo and other varieties. They are fermented in 500-litre pine barrels and are often kept for years in troglodyte wineries so that they come to resemble *rancios*. They are not bottled but can be bought at the door or in bars.

Some leading bodegas

BODEGAS BUTEN

San Nicolás 122, El Sauzal, Santa Cruz de Tenerife. Tel: +34 922 57 32 72; Fax: +34 922 56 18 15; Email crater@bodegasbuten.com

A small bodega founded in 1998 that exports part of its output. Its Cráter 2003, made from seventy per cent Listán Negro and thirty per cent Negramoll, gained high praise.

EL LOMO (AFCAN)

Carretera El Lomo 52, 38280 Tegueste, Tenerife.
Tel: +34 922 54 52 54; Fax: +34 922 24 15 87;
Email: afecan@bodegaellomo.com; Website: www.bodegaellomo.com

Founded in 1990, this estate has nine hectares of vines, mostly Listán Negro, and produces red and white wines, including a red made by carbonic maceration. For the whites it is experimenting with both stainless steel and barrel fermentation.

INSULARES TENERIFE

Vereda del Medio, 8B - 38350 Tacoronte, Santa Cruz de Tenerife.
Tel: +34 922 57 06 17 Fax: +34 922 57 00 43;
Email: bitsa@bodegasinsularestenerife.es; Website:
www.bodegasinsularestenerife.es

A modern bodega founded in 1992, it is an SAT acting as a cooperative for 600 growers, making it by far the biggest bodega on the island and producing some of the best wines of all colours. They are sold under the names

Viña Norte and, for the whites, Humboldt. Some of the reds are made by carbonic maceration, and the straightforward Viña Norte is a good example. There are also *crianzas*, its finest being Selecciónada. Some red and white wines are also sold under the name Brezal, and the white, made from Listán, is a very good expression of that grape.

LA ISLETA

José Rodríguez Amador 21, 38260 Tejina-La Laguna, Santa Cruz de Tenerife.

Tel: +34 922 54 18 05; Fax: +34 922 54 00 82

Produces some of the best white wines in the island, particularly sweet ones.

MONJE

Camino Cruz de Leandro 36, 38359 El Sauzal, Santa Cruz de Tenerife.

Tel/Fax: +34 922 58 50 27; Email: monje@bodegasmonje.com;

Website: www.bodegasmonje.com

A modern bodega founded in 1956 by a family with wine-growing traditions stretching back to 1750. It has fourteen hectares of old-established vineyard, 500 metres (1,640 feet) above sea level, growing Listán Blanco, Listán Negro, and Negramoll. The basic red *joven* contains a small proportion of Listán Blanco. Hollera Monje is a good red made by carbonic maceration. The red Monje de Autor *crianzas* and *reservas*, each dedicated to someone notable in the arts, are good, interesting wines that are hard to find but well worth seeking. Its white wines can be good, too, the Evento being barrel fermented. It has a good sideline in vinegar.

VALLE DE GÜÍMAR

Geography

The vineyards are on the arid south-facing slope of the volcanic Teide peak, in a strip parallel to the coast along the motorway to Santa Cruz. It is really a continuation of the Abona region and has the same quality dividing line of 600 metres (1,968 feet) above sea level, the best vineyards being above it. In all they stretch from 200–1,500 metres (656–4,921 feet).

Climate

A summer average of 18°C (64.4°F) and a winter average of 12°C (53.6°F). Rainfall is 400 millimetres (15.7 inches). There are 2,900 hours of sunshine.

Soils

The terrain is very varied, but the soil mostly volcanic.

Grapes

Red varieties: Listán Negro and Negramoll, with some Malvasía Rosada.
White varieties: Listán Blanco (seventy-three per cent of the vineyard); Forastera (fourteen per cent); with small quantities of Malvasí; Moscatel; Gúal; Vijariego; Marmajuelo; etc.

Planting

This follows local traditions with many different styles of cultivation, but recently planted vineyards tend to be on wires.

Vineyard area

The total area is 913 hectares but only 883 are registered. These are the official figures, but others are quoted.

Authorized yield

70hl/ha, but in 1995 the actual yield was 13.33hl/ha.

Wines

Mostly white *jóvenes*, but also *rosados* and reds, with some of the reds seeing oak. The minimum strengths are: whites 10% ABV; *rosados* 10.5% ABV; reds 11.5% ABV; sweet wines 15% ABV; and sparkling wines 11% ABV. Some of the reds are made by carbonic maceration. The most recent development, since 1999, is the production of sparkling wines from the Listán Blanco.

Production

6,000 hectolitres (1995).

Split off from Abona, this is not as yet an area to be taken very seriously, though some of the white wines grown in the higher vineyards can be good. Traditionally, it was a place of small family vineyards producing old fashioned wines. Now there is a cooperative movement and new technology is moving in, so some interesting wines are emerging.

Some leading bodegas

ARCA DE VITIS

Chinguaro 26, 38500 Güímar, Tenerife. Tel/Fax: +34 922 51 25 52;
Email: arcadevitis@arcadevitis.com; Website: www.arcadevitis.com

Founded in 2003, with thirteen hectares of vines, so it is early days yet, but its first releases have been praised.

COMARCA DE GUIMAR

Carretera Subida Los Loros km 4, 38550 Arafo, Tenerife.
Tel/Fax: +34 922 51 04 37; Email: infor@bodegacomarcalguimar.com

Founded in 1991, it has some export trade and sells its wines under the name Brumas. Its white wines have been praised, and it also makes a sparkler.

VALLE DE LA OROTAVA

Geography

This is not a valley at all, but a famously beautiful vineyard area on the western foothills of the volcanic Mount Teide, extending from near sea level to 800 metres (2,625 feet) or more.

Climate

Notably humid with a rainfall of 650 millimetres (25.6 inches) and additional water from sea mists. A summer high of 28°C (82.4°F) and a winter low of 8°C (46.4°F) gives an average temperature of 15°C (59°F), with 2,600 hours of sun.

Soils

Very acid and generally volcanic with some clay.

Grapes

Red varieties: Bastardo Negro; Listán Negro; Malvasía Rosada; Moscatel Negra; Negramoll; Tintilla; and Vijariego Negra.
White varieties: Bastardo Blanco; Gúal, Forastera; Listán Blanco; Malvasía; Marmajuelo; Moscatel; Pedro Ximénez; Torrontés; Verdello; and Vijariego.
In practice the two Listáns account for practically the whole of the planting, and some of the other varieties are hardly found at all.

Planting

This is by a unique local method, along horizontal poles about 60 centimetres

(24 inches) above the ground. It is known as *cordón*, but is totally different from *cordón* training as practised in Europe. The density is 1,000–2,000 vines per hectare.

Vineyard area

The total is 926 hectares, but only 679 are in production.

Authorized yield

70hl/ha, but as usual this is not achieved in practice.

Wines

These are mostly white *jóvenes* made with no malolactic fermentation; there are also reds, including some *crianzas*, but practically no *rosados*. There are also some sweet wines. The minimum strength is 11% ABV for whites and *rosados*, 11.5% ABV for reds, and 15% ABV for sweet wines. The sweet wines are of two kinds: *vino dulce clásico* made from Malvasía and Moscatel grapes left to shrivel on the vine or partially dried by sunning; and *vino de licor* made by stopping the fermentation by the addition of alcohol. To be sold under a varietal name they have to be made from eighty-five per cent of that variety.

Production

5,175 hectolitres (1996).

Initially these wines were made by small growers who sold them in bulk, but now technology is moving in, more are being bottled, and quality is on the up. They need to go a lot further, though, before anyone need seek them out. The three largest producers are SAT Union de Viticultores Valle de Orotava, which sells its wines under the name Valleoro; El Penetente; and Bodegas Montijo.

YCODEN-DAUTE-ISORA

Geography

The DO is on the western tip of the island with two distinct orientations: north and west. In the north there is a mountain range that at first descends steeply and then more gradually until it ends in a fairly flat, low plain. In the west, it is much more irregular with mountains, ravines, and cliffs. The best wines generally come from the higher vineyards.

Climate

This is one of the warmest parts of the island, but it is impossible to define its climate as there are many different microclimates, depending on orientation and altitude. West-facing vineyards are generally hotter and drier than those facing north, the former having a rainfall of 200–300 millimetres (7.9–11.8 inches) and the latter 400–500 millimetres (15.7–19.7 inches). As you get higher, the temperature goes down and the humidity up. Taking the area as a whole, the average temperature is 19°C (66.2°F) with a maximum of 35°C (95°F).

Soils

Here again there is considerable variation, but they are generally sandy along the coast with some clay over the inevitable volcanic rock inland.

Grapes

Red varieties: Bastardo Negra; Listán Negro; Malvasía Rosada; Moscatel Negra; Negramoll; Tintilla; and Vijariego Negro.
White varieties: Albillo; Bastardo Blanco; Bermejuela (Marmajuelo); Forastera Blanca; Gúal; Listán Blanco; Malvasía; Marmajuelo; Moscatel; Pedro Ximénez; Sabro; Torrontés; Verdello; and Vijariego.
The Listán Blanco accounts for seventy-eight per cent of the vineyard and the Listán Negro for twenty per cent.

Planting

This is somewhat haphazard with two local forms of cultivation, but some of the more recent vineyards have wires. Most of the vineyards are small and cannot be cultivated by machinery. The density is from 2,000–3,400 vines per hectare. The altitude varies between 50–1,400 metres (164–4,593 feet).

Vineyard area

The total is 1,243 hectares, but only 435 hectares are planted.

Authorized yield

70hl/ha, but the actual yield in the 1995 vintage was 8.75hl/ha!

Wines

Whites, with a minimum of 11% ABV, account for fifty-five per cent; *rosa-*

dos, with a minimum of 11.5%, ABV for thirty per cent; and reds, with a minimum of 12% ABV, for fifteen per cent of the "table wine" production. All have a maximum strength of 14% ABV. Most are sold as *jóvenes.* But in addition there is a small production of *Malvasía clásico* made by sunning the grapes to produce a minimum of forty-five grams of sugar per litre, with a minimum strength of 15% ABV and a maximum of 22% ABV.

Production
About 2,250 hectolitres.

Known in the past as Icod de los Vinos, this area has one of the longest wine-growing traditions in the islands and used to be noted for those rich Malvasías, which now form only a small part of its production. The tradition here has been a large number of very small family bodegas making the wines as their grandfathers did and maturing them in chestnut casks until they are sold, but many of these have now disappeared. Although most of the bodegas are still quite small, they use modern technology to produce excellent wines. The *rosados* are particularly good. It is a very active, exciting, and expanding area; in 1992 there were only seven bodegas registered with the *consejo regulador*, but in 2004 there were twenty-seven. One of the leading producers is Bodegas Viñatigo, which produces a good white wine called Añaterve from a combination of Malvasía, Gúal, Marmajuelo, and Vijariego grapes, and an excellent Viñatigo Blanco Allier, oak-fermented but not overoaked. The local cooperative, Viña Donia, has 125 members with more than 600 hectares between them, and is making good wines. This district is worth watching.

Some leading bodegas

BODEGAS BILMA
Carretera al Teide desde Chío, km 0.5, Guía de Isora, Tenerife.
Tel: +34 922 850 641; Fax: +34 922 852 318
Email: tagara@bodegasbilma.com; Website: www.bodegasbilma.com
Sold under the name Tagara, the white wines are very well made, fragrant, with considerable finesse; they show what can be achieved with Listán.

BODEGAS VINATIGO
Calle Cabo Verde s/n, 38440 La Guancha, Tenerife. Tel: +34 922 82 87 68; Fax: +34 922 82 99 36; Email: vinatigo@vinatigo.com; Website: www.vinatigo.com

Founded in 1990, this bodega produces a wide range of wines and has an export trade. The reds include varietals from Listán Negro (one version of which is made by carbonic maceration), Negramoll, and Tintilla. The *rosado* is a varietal Listán Negro. The dry whites include varietals from Gúal, Marmajuelo, and Listán Blanco (one version of which is fermented in Allier oak) together with one made from four indigenous varieties: Bujariego, Gúal, Verdello, and Malvasía, sold under the name Añaterve. There is a sweet wine made from ninety per cent Listán Blanco and ten per cent Moscatel together with a very sweet, traditional varietal Malvasía. The best and most interesting of the whites is the Añaterve, but others are good, particularly the *rosado* and the Malvasía, which avoids being over-stated.

EL HIERRO

Geography
The most westerly and smallest of the Canary Islands. The vineyards are 125–700 metres (410–2,296 feet) above sea level.

Climate
It enjoys the benign Canary Islands climate, the temperature rising to a maximum of 28°C (82.4°F) in summer and falling to a minimum of 18°C (64.4°F) in winter, with widely varying rainfall of 125–525 millimetres (4.9–20.6 inches) and 3,000 hours of sunshine.

Soils
Volcanic with good water retention.

Grapes
Red varieties: Listán Negro; Vijariego Negro; Baboso Negro; and Negramoll.
White varieties: Vijariego Blanco; Bremajuelo; Baboso Blanco; Bual; Malvasía; Verdello; Pedro Ximénez; and Listán Blanco.

Planting
Mostly *en vaso*.

Vineyard area
192 hectares.

Authorized yield

18hl/ha.

Wines

Whites and *rosados* have a minimum strength of 11% ABV, and reds (with provision for going up to gran *reservas*) have a minimum strength of 12% ABV. Sweet wines have a minimum of 15% ABV.

Production

2,800 hectolitres (2004).

For centuries, before the advent of Greenwich (after some fierce competition from other places, notably Paris), El Hierro had the distinction of being the site of zero longitude, and it has a long vinous history going back to the days of Canary Sack; indeed some of the wines it produces today may well show what historic wine tasted like. Politically it is integrated with Santa Cruz de Tenerife. Although, unlike most of its bigger neighbours, it does have an export trade (to Venezuela), most of the wines are sold and drunk locally. There are nine bodegas, up from seven, and production is rising. They have modern equipment. The first vines are said to have been planted by John Hill in 1526.

Principal bodega

VIÑA FRONTERA

El Matorral s/n, 38911 Frontera, Tenerife. Tel: +34 922 55 60 16;
Fax: +34 922 55 60 42; Email: coopfreontera@cooperativafrontera.com;
Website: www.cooperativafrontera.com

A general cooperative dealing in all the island's agricultural produce. It was founded in 1986 and has 600 members. Its wines are mostly young whites sold under the mark Viña Frontera, but reds go up to a *crianza*. Its best wine is the sweet white Gran Salmor, which is given some oak ageing.

LANZAROTE

Geography

This is the most easterly of the islands, and an astonishing place. In the 1730s there was a volcanic eruption that lasted six years and left a vast expanse of black, solidified lava that grows nothing: the Timanfaya National Park. While the DO covers the whole island, it is divided into three sub-zones: La Geria in the south, Tinajo/San Bartolomé in the middle, and Haría in the north. Its highest peak is La Peña del Chache, which rises only to 670 metres (2,198 feet). The vineyards are on the mountain slopes.

Climate

Being nearest to Africa, this is unique. The temperature is very even, with a mean minimum of 16°C (60.8°F) and a mean maximum of 24°C (75°F), with an overall mean of 23°C (73.4°F). The rainfall, averaging 150 millimetres (5.9 inches), is very low, with the rain falling irregularly. When it does fall it is torrential, but the volcanic soil retains the moisture. The humidity is high, with a mean of seventy per cent, but when the east wind blows from Africa (and it can blow for a fortnight at a time), this goes down dramatically and the heat goes up. Even when this wind is not blowing, it is still a very windy place. There are 2,700 hours of sunshine.

Soils

Vines will not grow in the volcanic ash (*picón*), but the soils beneath it are fertile, ranging from sand to clay over limestone.

Grapes

Red varieties: Listán Negro (Negra Común) and Negramoll (Mulata).
White varieties: Burrablanca; Breval; Diego; Listán Blanco; Malvasía; Moscatel; and Pedro Ximénez.
Other varieties, however, may be found in old vineyards. Malvasía is the dominant variety.

Planting

This is extraordinary, and the only other vineyard practising anything remotely like it is Colares in Portugal. The vines have to be planted in the soil beneath the volcanic ash. To achieve this great pits known as *hoyas*, or trenches called *sanchas pedrimentales,* are dug. Some of these have to go down as much as six feet. One to three vines are planted in the bottom. Naturally this results in a very low density of planting: 200–600 vines per hectare. It is then necessary to make a pile of stones, known as an *abrigo*, to protect the vines from the prevailing wind. Some of these are walls and others look like pyramids.

Vineyard area

The total area of the zone is 3,567 hectares, but only 2,209 hectares are in production.

Authorized yield

35hl/ha, but in practice this is never approached.

Wines

All sorts are made: red (11–14.5% ABV); *rosado* (11–14% ABV); white (10.5–14.5% ABV); *vino dulce clásico* (15–22% ABV); *vino de licor* (15–22% ABV); and even some sparklers. *Vino dulce clásico* is made by leaving the Malvasía or Moscatel grapes on the vine until they are practically raisins or by sunning them. *Vino de licor* is made by stopping the fermentation by the addition of alcohol.

Production

10,240 hectolitres (2003).

This island is certainly unique in its wines and in the way it grows them. It is not surprising that many of the vineyards are forty years old or more. Planting is so labour intensive that new vineyards are likely only because it is the traditional family occupation and nothing else will grow. And it can be no wonder that the wines are expensive. Nowadays labour is drawn off into the flourishing tourist trade; but tourists drink wine. Most of the wine is white, and generally fairly or very sweet, from Malvasía grapes with some Moscatel. The many small proprietors used to vinify their grapes individually using old-fashioned methods, and the quality was usually not such as would appeal today. This was one of the homes of Canary Sack. Such wines are still made but now there are modern bodegas making lighter, more modern wines. The principal grape is still the Malvasía, though, and when this is vinified to give a dry wine the results are rather unusual: there is a striking degree of fragrance, but a degree of sheer bulk, even at 12% ABV, detracts from the finesse. Nevertheless they make agreeable drinking and there are some good sweet and semi-sweet ones.

There are nine bodegas in all, though there appear to be some very small ones not included in this figure.

Some leading bodegas

BODEGAS EL GRIFO

El Islote 121, 35550 San Bartolomé, Las Palmas de Gran Canaria.

Tel: +34 928 52 40 36; Fax: 928 83 26 34;

Email: bodegas@elgrifo.com; Website: www.elgrifo.com

A substantial family bodega dating from 1775, it led the way to more modern wines, producing a wide range from its own forty hectares of vineyards, with other grapes bought in. It is noted for its whites, particularly the sweet ones, which include Moscatel de Ana, matured on the *solera* system. The Malvasía Dulce is also very good. It is well geared up to the local tourist trade and has a wine museum in its vineyards.

MOZAGA

Carretera Arrecife a Tinajo km 8, 35562 Mozaga, Lanzarote.

Tel: +34 928 52 04 85; Fax: +34 928 52 14 09;

Email: bodegasmozaga@hotmail.com

Founded in 1973, Moscatel Mozaga is also matured on the *solera* system. Other wines include a varietal Diego.

TIMANFAYA

Camino Volcán 1, 35550 Macher-Tias, Las Palmas de Gran Canaria. Tel: +34 606 32 38 11; Fax: +34 928 51 00 61

A smaller and more recent establishment, founded in 1999, it has a wide range of wines that have been praised, particularly the Moscatel.

LA PALMA

Geography

Like all the Canary Islands this is volcanic; but it is more volcanic than most, as the Teneguía volcano erupted as recently as 1971. It is dominated by La Caldera de Taburiente, an enormous volcanic crater. The vineyards are in three zones: Fuencaliente in the south; Hoyo de Mazo in the centre; and Norte de La Palma in the north. They are generally planted around the coasts, at altitudes from 200–1,200 metres (656–3,937 feet). The great rival crop is bananas, and the best bodegas will not buy grapes from banana growers. It is not through prejudice, but because the bananas take the goodness out of the soil and starve the grapes.

Climate

The average annual temperature is 18–20°C (64.4–68°F) with a minimum of 13–16°C (55.4–60.8°F) and a maximum of 23–24°C (73.4–75°F), but this gives only a small part of the story. There are wide variations and many microclimates. The humid northeast trade winds bring rain, particularly at altitudes between 500–1,500 metres (1,640–4,921 feet). At elevations below 300 metres (984 feet) and on east-facing slopes the climate is drier and can be semi-arid on the coastal strip. Fuencaliente is the most arid part of all. Drip irrigation is allowed.

Soils

These are volcanic and rich.

Grapes

Red varieties: Almuñeco (Listán Negro); Bastardo Negro; Malvasía Rosada; Moscatel Negro; Negramoll; and Tintilla.
White varieties: Albillo; Bastardo Blanco; Bermejuela; Bujariego; Burrablanca; Forastera Blanca; Gúal; Listán Blanco; Malvasía; Moscatel; Pedro Ximénez; Sabro; Torrontes; and Verdello.
Many of these grape varieties, however, are little planted. The Listán Blanco accounts for forty-six per cent, the Negramoll forty-one per cent, the Malvasía two per cent, and all the others eleven per cent between them. The Gúal and the Verdello are officially favoured, but the Listán Blanco is not and its spread is discouraged. Part of its production, however, is eaten as table grapes.

Planting

Some of the vineyards, especially in Fuencaliente, have to be planted in the way already described for Lanzarote. In the Norte de La Palma the planting is more normal, though very varied: bushes; wires; and even pergolas. Some of the vineyards are on terraces supported by dry stone walls. Generally vines are planted wherever they will grow.

Vineyard area

The total area is 1,666 hectares but only 869 hectares are registered with the *consejo regulador* as being in production.

Authorized yield
56hl/ha, but the actual yield is very much less.

Wines
Whites (11–14.5% ABV), *rosados* (11–13% ABV), reds (12–14% ABV), *Malvasía clásico* (15–22% ABV), *Malvasía seco* (14–16% ABV), and *dulce* (15–22% ABV). Wines sold as varietal (mostly Malvasía and Sabro) must have at least eighty-five per cent of the named variety. *Malvasía clásico* is made by late gathering or sunning and must have at least forty-five grams of residual sugar per litre. Two thirds of the wine is white and almost a third red, with very little *rosado* and only small amounts of the others. In addition to these, a wine unique to the Canary Islands is also grown in the area Norte de La Palma: *vino de tea*. Tea has nothing to do with the familiar infusion. It is the local name for the Canary pine (*Pinus canariensis*) and these wines, which may be white, *rosado*, or red, are matured in pine casks for up to six months, giving them a resinous flavour. They may be aged for a long time to resemble *rancios*.

Production
5,440 hectolitres (1996).

This very beautiful island is well known to holidaymakers who drink their fair share of its wines. Agriculturally it is by no means a monoculture and has flourishing trades in bananas and avocado pears. Of the wines, whites predominate and come in all degrees of sweetness, grown mostly in Fuencaliente. The best reds are grown in Hoyo de Mazo and some of the *jóvenes* are made by carbonic maceration. The general standard is high and the sweet Malvasías can be delicious. This is helped by the maturity of the vines, ninety per cent of which are over forty years old. I must confess that I have never drunk a *tea* wine. These fall within the ambit of the DO, but in practice never get the certification as they are not bottled, but are sold in bulk at the door to all comers. They have a strong local following and are said to be good for you.

Some leading bodegas

BODEGAS CARBALLO

Carretera Las Indias 74, 38740 Fuencaliente, La Palma, Tenerife. Tel: +34 922 44 41 40; Fax: +34 922 44 41 40

A small, privately owned modern bodega, founded in 1990, that produces mostly whites with some good Malvasías.

LLANOVID SOCIEDAD COOPERATIVA

Los Canarios s/n, 38740 Fuencaliente, La Palma, Tenerife. Tel: +34 922 44 40 78; Fax: +34 922 44 43 94; Email: informacion@vinosteneguia.com; Website: www.vinosteneguia.com

Founded in 1948 this cooperative is the largest producer. It is modern and well equipped. It sells its wines under the trade mark Teneguia. Most are whites, including a range of varietals, but it makes the others as well, apart from *tea*. The ones to look for are Vinos de Autor, Negramoll, and Malvasía. The delicious *reserva Malvasías* give one an inkling of what Canary Sack may have been like.

SAT EL HOYO

Carretera Hoyo de Mazo 60, Callejones, 38738 Villa de Mazo, Tenerife. Tel: +34 922 44 06 16 ; Fax: +34 922 42 85 69; Email: info@bodegaselhoyo.com; Website: www.bodegaselhoyo.com

An SAT founded in 1994 with 110 hectares of vineyards, producing a range of good wines under the Hoyo de Mazo label.

GRAN CANARIA

Formerly a VdlT, Gran Canaria El Monte, this was given DO status at the end of 2003, so these are early days and it remains to be seen how it will develop. All the vineyards are in the northeast of the island, in areas formerly known as Santa Brígida and San Mateo. There are 450 hectares of vineyard growing the usual bewildering variety of vines in volcanic soil. Red wines have a minimum strength of 12% ABV, *rosados* and whites 11.5% ABV. Much of the production is *rosado*, but the most highly regarded wine is the notably robust Tinto del Monte (Mountain Red).

MONTE DE LENTISCAL

Although enjoying the status of a separate DO, this is within Gran Canaria and the two DOs may well be amalgamated. Judgment will have to be reserved.

LA GOMERA

This new DO was granted at the same time as Gran Canaria and likewise used to be a VdlT covering the whole island. Again we shall have to see how this develops. There are 350 hectares of vineyard in the northwest growing the usual bewildering number of grape varieties in volcanic soil. The red wines have a minimum strength of 12% ABV, the *rosados* and whites 11.5% ABV; but the most notable wines are the powerful whites made from the Forastera grape, going up to 15% ABV. The reds are sometimes lightened with the addition of white grapes.

13

Cava

Geography

Cavas are made in many of the leading wine-growing areas of Spain, altogether from 160 municipalities in seven regions, but ninety-five per cent come from Cataluña, where they originated. They must be made from grapes grown in designated vineyards. The capital of the trade is San Sadurní d'Anoia (San Sadurní de Noya) in the area producing Penedès table wines, which accounts for seventy-five per cent.

Climate

As the vineyards are split between so many provinces and areas within those provinces, it is impossible to generalize save to say that grapes for cavas are grown in cooler sites and those that produce the lightest wines within those areas.

Grapes

White varieties: Macabeo (Viura); Parellada; Xarel.lo; Chardonnay; and Subirat Parent (Malvasía Riojana).

Red varieties: Garnacha; Monastrell; Pinot Noir; and Trepat. The last two may be used only for *rosados*.

In Cataluña, the traditional mix is of the first three named white varieties, which are officially considered to be the principal ones. There is more Macabeo in the rest of Spain. Macabeo contributes freshness and acidity, Xarel.lo gives body, and Parellada gives fragrance and finesse. The red varieties are used in making *rosados*, often sold under the French word rosé. There is much heated argument over the use of Chardonnay. The traditionalists claim that it is a foreign grape that will detract from the unique style of their very successful cavas, which do not attempt to be Champagne, but are their own thing. The modernists say that it is a world variety that will improve the wines and add to their appeal. Its use is clearly on the increase.

Planting

Traditional *en vaso* viticulture is giving way to growing on wires. Macabeo and Parellada vines are sometimes grown on the Royat principle, but Xarel.lo on the Guyot. There must be between 1,500–3,500 vines per hectare.

Vineyard area

32,000 hectares.

Authorized yield

White 80hl/ha; red 53hl/ha. An increase of twenty-five per cent may be allowed, but above that the must may not be used for cava.

Wines

The wine is made essentially in the same way as Champagne. It has to spend at least nine months in bottle on its lees before it is disgorged, and it must achieve a carbon dioxide gas pressure of four atmospheres. The alcoholic strength of the finished wine lies between 10.8–12.8% ABV. There are six degrees of sweetness, according to sugar content:

Extra brut: less than 6 gm/litre.
Brut: 6-15 gm/litre.
Extra seco: 12-20 gm/litre.
Seco: 17-35 gm/litre.
Semi-seco: 33-50 gm/litre.
Dulce: over 50 gm/litre.

In practice the wines are usually matured for well over the minimum period (though one noted house was questioned about it some time ago), and they may well have as many as five years, or occasionally even more, in bottle.

Production

1,609,860 hectolitres (2000).

Vintages

1993 (4); 1994 (3); 1995 (3); 1996 (4); 1997 (3); 1998 (4); 1999 (4); 2000 (5); 2001 (4); 2002 (4); 2003 (4); 2004 (4).

Cava is undoubtedly one of the world's great sparkling wines, and its popularity has been increasing every year, so much so that there were great rejoicings in 2001 when exports exceeded those of Champagne. In 1980 there were eighty firms producing it; by 2005 there were 271. Spain is now the second-largest producer of sparkling wines after France and most of them are cavas. There were early attempts to produce wine in Spain on the model of Champagne, but these failed. The breakthrough came in 1872. Josep Raventós i Fatjó, who was born in 1825, got together with a group of friends known as the "seven sages" to try to create a good sparkling wine. He was already a leading wine-grower and head of his family bodega Codorníu. In 1872 he laid down the first wine in his cellar for bottle fermentation, and in 1879 the first six dozen bottles were sold. They were highly successful, and by the time he died in 1885 he had effected further improvements with the aid of a French oenologist. His descendants are still leading shippers.

But why "cava"? The word *cava* (or in Catalán *cave*) means cellar, as does bodega, but a *cava* has to be underground. At first the wine was called "Champán" (Champagne) or in Catalán, "Xampán", but not unnaturally the French objected. At the time it was not as iniquitous as it may now seem, as the name was used generically for sparkling wine all over the world and still is, for instance, in the USA. The first action was taken in England, where a criminal prosecution failed; but a case brought in the Chancery Division in 1959 succeeded, preventing the sale of any wine as "Spanish Champagne". However things elsewhere went on as before until Spain joined the EEC in 1986, when the name had to be dropped throughout the Community and the new name, cava, was found. In 1989 it was recognized by the Community, but to achieve this it had to have a geographical basis, and this was done by delimiting the areas where it had traditionally been produced and designating vineyards. The vast majority are in Cataluña, and of these most are in Penedès; but the name of Penedès cannot be used on cava labels as it is a geographical origin limited to table wines. All cava is made, however, by the method that used to be universally known as the *méthode Champenoise* or, in Spanish, as the *método champañés*. Unfortunately, and perhaps rather churlishly, as it accurately described a method of preparation rather than a geographical origin, the French objected to this, too, and it had to go. Now it is called the *método tradicional*.

The grapes are picked early so that they have plenty of acidity, and often early in the morning before the heat of day. Then they are brought in for pressing as quickly as possible, to avoid oxidation, and are pressed very gently, sometimes with very modern presses using a continuously moving rubber band. The must is cold fermented to produce base wines, which must have an alcoholic strength of between 9.5–11.5% ABV. These are then blended the following year to produce *cupadas* (*cuvées*) of the various styles that the shipper needs. Sometimes, as in Champagne, reserve wines are added to form part of the *cupada*.

The next task is to add the bubbles. Four grams of sugar in the *licor de tiraje* (in French, *liqueur de tirage*: the mix added to start the second fermentation) are needed to give the right pressure; in practice a little more is used, but the alcoholic strength of the wine must not be increased by more than 1.5% ABV. The bottles are tightly sealed, originally using a cork held down with a strong steel clip or *agrafe*, but now usually with a plastic insert held in by a crown cap. The give away (as with Champagne) is whether the top of the bottle has a lip for the crown cap. The wine has to be left in contact with the yeast for at least nine months, and the best are left for a good deal longer, often for several years. This results in an autolysis of the yeast, releasing flavouring elements, mostly amino-acids, into the wine, which gives all wines made this way a characteristic yeasty aroma.

A few of the very small bodegas still do *removido* (in French *remuage*: the process of settling the dead yeast on the cork of the bottle so that it can be removed) by hand, but nowadays it can be done much more quickly by the use of techniques invented in Cataluña and adopted in Champagne. The first was the *girasol* (sunflower), which is a metal cage containing about 60 bottles, initially at an angle of forty-five degrees; this can be moved a little every day, which shakes the sediment down onto the corks in exactly the same way but with much less effort. The second is the giropalette, again operating with a large number of bottles stored in a number of containers, which are moved every six hours in a pattern controlled by a computer. This is quicker, just as good, and involves even less effort, but the machine is relatively expensive.

The next and final step is the *degüelle* (in French *dégorgement*) to disgorge the deposit from the bottle. The necks of the bottles are dipped into a freezing solution. The bottles are then turned the right way up, the cork removed, and the sediment, encased in a little block of ice, blows out. At the same time the *licor de expedición* (in French *liqueur d'expédition*) is added. This may contain a number of things, and each bodega keeps its exact formulation secret, but essentially it consists of wine, sugar, and perhaps a little alcohol. The amount of sugar added at this stage determines the style of the wine (*see* above). But the alcohol may not be increased by more than 0.5% ABV. Small producers do this manually, but in the big bodegas the whole process is automated, the bottles being picked up at one end of the line and emerging at the other with their final corks (*tapones de expedición*) held in by a wire *bozal* (muzzle).

The most popular styles in Spain used to be the *seco* and the *semi-seco,* but now there is a general move toward the extra brut and the brut. Wine snobs in particular eschew anything sweet. But they miss a lot. A small degree of sweetness, softening the flavour of the wine, can be attractive, especially in a northern climate. Wines with a degree of sweetness, even *semi-seco*, often go down very well at a party, and the *dulce* wines are perhaps most suitable for drinking with a Christmas pudding. Cava is best served, like Champagne, in flute glasses and, like Champagne, chilled, but definitely not frozen; if a cava is too cold, essential aromas and complex flavours are masked. But cava is not Champagne and does not pretend to be. The wines should be judged on their own, very considerable, merits.

Some leading bodegas

ALBET I NOYA
See Penedès.
Vines are grown organically at its Can Vendrell estate at Costers de l'Ordal in Alt Penedès. The three main varieties are used with Chardonnay in most of the blends. For example, the Brut Barrica 21, made in Allier oak, has seventy per cent Chardonnay with thirty per cent Parellada. The Brut Rosé is a varietal Pinot Noir. *Semi-seco* and *dulce* wines are given a year in bottle on the lees, and 2–4 years for the remainder. They are disgorged by hand and sold immediately.

CAN FEIXES (HUGUET)
See Penedès.
The excellent cavas are sold under the name Huguet. Using plenty of

Parellada and Chardonnay they have an unusual degree of finesse. The *reserva*, for instance, is from fifty per cent Parellada, twenty-six per cent Macabeo, and twenty-four per cent Chardonnay.

CARMENET

Pelegrí Torelló 14, 08770 Sant Sadurní D'Anoia, Barcelona.

Tel: +34 934 64 49 49; Fax: +34 934 64 24 01; Email: carmenet@carmenet.es

Carmenet's cavas are unusual in that most of them, sold under the mark Privat Laità, are varietal Chardonnays. The Privat Reserva, however, is from the three traditional varieties.

CASTELL DE VILARNAU

Crta. d'Espiells, Km, 1.4 "Finca Can Petit" 08770 Sant Sadurni d'Anoia, Barcelona.

Tel: +34 938 91 23 61; Fax: +34 938 91 29 13;

Email: castelldevilarnau@castelldevilarnau.es; Website:www.gonzalezbyass.es

Established in 1982 as a subsidiary of the great sherry and brandy house Gonzalez Byass, this bodega makes cavas of exceptional quality. Vilarnau Brut is from fifty-five per cent Macabeo, thirty per cent Parellada, and fifteen per cent Chardonnay, while the Brut Gran Reserva Vintage is from thirty-five per cent Macabeo, thirty per cent Parellada, and thirty-five per cent Chardonnay. Albert de Vilarnau *fermentado en barrica* is from fifty per cent barrel-fermented Macabeo, twenty per cent from the same grape normally fermented, twenty per cent Parellada, and ten per cent Chardonnay. There is also a varietal Chardonnay. The *rosado* is from ninety per cent Trepat and ten per cent Pinot Noir.

CASTELL SANT ANTONI

Passeig del Parc 13, 08770 Sant Sadurní D'Anoia, Barcelona.

Tel/Fax: +34 938 18 30 99; Email: cava@castellsantantoni.com;

Website: www.castellsantantoni.com

This small family bodega was started in a cellar behind the family house; although it now has moved to larger premises it is still proud of being small. The Castell Sant Antoni brand was introduced in 1989 and uses the three traditional varieties save for the *rosados,* which are varietal Garnachas. Its wines enjoy a very high reputation.

CASTELLBLANCH

Avenida Casetes Mir s/n, 08770 Sant Sadurní D'Anoia, Barcelona.

Tel: +34 938 91 70 25; Fax: +34 938 91 01 26;

Email: castellblanch@castellblanch.es; Website: www.castellblanch.com

Founded as a small family business in 1908, it now belongs to Freixenet. Its cavas are very reliable. Brut Zero, aged for two years, is from sixty per cent Parellada, thirty per cent Macabeo, and ten per cent Xarel.lo. Dos Lustros, aged for four years, is from forty per cent each of Macabeo and Parellada, with twenty per cent Xarel.lo. The top wine Gran Castell is forty per cent Parellada, twenty-five per cent Macabeo, twenty per cent Xarel.lo, and fifteen per cent Chardonnay.

CAVAS CASTILLO DE PERELADA

See Ampurdán-Costa Brava.

This very reputable family-owned cava house had the unfortunate distinction of being the supplier of the wines that were banned from sale in England as "Spanish Champagne" following the litigation referred to above. In addition to Castillo de Perelada it uses the name Gran Claustro for its top wine. Most of the wines are made from the traditional grapes, but there is also a varietal Chardonnay, and the Gran Claustro 2002 contained forty per cent Chardonnay. The *rosados* are made from Garnacha and Monastrell.

CODORNÍU

Avenida Jaume Codorníu s/n, 08770 Sadurní D'Anoia, Barcelona.

Tel: +34 938 18 32 32; Fax: +34 938 91 08 22;

Email: codorniu@codorniu.es; Website: www.grupocodorniu.com

The seminal part played by Josep Raventós i Fatjó in creating cava has already been described, and happily his bodega, now run by his descendants, remains a pre-eminent producer. It is not known when the Codorníu family started to grow wine, but in 1551 Jaime Codorníu left an established business to his heir. Just over 100 years later, María Anna Codorníu married Miguel Raventós and the present owners are all descendants. When Josep Raventós decided to make sparkling wine, he was taking a huge risk. No one could be sure that really good sparkling wine could be made or that it would sell well if it were. The investment was enormous, beginning with digging vast underground cellars, but it paid off magnificently.

Happily the family is as inspired in its judgment of art and architecture as it is in wine. When Josep's son Manuel decided to build a fine new bodega in 1898, he tried to get the great Catalán architect Antoni Gaudí to design it. Gaudí was too busy so one of his rivals, Josep María Puig i Cadafalch, did it instead, producing outstanding art nouveau buildings. It is now a national monument, as much a place of pilgrimage for students of architecture as for wine lovers. And the first advertising posters were painted by Casas, Utrillo, and Junyent. That is flair.

The underground cellars are now said to be the largest in the world, stretching for twenty-four kilometres (fifteen miles) on five levels – and still growing. The bodega has 1,200 hectares of its own vineyards and is supplied by 1,000 growers, who receive complete technical back-up and are carefully supervised. Satellite imagery is used to locate the best grapes in each plot. The grapes mostly are pressed with the latest Italian Sernagiotto presses, but only the first, free-run juice is used for cava, the rest sold off to winemakers. All the traditional grape varieties are used, but Codorníu is uninhibited in the use of Chardonnay, which has brought it into conflict with some of its rivals, the question being whether cava should follow its uniquely Spanish style or go international. The success of Chardonnay in the market place provides the answer, and most of the *cuvées* now include some. As another step, Codorníu has developed its own clone of Parellada, called Montonegra, giving extra fragrance.

There is an unusually wide range of excellent wines, backed by a stock of 100,000,000 bottles. In order of price, from the cheapest to the most expensive, it includes: Prima Vides; Anna de Codorníu (seventy per cent Chardonnay with ten per cent each Macabeo, Parellada, and *reserva* wine), Non Plus Ultra Reserva, Cuvée Raventós, Jaume Codorníu (fifty per cent Chardonnay, thirty per cent Macabeo, and twenty per cent Parellada), and Magnum Jaume Codorníu 450 Aniversario. The *rosado* is from Pinot Noir.

BODEGAS FAUSTINO
See Rioja.
This famous Rioja house produces a good cava from Macabeo and Chardonnay.

FREIXENET
Joan Sala 2, 08770 Sant Sadurní D'Anoia, Barcelona.
Tel: +34 938 91 70 00; Fax: +34 938 91 30 95;
Email: freixenet@freixenet.es; Website: www.freixenet.es
There are two giants in the cava market: Freixenet and Codorníu. For anyone arriving at San Sadurní de Noya by train, this is the first bodega they

see, as its impressive buildings are next to the railway station. It is the leading cava exporter and, with its subsidiaries, the largest sparkling wine maker in the world. Still family owned, it was founded by Pedro Ferrer Bosch at the beginning of the twentieth century. He was the youngest son of a family that had owned an estate called La Freixenada (in Catalán, A Plantation of Ash Trees) in the Alt Penedès since the thirteenth century. His wife was Dolores Sala Vivé, whose grandfather had founded a wine company that gave a basis for the new enterprise, in which she joined him. It was wonderfully successful. From the beginning it went in for imaginative advertising and was one of the first to use television. A galaxy of stars took part in its campaigns, including such names as Gene Kelly, Plácido Domingo, José Carreras, and Paul Newman.

From the beginning the emphasis was on tradition. All but one of its wines are made with varying proportions of the three traditional varieties. These include Carta Nevada, which became instantly popular when it was launched in 1941 in white ground-glass bottles. Its most popular wine today, especially on the export markets, is Cordón Negro, sold in black ground-glass bottles. Cuvée DS, a delicate and subtle wine, is named after Doña Dolores Sala, who was the winemaker and was killed by the communists in the Civil War; a very good *gran reserva*, it is made from forty per cent each of Macabeo and Xarel.lo, with twenty per cent Parellada. A recent introduction was Monastrell Xarel.lo, made from equal quantities of the two grapes. The Monastrell is, of course, a black grape, but careful winemaking (as when using the black Pinot Noir in Champagne) results in there being only the least trace of colour; but the Monastrell is very evident in the nose and flavour, producing a fascinating and unique cava. Chardonnay is disapproved of, though some (twenty per cent) is used in the top, superb, Reserva Real. There are also varietals from Trepat and Malvasía.

The Freixenet empire is spread worldwide. In Penedès it includes Segura Viudas and Castellblanch, acquired in 1984 after the disappropriation of RUMASA, and René Barbier (quite separate from the company of the same name in Priorato). In the US it has an estate in Sonoma. In France it actually owns one of the oldest Champagne houses: Henri Abelé. It also has wine interests in Mexico and offices in many countries, including England. Its subsidiaries are left to go their own ways and make their own, quite distinct and competing, ranges of wines.

GRAMONA

See Penedès.

The cavas produced by this family bodega, now in the fourth generation, are among the best. They used to be made with the three traditional varieties in roughly equal amounts, but this is still true of just some of them, for instance La Suite *gran reserva*. Celler Batile is a Brut wine made from seventy per cent Xarel.lo and thirty per cent Macabeo and given at least six years in bottle. It is named after Doña Pilar Batlle Gramona, who was the mother of the third generation of the family. Chardonnay has now entered the picture as ten per cent of the *gran reserva* Imperial, and Argent is a varietal Chardonnay. The *rosado* is a varietal Pinot Noir. The cavas from this bodega keep unusually well in bottle.

CAVAS HILL

See Penedès.

It makes a complete range of good cavas using the traditional grapes.

JUVÉ & CAMPS

See Penedès.

It is perhaps rather unfair to ask wine-growers whose wines they would drink in a restaurant that did not have their own. Asking cava producers, the one name that always comes up is Juvé & Camps, a family firm now in its third generation. The wines are very well made from the traditional varieties, typically in roughly equal quantities, kept on the lees for thirty months to five years, and sold in numbered bottles. The Reserva de Familia and the top Gran Juvé y Camps are especially worth seeking out.

LANGA HERMANOS

See Calatayud.

One does not normally look to Calatayud for a cava, but those from this bodega, sold under the name J Langa, and made from Macabeo with a high proportion of Chardonnay, are good.

LAR DE BARROS-INVIOSA

See Ribera del Guadiana.

This is rather an oddball, in Extramadura, right across from Penedès in the west of Spain. It makes a cava from Macabeo, given eighteen months in bottle and sold under the name Bonaval. It is quite unlike the usual run of cavas, but good.

CAVAS LLOPART

Carretera de Sant Sadurni – Ordal km 4, 98739 Subirats, Barcelona.

Tel: +34 938 99 31 25; Fax: +34 938 91 17 79;

Email: llopart@llopart.es; Website: www.llopart.es

This family bodega in San Sadurní de Noya has been making cava since 1887 and uses the trade names Llopart, Integral, and Leopardi. While its wines are mostly from the three traditional varieties, it is not afraid of Chardonnay. For instance, its Vintage Leonardo Brut Nature is from forty per cent Monastrell, thirty per cent Xarel.lo, fifteen per cent Parellada, and fifteen per cent Chardonnay, while the Integral Brut Nature has thirty per cent Chardonnay.

ANTONIO MASCARO

See Penedès.

Although Mascaró is most famous for his brandies, everything he makes is good, and not least his cavas. The traditional varieties are used, but with an emphasis on Parellada. The *gran reservas* have an addition of 10–15 per cent Chardonnay.

CAVES MONT-FERRANT

Abat Escarré 1, 17300 Blanes, Girona.

Tel: +34 934 19 10 00; Fax: +34 934 19 31 70;

Email: montferrant@montferrant.com; Website: www.montferrant.com

Up in the Costa Brava, this bodega, established in 1865, was one of the cava pioneers. It is now making some of the best, mostly from the three traditional varieties, but some including minor proportions of Chardonnay. Among the best of those from the traditional varieties are Agustí-Villaret and Luis Justo Villanueva. Rudolph Bourlon Extra Brut is from fifty-five per cent Parellada, twenty-one per cent each of Macabeo and Xarel.lo, and three per cent Chardonnay.

PARXET

See Alella.

Just up the coast from Penedès, this is a good example of small being beautiful. Its cavas are certainly good. Brut Nature is from forty per cent Pansá Blanca (a clone of Xarel.lo) and thirty per cent each of Macabeo and Parellada. It is rather given to original packaging, and the Aniversario range (excellent Chardonnays) comes in silver-coloured bottles.

RAVENTÓS I BLANC

See Penedès.

Raventós uses the traditional varieties plus Chardonnay to produce a small range of good wines. L'Hereu is from sixty per cent Macabeo with twenty per cent each of Xarel.lo and Parellada. *Gran reserva* Brut Nature is from the same grapes and aged for three years. Elisabet Raventós Brut Nature is fifty per cent Xarel.lo, thirty per cent Chardonnay, and twenty per cent Monastrell, aged for four years. *Gran reserva* Personal Manuel Raventós is from forty per cent Parellada, twenty-five per cent each Macabeo and Xarel.lo, and ten per cent Chardonnay, aged for six years. The last two are exceptionally mature and worth seeking.

CAVAS RECAREDO

Tamarit 10, 08770 Sant Sadurní D'Anoia, Barcelona.
Tel: +34 938 91 02 14; Fax: +34 938 91 16 97;
Email: cava@recaredo.es; Website: www.recaredo.com

A small family bodega founded in 1924 . Its cavas, made from the traditional varieties, are well regarded.

RIMARTS

Avenida Cal Mir 42, 08770 Sant Sadurní D'Anoia, Barcelona.
Tel/Fax: +34 938 91 27 75;
Email: rimarts@rimarts.net; Website: www.rimarts.net

This small bodega started at San Sadurní de Noya in 1987, has established a formidable reputation for its cavas. It is a family business where everything is done by hand. While based on the traditional varieties, the top wines now include Chardonnay. The Brut Nature Grand Reserve is aged for thirty-six months, the Grand Cuvée L'Avi Comes for fifty-two.

ROURA

See Alella.

Apart from its table wines, this young bodega also makes good cavas from fifty per cent each of Chardonnay and Xarel.lo.

SEGURA VIUDAS

Carretera Sant Pere Riudebitlles, Km 5 08775 Torrelavit, Barcelona.

Tel: +34 938 91 70 70; Fax: +34 938 99 60 06;

Email: seguraviudas@seguraviudas.com; Website: www.seguraviudas.com

Although a member of the great Freixenet group, it is run independently. It is one of the major producers of cava and makes many wines sold under the buyers' own brands. Its wines are made from the three traditional varieties in varying proportions. The Brut Reserva, for example is from fifty per cent Macabeo, thirty-five per cent Parellada, and fifteen per cent Xarel.lo, while the Lavit Brut Nature is from sixty per cent Macabeo and forty per cent Parellada. These cavas are always good and generally very good.

SIGNAT

Escultor Llimona s/n, 08328 Alella, Barcelona.

Tel: +34 935 40 34 00; Fax: +34 935 40 14 71;

This boutique bodega at Alella, founded as recently as 1987, is producing cavas that are very highly regarded.

AGUSTÍ TORELLÓ

PO Box 35, La Serra s/n, 08770 Sant Sadurní d'Anoia, Barcelona.

Tel: +34 938 91 11 73; Fax: +34 938 91 26 16;

Email: info@agustitorellomata.com; Website: www.agustitorellomata.com

The roots of the Torelló family as wine-growers are said to go back to 1395, but Agustí Torelló Mata started making cava in 1950 and entered the market in 1979. He is still in charge, assisted by his children, and it is very much a family bodega. The estate and vineyard, Can Marti de Baix, are five kilometres (three miles) outside San Sadurní de Noya in the direction of Barcelona. A full range of very good cavas is produced from the three traditional grape varieties, notably Mata Gran Reserva and Kripta. The latter is made from the oldest vines, and sold in a special "traditional" bottle based on the shape of an amphora, which looks wonderful, but has the disadvantage that it cannot be stood up. The *rosado* is a varietal Trepat.

CAVAS Y VINOS TORRE ORIA

Carretera Pontón – Utiel km 3, 46390 Derramador-Requena, Valencia.

Tel: +34 962 32 02 89; Fax: +34 962 32 03 11;

Email: info.torreoria@natra.es; Website: www.torreoria.com

From a rather improbable part of Spain, this bodega produces some good cavas from combinations of Macabeo, Parellada, and Malvasía.

MASIA VALLFORMOSA

See Penedès.

Good cavas are made, particularly Gala de Vallformosa Brut, the vintage version from equal parts of Chardonnay, Macabeo, Parellada, and Xarel.lo, a well-matured wine of considerable character.

JANÉ VENTURA

See Penedès.

Another family firm now in its fourth generation. A small range of good and reliable cavas, especially the Brut nature, made from the traditional varieties in roughly equal amounts as *gran reserva*, brut *nature,* and Brut. The first two have no *dosage* and the third very little. The *rosado* is a varietal Garnacha.

14

A guide to vines

Most vines originated in the Middle East, and many have come to western Europe via Greece. New vines are created by crossing existing ones. Vines have to be propagated by cuttings; if you grow one from a pip almost anything may happen. Vines spontaneously mutate, too. Tempranillo – certainly one of the world's best black grape vines – grows thicker skins in hotter places and is often given different names. In Ribera del Duero it becomes Tinto del País, and in Toro it becomes Tinto de Toro – though some would deny that this is in fact the same vine. And many authorities suggest that the Tempranillo may be the Burgundian Pinot Noir, transplanted to Spain centuries ago and developing its own character there. A form of DNA testing is being used for vines and some unexpected relationships are emerging.

Complicated as the picture is, knowing what vines are cultivated where and the various names they are given, lies at the root of understanding wines, and the purpose of this chapter is to throw some light on it.

In Spain the gender of the names of many vines appears uncertain: they can be masculine or feminine, depending on where you are and to whom you are speaking. The more usual gender, when this applies, is used in the list that follows.

Red wine vines

AFARTAPOBRES
Once cultivated in Cataluña, but now very rare indeed and regarded as a table grape.

ALCAYATA
See Monastrell.

ALICANTE
See Garnacha Tintorera.

ALMUNECO
See Listán Negro.

ARAGÓN, ARAGONÉS
See Garnacha Tinta.

ARAUXA
See Tempranillo.

ARINAMOYA
Rare. A cross of Merlot and Petit Verdot grown in Penedès.

BABOSO NEGRO
Grown in the Canary Islands.

BARBARA
An Italian variety known as Barbara, widely planted in other countries and being tried experimentally in Spain.
Grown in Navarra.

BASTARDO NEGRO
Otherwise as for Bastardo Blanco.

BLANQUIRROJA
See Subirat-Parent.

BOBAL
The fourth most commonly cultivated vine in Spain. It does well in arid and semi-arid places. If its wines tended to be rather rustic, they were notable for colour, tannin, and acidity, while modern winemaking has much diminished the rusticity. It also makes good *rosados*.
Grown in Alicante, Los Arribes del Duero-Fermoselle, Manchuela, Ribera del Guardiana, Ribera del Júcar, Utiel-Requena, and Valencia.

BOLICAIRE
Being grown experimentally in Navarra.

BRANCELLAO

A native of Galicia, this vine is capable of producing good wines, but is very rare and in danger of disappearing as the emphasis in that area is now on the very successful whites.

Grown in Rías Bajas, Ribera Sacra, and Ribeiro.

Another name (in Portugal) is Brancelho.

BRUJIDERA

See Moravia.

CABERNET FRANC

A top French variety now being grown on a small scale in Spain. In world reputation it is overshadowed by Cabernet Sauvignon, but produces a rather lighter style of wine that ages well and may well become more widely grown. *See* also Mencía.

Grown in Cataluña, Navarra, Penedès, Pla de Bages, Sierras de Málaga, and Valencia.

CABERNET SAUVIGNON

A top French variety grown worldwide. It is at present the fashionable red grape. It has long been grown in Spain, at Vega Sicilia, in what is now the Ribera del Duero (though it was not so named when the grape was introduced there) and in Rioja. It is now giving superb wines in Penedès. It provides plenty of backbone and blends well with other varieties (as Bordeaux has shown for years) in Spain, notably with Tempranillo.

Grown in Alella, Alicante, Almansa, Ampurdán-Costa Brava, Biezo, Bullas, Calatayud, Campo de Borja, Cariñena, Castilla y León, Cataluña, Cigales, Conca de Barberá, Costers del Segre, Dominio de Valpusa, Finca Elez, Jumilla, La Mancha, Manchuela, Méntrida, Mondéjar, Monterrei, Montsant, Navarra, Penedès, Pla de Bages, Priorato, Ribera del Duero, Ribera del Guadiana, Ribera del Júcar, Rioja, Rueda, Sierra de Alcaraz, Sierras de Málaga, Somontano, Tarragona, Terra Alta, Tierra del Vino de Zamora, Toro, Utiel-Requena, Valdeorras, Valdepeñas, Valencia, VdlT Castilla, VdlT Granada Suroeste, Vinos de Madrid, Yecla, and in a number of leading bodegas producing non-DO wines, such as Bodegas Alta Pavina, Bodegas SAT Los Curros, Finca Retuerta, and Valle de Cinca.

CAINO

Two versions: red and white. Neither of these Galician varieties is widely grown but each is capable of giving good wines.

Grown in Rías Bajas, Ribeira Sacra, and Ribeiro.

CALADOC
Rare. A cross of Malbec and Garnacha grown in Penedès.

CALLET
It is said to be a native of Mallorca, where it is still widely planted, but nowhere else. Its wine are highly coloured but with little extract.
Grown in Binisalem and Plá i Llevant de Mallorca.

CARINENA
See Mazuelo. Which name is used depends on where you are.

CASTELLA NEGRA
Grown in Abona, Tenerife.

CATALAN
See Mazuelo.

CENDRON
See Graciano.

CINSAULT
This vine from the south of France is promising, not least because of its ability to thrive in hot places, but so far has made no headway and is only experimental.
Grown in Navarra.

CRUJIDERA
See Moravia.

CRUJILLON
See Mazuelo.

CRUSILLO
Grown in Cataluña.

ESPADEIRO
A native of Galicia. Very rare.
Grown in Rías Bajas and Ribera Sacra.

FERRON
Not widely grown.
Grown in Ribera Sacra and Ribeiro.

FOGONEU

Grown in Mallorca but not authorized for a DO. Produces undistinguished young red wines.

FORCAYAT

High yielding and not very good.

Grown in Valencia.

GAMAY

The Beaujolais grape from France. In Spain only being tried experimentally.

Grown in Navarra.

GARNACHA PELUDA

Another mutant of Garnacha Tinta, it crops more regularly, giving wines with plenty of alcohol, but tending to be deficient in colour and to oxidize easily.

Grown in Alella, Cataluña, Montsant, Terra Alta, and Priorato.

Another name is Liedoner Gris.

GARNACHA ROJA

Yet another mutant.

Grown in Cigales.

GARNACHA TINTA

Spain's most popular red grape vine and also very well known in France as Grenache, it is the world's second most widely planted vine. It has been maligned in the past, but this is the result of over-cropping, which is only too easily achieved. With the yield kept down it can produce great wines, as in Priorato; and Garnacha grown in Rioja Baja adds smoothness to many of the Rioja blends. The alcohol level can be almost dauntingly high. It also makes very good *rosados*. Care needs to be taken, though, to avoid oxidation.

Grown in Alella, Alicante, Ampurdán-Costa Brava, Los Arribes del Duero-Fermoselle, Bullas, Cariñena, Calatayud, Campo de Borja, Cariñena, Castilla y León, Cataluña, Cava, Cigales, Conca de Barberá, Costers del Segre, Jumilla; La Mancha, Manchuela, Méntrida, Navarra, Penedès, Pla de Bages, Priorato, Ribera del Arlanza, Ribera del Duero, Ribera del Guadiana, Ribeiro, Rioja, Rueda, Sierras de Málaga, Somontano, Tarragona, Terra Alta, Tierra del Vino de Zamora, Toro, Utiel-Requena, Valencia, Valdepeñas, VdlT Castilla, Vinos de Madrid, and Yecla; as well as by a number of bodegas making good non-DO wines.

Other names are Aragón, Aragonés, Garnatxa, Lladoner, and Tinto Aragonés.

GARNACHA TINTORERA

It is unusual in being a Teinturier, producing red juice. It is not, however, in the top quality league. It is widely planted in France, where it was bred in the nineteenth century by Henri Bouschet who crossed Aramon, Teinturier de Cher, and Grenache.

Grown in Alicante, Almansa, Bierzo, Cataluña, Jumilla, Monterrei, Navarra, Ribera del Guadiana, Ribeira Sacra, Valdeorras, Valencia, and Yecla.

Another name is Alicante.

GARNACHA TREPAT

See Trepat.

GARNATXA

See Garnacha.

GARRO

A Catalan variety that almost died out, but is now being grown again.

GOTIM BRU

See Tempranillo.

GRACIANO

A very high quality, very low yielding grape believed to be a native of the Rioja, where it is finding increasing favour. Its name is said to be derived from *gracia* (grace). Its wines are not highly alcoholic but are tannic, rough, and acid when young. It is deeply coloured (though the colour tends to go brown with age), age very well, and when mature shows great fragrance and finesse, so it is used, for example, in Rioja *grandes reservas*. It will not ripen well if grown too high up.

Grown in Dominio de Valpusa, Navarra, Ribera del Guadiana, Rioja, Somontano, and VdlT Castilla.

Other names are Morastell, Cendrón, and (in France) Morrastel, and Tanat Gris.

GRAN NEGRO

Grown in Monterrei and Valdeorras.

GRAU

A native of Galicia and very rare. Grown in Valdeorras.

JAEN
A high yielding vine of no great distinction.
Grown in Contaviesa-Alpujarra, Ribera del Guadiana, and Vinos de Madrid.

JUAN GARCIA
Grown in Los Arribes del Duero-Fermoselle.

JUAN IBANEZ
Not widely grown.
Grown in Calatayud and Cariñena.
Another name is Miguel de Arco.

LISTAN NEGRO
Grown in the Canary Islands.

LIEDONER GRIS
See Garnacha Peluda.

LLADONER
See Garnacha Tinta.

LOUREIRA
There are both red and white versions – respectively Tinta and Blanca. Natives of Galicia, both are rare, the red version very rare indeed, but give good wines.
Grown in Monterrei, Rías Bajas, Ribeira Sacra, and Ribeiro.
Another name is: Loureira Blanca, which is also known as Marqués.

MALBEC
A French variety from Bordeaux, introduced into what is now Ribera del Duero during the nineteenth century and occasionally found elsewhere, but little grown.
Grown in Navarra and Ribera del Duero.

MALVASÍA ROSADA
Grown in the Canary Islands.

MANDO
Grown in Valencia.

MANTO NEGRO
A native of Mallorca where it produces very good wines.
Grown in Binisalem.

MARIA ARDONA
See Maturana.

MATURANA
A red variety that once grew in Rioja, practically disappeared, and is now being tried again experimentally. There is also a white version. In Galicia it appears also to be known as Bastardo, but whether this is the same as the Portuguese grape is uncertain. Rare.
Grown in:Rioja and Galicia (Monterrei, Ribeira Sacra, and Valdeorras).
Other names are Merenzao, María Ardoña, and Bastardo.

MAZUELO
One of the basic red vines of Rioja, it is found in the oldest vineyards there and also in Navarra, where it is thought to have originated. But it is equally well known as Cariñena and is thought to have crossed the Pyrenees from the eponymous town (which does not grow much of it nowadays), to become well established in France, and in other countries, as the Carignan. In Spain it is low yielding and difficult to grow. It gives wines that are rather variable in alcohol, but which have high natural acidity and tannin, so that they require some time to mature. This makes them unpopular with bodegas selling young wines, but make them valuable for blending.
Grown in Ampurdán-Costa Brava, Calatayud, Campo de Borja, Cariñena, Cataluña, Conca de Barberá, Costers del Segre, Montsant, Navarra, Penedès, Priorato, Rioja, Ribera del Guadiana, Tarragona, and Terra Alta.
Other names are Cariñena, Catalan, Crujillón, and in other countries, it is known as Carignan.

MENCIA
Generally equated now with the Cabernet Franc, and where it is grown it certainly produces excellent wines of a similar style. It is not easy to ripen,though.
Grown in Bierzo, Castilla y León, Monterrei, Rías Bajas, Ribera del Arlanza, Ribera Sacra, Ribeiro, Valdeorras, and Valle de Benevente.

MENTRIDA
See Tinto de Madrid.

MERENZAO
See Maturana.

MERLOT

A major French variety from Bordeaux, widely planted around the world. It is now finding favour in Spain, where it is producing excellent varietals.

Grown in Almansa, Ampurdán-Costa Brava, Alicante, Bierzo, Bullas, Calatayud, Campo de Borja, Cariñena, Castilla y León, Cataluña, Cigales, Conca de Barberá, Costers del Segre, Dominio de Valpusa, Finca Elez, Jumilla, La Mancha, Manchueal, Méntrida, Montsant, Navarra, Penedès, Pla de Bages, Ribera del Duero, Ribera del Guadiana, Ribera del Júcar, Rioja, Rueda, Sierras de Málaga, Somontano, Tarragona, Terra Alta, Utiel-Requena, Valdepeñas, Valle de Cinca, VdlT Castilla, VdlT Granada Suroeste, Vinos de Madrid, and Yecla. Also in some non-DO vineyards producing good wine, such as Finca Retuerta.

MIGUEL DE ARCO

See Juan Ibañez.

MONASTRELL

It is a Spanish variety taking its name from Murviedro in Valencia, but has spread around the Mediterranean, especially in the south of France, where it is known as the Mourvèdre, and in many other world vineyards. It is easy to grow and very resistant to disease, even to phylloxera, so it is sometimes found on its own roots. It needs sun but dislikes wind. It produces very fine wines noted for their colour and tannins (which can be rather aggressive in young wines) and plenty of extract, with a strong varietal aroma. Although they can be drunk young, and usually are, they age well and often need to breathe for a time before they can give of their best.

Grown in Alicante, Almansa, Binisalem, Bullas, Calatayud, Cariñena, Cataluña, Cava, Conca de Barberá, Costers del Segre, Jumilla, Manchuela, Montsant, Navarra, Penedès, Plá i Llevant de Mallorca, Ribera del Guadiana, Valencia, and Yecla.

Other names are Alcayata and Valcarchella. In France, Mourvèdre. In California and Australia, Mataro.

MORASTELL

See Graciano.

MORAVIA

Grown in La Mancha and Manchuela.

Other names are Crujidera, Moravia Dulce, Brujidera, and Trujidera.

MORAVIA DULCE
See Moravia.

MORISTEL
Grown in Somontano.

MOSCATEL NEGRA
Grown in the Canary Islands.

MOSCATEL ROMANO
See Moscatel de Alejandría.

MOURATON
Grown in Ribiera Sacra and Monterrei.

MULATA
See Negramoll.

MURATON
Grown in: Sacra.

NEGRA COMUN
See Listán Negro.

NEGRA DE MADRID
Although planted in a number of vineyards in central Spain, it does not come into any of the DOs.

NEGRAMOLL
It produces good wines to be drunk young.
Grown in: Canary Islands.

NEGREDA
Grown in Ribera Sacra.

OJO DE LIBRE
See Tempranillo.

ONDARRIBI
There are two versions: Ondarrubi Zuri, which is white, and Ondarrubi Beltza, which is red.
Grown in the Chacolís.

PARRALETA
Grown in Somontano, where it originated.

PEDRO JIMENEZ
See Pedro Ximénez.

PELUDA
Grown in Terra Alta.

PETIT VERDOT
A Bordeaux variety. There it is noted for its colour and the robust nature of its wines, but it does not often fully ripen. In Spain it looks very promising and has given an excellent varietal.
Grown in Castilla y León, Dominio de Valpusa, Finca Retuerta, Jumilla, Sierras de Málaga, Valdepeñas, and Yecla.

PICUDO PRIETO
Grown in Valdevimbre-Los Oteros and Valle de Benevente.

PINOT MEUNIER
A French variety from Champagne.
Grown in Terra Alta.

PINOT NOIR
This French grape is the leading red variety in Burgundy and Champagne, and has been tried in many countries with varying degrees of success. It is a rather difficult grape to grow and to vinify.
Grown in Alella, Alicante, Bierzo, Cataluña, Cava, Conca de Barberá, Costers del Segre, Mallorca, Navarra, Penedès, Pla de Bages, Priorato, Ribera del Guadiana, Rioja, Sierras de Málaga, Somontano, and Terra Alta. Also for some serious non-DO wines such as Bodegas Alta Pavina.

PRIETO PICUDO
See Picudo Prieto.

ROME
Grown in Sierras de Málaga.

ROYALTY
A new variety from the US. Being grown experimentally in Navarra.

RUBY CABERNET
A Cabernet Sauvignon x Cariñena cross being grown experimentally in Navarra and Valencia.

RUFETE
It gives light wines that oxidize easily. Grown in Las Arribes del Duero-Fermoselle.

SAMSO
Not widely grown now. It has been identified as an ancient clone of the Cinsault. Now being grown again commercially in Cataluña and Conca de Barberá.

SANGIOVESE
Italian.
Grown in Navarra.

SHIRAZ
See Syrah.

SOUSON
A rare Galician variety.
Grown in Rías Bajas, Ribeira Sacra, and Ribeiro.

SUNOL OR SUMOLL
Once popular in Penedès, but now distinctly on the decline, it gives aromatic but very acid wines which make excellent brandies.
Grown in Penedès, Pla de Bages, and Tarragona.

SYRAH
A classic variety from the Rhône Valley in France, it seems a natural to try in Spain and is being experimented with in a number of places, but has not yet started to be grown in large quantities.
Grown in Alicante, Almansa, Ampurdán-Costa Brava, Bullas, Calatayud, Campo de Borja, Cariñena, Castilla y León, Cataluña, Conca de Barberá, Dominio de Valpusa, Finca Elez, Navarra, Jumilla, La Mancha, Manchuela, Méntrida, Mondéjar, Montsant, Pla de Bages, Plá i Llevant de Mallorca, Priorato, Ribera del Guadiana, Ribera del Júcar, Rioja, Sierras de Málaga, Somontano, Terra Alta, Utiel-Requena, Valdepeñas, Valencia, Valle de Cinca, VdlT Castilla, VdlT Granada Suroeste, Vinos de Madrid, and Yecla. Also for good non-DO wines such as Finca Retuerta.
Another name is: Shiraz.

TEMPRANILLO
This native Spanish vine is undoubtedly one of the world's greats and Spain's

best. It is not a high yielder, but the quality of its wines is excellent: fragrant; deeply coloured tending toward purple; with lots of fruit; enough alcohol; acidity; and the ability to age well with little tendency to oxidize. Its wines tend to contain a certain amount of glycerine, giving them an agreeable unctuousness. And it makes remarkably successful blends with other varieties. It has been grown for a long time and in many places, so that clones have developed their own characters producing, for instance, the thick-skinned Tinto del País. And it has many other local names such as Ull de Liebre in Penedès. There is a theory that it is descended from Pinot Noir vines imported from France centuries ago, while others would suggest the Cabernet Franc, but no such connections have been established. It is said to get its name from *temprano* (early), because it ripens earlier than the Garnacha, with which it is associated in Rioja.

Grown in Alella, Alicante, Almansa, Ampurdán-Costa Brava, Los Arribes de Duero-Fermoselle, Bierzo, Binisalem, Bullas, Campo de Borja, Calatayud, Cariñena, Castilla y León, Cataluña, Cigales, Conca de Barberá, Costers del Segre, Finca Elez, Jumilla, La Mancha, Manchuela, Mondéjar, Bodegas Mauro, Méntrida, Monterrei, Montsant, Navarra, Penedès, Pla de Bages, Pla i Llevant de Mallorca, Ribera del Júcar, Ribeira Sacra, Ribera del Arlanza, Ribera del Duero, Rinera del Arlanza, Ribera del Guadiana, Ribeiro, Rioja, Rueda, Sierra de Alcaraz, Sierras de Málaga, Somontano, Tarragona, Terra Alta, Tierra del Vino de Zamora, Toro, Utiel-Requena, Valdeorras, Valdepeñas, Valencia, Valle de Benevente, Valle de Cinca, VdlT Castilla, VdlT Castilla y León, VdlT Granada Suroeste, Vinos de Madrid, and Yecla. Also for good non-DO wines such as those of Bodegas SAT Los Curros, and Finca Retuerta.

Other names are Arauxa; Cencibel; Gotim Bru; Tinta Madrid; Tinto Fino; Tinto del País; Tinto de Toro; and Ull de Liebre. In Portugal: Aragonez and Tinta Roriz.

TINTILLA
Black. Grown in the Canary Islands.

TINTO ARAGONÉS
See Garnacha.

TINTO BASTO
See Tinto de Madrid.

TINTA MADRID
See Tempranillo.

TINTO DE MADRID

Quite widely planted, but rather curiously not in Vinos de Madrid, only in Mondéjar, and it has been dropped from there.

Other names are Méntrida, and Tinto Basto.

TINTO DE NAVALCARNERO

See Garnacha.

TINTO DE TORO

See Tempranillo. But it is certainly a special clone and could be a separate variety. The standard grape in Toro. Being grown experimentally in Navarra.

TINTO DEL PAIS

See Tempranillo.

TINTO FINO

See Tempranillo.

TOURIGA NACIONAL

One of the best Portuguese vines and a favoured vine for port. Some think it is related to Syrah. Grown experimentally in Manchuela.

TREPAT

A productive variety that likes heat and is thought to be related to the Garnacha. Its area is declining.

Grown in Cataluña, Cava, Conca de Barberá, Costers del Segre, and Montsant. Other names are Garnacha-Trepat, Trobat, and Tropat.

TROBAT/TROPAT

See Trepat.

TRUJIDERA

See Moravia.

ULL DE LLEBRE

See Tempranillo.

VALCARCHELLA

See Monastrell.

VIDAU

A rare variety found in the Rioja Baja and said to be a mixture of Tempranillo and Garnacha, with the latter predominating.

VIJARIEGO NEGRO
Grown in Abona, Tenerife.

White wine vines

AGUDELO
See Godello.

AIREN
Spain's most commonly cultivated grape and probably the most common in the world. It covers vast areas of La Mancha, where it used to give a very high yield of dull wines, many of them used for distilling and some for blending with the heavy reds that used to be grown there. It has been transformed, though, by modern winemaking. Cultivated for a low yield, picked early enough to have sufficient acid, and given a temperature controlled fermentation, it now provides fruity, aromatic, and agreeable table wines.
Grown in Alicante, Bullas, Jumilla, La Mancha, Málaga, Montilla-Moriles, Navarra, Sierras de Málaga, Valdepeñas, VdlT Castilla, Vinos de Madrid, and Yecla.
Other names are Lairén and Valdepeñera.

ALAMIS
See Pedro Ximénez.

ALARIJE
Popular in Extremadura.
Grown in Ribera del Guadiana.

ALBAN
See Palomino.

ALBARELLO
A rare vine grown in Ribera del Ulla, where it produces very aromatic wines.

ALBARINO
The leading vine in Rías Bajas, where it likes shallow, sandy soils and produces remarkably fragrant wines of great quality. Its cultivation is rapidly expanding. It was certainly growing in Galicia in the eighteenth century and

there are various theories about its origin: some claim it was originally French and others that it is Riesling, brought in by German monks.

Grown in Costers del Segre, Penedès, Rías Bajas, Ribeira Sacra, and Ribeiro. A synonym (in Portugal), is Alvarinho.

ALBILLO

Capable of producing very good wines, this has been variously identified with Pardillo and Viura, but whether it is related to one or the other it now has a separate identity.

Grown in Castilla y León, Cigales, La Palma, Manchuela, Méntrida, Ribera del Arlanza, Ribera del Duero, Ribeiro, Tierra del Vino de Zamora, and Vinos de Madrid.

ALCANON

This produces good, fragrant, light wines in Somontano, where it is thought to have originated, though some claim it is related to the Viura.

Grown in Somontano.

Another name is Alcañól.

BALARDI

Rare.

Grown in Montilla-Moriles.

BABOSO BLANCO

Grown in the Canary Islands.

BASTARDO BLANCO

Of Portuguese origin and may have arrived by way of Madeira.

Grown in the Canary Islands.

BERMEJUELA

Grown in: the Canary Islands

BORBA

Noted for its yield rather than for its quality, it is popular in Extremadura.

Grown Ribera del Guardiana.

BRAVE

Grown in the Canary Islands.

BREMAJUELO

Grown in the Canary Islands.

BREVAL
Grown in the Canary Islands.

BUAL
Grown in the Canary Islands.

BUJARIEGO
Grown in the Canary Islands.

BURRABLANCA
Grown in the Canary Islands.

CAINO
Two versions: red and white. Neither of these Galician varieties is widely grown, but each is capable of giving good wines.
Grown in Rías Bajas, Ribeira Sacra, and Ribeiro.

CALAGRANO
This was one of the traditional varieties in Rioja, but is now prohibited there and is practically extinct. It was not highly regarded. But it may be the same thing as Cayetana Blanca (*see* below), and if so is by no means extinct.
Other names are Cazagal and Naves.

CARREGA-RUCS/CARREGA-SUMS
See Escanyavelles.

CANARROYO
An obscure variety grown in Ribera del Arlanza.

CANOCAZO
Once fairly common in the sherry vineyards, it is now very rare indeed and no longer authorized. It is grown, however, in Australia, where it is sometimes wrongly called Palomino.

CAYETANA BLANCA.
This grape is high yielding and not at all well regarded. It is quite widely planted, though generally not in DO areas; some of its wines are used for distillation. It may or may not be the same as the Calagraño formerly grown in Rioja.
Grown in Ribera del Guadiana.
Other names are Cayazal, Jaén (but not to be confused with the red Jaén), Jaina, and Nava.

CAZAGAL
See Calagraño.

CHARDONNAY
If Cabernet Sauvignon has swept the world as a red, then Chardonnay, from Burgundy, has done the same thing as the fashionable white. It is easy to grow almost anywhere. It is also unusually easy to handle, adapting itself to the tastes of the oenologist by absorbing oak (only too often too much) and blending easily with the wine of other varieties, as Champagne found out years ago. Deplored by traditionalists, who would stick to the native varieties, but loved by the public, it has been a great success in Spain, particularly in the new regions which are uninhibited by tradition. Controversy rages over its use in making cavas, but its use is authorized. It is increasing its hold and is undoubtedly there to stay, producing a remarkable range of very good wines.

Grown in Alella, Alicante, Almansa, Ampurdán-Costa Brava, Bierzo, Calatayud, Campo de Borja, Cariñena, Cataluña, Cava, Conca de Barberá, Costers del Segre, Dominio de Valpusa, Finca Elez, Jumilla, La Mancha, Méntrida, Montilla-Moriles, Montsant, Navarra, Penedès, Pla de Bages, Plá i Llevant de Mallorca, Ribera del Guadiana, Rioja, Sierra de Alcaraz, Sierras de Málaga, Somontano, Tarragona, Terra Alta, Utiel-Requena, Valdepeñas, Valle de Cinca, VdlT Castilla, Vinos de Madrid, and Yecla.

CHELVA
Grown in Ribera del Guadiana.

CHENIN BLANC
This very fine French variety, originating in the Loire, has spread all over the world, notably into California and South Africa. Like all other vines, but to a greater extent than some, it changes its character notably when transplanted. In Spain it is as yet rather tentative, but is producing some very fruity and flavoursome wines.

Grown in Alella, Ampurdán-Costa Brava, Cava, Navarra, Penedès, and Priorato.

CIGUENTE
Grown in Ribera del Guadiana.

COLOMBARD
Originating in the Charente area of France, this variety has been very suc-

cessful in California and generally thrives in hot places, but in Spain it is only experimental.

Grown in Navarra, Sierras de Málaga, and Terra Alta.

DIEGO
See Vijariego.

DONA BLANCA
Grown in Bierzo, Ribeira Sacra, Monterrei, and Valdeorras.

DONA BRANCA
See Doña Blanca.

DORADILLA
Grown in Málaga and Sierras de Málaga.

ESCANYAVELLES
Thought to be a white mutation of the red Monastrell. Once grown in Cataluña, but now almost extinct.

ESQUITXAGOS
Found in Tarragona and Castellón. It may be a clone of Mersegura.

EVA
Grown in Ribera del Guadiana.

FOLLE BLANC
This is the French Folle Blanche, once popular for making wine to be distilled for brandy.

Grown in Chacolí de Vizcaya.

FORASTERA
Grown in the Canary Islands.

GARNACHA BLANCA
The Garnacha grapes are Spanish, probably natives of Aragón or Alicante. They crossed the border into France and have become very popular there as Grenache. The white vine is believed to be a mutation of the red. In Spain it is a popular grape, but usually found in blends rather than as a varietal, though Torres has produced an experimental varietal. It produces enough alcohol, but has to be vinified well if there is to be enough acidity, and it is easily oxidized.

Grown in Alella, Ampurdán-Costa Brava, Campo de Borja, Calatayud, Cariñena, Cataluña, Costers del Segre, Montsant, Navarra, Penedès, Priorato, Rioja, Somontano, Tarragona, and Terra Alta.

Other names are Alicante Blanca, Garnacha Blanca de Rioja, and Garnatxa Blanca.

GARNACHA GRIS
Another mutant being grown experimentally in Penedès.

GARRIDO FINO
Grown in Condado de Huelva.

GEWURZTRAMINER
Although this variety is usually associated with Alsace, it originated in Italy, at Tramin, or Termano, in the Italian Tyrol. Its arrival in Spain, pioneered by Torres, is comparatively recent. The wines retain their notable aroma when grown in Spain, while avoiding the excesses sometimes achieved in Alsace.

Grown in Ampurdán-Costa Brava, Bierzo, Cataluña, Navarra, Penedès, and Somontano.

GODELLO
This excellent vine, producing fine wines with a distinctive aroma, is a native of Galicia. After phylloxera, its vineyards were replanted with high-yielding varieties and it almost became extinct, but was saved by the efforts of REVIVAL (*Reestructuración de los Viñedos de Valdeorras*), formed in 1974 to bring the vineyards of Valdeorras back to their former distinction. This has been a great success and the variety is on the up and up.

Grown in Bierzo, the Canary Islands, Monterrei, Rías Bajas, Ribeira Sacra, Ribeiro, and Valdeorras.

Other names are Agudelo and Verdello.

GROS MANSENG
Originally from Jurançon, France.

Grown in Chacolí de Alava.

GUAL
Grown in the Canary Islands.

HORGAZUELO
See Palomino.

INCROCCIO MANZONI
A Pinot Blanc x Riesling cross from Italy grown in Penedès.

JEREZ
See Palomino.

LADO
Although it is little grown, it is well regarded, producing light, aromatic wines. Grown in Valdeorras.

LAIREN
See Airén.

LISTAN
See Palomino. But the vine grown under this name in Condado de Huelva would appear to be a different variety, sometimes called Listán de Huelva.

LOUREIRA
There are both red and white versions – respectively Tinta and Blanca. Natives of Galicia, both are rare, the red version very rare indeed, but give good wines.
Grown in Monterrei, Rías Bajas, Ribeira Sacra, and Ribeiro.
Another name is Loureira Blanca, which is also known as Marqués.

MACABEO
See Viura.

MADRIGAL
See Verdejo.

MALVAR
This may be a clone of Airén, but it is distinctly different, giving lower yields, ripening earlier, and giving generally better wines (though modern practices have, as noted above, greatly improved the Airén).
Grown in Mondéjar, Ribera del Guadiana, and Vinos de Madrid.

MALVASIA
Originating in Greece and associated with the legendary Malmsey, this has been established as a Spanish favourite for centuries. It has been about the place long enough to develop distinctive clones, and there is now really a family of Malvasías, some of which are listed below. Most, but not all, of the wines it produces are sweet and all have a distinctive aroma.

Grown in Los Arribes del Duero-Fontanelle, Bierzo, Calatayud, the Canary Islands, Cataluña, Jumilla, Navarra, Penedès, Tierra del Vino de Zamora, Toro, Valencia, and Yecla.

MALVASIA DE ALICANTE, MALVASIA FRANCESA, MALVASIA RIOJANA
See Subirat-Parent.

MALVASIA DE SITGES
Another clone. Grown in Penedès.

MANTUA
See Montúa.

MARMAJUELO
Grown in the Canary Islands.

MARQUES
See Loureira Blanca.

MARSANNE
A white French variety. Grown in Rioja.

MERSEGUERA
One of the best white varieties, especially favoured in the southeast of Spain. Grown Alicante, Almansa, Utiel-Requena, Valencia, and Yecla.

MOLL
It produces light, agreeable wines in Mallorca.
Grown in Binisalem.
It is sometimes said to be the same as Prensal, but this doubtful.

MONTEPILA
Grown in Montilla-Moriles

MONTUA
Grown in Ribera del Guadiana.

MONTONEC
See Parellada.

MONTONEGA
A fragrant clone of Parellada developed by Codorníu, *see* Cava.

MOSCATEL
The basic name of a whole family of vines, of which there are at least 200 rec-

ognized members. Otherwise known as the Muscat or Muscatel, it has been known at least since Roman times. It is said to have got its name from the fact that flies are attracted by its sweet and fragrant juice, and it was known to Pliny the Elder as *uva Apiana* (grape of the bees), but is more likely to have originated in Muscat. Grown all over Spain, and indeed all over the world, the sweetness and unique fragrance are its hallmarks. It is the best possible table grape. Although it is possible to make relatively dry wines from them, most of these grapes are used for sweet dessert wines.

Grown in Campo de Borja, the Canary Islands, Condado de Huelva, Málaga, Montilla-Moriles, Montsant, Navarra, Plá i Levant de Mallorca, Jerez, Sierras de Málaga, Tarragona, Terra Alta, Tierra del Vino de Zamora, and VdlT Granada Suroeste. But there are few places where you will not find one of the family growing at least on a modest scale.

MOSCATEL DE ALEJANDRIA

Said to have been named after Alessandria in Italy rather than Alexandria in Egypt, but this is doubtful. It is sometimes named specifically in DO regulations; if a specific clone is not named, this is likely to be the one grown – for instance in the districts named above.

Grown in Alicante, Campo de Borja, Calatayud, Cariñena, Cataluña, Ribera del Guadiana, Jerez, and Valencia.

Other names are Moscatel de Chipiona, Moscatel de España, Moscatel Gordo, Moscatel de Málaga, and Moscatel Romano.

MOSCATEL DE GRANO MENUDO

The small-berried Muscat, the best kind of Moscatel for winemaking, providing a special fragrance. One strain has the odd characteristic that it mutates easily from pink to reddish brown and back again, but the one grown in Spain generally stays white.

Grown in Jumilla, Navarra, Penedès, Ribera del Guadiana, Valdeorras, Valdepeñas, and Vinos de Madrid.

Other names are Moscatel de Grano Pequeño, Moscatel Dorado, (in France) Muscat Blanc à Petits Grains, Muscat d'Alsace, Muscat de Frontignan, (in Italy) Moscato d'Asti, Moscato Bianco.

MOSCATEL DE MALAGA

See Moscatel de Alejandría.

MOSCATEL MORISCO

Grown in Málaga.

MOZA FRESCA

It has said to be a clone of Merseguera. It is not highly regarded and is often confused with Doña Blanca.

Grown in Bierzo, Monterrei, Ribeira Sacra, and Valdeorras.

Another name is Valenciana.

MULLER-THURGAU

A German cross grown experimentally in Penedès.

MUNEMAHATSA

Said to be the Folle Blanche of Cognac.

Grown in Bizkaiko Txakolina.

MUSCAT D'ALSACE

Grown in Penedès.

NAVES

See Calagraño.

ONDARRIBI

There are two versions: Ondarrubi Zuri, which is white; and Ondarrubi Beltza, which is red.

Grown in the Chacolís.

PALOMINO

This widely planted variety is most important in the sherry vineyards, which are practically monovarietal. There it gives a good yield and produces one of the greatest wines in the world. Planted in other places for "table wines", it likewise gives a good yield, but the wines are usually very second-rate. Now that the emphasis throughout Spain is on quality, it is beginning to be replaced in many areas.

Grown in Los Arribes del Duero-Fermoselle, Bierzo, the Canary Islands, Cigales, Condado de Huelva, Jerez, Monterrei, Navarra, Ribeira Sacra, Ribeiro, Ribero de Alanza, Rueda, Tierra del Vino de Zamora, and Valdeorras, among other places.

Other names are Albán, Horgazuela, Jerez, Jerez Fino, Listán, Palomino de Chipiona, Palomino de Pinchito, Seminario, Temprana, and Xeres.

PANSA BLANCA

See Xarel.lo.

PANSA ROSADA
Grown in Alella.

PANSAL
See Pansá.

PARDILLO
Although this is not a highly esteemed variety, if the yield is low and the must cold-fermented it can give very respectable wines.
Grown in Ribera del Guadiana, and Rioja.
Another name is Pardina.

PARDINA
See Pardillo.

PARELLADA
This is Cataluña's best vine. Grown in poor soils and cool areas, it produces light, aromatic, and elegant wines with ample acidity. If the soil is fertile, though, the yield goes up and the elegance down. It is one of the three traditional varieties for making cava, but also makes very good, light white "table wines".
Grown in Ampurdán-Costa Brava, Binisalem, Cariñena, Cava, Conca de Barberá, Costers del Segre, Montsant, Navarra, Penedès, Pla de Bages, Plá i Llevant de Mallorca, Priorato, Ribera del Guadiana, Tarragona, Terra Alta, and Vinos de Madrid.
Another name is Montonec.

PEDRO XIMENEZ
One of Spain's great vines, it is low yielding and gives musts rich in sugar but lacking in acid. The wines nevertheless age well and it is a major variety for fortified wines and *rancios*, as well as producing some very good table wines. In *vinos generosos* it is usually used for making sweet wines, but it can also be vinified to give quality dry wines.
Grown in the Canary Islands, Cataluña, Jerez, Jumilla, Málaga, Montilla-Moriles, Penedès, Priorato, Ribera del Guadiana, Sierras de Málaga, and Valencia.
Other names are Alamis, Pedro Jimenéz, Pedro Ximen, and Ximénez.

PERRUNO
Grown in Ribero del Guadiana.

PETIT CORBU
An obscure variety presumably originating in France.
Grown in Chacolí de Alava.

PETIT MANSENG
Originally from Jurançon, France
Grown in Chacolí de Alava.

PICAPOLL
Originates in the French Languedoc, where it is known as Picpoul or Piquepoul, and where it also exists in a black version.
Grown in Cataluña, Montsant, and Pla de Bages.

PIMPT BLANC
Possibly a mutation of Pinot Noir.
Grown experimentally in Navarra.

PLANTA FINA DE PEDRALBA
Grown in Alicante, and Valencia.
Another name is Planta Pedralba.

PLANTA NOVA
Grown in Utiel-Requena and Valencia.
Another name is Tardana.

PRENSAL
Probably another name for Xarel.lo.
Grown in Binisalem, and Plá i Llevant de Mallorca.

RIESLING
This is one of the great world varieties.
Grown in Alicante, Ampurdán-Costa Brava, Cataluña, Montilla-Moriles, Navarra, Penedès, and Valdeorras.

ROSANA
Grown in Penedès.

ROUSSANNE
French.
Grown in: Rioja.

SABRO
Grown in the Canary Islands.

SAUVIGNON BLANC

One of the major French varieties now being grown all over the world. It has a very distinctive aroma, which can nevertheless exist in a number of forms depending on site, ripeness, and microclimate, sometimes compared with grass and at other times with cats' pee. Happily in Spain the former prevails. Grown in Alicante, Almansa, Cataluña, Costers del Segre, Cigales, Jumilla, La Mancha, Machuela, Méntrida, Montilla-Moriles, Penedès, Ribera del Guadiana, Rioja, Rueda, Sierras de Málaga, Utiel-Requena, Valdepeñas, Valencia, and VdlT Castilla.

SEMILLON

One of the major French varieties now being grown in Valencia and experimentally in Navarra.

SUBIRAT-PARENT

One of the Malvasía family, now falling out of favour.
Grown in Penedès; Rioja; and for Cava.
Other names are Malvasía de Alicante, Malvasía Francesa, and Malvasía Riojana.

TARDANA

See Planta Nova.

THOMPSON SEEDLESS

Also known *as* Sultana.
Grown experimentally in Navarra.

TORRONTES

Originating in Galicia, this variety has spread far.
Grown in the Canary Islands, Mondéjar, Montilla-Moriles, Rías Bajas, Ribeiro, Ribeira Sacra, and Vinos de Madrid.

TORTOSI

Grown in Valencia.

TREIXADURA

A Galician variety that thrives in the mountains, giving good, highly aromatic wines.
Grown in Monterrei, Rías Bajas, Ribeira Sacra, and Ribeiro.

VALDEPENERA

See Airén.

VALENCIANA
See Moza Fresca.

VERDEJO
Although it is said to have been brought from Africa by the Moors, this is now considered to be a native Spanish grape – and one of the very best, providing aromatic, big-bodied wines of great character. It can withstand extreme cold and drought.

Grown in Almansa, Los Arribes del Duero-Fermoselle, Cigales, Dominio de Valpusa, Machuela, Navarra, Ribera del Guadiana, Ribera del Alanza, Rueda, Tierra del Vino de Zamora, Toro, and Valdepeñas.

Another name is Madrigal.

VERDELLO
See Godello. There is some doubt about this, as Verdello in the Canary Islands is said the be the same as the Madeira Verdelho.

VERDELLO LOURO
See Treixadura.

VERDIL
Grown in Alicante and Valencia.

VERDONCHO
This is not considered to be a quality grape.

Formerly grown in La Mancha.

VERIJADIEGO
See Vijariego.

VERMEJUELA
Grown in the Canary Islands (El Hierro).

VIJARIEGO
There is also a red version, Vijariego Negra.

Grown in the Canary Islands.

VIOGNIER
French, originally from the Rhône.

Grown in Finca Elez, Penedès, Rioja, Sierra de Alcaraz, VdlT Castilla, and Terra Alta.

VIURA

This is one of Spain's most important varieties, probably originating in Aragón, and is very widely grown. It is equally well known under its alternative name Macabeo. Highly productive, it can give wines of very high quality, but needs careful handling. If it is unripe the wines can be over-acidic and bitter. If it is overripe, the wines are dull. But harvested at the right time and cold fermented, it gives wines of ample acidity, but good balance that age well.

Grown in Alella, Alicante, Ampurdán-Costa Brava, Binisalem, Bullas, Calatayud, Campo de Borja, Cariñena, Cataluña, Cava, Cigales, Conca de Barberá, Costers del Segre, Dominio de Valpusa, Jumilla, La Mancha, Manchuela, Méntrida, Mondéjar, Montsant, Navarra, Penedès, Pla de Bages, Plá i Llevant de Mallorca, Priorato, Ribera del Tea, Ribera del Arlanza, Ribera del Guadiana, Ribeiro, Rioja, Rueda, Sierras de Málaga, Somontano, Tarragona, Terra Alta, Utiel-Requena, Valdepeñas, Valencia, VdlT Castilla, Vinos de Madrid, and Yecla.

Other names are Alcañol; Alcañon; Forcalla; and Macabeo. In France,Macabeu.

XAREL.LO

A Spanish, specifically Catalan, variety that is principally noted as one of the traditional varieties for cava. It is generally grown in low lying vineyards and gives aromatic wines with plenty of body, adding a useful dimension to the other varieties. In the past it tended to oxidize, but this problem has been overcome by modern vinification.

Grown in Alella, Ampurdán-Costa Brava, Cataluña, Cava, Costers del Segre, Montsant, Navarra, Penedès, and Tarragona.

Another name is Pansa Blanca (but this is a specific clone).

XIMEN/XIMENCIA

See Pedro Ximénez.

ZALEMA

A very productive variety that is easy to grow and much esteemed for those reasons in Condado de Huelva, but it gives rather dull wines and these are unlikely to improve unless it is replaced or, at the very least, its yield is drastically reduced.

Glossary

Abocado – slightly sweet.

ABV – the EU standard for measuring strength: alcohol by volume at 20°C. Formerly known as Gay-Lussac, after the French chemist who invented a volume alcoholometer.

Adega – Galician for a bodega.

Aftertaste – the flavour that is detected after the wine has been swallowed.

Agrife – a steel clip used to keep the cork in a sparkling wine during its bottle fermentation and sometimes after the final corking.

Aguapie – must from the second pressing.

Aguardiente – grape spirit.

Aguja – a very slightly sparkling wine.

Alambiaco – a wire cage placed round a bottle, originally to prevent fraud.

Albariza – the name given to the best soil in the sherry district. It is white in colour and contains a high proportion of calcium.

Allier – Oak from the *département* of the same name in France.

Almacenista – a store keeper; someone who makes wines and keeps them for onward wholesale sale.

Almija – the yard outside a vineyard building where, especially in the sherry area, grapes were traditionally dried in the sun before being pressed.

Alta expresion – a term used to describe the new style of wine, particularly in Rioja, where the emphasis is on fruit and vineyard characteristics.

Amontillado – a style of sherry obtained when fino is aged for a long time in wood. It resembles wines formerly prepared only in Montilla. They are still prepared in Montilla, and in Spain the term is used for both sherries and Montilla-Moriles wines of the appropriate style, but cannot be used this way in the UK owing to legal action taken by the sherry shippers.

Amoroso – a term used chiefly in the UK for a type of light and slightly sweet oloroso sherry.

Ampelography – the comparative study of the vine.

Añada – a vintage wine; a wine made from grapes grown in a single year.

Añejo – wine aged for not less than two years.

Añina – the fourth, in order of merit, of the four leading districts with albariza soil around Jerez.

Apaleador – a stick used for stirring wine during fining.

Aranzada – a measure of vineyard area. One aranzada = 0.475 hectares or 1.1737 acres.

Arena – sand.

Arroba – a measure of weight or volume that is confusing because it is different in different parts of Spain. In Jerez it is equivalent to about 11.5kgs or 16.66 litres.

Arrope – a syrup used in blending sherry, made by simmering must down to one fifth of its original volume.

Autonomía (or Autonoma) – Spain is a federation of seventeen autonomous areas, plus two more offshore. These are further subdivided into *provincias*, or provinces, which themselves are subdivided into *comarcas*, or counties, which are yet further subdivided into *municipios*, or municipalities.

Autovinifier – a modern machine for making red wine, effecting maceration, fermentation, and temperature control by means of a rotating stainless-steel tank, rather like a cement mixer. Another form exists for making white wines but is seldom found in Spain. Also known as a Vinimatic.

Backbone – the combination of elements that provide a wine with structure.

Balbaina – the third, in order of merit, of the four leading districts with albariza soil around Jerez.

Barrica – a 225-litre oak cask.

Barro – clay.

Baumé – a measure of the sugar in must, obtained by using a hydrometer. If a 15° Baumé solution is fermented dry it gives a wine of 16.4°. Very roughly, each degree Baumé results in a degree of alcohol on fermentation. Its inventor was Antoine Baumé (1728–1804), a French pharmacist.

Biological ageing – the maturation of wine under a film of yeast cells, as with fino sherry.

Bocoy – an odd-shaped butt usually containing about 40 *arrobas*.

Bodega – winery. The word is used in two ways: a winemaking establishment or a building in such an establishment.

Bota – butt. The usual size contains 500 litres (30 *arrobas*), but there are also special sizes such as Bota Gorda, which is used in sherry bodegas for storing and maturing wine and which contains 36 to 40 *arrobas*.

Bozal – literally muzzle; the wire placed over the cork of a bottle of sparkling wine to stop it blowing out.

Cabaceo – the formula for a blend of wine.

Campaña – season. The period from one vintage to the next.

Canasta – a cane basket used in vineyards.

Carbonic maceration – a method of vinification for red wine used all over Europe. Whole bunches of grapes are put into a sealed container from which oxygen is excluded, usually by adding carbon dioxide. The fermentation starts within the grapes themselves, which then begin to break under their own weight; a normal fermentation then follows. There are many variations of the technique. Known in Spanish as *maceración carbónica* and French as *macération carbonique*.

Carrascal – the second, in order of merit, of the four leading districts around Jerez.

Casco – cask.

Casse – a generic term for various kinds of wine faults.

Cava – the best kind of Spanish sparkling wine, *see* Chapter 12. The literal meaning of the word is a subterranean cellar.

Cepa – vine.

Clarete – a light-coloured red wine.

Claro – a clear wine.

Claros de Lias – clear wine obtained from the lees of must.

Claros de Turbios – clear wine obtained from filtering the lees of wine.

Clone – a stock of vines raised by vegetative multiplication from a single parent.

Color, vino de – a wine used for deepening the colour of sherry blends.

Comarca – county; see Autonomía.

Cono – name given to a *tinaja* in Condado de Huelva.

Consejo Regulador de la Denominación de Origen – An official government body appointed to supervise a specific recognized wine area.

Corredor – a broker who buys and sells wine.

Cosecha – harvest, vintage.

CRDO – Consejo Regulador de la Denominación de Origen.

Criadera – literally a nursery. A series of butts that are never moved and from which wine is periodically drawn to refresh a *solera* or another *cri-*

adera, the wine drawn out being replaced by an equal quantity of younger wine drawn from another *criadera* or from a stock of *añada* wine.

Crianza – literally "brought up". Applied to a wine given oak ageing.

Cuarto (bota) – quarter cask (° butt).

Cupada – a blend of various wines prepared, for instance, as the base wine for a cava. In French, a *cuvée*.

Deposito – vat, tank

DE – Denominación Especifica.

Degüelle – disgorging, in French *dégorgement*; the removal of the deposit formed during the bottle fermentation of a sparkling wine.

DEP – Denominación Especifica Provisional.

Desfangado – literally "demudding", the separation of must from heavy impurities before fermentation.

DO – Denominación de Origen.

Doble pasta – after fermenting one lot of wine, the skins are left in the vat and a second fermentation of wine is done on top of them. This makes very deeply red wines, which are generally used for blending. *See* the descriptions of Valencia and Alicante.

Double cordon – a system of pruning. Two horizontal arms, trained along wires, extend from the vine's vertical trunk, with shoots growing upwards from the arms.

DOC, DOCa, DOQ – Denominación de Origen Calificada.

Dulce – sweet

Dulce apagado – a form of sweet wine made by adding alcohol to unfermented must and then fermenting it.

Embottelado – bottled.

Enology – a modern spelling of oenology – the science of winemaking.

En cabeza – a method of pruning vines. Literally it means "in a head". The vine is cut down drastically so that the portion quite near the ground thickens to form a sort of head that sprouts a number of shoots (five or six) which are cut short and form a crown.

En espaldera – the method of training vines on a wire fence, which is rapidly increasing.

En vaso – the most common method of pruning vines in Spain. The vine is grown like a bush and pruned short. Over a period of three years the pruning is done to leave a vertical trunk with two shoots sticking out at an angle and leaving what looks like a vessel, or *vaso*, between them. Subsequently it may be allowed more shoots.

Espalderas – the structure of wires used for supporting vines in vineyards. This is to be contrasted with the traditional method, which grew them as bushes.

Espirraque – a third, heavy pressing. The wine obtained from it is generally distilled.

Espumoso – sparkling.

Etiqueta – label.

Extract (or dry extract) – the non-volatile components of wine; the solids.

Fining – clarifying wine by precipitating out the colloids and particles that cause opacity.

Fino – fine. It is used to define a kind of sherry on which *flor* has bred freely.

Flabby – a wine lacking in acidity and grip.

Flor – literally "flower"; a film of yeast cells growing on the surface of certain wines, notably fino sherries and Montillas.

Fondillón – a strong, oxidized wine that is a speciality of Alicante.

Gay-Lussac – French chemist who invented a volume alcoholometer. *See* abv.

Generoso – alcoholically strong wines made mostly in Andalucía.

Girasol – literally "sunflower"; a device used for shaking down the deposit formed in the bottle fermentation of sparkling wines, handling a number of bottles at the same time instead of shaking them individually.

Giropalette – an automated form of girasol.

Glycerine – the name given to the trihydric alcohol glycerol that is a natural product of fermentation and a major constituent of wines; it is rather sweet tasting and can give a sweet sensation in the mouth even when the wine contains no sugar.

Gran reserva – the top grade of aged wine; a wine made in a good year and given a substantial period of ageing.

Guyot – a common method of pruning, named after its French inventor. Traditionally known in Spain traditionally as *poda de pulgar y vara* (thumb and stick pruning), but the French term is now commonly used. As its name suggests, the vine is trained to have one long and one short shoot. In the single Guyot method, one long shoot is trained horizontally along a wire; in the double Guyot method there are two, one in either direction. In Spain, the system is considered especially suitable in cool areas.

Hecho – literally "made"; a term applied to wine that is fully mature.

Hectare – the European measure of area: 100 acres or 10,000 square metres = 2.471 acres.

Hogshead – a cask holding 250 litres, half the size of a butt.

Injerta – grafting.

Inox – stainless steel.

Jerez cortado – the name given to palo cortado in Sanlúcar de Barrameda.

Joven – young. A wine not aged in cask and intended for immediate drinking.

Lagar – a wooden wine press.

Lago – its usual meaning is "lake", but in a wine context it is the fermenting tank used traditionally by small wine-growers.

Lágrima – free-run must.

Lees – the cloudy and sometimes solid deposits that form at the bottom of casks of wine; they consist of yeasts, tartrate crystals, and other matters.

Length – the time a wine's flavour lingers in the mouth after being swallowed.

Lías – the lees of must or wine.

Licor de expedicion – the preparation added before the final corking of a sparkling wine to give it the necessary degree of sweetness and to top it up after the disgorgement. In French, *liqueur d'expédition*.

Licor de tiraje – the mixture of wine, sugar, and yeasts used to bring about the fermentation to make sparkling wines by the *método tradicional*.

Limousin – oak from the region of Limoges in France.

Macharnudo – the first, in order of merit, of the four leading districts with albariza soil around Jerez.

Maceración carbonica – *see* Carbonic Maceration.

Maceration – contact between must or wine and grape skins.

Maderization – the oxidation of white wines causing them to turn brown and to have a smell that is somewhat reminiscent of Madeira – hence the name.

Magnum – a bottle containing twice as much as an ordinary bottle, i.e. 1.5 litres.

Malic acid – an acid found in grape must and also in apples. It imparts an acid flavour (which is sometimes desirable) and an appley smell. When it is not required it is removed by means of a malolactic fermentation, which is an entirely natural process but which can now be controlled.

Malolactic fermentation – the bacteriological transformation of malic acid into the less aggressive lactic acid, with the evolution of carbon dioxide.

Manzanilla – a form of sherry matured at Sanlúcar de Barrameda. It also means "camomile", and the unwary who ask for it in the parts of Spain where sherry is not a usual drink are apt to be given a cup of camomile tea.

Marc – grape residues after pressing.

Marco real – a square pattern used in planting out vineyards.

Media bota – a hogshead.

Meseta – Spain's central plateau.

Método tradicional – the method used to produce cava and some other sparkling wines.

Mistela – a strong and sweet wine made by inhibiting the fermentation with the addition of alcohol, leaving natural sugars.

Mitad y mitad (miteado) – a fifty-fifty mixture of alcohol and wine used for fortifying wines.

Mosto – must; the juice of grapes. It ceases being must and becomes wine as soon as fermentation is complete. In the sherry country, however, the term is used more loosely, both before and after fermentation and until the wine has been racked from the lees.

Mosto de yema – free-run must.

Municipio – municipality; *see* Autonomía.

Must – *see* mosto.

Mycoderma aceti – a ferment that turns wine into vinegar.

Noble – a wine with a year in oak of not more than 600-litre capacity, or in bottle.

Oak – several kinds of oak are used for wine casks.

Octavo – an octave (eighth of a butt).

Oenology – the science of winemaking, now often spelled "enology".

Oidium – a fungoid parasite of the vine.

Oloroso – fragrant. A term used to define a style of sherry in which either there has never been much *flor* or in which the growth of *flor* has been stopped by additions of spirit: a dark and full-bodied wine.

Orujos – grape skins; the spirit distilled from grape skins; *marc* in French.

Oxidation – the interaction of oxygen with various chemical compounds in the wine. Correctly used, this forms part of the normal process of ageing, and is essential for the ageing of wines like oloroso sherry. But if it is uncontrolled, or if a wine has been kept too long, it loses its edge of flavour, goes brown, and gets spoiled.

Pago – a distinct, named vineyard.

Palma – a high quality fino sherry.

Palma cortada – a rather stouter fino tending toward amontillado.

Palo – a stick. Also an iron rod with a brush attached used for fining wine.

Palo cortado – a rather full-bodied sherry of a particularly good style.

Pasado – a wine, particularly a sherry, that has developed with age.

Pata de gallina – literally "hen's foot"; a style of oloroso sherry that is dry but tastes slightly sweet owing to the presence of glycerine.

Paxarete – a sweet wine partly consisting of Pedro Ximénez, used for sweetening blends of sherry and for colouring whisky.

Pedro Ximénez – a grape which, when dried and pressed, makes the best sweet wine, in Jerez, Montilla-Moriles, and Málaga. It is also used in all those districts to make dry wines.

Persistence – the lingering flavour of wine after it has been swallowed.

Pétillance – the presence of a very small amount of carbon dioxide, which gives a slightly tickling sensation.

pH – hydrogen power. It is an inverse measure of acidity, 7 being neutral, anything above 7 alkaline, and anything below 7 acid. All wines are acid to some degree and usually have a pH between 3 and 4.

Phenolics or polyphenols – a naturally occurring group of compounds based on phenol. They include tannins and important elements of colour and flavour.

Phylloxera – the "vine louse", an aphid; a destructive insect parasite of the vine, originating in America.

Plastering – the addition of gypsum to grapes to increase the acidity of the must.

Prensa – a wine press.

Pricked – a wine tainted with acetic acid (vinegar).

Provincia – province; *see* Autonomías.

Pupitre – literally "desk"; the device used for holding sparkling wines while the deposit formed by the second fermentation in bottle is shaken down on to the cork.

PX – Pedro Ximénez.

Quercus – oak.

Quina – quinine, sometimes used as a flavouring element in medicinal wines and the like.

Racimo – a bunch of grapes.

Racking off the lees – drawing the clear wine off the lees that have accumulated at the bottom of the cask.

Rancio – a traditional style of wine going back to Roman times that is deliberately oxidized, sometimes in glass demi-johns kept outside, which hasten the oxidation by the heat of the sun and the cool of night.

Raya – a term used in classifying sherry musts. Also a coarse form of oloroso sherry.

Raya olorosa – a light raya.

Redondo – a term used to describe a wine that is "round", or well balanced.

Remontaje – a process used in making red wine. The must is drawn from the bottom of the fermentation vessel and pumped after the "cap" of skins that forms at the top.

Removido – the process of removing the deposit formed during the bottle fermentation of sparkling wines. In French, *remuage*.

Rendimiento – Pressing very hard can usually get one litre of must from each kilogram of grapes. But such pressure makes bad wine, so a *rendimiento,* or limit of 65–70 per cent is set to limit production.

Reserva – a wine given a substantial period of ageing.

Reserva de familia – family reserve.

Reserve wines – wines from a previous vintage or vintages put to one side for use in blending the base wine for high quality cavas.

Roble – oak. The word is also used to indicate a wine that has had some oak maturation but not enough to qualify as a *crianza*.

Rosado – pink wine. In French *rosé*, a term sometimes used on Spanish wine labels.

Royat – a system of pruning known in France as Cordon de Royat, in which the vine is trained into a curve and then horizontally along a wire.

Sacar – to draw off wine from a cask.

Sack – a historic term formerly used to describe wines for export, notably Sherry Sack, Malaga (or Malligo) Sack, and Canary Sack.

Sacristía – the area in a bodega that contains the oldest wines kept for special occasions.

Sancocho – a syrup made in the sherry district by simmering must until it is one third of its original volume.

Sangría – a long drink served in a jug and made basically from red wine and fruit with soda water or sparkling lemonade, sometimes sugar and (in Spain) a dash of brandy. Bottled versions are now available.

SAT – Sociedad Agraria de Transformación; a company of growers more exclusive than a cooperative.

Seco – dry.

Semi-crianza – a wine given some oak ageing but not enough to make it a *crianza*.

Short – a wine whose flavour rapidly disappears after it has been swallowed.

Soleo – the process of increasing the sweetness of grapes by drying them slightly in the sun.

Solera – a series of butts that are never moved and from which wine is periodically drawn, whereupon the *solera* is refreshed with an equal quantity of wine from a *criadera*. This system is particularly used for sherry and for Montillla-Morales. It is also used loosely to describe the complete unit, consisting of the *solera* itself and all its *criaderas*. The word may not properly be used to describe a style of wine.

Structure – the flavouring elements that combine together to make a complete wine.

Tannins – naturally occurring polyphenols that give an astringent taste but which are essential elements in good red wines, contributing to their ability to mature and last.

Tapón – cork.

Tears – the little drops of wine that cling to the side of a glass and descend very slowly. They are largely made up of alcohol and glycerine, and are found mostly in wines of good quality.

Tent – a style of wine formerly made at Rota in the sherry area.

Tina – a large wooden vat.

Tinaja – large jars, formerly of earthenware but more recently made of concrete, used for fermenting and storing wine. *Tinajas* are still used but are becoming obsolete. The term is also used for earthenware jugs sometimes used in bodegas.

Toast – the charring given to the insides of the staves when a barrel is made.

Tolva – a hopper in which the grapes are received at the bodega.

Tonel – a very large storage cask containing two, three, four, or more butts.

Tonelero – cooper.

Tresbolillo – a diagonal pattern used for planting out vineyards.

Turbios – the lees of wine, as opposed to *lías*, the lees of must.

Ullage – empty space in cask or bottle.

Uva – grape.

VC – *vino comarcal* (local wine).

VCPRD – *vinos de calidad producidos en regiones determinadas*, quality wines produced in specific regions.

VdlT – *vino de la tierra* (country wine).

VdM – *vino de mesa* (table wine).

Varietal – a wine made from a single grape variety.

Velo – the surface film of *flor*.

Vendimia – vintage.

Venencia – an instrument consisting of a small silver cup on the end of a long whalebone handle (though now usually made of stainless-steel and plastic) used for drawing small quantities of wine from casks for tasting; an alternative form is made of split bamboo.

Vid – vine.

Viejo – old; a wine not less than three years old and showing oxidative ageing.

Viejísimo – very old.

Vinimatic – *see* autovinifier.

Viña – vineyard.

Vino – wine.

Vino blanco – white wine.

Vino Común, or Vino Corriente – wine of ordinary quality.

Vino de Crianza – wine given oak ageing.

Vino de Mesa – table wine.

Vino de Pasto – in Spain a pale, cheap table wine; in the UK a sherry blended as an apéritif (but an obsolescent term).

Vino de Prensa – wine produced from must obtained by pressing the grapes.

Vino de Xérès – sherry.

Vino Joven – young wine.

Vino Tinto – red wine.

Viticulture – the cultivation of vine grapes.

VT – see VdlT.

Xenérico – Galician for generic.

Yema – bud. *See* "mosto de yema".
Yeso – gypsum (calcium sulphate), a small quantity of which is traditionally sprinkled on grapes before they are pressed in areas making fortified wines.

Zona de Crianza – the area in which a DO wine may be matured.
Zurra or Zurracapote – a *sangría* made with white wine instead of red.

Index

Hidalgo-la Gitana, Bodegas 321
Hierro, El 364–5
Hijos de Rainera Perez Marin 322–3
Hill, Cavas 19
Horgazuelo vine 406
Hoyo, Sat El 371

I

Ibiza 351
Ignacio Marin, Bodega 75
Ijalba, Bodegas Viñña 111–12
Illa de Menorca 351
Incroccio Manzoni vine 407
INDO *see* Instituto Nacional de Demoninaciones de Origin
Iniestense, Cooperativa Union Campesina 279
Instituto Nacional de Demoninaciones de Origin (INDO) 7
Insulares Tenerife 357
Inviosa, Lar de Barros/ 300–1, 382
Isidro, Sociedad Cooperativa Comarcal Vitivinicola San 282
Isleta, La 358
Itsasmendi, Bodega 207
Izadi/Viñña Villabuena, Viñña 112

J

J & F Lurton 190
J Belda 255
Ja Megia e Hijos, Bodegas 291
Jaen vine 393
Jalóón, Bodegas y Viññedos de 68
Jane Ventura 25–6, 386
Jaume de Puntiro 346
Jaume Mesquida 349
Jean Leóón 19–20, 62
Jerez vine 407
Jerez y Manzanilla de Sanlúúcar de Barrameda 305–25
  authorized yield 306
  bodegas 316–25
  climate 305
  geography 305
  grapes 306
  history 307–16
  planting 306
  production 307

soils 306
vineyard area 306
vintages 307–16
wines 307
Jeromin, Vinos 266–7
Jesus del Perdon, Cooperativa 275
Joan d'Anguera 60
Joan Raventóós Rosell 21–2
Joaquin Rebolledo 229
John Harvey, Pedro Domecq/ 317–18
Jose, Adegas San 222
Jose de Soto 318–19
Joséé Estééved/Valdespino 318
Jose L Ferrer (Franja Roja) 345–6
Josep Maria Raventóós i Blanc 22
Juan Alcorta, Bodegas 112–13
Juan Garcia vine 393
Juan Ibanez vine 393
Julia Roch e Hijos 248
Julian Chivite, Bodegas 147–8
Jumilla 243–8
  authorized yield 244
  bodegas 246–8
  climate 244
  geography 243–4
  grapes 244
  planting 244
  production 245
  soils 244
  vineyard area 244
  vintages 245–6
  wines 245
Juvéé & Camps 382

L

La Casa de las Cuatro Rayas 282
La Encina Bodegas y Vinedos 108–9
La Gomera 371–2
La Guita 322–3
La Isleta 358
La Mancha 270–7
  authorized yield 271
  bodegas 273–7
  climate 270–1
  geography 270
  grapes 271
  map 263
  planting 271
  production 272
  soils 271
  vineyard area 271

vintages 272–3
wines 271
La Palma 368–71
  authorized yield 369
  bodegas 370–1
  climate 368–9
  geography 368
  grapes 369
  planting 369
  production 370
  soils 369
  vineyard area 369
  wines 370
La Rioja Alta 130–1
Lacalle, Bodega Lezcano 160
Ladairo, Adegas 210
Ladera de Pinoso 237
Lado vine 407
Lagar de Fornelos 216–17
Lagunilla 113
Lairen vine 407
Lan, Bodegas 113–14
Langa Hermanos 382
Lanzarote 365–8
  authorized yield 367
  bodegas 367–8
  climate 366
  geography 365
  grapes 366
  planting 366
  production 367
  soils 366
  vineyard area 366
  wines 367
Lar de Barros/Inviosa 300–1, 382
Larios 338
Laurona, Celler 60
Lentiscal, Monte de 371
Leóón, Castilla y 155–96, 296
Leóón, Jean 19–20, 62
Leóón, VdlT Castilla y 193–5
Lezcano Lacalle, Bodega 160
Liedoner Gris vine 393
Listan Negro vine 393
Listan vine 407
Lladoner vine 393
Llanos/Cosecheros Abastecedores, Bodega los 290–1
Llanovid Sociedad Cooperativa 371
Llopart, Cavas 383
Lomo (Afcan), El 357
Lóópez de Heredia - Viñña Tondonia, Bodegas Rafael 114–15